QUIET
HEROES

*True Stories of the Rescue
of Jews by Christians
in Nazi-occupied Holland*

André Stein

LESTER
&ORPEN
DENNYS

PUBLISHERS

*To the memory of my friend Jeffrey Bishop and my sister,
Agnes Carlton Stein — they both died much too young*

Copyright © 1988 by André Stein

FIRST EDITION

Canadian Cataloguing in Publication Data

Stein, André
  Quiet heroes

ISBN 0-88619-133-5

1. World War, 1939-1945 - Jews - Rescue -
Netherlands.   2. World War, 1939-1945 - Underground
movements - Netherlands.   3. Netherlands - History -
German occupation, 1940-1945.   I. Title.

D802.N4S85 1988   940.53'492   C88-093077-2

Cover design by Bernice Eisenstein

Printed and bound in Canada by Metropole Litho Inc.

for
Lester & Orpen Dennys Limited
78 Sullivan Street
Toronto, Canada
M5T 1C1

If men cannot always make history have a meaning, they can always act so that their own lives have one.

Albert Camus

Thou shalt pursue light even in the darkness, for light remains light.

*from "The Dutch Ten Commandments
to Foil the Nazis", which were distributed throughout The Netherlands*

Acknowledgements

This book would never have been written without the recognition Elie Wiesel and Harry James Cargas paid to my testimonial volume, *Broken Silence*. After having read my book, they invited me to address the rescuers, scholars, and other participants at the Conference on Faith in Humankind, held at the U.S. State Department in Washington, D.C., in September 1984. That is where I met rescuers for the first time in my life. This meeting proved to be a turning point in my dealing with the events of my past.

At a time in my life when I was becoming increasingly tormented by memories, I met a handful of elderly people who were generous to others and yet entirely self-effacing about their heroic activities. This volume tells their stories. I thank the rescuers for trusting me with their own memories.

I wish to thank Gregory Baum, who, shortly before the publication of *Broken Silence*, wrote to me: "I hope that writing this book has healed you and that your next book will heal the reader." In a very real sense, it is the writing of this book that helped me along the path to my own healing. And yes, I do hope that the stories of these extraordinary people will heal many of my readers.

Once I had made the decision to find out about the rescuers, Samuel Oliner of the Altruistic Personality Project and Sister Carol Rittner of the U.S. Holocaust Memorial Committee—one of the organizers of the Conference on Faith in Humankind—generously shared with me their lists of Dutch rescuers living in The Netherlands and in Canada. Without their co-operation, I would never have been able to embark on this project. Sam later proved to be a compassionate, generous, and wise colleague, and he and his wife, Pearl, along with Jack Shaffer (another member of the project), gave me welcome assistance in unfolding my personal inquiry into the world of rescuers.

When unexpected obstacles cluttered the road towards my final destination point, there were friends who did their best to clear the passage for me. I would particularly like to thank Wayne Walder, Linda Finkelstein, Judy and Ivan Flaschner, Ted Grosberg, and Tomas Rejto for their unwavering support, patience, and affection. My gratitude also goes to Kenny Dancyger, Lucy Hall, and Kevin Sullivan for responding so enthusiastically to my recounting of the rescuers' stories. And without the help of my friend and editor, Sarah Shadowitz, this book would never have seen the light of day.

There is nothing more thankless than doing clerical work on someone else's brainchild. And yet, so many people offered me their time and effort. Among them were Cybèle, Tristana, and Vicki Stein, Wendy Balaban, and Shelley Grosberg.

I would also like to thank my publisher, Malcolm Lester, for his support of this project throughout its development. From the first time I spoke to him about the Washington meeting right up to the final stages of producing this book, he has been of tremendous assistance.

My children—Cybèle, Tristana, Adrian, and Eliana—all deserve a special word of thanks for the interest and patience they have shown during the sometimes difficult periods I spent writing this book. And without the assistance of my wife, Vicki—both in the interviewing and in the writing processes—this book would have been greatly diminished. In a very real sense, working on this project has been a "family affair".

Finally, my gratitude goes to all those individuals and institutions who helped me, one way or another, to secure the funds necessary for this project: Lenny and Roz Rosner, Robert Krell, The Canada Council, The Office of the Secretary of State (Judy Young and Barbara Preston in particular), and the Ontario Arts Council.

CONTENTS

Foreword

This is a book of stories too long untold. Published accounts of those quiet heroes who helped save Jews during the Holocaust have been few and far between. Only recently has there been more of an effort to collect and relate these stories of simple goodness in a time of terror.

It is understandable that these stories about quiet heroes are among the last, from that terrible time, to be told. In the aftermath of the Second World War, as the world began to piece together the wreckage from the Nazi experiment, there was an intense effort to try and comprehend those who had committed such crimes against humanity. Only slowly did Jewish survivors themselves begin to find the words to convey the inexpressible horrors which culminated in the murder camps. One of these survivors is André Stein, whose book *Broken Silence* is a shattering testimony from those times. Stories such as his expose the dark underside of the history of the Christian West. The myth of human progress crashed upon the shoals of the reality of the twentieth century.

Significantly, it was often those who saw that the total darkness of the Holocaust was undeniable who also looked for small signs of light within that darkness—perhaps to make the future at least bearable. There was serious reflection on survival itself as the final form of human freedom in a situation of organized murder. There was increased historical research on the various types of Jewish resistance during the Nazi era. And now there is also a desire to seek out those quiet heroes, those non-Jews who were willing to risk their own lives so that others would not die. One can only stand in awe of the fact that a survivor, like André Stein, could not deny the illumination these rescuers provided in the midst of what he experienced as the unbearable darkness of the Holocaust.

The importance of this book lies in the perspective from which it was lived and is related. It is, as it were, the view from ground-level. This angle of vision provides a necessary complement to the other reflections on the Holocaust that view it "from above".

There are, it should be noted, relevant insights to be found from examining what happened from above. From this perspective, it appears that the organized murder of millions of people took place within a particular political form—the totalitarian system. Indeed, the Holocaust reveals the outlines of what can be called systematic evil.

This system functioned (and this is the frightening fact) because thousands of ordinary people simply went about their business. By actively or passively co-operating with this system, the most ordinary people contributed, cumulatively, to the most extraordinary evil. The most ordinary activities (driving trains, filing papers, rubber stamping) were systematically co-ordinated into a consequence of immense proportions. It was a system of organized complicity in which everyone, by simply participating in the system, became implicated in enormous crimes. When everyone becomes guilty, it becomes more difficult for individuals to feel responsible, to feel that they *can* be responsible. Within an all-pervasive yet elusive system, moral responsibility seems illusory. It seems as if many who participated in this evil felt as powerless within it as did those who were its victims.

Such is the shape of much of the evil done in the world today. Contemporary historical struggles are rarely between individual heroes and villains. It is not like the old days. More often than not, ordinary people suffer the cruel consequences of a system fuelled by the energies of countless nameless, faceless people. Such are the dark revelations which appear when viewing the Holocaust from above.

Yet the view from below, presented so concretely in this book, reveals something which might otherwise remain concealed. From this perspective, the possibility of individual choice and responsibility emerges more clearly. The rescuers state, through their actions, that non-cooperation with an evil system remains an option even in the darkest of times. Their acts of resistance, however quiet, reclaim some ground for human beings to act upon: if systems are constructed through the efforts of ordinary people, then systems can be changed or even destroyed by ordinary people. In acting as they did, these quiet heroes became hold-outs for humanity. And they became so not by being bigger than life, but by remaining life-size in a time when most people were diminished by terror.

Nevertheless, the hope which these people hold out must remain for ever partial. The fact that their actions seem so exceptional simply proves the rule—that the majority of the non-Jewish population did nothing to help their fellow citizens. The actions of the quiet heroes, who were explicitly Christian, speak volumes about what many other Christians and church officials did not do and did not say. While some Jews were rescued, millions perished. There simply were not enough good people to go around.

If there is any lesson to be learned in this, it is that no one, no group, should ever be placed in a position of being dependent only on the good will of a few people. What was needed then, as now, is a condition of social justice in which the rights of all have the necessary political and legal guarantees. The strands of society must constantly be woven together on a framework of equality. The reality, however, is that the social fabric sometimes becomes frayed at the edges and begins to come apart at the seams. In such times, only tensile threads of human mercy remain to tie human beings to one another. It is these human threads that can sustain a fragile hope of mending the world.

As this book follows the threads of various lives, it becomes clear that these people do not fit easily into any pattern. There were some who helped Jewish friends and others who rescued total strangers. There were those who were eager to help and some who were more reluctant. While some reflected about what they were doing, others did not. There is every shade and stripe of motivation in between the lines of these lives—religious beliefs, pacifist convictions, simple humanitarianism. These people are alike, however, in that they acted, they did something. In this they provide us with an important example of how to respond humanly in the face of vast socio-political problems today. These quiet heroes did not respond to an overwhelming situation in either of the two extreme ways which are so prevalent now. On the one hand, they did not take upon themselves the impossible burden of their times. They did not feel responsible for everything and everyone. On the other hand, they did not choose to do nothing. They chose, instead, a way of response which was as effective as it was humble. They did not do everything but they did do something.

Why did these people do something when so many others did nothing to help? This book does not answer this question but rather deepens it. Although we know something about why people are cruel and violent, we need to learn more about why human beings are good and merciful. This book invites us to learn from such people, to find in them not so much an *answer* to our questions as a *desire* to respond to those questions within our own lives.

There are few really happy endings in this book. Like so many of those whom they sheltered, these quiet heroes did not emerge unscathed from their experiences during the war. Most seem to feel that, while they came out of it with their integrity intact, there was much more that should have been done. This feeling is indicative of how the shadow of the Holocaust reaches even now into their lives and into our times. It was typical of the inverted world created by the Nazi ideology that those who were responsible for the crimes felt little guilt while those who resisted a criminal system felt that resisting wasn't enough.

But for those of us who read the stories of these quiet heroes, what they did is enough to go on.

Mary Jo Leddy, NDS
Editorial Team, *Catholic New Times*
Toronto
January, 1988

Introduction

In September 1984, I was invited to address the first conference ever held on "Righteous Gentiles", in Washington, D.C. In addition to hearing scholarly papers read and discussions undertaken by Christians and Jews, we paid homage to seventy-five rescuers of Jews. They were the honoured guests of the U.S. Holocaust Memorial Council of the State Department, and the Honorable Elie Wiesel presided.

The most outstanding feature of this historical event for me was the opportunity to meet with the handful of rescuers who attended. They were quiet, seemingly ordinary human beings. Only one thing distinguished them from the other workers, farmers, and homemakers whom I had met in my life: while so much of the world had been busy killing Jews or looking the other way and allowing the massacres to take place in an orderly fashion, these people had chosen to save Jewish lives. Not for money, not for fame, not for any personal gain—they just did it.

I was touched by the self-effacing shyness, the awkward bewilderment on these time- and weather-beaten faces. While these people expressed gratitude for the recognition they received, they seemed lost and ill at ease. In their judgement, the celebration of their particular version of heroism was largely misplaced and overstated. "Since when does a man deserve praise from the highest human sources for being just that, a man?" Some voiced this question in muffled voices, others wore it silently on their puzzled faces.

I, too, felt out of place. In the course of the previous few years, I had addressed dozens of audiences on three continents on the story of my family's demise as well as giving scholarly lectures on various aspects of the destruction of European Jewry. The tone of these meetings was always sombre and awesome. This time, however, an atmosphere of discreet celebration animated the lacklustre halls and corridors of the State Department: we were paying tribute to the good news, to tangible, breathing evidence of the existence of decency in human kind despite the overwhelming attestations to the contrary.

My opening address was the only bad news. You see, I spoke for the unburied—those whose lives were not significantly touched by the spiritual generosity and the courage of a "righteous Gentile". I didn't like my role as the bearer of bad tidings. So I sheltered myself in a corner of the main corridor while the rest of the participants abandoned themselves to the joy of meeting real live rescuers.

An elderly couple hesitantly approached me and interrupted my solitude. "We were touched and shamed by your testimony this morning," the man said haltingly, his words uttered with an obviously Dutch accent. "Please, don't take this as prying but we would be honoured if you would send us a copy of your book *Broken Silence* when it becomes available."

My interlocutors turned out to be Dutch, indeed, and now resided in rural Ontario. They had saved six Jewish people during the war, and now, seeing my discomfort, they had reached out to me. For that, and for their courage forty years earlier, I was grateful to them.

It was then that I decided that I wanted, that I needed to get to know as many rescuers as possible and to learn how they became life-savers in a landscape dominated by violent death. On that day, I decided to collect and recount their stories and also to put my training as a social scientist to the task of making sense of rescue in the context of killing.

To put one's own life and that of one's children in danger, I thought, must require extraordinary compassion and courage. And the number of those who possessed both was pitifully small. It didn't take me long to realize that, while these wonderful people deserved to be honoured, their existence is also cause for concern and suspicion: Why were there so few of them? Why weren't they joined by their brothers and sisters, their neighbours and friends, their ministers and teachers? While we may not fully comprehend the heroism of a Raoul

Wallenberg or an Oskar Schindler, it is easier to take hope from it than it is to make sense of the noble gestures of these common folk. It would have been so easy and so "natural" for them to follow the example of most of the Western world! And yet, they didn't.... Why?

A quick glance at the list of rescuers attending the conference in Washington revealed to me some noteworthy facts: There were more Dutch people among them than any other nationality. Furthermore, many of these Dutch people had resettled in Ontario, mostly in small towns and rural communities. It turned out that most of them were born and raised in the northern Dutch province of Friesland.

I knew I had to gather their stories before it was too late. I also knew that I must make my way to The Netherlands to see the places where the rescuing had taken place. I wanted to meet the families and neighbours of these people, to learn more about them and about those who had chosen to remain uninvolved in rescuing. I also wanted to meet and hear the stories of those Dutch rescuers who had chosen to remain in their country—often in the very same house in which they had saved Jewish lives.

Since most of the rescuers were married couples, I decided to ask my wife, Vicki Rosner Stein, to collaborate with me in the interviewing process. For one thing, the women would open up more readily to another woman and would feel more comfortable speaking about topics they would never have been able to discuss with a strange man. For another thing, Vicki is a psychotherapist, a skilled and compassionate interviewer in whom I placed my utmost professional and personal trust. The women's stories were indispensable. Typically, but not always, their husbands were out in the public world while the wives tended to the exigencies of the home. That meant, of course, that the wives did the lion's share of the actual hiding of and caring for their forbidden wards.

We used no questionnaire or schedule for the interviews. We asked common-sense questions and let the rescuers remember. Most of the time, they needed little prodding. With very few exceptions, the interviews were done in one sitting, taking anywhere from four to six hours. I kept in telephone contact with several of the rescuers, calling them for additional information or just to say hello. They often called me to inquire about the status of the project or just to tell us that they were thinking about us. One invited us fishing, another wanted to chat about her bad back, a third to find out when we could drop by for dinner.

Quiet Heroes

My experience with the rescuers in The Netherlands was a bit more complicated. First, I speak neither Dutch nor Frisian. Second, it was a lot more difficult to contact them. I received heart-warming assistance in the effort from Sister Carol Rittner, one of the organizers of the conference in Washington, D.C., and from Professor Samuel Oliner, the director and principal investigator of the "Altruistic Personality Project". Both of these researchers shared with me their list of Dutch rescuers.

With the assistance of a professional interpreter and translator from the State University of Groningen, we secured the co-operation of about a dozen rescuers.

The seven stories contained in this volume are factual accounts. Most of the rescuers, in order to preserve their privacy, insisted that we not use their real names. The Miedemas were the exception. Most of the time, in retelling the stories, I aimed at preserving the subject's style but not necessarily his or her exact words. Finally, I need to remind you, the reader, that the events are recalled from the distance of forty years, by people who are mentally and physically tired. While they cannot guarantee that every date, place, and name is accurate, they all insist on the truthfulness of the facts of their accounts. As such, I do not view these stories as literal renditions of "the truth" as much as consider them to be within the framework of truth and integrity. There is no doubt in my mind that these quiet heroes have done what they claim to have done. The survivors are living documentary evidence that the rescuers' stories are true. That's enough truth for me.

A brief historical overview will help the reader understand the reality the rescuers faced forty years ago.

On May 10, 1940, at 1:00 a.m., German bombers took off in the direction of the Dutch skies in an all-out air attack on The Netherlands. The pilots kept their navigation lights on to make sure that everyone could see the bombing run. The flights continued until 3:00 a.m. The Dutch thought that the bombers were heading for an air attack on England, but once the planes reached the North Sea, they turned around and, in an hour, they were over their Dutch targets. The people of The Netherlands were stunned.

The Dutch marshalled their troops and, relying heavily on their water defences, they fought valiantly. The battle was desperate and the losses were heavy. The Nazis were taken off guard by the

Introduction

unexpected feisty resistance and decided to break it at once, at any cost. The port city of Rotterdam was attacked viciously, the inner core of the city destroyed, leaving behind about a thousand dead and tens of thousands wounded and homeless. To prevent further devastation, the Dutch surrendered. In the first show of armed resistance the German forces had met, the tiny Dutch army held out for five days against the might of the Third Reich.

After issuing a strong protest against the invasion, Queen Wilhelmina and her family fled to England, the Dutch government following them and leaving the country totally under the power of the German occupying forces, commanded by Austrian Nazi Dr. Artur Seyss-Inquart. He promised the fretful population a return to normal life. The situation, as he described it, was simple: he made the rules; the Dutch had to obey them to avoid reprisals. Indeed, for a while, life did seem relatively normal and routine and the people were reassured. But not for long.

The Nationaal Socialistische Beweging (NSB), a right-wing authoritarian party founded in 1931 by Anton Mussert and C. van Geelkerken, couldn't have been happier with the takeover. This Dutch version of the German Nazi party, with membership amounting to about 8 per cent of the population, was elated at what they saw to be a golden opportunity to become the rulers of the land. But Hitler didn't trust them. Seyss-Inquart retained all the power and reduced the role of the NSB to that of his enforcers, ensuring that his rules were followed and that any resistance or sabotage activity was halted. The general populace despised and feared these vicious traitors.

It didn't take the Nazis long to beian their anti-Jewish activities in The Netherlands. Just as everywhere else, their plan was the deportation and liquidation of all Jews. By September 1941, all Jews had to register their names and addresses with the authorities. With about 140,000 names thus collected, the stage was set for the systematic removal of Jews from Dutch society and for their annihilation. The round-ups and the subsequent transports, euphemistically referred to as "labour assignments", began. For the first time since the Nazis put in place the "Endlösung der Judenfrage" (the "Final Solution" to the "Jewish Problem"), they met with actual resistance to their brutal treatment of the Jews: workers and public employees went on strike in Amsterdam. But this resistance was instantly crushed and the retaliation was merciless. The round-ups became devastating in

1942. Anti-Jewish laws proliferated with diabolical speed. For example, all Jews were required to wear the yellow star with the word "Jood" (Jew) printed in mock Hebrew letters in the centre. Jewish teachers and professors were fired. No Jews were allowed in cafés, restaurants, libraries, swimming pools, theatres, or cinemas; a curfew was set for Jews, prohibiting them from being outside between 6:00 p.m. and 8:00 a.m. Jews were allowed to shop for food only in the afternoon hours and, by then, there was hardly anything left on the shelves. Jews were relocated to one area of Amsterdam, near the central synagogue. The Nazis then set up a Jewish council to lull the fears of the panic-stricken Jews and to have it do the dirty work of compiling lists of who was to be deported and when.

The deportation of the Jews crowded into the Amsterdam ghetto during the previous months began. They were sent to Westerbork, a dismal transit camp in the north-eastern province of Drenthe. In existence since autumn 1939, the camp didn't become a warehouse of human beings marked for mass murder until July 1, 1942, when the camp passed from Dutch in to German hands. Renamed by its new masters "Police Transit Camp Westerbork", it was to be the last station in the Jews' lives prior to deportation to Auschwitz or other death camps. Of the 140,000 Jews in Holland, 104,000 passed through Westerbork. At the war's end, a total of 909 survivors were found in the camp. The Dutch disaster can be compared only to the liquidation of Polish Jewry. When Holland was liberated in May 1945, 90 per cent of its Jewish population had been murdered.

The Dutch wartime record of the rescue of condemned Jews belongs mostly to a relatively tiny number of ordinary, and often isolated, citizens who risked their lives to save some 15,000 Jews.

The volume you have in your hands is the testimony of a handful of these life-savers. Their stories are a balm to our sense of loss and a beacon in the dark history of humankind.

The Farm on the Dyke:
Bill and Margaret Bouwma

We knocked on the Bouwmas' front door several times without success. Vicki checked the appointment schedule, but there was no mistake. "It's warm outside; perhaps they're in the backyard," she suggested. Loaded down with recording and camera equipment, we followed the stone path around the house and discovered a wiry elderly woman tending to flowers. From the modest façade of this small house on the outskirts of Kingston, Ontario, I would have never guessed that there would be such a deep backyard behind.

"You must be the Steins," she said, looking up at us, her words marked with a strong Frisian accent. "Don't mind us, we have some work to finish in the yard. Just make yourselves at home. Put down your things; help yourself to a glass of water if you are thirsty."

I unloaded my equipment among the gardening supplies in their cluttered mudroom and returned to the yard. The woman was explaining to Vicki what she was doing. "Come, young man, let me show you what we have planted this year." She was so casual, so relaxed, so patient with our urban ignorance about the land, that I had an immediate intuition about how it had happened that she had reached out to people in trouble. And yet, I felt a bit ill at ease with my clumsiness in her presence.

"My husband is somewhere in the fruit trees, I'm sure," she said, looking straight into my eyes without staring. Her skin was tanned from a life spent outdoors. Her face was open, uncomplicated.

"Here I am." We heard a man's voice without seeing the person to whom it belonged. "Come on over here and let me brag about our fruit orchard."

After passing beneath a dozen fruit trees, we met our host. He was a sturdy replica of his small-boned wife. I would have been more inclined to take them for siblings than for husband and wife.

"Just call me Bill," he said, extending to me a dirty hand. "Things aren't always what they seem to be. The dirt on my hand is clean soil. And my name is not really Bill." He flashed a radiant smile at the both of us. That smile, the broad, open face, and the rich white mane on his head, all contributed to inspire the same kind of trust in me that he seemed to have for the soil.

After identifying the variety of each fruit tree, we filed into the house. Our hosts left their *klompen* by the door, as they had learned to do as children, about seventy years before.

"We do our best talking in the kitchen," Bill said, inviting us to join them at their grey formica-covered table. "Later, we may wish to resettle in the living room, just for a change of scenery."

"We are very pleased to co-operate with the two of you, Vicki and André," the lady of the house told us, articulating her words slowly and carefully. "I hope you're not offended by our familiarity. Living close to nature, we never had any use for formality. We'll tell you what happened to us during the war. Not because it is so extraordinary—the way we see it, it's hardly worth the trouble or the time—but because you seem to think that others could find worth in reading about it, and we respect your judgement."

"But we certainly don't want any praise or fame for it," Bill chimed in. For the first time, he looked serious. "That's why we prefer that you don't use our real names. You know our family name, obviously. And perhaps our Christian names, as well. But from here on, please refer to us as 'Bill' and 'Margaret'. No one in this community knows about our rescue activities and we prefer to keep it that way. People in the New World tend to make a big deal out of small things. We appreciated the respect Elie Wiesel's people paid us in Washington because it came from Elie Wiesel, a man we admire. But when he asked that the rescuers stand to be honoured, my legs were shaking:

I was ashamed and embarrassed. I felt like a phoney basking in somebody else's glory. Do you understand what I mean?"

"I don't, to be truthful," I replied, a bit confused, "but I will respect your wish."

"I, too, have a wish," Margaret spoke up. "Bill and I agreed that while everything we did, we did together, he will speak most of the time. As you must have noticed, my English is quite clumsy, and I get tongue-tied. If it's necessary, I'll interrupt him. Or if you have a question to which I know the answer and he doesn't, I'll speak up."

"Well, Bill, how did it all start?" I asked my opening question.

"I don't remember how it all started. All I know is that when Edith Cohen's name came up, there was little to say and, in fact, little to do other than to say, 'But, of course, let her come, naturally!' And that was that.

"Margaret and I were not actively searching for a way to intervene. That was just not our style. But when someone told us that there was a Jewish woman in her thirties who needed shelter, we were ready. We hadn't discussed all the details of such a dangerous undertaking. All that seemed to matter was that a person had an urgent need to hide. What was there to be discussed? We had the place; food was not a concern as we had a potato farm. Our own safety? Not relevant in the presence of a hunted Jew. Anyway, we were sure we could outwit anyone who saw fit to poke his nose into our business. The nearest German garrison was about five kilometres from us. The farm lay outside of the village, often lost in milky mist.

" 'This is our domain; we govern it as we see fit,' Margaret and I agreed without consulting each other. Discussion was not necessary. If it had been, most likely we would have remained uninvolved.

" 'When the law of the land turns on the people, it has to be amended or ignored. After all, what kind of law is it that demands the lives of children and the elderly, of people who have nothing but peace in their hearts?' I would ask myself time and again. To be sure, I knew the answer but I was not one to throw up my hands in resignation. Have no doubt, we were exemplary citizens, but we would never have agreed to serve a hostile master. We were loyal members of a community, a nation. We loved the House of Orange. It has always conducted itself with respect for all of its subjects. But now that Queen Wilhelmina had chosen exile rather than being party to the destruction and humiliation of her subjects, it was a natural matter for us to pledge allegiance to the hunted and against the hunter.

" 'But, of course, let her come, naturally,' Margaret agreed. 'She is welcome to stay as long as the Nazis are after her. Should she wish to extend a helping hand with the kids or the household, that assistance would be welcome, but it is not a condition of her coming. She is not coming to work. She is coming to live.' And that was that."

"Who was the link between Edith and you?" I inquired.

"A shadow from the underground," Bill replied. "A man? A woman? Young? Old? Neighbour? Stranger? Not only were the details irrelevant, but it was imperative that the shadow's identity remain a secret. Encounters among those in the resistance movement often had to be furtive—without so much as a handshake. The task of saving lives took precedence over overt signs of friendship and civility. Knowledge of the identity of a courier could lead to his or her torture or even death, not to mention the potential collapse of the underground railroad. How many links connected Edith to us? No one could tell and that was the best way for all involved.

"Naturally, we had to invent a story to account for her sudden appearance in our midst. Ternaard was a small town, everyone knowing everyone. Our children and the outside world were to be told that my second cousin, Edith, was going to spend some time with us because her place had been hit during the bombing of Rotterdam. There were quite a few evacuees in Friesland.

"Later we learned from Edith that she had lost her husband in a raid. The butcher who had employed her as a bookkeeper had chosen to flee. She set out to visit her sister in The Hague to find shelter and solace with her. However, by the time she made her way to the railway station, the order prohibiting Jews travelling was in force. Defeated and anguished, she returned to her apartment. When she arrived, her front door had been sealed by the authorities. In desperation, she sought temporary refuge with some friends of her husband. It was they who set in motion her vanishing act.

"A week passed, then a silent stranger came to escort her to a truck, which drove her to a northern suburb of Amsterdam. There she was met by a young woman who, without introducing herself, took her by the arm and led her to the bus stop where she was met by an elderly couple. They sat Edith between them, acting quite solicitous, as parents do towards an unwell child.

"They made it to Leeuwarden, the Frisian capital, without incident. They took a long walk along the river. There they met another stranger who led Edith to another bus. When the bus reached Ternaard, her escort suggested that she get ready to get off, wishing her good luck. By way of luggage all Edith had was the small suitcase that she had packed for the trip to The Hague. Except for some cash and a few pieces of jewellery, she had left all her belongings behind in the apartment. Edith left the bus without her companion. By then she knew the routine: there would be someone to meet her who would recognize her without ever having laid eyes on her. When she set foot on the cobble-stones of our village, I moved towards her. When I was a few steps from her, I welcomed her heartily: 'Hey, cousin Edith, over here, it's me, Bill. It's been a while, hasn't it? Margaret and the kids are waiting for your arrival. So is my mother.' With that, we shook hands. Although Edith was tired and disoriented, she knew her part in this charade. She managed to greet me with a smile.

" 'Cousin Bill, so nice to see you. I'm so much looking forward to spending some time with your family. How is everyone?'

"I took her suitcase and secured it to the back of my bicycle. Then I pointed at the bike next to it. 'This one is for you. We have about six kilometres to ride. I hope you can still hold your own on one these things, you city-dweller.' I teased her without looking at her. I was making an oblique allusion to the insane law that forbade Amsterdam Jewry to ride their bicycles. And we set out on the westbound road leading to the sea, to our home across the road from the dyke."

"How was it for you to share your home with a total stranger?" Vicki asked.

"Edith settled into our lives as if she was a member of the family. Being a woman of intuition and spiritual strength, as soon as she learned that our sea-sprayed potato farm would be her home and that we would be her hosts she knew that she had to fit into our world as smoothly as one slips into a familiar shoe. She was a frail-looking woman, slender and short. Her olive-skinned, oval face was exotically crowned by dark hair. Maybe even dangerously so. We all agreed that there was nothing in her appearance of a Frisian woman. Thus, we quickly resolved that Edith would not venture into Ternaard. She would be free to move about on the farm, but it was in everyone's best interest that she not stray beyond its boundaries.

"It took her no time to settle into the household. She had a keen feel for when her participation in the family's routine was welcome and when it would have been awkward and intrusive. She tried to make herself useful by helping Margaret with the daily chores. My wife, however, felt uncomfortable about Edith doing housework.

" 'You are not here as a domestic,' Margaret told her. 'You are our guest. We don't want to exploit or profit in any way from your predicament. So, please, don't worry about work. I managed before you arrived, and I will continue to manage.'

"Edith didn't like to remain idle, but she didn't push the issue. And yet, confined to the farm, she needed something to fill her free time....

" 'Do you have a radio?' she inquired. Listening to music and news would not only allow her to let her imagination fly way beyond the limits of the farm, but also keep her informed about whether or not there was hope for the Jews—for Simon, her husband; for Gerda, her sister; and for the rest of her family and friends. For Holland.

" 'Well, we do and we don't,' I told her. 'When the order came to hand in our sets, I surrendered one cheap one and buried the good one in the field. It's our property. The bastards have no right to it.' I dug it up for her.

"Food was not a problem: we had plenty of potatoes, of course, and also bread and dairy products. And while it was strictly forbidden to slaughter a pig, we took the risk of secretly providing ourselves with meat, bacon, and fat."

"Was your home large enough to accommodate another person comfortably?" Vicki inquired.

"We were a bit cramped for space. The three kids shared one bedroom; we had another one. Edith occupied an alcove behind the kitchen. In fact, Margaret wanted to hide more fugitives. I was frequently absent from home during the evening and early night hours. I didn't say where I spent all that time. But Margaret knew: I was helping to place and to escort Jewish refugees in the area. I had that freedom of movement. But Margaret had no such way to make herself useful in the rescue operations. She was a feisty woman, my wife.

"A few weeks after Edith's arrival, one night after the children went to sleep, the two women were sitting in the kitchen, chatting, when I came in, dropped my coat, straddled a kitchen chair, and without any introduction announced: 'Edith, your niece Sonja has been placed in my mother's house. She will stay there as long as is necessary or safe.'

" 'My nine-year-old niece, Gerda's daughter, safe and only five kilometres from here? That's a miracle!' Edith was moved to tears, but she choked them back as well as she could. 'Oh, my God, that's incredible.... How in the world...?' But then she checked herself, obviously remembering the absolute secrecy that had cloaked her journey from Amsterdam to our farm. What did it matter really who and how? Sonja was safe and in Ternaard with my mother.

" 'I can't tell you how grateful I am,' she said awkwardly. 'You can't imagine what it means to me to know that my sister's only child is going to live in safety and without deprivation. And I am deeply touched that you would risk your own lives to shelter us, the pariah. You are indeed heroes — quiet heroes. You share your homes without reward of any sort. You wouldn't even accept the modest sum I offered to you for my board.'

" 'A guest doesn't pay,' I said.

" 'We are grateful to *you* for providing us with the opportunity to do the right thing in these troubled times,' my wife added in that moral style she learned from her mother. Margaret was about Edith's age. Given the different upbringing of the two women, it would have been quite understandable if they had remained strangers. Instead, they became quite close. 'You have never done me any harm, you are a creature of God just as I am, you lost your world because of what so-called Christians have done to you—what better bond could there be between you and me? Besides, you are so gentle with my kids. I love to listen to you tell them stories, to watch you play and become almost like a child yourself. I could never let myself go like that, not even with my own kids. I'm too self-conscious, too afraid that they would end up thinking that I am silly. But you, you just jump in as if you had never left your childhood. You and I have very different ways of expressing ourselves, but you carry in you the wisdom of a woman who has seen more than just what lies between the village and the dyke. I hope that when the world turns right-side up, we will remain friends.'

" 'The Nazis and those boot-licking NSB-ers dump everything of which they are guilty, of which they should be ashamed, on the backs of the Jews. It is almost as if they look at the Jew and see in him, like in a mirror, their own reflection. They hate what they see, so they want to smash it. Don't worry, Edith, an ill wind always blows itself out. It's tragic, however, that it leaves so much destruction in its wake,' I told her.

"Then, suddenly, I had an idea. I hastily left the house and late that night when I came home, Edith was sitting silently in the dark family room, looking at the ceiling. I noticed her, motionless in the armchair. Thinking that she was asleep I made a special effort to navigate the unlit house without making a sound. Then Edith rose to her feet to retire for the night.

"'Oh, you're awake, Edith. I hope I didn't wake you, but as long as you're up, I have some news for you. I just came from my mother's house. She and I agreed that it would be quite safe for you to walk over to visit her and Sonja after dusk. You may take Hendrik and Aafke with you. They would enjoy the visit, too, and it would look more natural for you to be taking them for a stroll than for you to be out alone. With those two in tow, you'll be quite safe. Do you feel brave enough to venture out?'

"You know what that crazy woman did? She jumped up and kissed me. 'I'm so happy—happy for the freedom to walk the road other normal people walk on, happy to see Sonja, and happy that you cared enough to cook up a plan to make my life more joyful, more normal. Now I'll be able to chat with Sonja, to find out what happened to Gerda and her husband.' Of course, I blushed.

"One night, after Margaret and the kids had retired for the day, Edith and I were sitting at the kitchen table sipping coffee. I was reading some religious text, and she was darning a sock. We exchanged a few words every once in a while. Somehow the topic of gratitude came up. I got worked up fast.

"'Cut that stuff out, Edith. What kind of a world is it when people think that doing the right thing deserves praise? You either do your duty—and there is nothing remarkable in that—or you don't do your duty, and then you pay the consequences. We know what we have to do and we do it the best we can.'"

"How *did* you know what you had to do about the Jews?" I interjected.

"Well, I'll be darned, that's exactly what she asked me. 'How do you know what the right thing is, Bill? I have been wondering ever since I met you what was in it for you to risk sharing the fate of the Jews. So why, Bill, why?'

"I sat for a while in silence, gathering my thoughts as if preparing an answer to a question during cross-examination before a jury. In a very private way, in fact, I was doing just that. I had never really stopped to examine my motivations. There was a job to be done. Farmers don't have the luxury of being able to consider whether or not to do what has to be done. Those who learn their wisdom as well as their rules of conduct from the land, don't have many choices—nature doesn't wait. If you don't sow today and today is the best day for it, by tomorrow you will have to pay a price for your delay. But when Edith questioned me, I gave it some thought. 'Yes, why *are* we doing this? Are we crazy to be risking the well-being of our kids, our parents, even if we don't mind being reckless with our own lives? Is it not wrong to be so concerned with the fate of others that you fail to secure the future of your own?' I felt my stomach begin to do somersaults. 'Maybe this is all wrong. Maybe I should just arrange for Edith and Sonja to go somewhere else where they'd be safe and to stop this whole Jewish business and mind my own potatoes. She is right, what business have I playing with fire? What am I trying to prove? That I am braver than the next man? Or that I am more righteous?' Suddenly I was very confused. 'I say that I know what's the right thing, but do I really know? What's right, saving my family or saving strangers?' You see, I was not used to analysing the reasons for my actions. The decisions I had to make were usually straightforward. I felt a tightness in my throat.

" 'I just don't have the answer for you, Edith, I just don't.' I got up and left.

"Whenever I needed to collect myself, I climbed on the dyke and lost myself in the hypnotic rhythm of the waves. But this time that soothing spectacle couldn't hold my attention. Instead, I paced up and down on the dyke like an expectant father. For me it was a very grave matter, finding an answer, and finding the right one. That answer would allow me to live in peace with my conscience for the rest of my life and would afford me the courage to prepare to meet my Maker when the time came.

"After hours of vacillating, I stopped suddenly. I had the answer. 'My God, it's so elementary, how could I be so blind....' I ran back to the house, and without worrying that I might disturb others, I stomped inside. Without slipping off my *klompen*, I clonked straight to Edith's alcove behind the kitchen. In my haste I forgot my manners: I just threw the curtain open and abruptly woke the sleeping woman.

" 'Bill, what's come over you?... I don't understand.... Is there something wrong? Are we having a raid?' Edith questioned me breathlessly, clutching her flannel nightgown around her.

"It dawned on me suddenly that I was invading her privacy. I felt like an idiot. 'I'm sorry, Edith,' I apologized. 'I don't have the right to barge in on you like this. After all, this is your home, too. It's just that your question really got me going. But now I know what the answer is. And since I'm rather clumsy with words, I want to explain before I lose the words.'

" 'Look, Edith'—I started to speak in a quiet and calmer voice—'I could tell you all kinds of stories. I could tell you that I was brought up by my parents to always help the weak. I could tell you that I know what it feels like to be the underdog. I was very poor when I started out on my own; it's not quite the same thing, but it opened my eyes to what it is like to be without resources. And that would be the truth. I could also tell you that my faith teaches me to open my door to the homeless, the refugee. Can you imagine Judgement Day? The Lord would ask me: "What did you do, Bill Bouwma, when the Nazis were tormenting My people?" And I would have to answer sheepishly: "Nothing, my Lord. I had other things to do." I could also tell you that I am predisposed towards this kind of risky adventure by virtue of my military training and experience. All these stories would be true.

" 'But the real explanation is simpler than all this. I am involved with helping Jews because a voice inside me told me that I had to do it. Regardless of everything else, that's all there is to it. If I disobeyed that voice in me, I would no longer be me. I don't know if this unsophisticated farmer-talk makes any sense to a city-educated Jewish woman, but it's as basic as planting potatoes. As for my family—well, I'm not ruminating about my fear for them all the time, but when I do think of it, or when danger presents itself, I'm plenty scared. But I'm not panicked to the point of being unable to weigh the risk. Their lives are not in danger most of the time, in fact, hardly ever; whereas you and the others have no tolerable choices. I have been reading in the resistance literature about gas chambers and other mass killing centres in the East. Compared to that risk, the ones we take are embarrassingly minute. And that's all there is to it, Edith. Your question stirred up in me a powerful storm. It had to be calmed down.'

"After that, life took on an ordinary cloak in our house by the dyke. Edith had become a regular member of the family. The children never asked who she was or why she had come to their home. Edith was Edith and that was that. She spent a great deal of her leisure time with Aafke and Hendrik, reading to them, playing games with them. On occasion, she would get down on the floor and pretend with them that they were animals in the jungle, making the sounds and gestures of wild beasts. In their delight, the kids would forget about the quiet nature of our homelife. One day, I had reached my limit.

" 'Stop that. We cannot have such a ruckus in the house. You never know who might walk by. I don't want trouble. I'd have thought you would know that.'

"Edith blushed. I think I shamed her. She retreated into her alcove, and for days she didn't say a word to anyone. It became obvious that she was in a deep depression. Everyone asked her what was wrong—was she ill, was she homesick, was she worried about her husband—but she just kept repeating that she needed to be alone. But if you ask me, that was the last thing she needed. She needed to be free and in her home, with her own people.

"I never would have guessed that my remark to the children would have such an impact on her. Had I realized how strongly my concern for safety, and my selfish preference for quiet, would affect Edith, I would never have spoken.

"When she lost interest in visiting Sonja, we started to worry. You see, she had become an entirely different person since the arrival of her niece. When she had spent a bit of time with the girl, she would forget the reality of her current life. Now and then, she would take Sonja for a quick walk on the dyke. The two city-slickers were soothed by the mysterious sea and the islands looming on the horizon. But now, Edith did not want to see even Sonja."

"It sounds to me like she was in the grip of depression," Vicki commented. "Your request for silence, Bill, could not have set off such a crisis."

"You see, I didn't know that. Margaret could not understand what was happening to her friend, either. Later she confessed to me that, for a while, she secretly harboured a growing resentment towards this woman whom she thought far more attractive than herself—certainly a lot more mysterious than anyone she had ever met. She grew increasingly uncomfortable with Edith and I spending evenings together in the dimly lit kitchen, talking about who-knows-what. At times, we didn't make a peep. Margaret tormented herself more and more with doubt. She would have rather died, of course, than confront either of us with her fears. Rather, she endured in silence, and that was the hardest part for her since silent suffering was not her style. She was used to being outspoken. But how could she level such accusations at either me or her friend? Some of her fears tainted her daily rapport with Edith—a sharp word here, a stubborn silence in reply to a question there. Once, for no good reason at all, she refused to allow Edith to take the kids for a walk. For a couple of weeks, the two women managed to avoid any situation that would have forced them to be alone with each other.

"But when Edith grew more and more gloomy, Margaret's feelings shifted rapidly from resentment to concern and guilt."

"What was your guilt about, Margaret?" I asked her directly.

"I had been insensitive to her plight, that's what." Margaret cast her eyes down as if she were still in the clutches of that guilt. "She was cut off from her past, without any knowledge of her husband's fate. Her entire universe had been reduced to our farm and the occasional stroll with Sonja. How could anyone *not* go crazy trapped in such a restricted version of life? I felt ashamed of myself for begrudging her the few moments of adult male attention she required to keep whatever was left of her memory of being a woman. She just needed to hear a man's voice; there is no harm in that."

"Margaret took the responsibility for Edith's mental and emotional exhaustion all onto her shoulders. Ashamed of her silly female jealousy, she tried to woo her friend out of her self-made cocoon, but to no avail.

"'Day after day,' Margaret reported to me about two weeks later, 'I hear sounds that could come only from physical pain.' But Edith was not speaking to her about it, and she was not about to pry. But, this time, I wasn't so shy. I, too, heard the occasional moaning and groaning coming from the alcove. 'What's hurting you, cousin Edith?' I asked point-blank one morning. She looked pale and hunched over, as if she had been kicked. In case you wonder, I called her 'cousin' more and more frequently. She began to feel like a cousin, and I wanted her to feel that she *was* part of our family and not an outsider.

"'Nothing in particular, Bill; I guess winter is coming. My bones are not as young as they used to be,' she replied, dispiritedly.

"Despite Edith's assurances, Margaret and I decided to have the doctor examine her. When I think about it, there was not much conviction in her protest. Dr. Dykstra was one of the most committed workers in the local underground. Countless Jewish children and women found safety and received medical care from him. He despised the Germans, even in peace time. I went to see him about Edith. He asked that Edith be in his office that same evening.

The Farm on the Dyke

"We waited until it grew dark. As bad luck would have it, we ran into two German soldiers on bicycles, riding in our direction. But Margaret took control of the situation at once. 'We'll pretend I am the sick one and the two of you are taking me to the doctor. It's always the sick one people pay attention to.' Without a word we sandwiched Margaret between the two of us, supporting her. The Germans climbed off their bikes and shone a flashlight in our faces.

" '*Was ist los?*' one of them asked without much interest.

" '*Meine Frau ist sehr krank. Wir gehen nach Artzhaus.*' My German was rough and my delivery hostile. But it did the trick.

" '*Schade...also, guten Abend,*' the soldier replied as he remounted his bicycle.

"Dr. Dykstra believed that Edith should see a gynaecologist friend of his as soon as possible in the provincial capital. We covered the distance back to the farmhouse in silence. I was trying to figure out how to take Edith to Leeuwarden. Travelling with a Jew had become most hazardous. There were random checkpoints, and Edith didn't even have a fake identification card. With her exotic appearance, she would be unmasked in no time.

"Around noon the next day an old man came with a message from the doctor. The lady had an appointment with Dr. van Hertum the following day at 7:00 in the evening at his office in the Diakonnessenhuis, the best hospital in Leeuwarden.

" 'Well, I'll have to do some quick thinking,' I muttered. 'There has to be a way because we have no alternative,' I added aloud for the benefit of the two women. Margaret silently agreed with me. One look at her and I saw panic in her eyes. Edith was in violation of so many laws! And what of her travelling companions? Traitors all of them, and we knew what fate 'Jew-lovers' could expect when caught in the act. But Edith certainly could never make it alone, so what other option was there? It was too late to get someone not directly involved with the underground, and if Dr. Dykstra said it was urgent, then we couldn't take chances with Edith's health. As for Edith, it was easy to see that she was tortured by remorse: she knew what was going through our minds.

"Later that evening, when I came home, I called the family together for an 'important announcement'. 'Listen to me, all of you, adults and children. I have something quite extraordinary to tell you. We are all, and I mean all, going to take a trip tomorrow into Leeuwarden. Cousin Edith has an appointment with the doctor, and the rest of us will go along just to keep her company. How does that sound to you?'

"The kids were loudly enthusiastic. A trip to Leeuwarden seemed as fabulous to them as a trip to America. They had never been past the limits of Ternaard. Margaret and Edith looked at each other, incredulity mixed with terror on their faces. Neither of them spoke a word for the rest of the evening.

"When Margaret and I retired for the night, Margaret looked like she wanted to speak to me about the plan, but, somehow, she couldn't get up the courage to oppose the trip. As I told you, I knew my wife.

" 'We have to take Edith to Leeuwarden, right?' I turned to her once we were in bed. 'We will take the kids with us. A family of six, with all those children, would raise fewer eyebrows than a man in the company of a woman who couldn't pass for Frisian under any light. In a way the kids are our best hedge against detection. Besides, we're in this together, all of us. It will be all or nothing, right?' "

"Are you a gambler by nature, Bill?" I asked.

"Far from it. But when you have no other choice, gambling is your only reasonable alternative, right? Besides, Margaret agreed with everything I said. 'These cursed Nazis, it's all their fault. I never thought the day would come when I wished harm to any human being, but these perverts should perish if their hatred is so strong that it might take the lives of my children. I wish I could do more to hurt them. I feel so terribly frustrated, like my hands are tied. We'll deliver Edith to the doctor, of course.' She spent most of the night praying.

"The trip to Leeuwarden was, in fact, completely uneventful. We arrived around 5:00, just in time for supper. I had taken a large amount of cash with me, or at least an amount that was large for me. We had never been to a restaurant or a hotel in our lives. I wanted to look respectable, and I thought it would be so audacious to take a Jew to a fancy place that no one would ever suspect anything. The Hotel Oranje was teeming with German and Dutch officials. Its restaurant was a local hot spot. I felt a lump in my throat at the thought of being so out of my element. 'Jews and Dogs Not Allowed' the sign on the door read. We ate in silence. The children were intimidated by so many strangers. All those uniformed men sounding and looking as if they owned the whole world made them sink into their chairs and concentrate on their food. We all breathed a sigh of relief when we found ourselves on the street.

The Farm on the Dyke

" 'I gave you an appointment for this hour because my last patient left at six. Most of the staff is gone. There is no point in risking unfriendly encounters. Don't you agree?' Dr. van Hertum spoke to Edith in a warm, caring voice.

"After the doctor finished the thorough check-up, he signalled to Margaret and me to join them in his office. There he informed us in a reassuring but grave tone that he thought Edith might have to undergo surgery and that he would like to admit her to the hospital. 'I'm fully cognizant of your particular "non-medical" predicament. It is my understanding that you don't have satisfactory identification papers. I'm quite prepared to take the necessary steps to procure for you adequate papers. If we get you in soon, you'll have no problems. If you should delay...'

" 'If I have to have surgery, I'll have it in Amsterdam. I am deeply touched by your kindness towards a stranger in my condition, but I still have to decline your offer. I want to go to Amsterdam,' Edith answered."

"She didn't much believe in making things easier, did she?" Vicki said.

"That's probably what the doctor thought also. And so did we. But in her place, who knows how any of us would have reacted. We never lost sight of that. So the doctor said: 'I don't know if you fully realize your own predicament.' Then he proceeded to enumerate all of the obstacles Edith knew only too well. She listened politely, looking into the doctor's eyes, watching the many wrinkles around them grow deeper as the old man became defeated by her stubbornness.

" 'I don't know what mystical force draws you so fatally to Amsterdam. But I am in the habit of respecting my patients' decisions. All I can do is to look after your medical condition to the best of my abilities. So I am going to give you the name of a colleague of mine in one of the suburbs of Amsterdam. He lives and practises in a quiet residential area. I will contact him for you and he will be expecting you by the time you get there. After the war, you can buy me a good bottle of cognac and we'll be even. It's not good to feel obligated to someone for the rest of your life.'

"When we left the office, my wife and I looked at each other. After what seemed like a long second, Margaret's eyes said a silent 'yes'. And I said: 'If we have come this far, we may as well push on to Amsterdam, if that's where you need to go. But we'll need a private means of transportation.'

"Edith just nodded. 'You just do whatever you need to,' she said, fatigue taking hold of her whole body. The day had exacted an enormous toll from the frail creature. I needed to speak to an acquaintance in the capital to make some arrangements. As we walked along the deserted side streets of Leeuwarden, I left the gang for about five minutes. I returned with good news.

" 'We will spend the night at a friend's house. From there, we will take a taxi to Amsterdam tomorrow morning very early.'

" 'A taxi!' the others repeated in disbelief.

" 'I can't afford a taxi,' Edith turned to me, 'and neither can you, nor would I let you spend that kind of money. There has to be another way.'

" 'This is no longer your concern,' I responded with the voice of authority. Then I added in a whisper: 'I now have a new mission.'

"At 4:00, when the sun did not seem sure whether or not to rise, our tired gang climbed into the weather-beaten automobile with the luminous sign on its roof extinguished. The road to the capital was not yet busy, so we made very good time. Then we hit a road block. I whispered: 'Edith, lie down, and let them hear the sounds of your pain. Margaret, give me your papers quickly.' My heart was in my throat. But the price of losing my composure could be six lives.

" 'Documents!' I slipped the policeman Margaret's ID first. He dignified it with only a cursory glance before returning it. Then, one by one, I handed over our papers. When it came to the last one, I slipped him Margaret's papers again. He took a longer look this time and then took a peek at the obviously agonizing woman sunk into a corner of the back seat.

" 'What's with your wife?'

" 'She is very sick. We have been told by our doctor to rush her to this clinic in Amstelveen before it's too late. That's why we hired a taxi.' The policeman glanced at Margaret who had most of her face buried in her coat and then looked back at Edith, then at Margaret again. Something seemed to be bothering him. Finally he said with a faint smile: 'Well, make haste. I wouldn't want anything to happen to your wife, not a thing, you understand,' and he waived us on. No one said a word. We were still not sure if it had really happened: we had just successfully passed a checkpoint. All it took was a desperate stunt and a decent policeman. I had no doubt whatsoever that the officer had suspected that something was fishy. Had he investigated the matter, he would have had to do something nasty.

"Edith was not only speechless, her entire body was shaking.

"Desperate times call for desperate measures. It's amazing how quickly you can find courage when you need some. So, we reached our destination without incident. The street seemed to be deserted. Most of the living in this neighbourhood took place behind closed doors. I rang the bell and the door was opened almost instantly.

" 'Yes, yes, come on in, all of you, please.' A silver-haired lady ushered us into an elegant but simple hallway. 'I am Nora Gerrits, the doctor's wife. My husband will be with the patient right away. Dr. van Hertum spoke to him last night. You'll be in good hands here, my dear,' she said, turning to Edith. She had no difficulty detecting the person in pain. 'The rest of you will have coffee or hot cocoa with me.'

"The doctor appeared from behind a white door at the end of the hallway. His thin, bony face seemed ashen. 'I just spoke to Corrie van Hertum. Wouter has been taken into custody for treating a Jew. She's already spoken to the *burgemeester* to intercede on his behalf, but without success. Apparently he has been under surveillance for quite some time and they have a long file on him. The NSB chief is hell-bent on sending Wouter to Vught. It seems to be a matter of vicious revenge. To guarantee his victory, he involved the Gestapo. Van Hertum is as good as dead.'

"Dr. Gerrits uttered all this in a faint whisper intended for his wife's ears, but we heard every tragic word. When he realized that his patient had overheard him, as if by pressing a button he replaced the gloom on his face with a fatherly but reserved smile. 'Just come with me, young lady. I know all about you. You need not worry. We'll take good care of you here; we'll make sure everything will be quite all right.' He opened the white door and gestured to Edith to precede him.

"About thirty minutes later, the door opened and they reappeared in the hallway. 'Excellent, then we are all clear on everything. The clinic is in the next street, just around the corner to the left. You see, I'll be very close to you. You may walk over right now, you'll be expected.' He extended a friendly hand to Edith.

" 'Dr. Gerrits, I'm profoundly touched by your willingness to risk everything for me, especially in the light of the tragedy that has befallen Dr. van Hertum.' Her voice was faint. 'You are a kind, generous man but I have very meagre funds at my disposal...'

" 'Did you hear me mention money?' The doctor interrupted her. 'Health is one of the few things in life that we are all entitled to regardless of the size of our wallets. As you can see I have more money than my wife and I need.'

" 'My dear, the patient is on her way to the clinic, and I will join her momentarily,' he said affectionately to his wife before disappearing behind another door. Mrs. Gerrits discreetly retired from the living room to allow us a few private moments.

" 'Well, Bill, Margaret, kids, this is it, the moment you have all been waiting for,' Edith said, with an unconvincing jollity in her voice. 'You'll be rid of cousin Edith. I'm going to enjoy the good doctor's hospitality for a while. God bless you all. I'll miss you, and now I'd better get out of here before I embarrass you, and myself, with silly tears. I won't thank you because what you have done for me is beyond gratitude.' She picked up her case, and dashed through the front door without saying goodbye.

" 'I was afraid my urge to shed tears might be stronger than my ability to suppress them. And Margaret was already busy foraging for her handkerchief in her handbag. The children, accustomed to not asking many questions when their parents sounded or looked serious, continued to inspect the tips of their shoes. They understood that cousin Edith was not coming back to the farmhouse with us. She came from the blue; she'll return to the blue. Life goes on, either way.

"We thanked Mrs. Gerrits for the treats and asked her to keep us posted through an intermediary, Uncle Harry, the codeword for the underground.

"The taxi-driver was patiently dozing in his seat. 'Next stop, please,' I said after everyone had shut the doors. The driver did not need any further directions. He seemed to know his way around. After a thirty-minute ride, he stopped in front of a two-storey brownstone home. There were a few people on the street, all busy and purposeful; no one was loitering. Judging from all the trappings of the street, we were in a working-class suburb. I got out, and knocked. Seconds later, a very large woman opened the door.

" 'I've come to pick up your niece. Uncle Harry sent me.'

" 'So, you're the one who's going to put her to work. Well, good riddance, she has been doing nothing but eat and sleep here. Maybe you'll make something out of this lazy girl. Ilga, your new boss is here,' she yelled upstairs with the tone of a fishwife. A slightly built, very pale young girl appeared on the threshold. She was not even carrying a handbag.

" 'Don't you have any luggage?' I asked, somewhat surprised.

" 'She came with nothing, she is leaving with nothing,' answered the woman.

" 'We'll have what you'll need. Let's go. We've a long ride before we're home.'

"Ilga left without even looking at the old woman. In the car, she let out a sigh of relief. 'Take me anywhere. Any place will be better than that hell.'

"It was night when we arrived back at Ternaard. The taxi drove us all the way to the house. We couldn't risk letting the newcomer be seen. Rescuing Jews was like fine surgery: one little mistake and the patient was dead. And so was the surgeon," Bill mused.

"We didn't have a chance to nurture our sorrow for having lost Edith because our new guest not only slipped into her scarcely cooled-off bed but she generated her own heat around the farm. Rachel, Ilga's real name, was as different from Edith as the sea is from the earth. She was fuelled by the exuberance of seventeen years spent in the lap of luxury. When she sat down with us for our first meal, she immediately told us the story of her life. Did she inform us about her lavish past as a veiled attempt to map out her expectations? While Margaret and I were keen to get acquainted with this young stranger who was going to share our lives, we were concerned about the children learning more about this new cousin than they could digest. Margaret invited the girl to join her in the kitchen where she asked her to hold off finishing her story until the kids were tucked in. As far as the kids were concerned, Ilga, too, was a distant cousin from Amsterdam, related to Aunt Edith.

"Her family occupied a commanding position on the Diamond Exchange of Amsterdam. She grew up in a residence overlooking the colourful spectacle on Prinsengracht, one of the canals that meanders through the city. Rachel had grown up in a vast room, with oriental rugs and a piano in front of her window. So, for Rachel to be torn away from a world that she had always taken for granted as her birthright was at first disorienting and then infuriating and frustrating. For a while she thought it all a nightmare. She threw tantrums, which confused and angered her first hosts who were taking a chance on sheltering her, but for a sum large enough to guarantee them a lifestyle to which they would have gladly become accustomed. As such, they tolerated the outbursts of the 'Ruby Brat', the name they gave to Rachel. They provided her with the meagre necessities of life, in addition to a tiny corner in a modest, partly rural suburb of Arnhem. The hosts tolerated Rachel's whims, which they neither understood nor cared for, because the longer she stayed, the closer they inched their way to owning the little farm they had longed for.

"One day, however, Rachel felt she was being pushed too far. They wanted her to take on the menial task of housekeeping, saying that it would occupy her and not leave her so much time to brood about her diminished circumstances. Rachel lashed out at her hosts, and the woman of the house pinned her to the hard stone floor.

" 'You shut up, you ungrateful, spoiled bitch,' she hissed, 'or I'll hand you over to the police and they'll kill you and all of your family.'

" 'And I'll tell them about how you have kept me here for the money my father gave you, and you will come with me to the grave, you greedy pig,' Rachel returned.

"That night the couple decided to make a deal with the woman's alcoholic sister: she would keep the brat and they would share the money with her. She wasn't the most patient or caring person in the world, but what did they care about that little bitch? Whatever happened to her, she had brought it upon herself.

"To Rachel it all sounded like a Grimm's fairy tale: the witches plotting the gloomy fate of the pretty young princess who had no way to save herself. She couldn't get in touch with anyone who could help her.

"Three days later, a neglected-looking old woman presented herself at the door. 'So, this is the runt that's supposed to keep me company and help spare my aching bones. Who're you kidding? She's of no use to me. She's got milk-and-honey-soaked hands; she won't do any work unless I beat her day and night. But I'll take her in anyway because I can use the money. I want two hundred guilders to be paid every Sunday. If I don't have the money in my hand, Monday morning she's in the street, is that clear?'

"No one argued with her. Rachel was told to get out, just like that. They did not allow her to take her personal belongings—not the gold locket that held the only pictures she had of her parents or the little ruby ring that had earned her the spiteful nickname 'Ruby Brat'. 'You'd better leave these with us for safekeeping,' they'd said."

"I wonder what happened to people like that after the war," Vicki mused.

"Most of the time, not much." Margaret's tone of voice was sombre.

"Her new host had no concern for her well-being. As soon as Rachel arrived, the woman began to lay down the rules. 'Here you're on your own, kid. Whatever I don't do, you do. I don't cook, I don't clean, I don't do the wash. The rest is none of your business: I drink and I sleep. Most of all I don't want to hear your yammering. You just keep your tongue from wagging. Nothing interests me. No one comes to visit and you can go out if you want to be picked up and taken to the gas chambers. If you get caught, I have never laid eyes on you.'

"Rachel found out that the woman was not exaggerating. After a week of blending into a room that looked and smelled the way she imagined sewers did, she lapsed into a coma-like sleep. When she awakened, she felt dizzy from hunger. There was nothing to eat in the house. She decided that she would rather die right there and then than waste away in that infernal hovel. She walked into the street alone. Her hostess, just as she had predicted, did not raise any objection to Rachel's running into the open arms of death. The young girl had been kept so sheltered from the grim realities of the day that she did not hesitate to go up to the first stranger she met.

" 'Sir,' she said, 'I am a young Jewish girl abandoned to a drunken old witch who hasn't fed me for a week. Please, help me find another place to hide out or I'll go to the police and ask them to arrest me.'

"The man looked at the kid as if he had just seen a ghost. 'You can't just go up to any stranger in the street and tell him you're Jewish. You aren't even wearing the yellow star. Don't you know you can be taken to a concentration camp just for that? Don't you know anything about the law of the land? Where are your parents? They must be fine people to just leave you like this. I've never cared for your people, you're all selfish, you think you own the world...'

"That's all Rachel heard. When she regained consciousness, she was lying on a hard bed. The walls around her in the tiny room were decorated with crucifixes and pictures of saints. The man she accosted in the street was sitting at a table, whispering to another man.

" 'Where am I?' Rachel wondered aloud. 'Are you the enemy?'

" 'No, we are not the enemy, but we are not friends, either,' said the man. 'I already told you I don't like your kind. You are not Christians and you have no souls. But it says in the Good Book that you are God's favourite people. That's because you're a challenge to God.

Well, if you are a challenge to God, then you are a challenge to man. You are a miserable bunch, but we'll have to love you anyway. You cheat us on our clothes, you cheat us on our food, you're the dentist, the doctor, the banker, and wherever we go, we find your cheating lot. It must be in your blood to cheat. No wonder you're a challenge to God; it would require all of His efforts and ours to make you into decent Christians. So, my brother and I will do the charitable work of God by helping you out. Don't ask how. The Lord has many ways, and we happen to know one of them. Just praise the Lord who sent you to us, and we praise Him for allowing us to do His work.' Then the man gave her a thick slice of bread and a hunk of cheese.

"A little while later she was told that they were going to take her back to where she was staying and that someone would come for her very soon to place her in a good Christian home where she would be converted. About a week later, I showed up on the scene.

" 'The devil has so many faces. Each time you think you've seen them all, he shows up with a new one,' I said to her. What I really thought was not fit for that kid's ears.

" 'You're more than welcome in this house,' Margaret added, putting her hand on the young girl's arm. 'Whatever we have, we'll share with you in good faith. It's not that we are friends of the Jews or their enemies. It is our human duty to open our home, our pantry, and our hearts to anyone who suffers. And who suffers more today than your people?'

" 'Don't worry, young lady,' I chimed in. 'We not only don't expect you to convert, we won't allow you to abandon your faith. The Lord put you on earth as a Jew; you have the right to live out your natural life as a Jew. We don't want to steal the faith He has given you. Anyone trying to convert you is as much a murderer as the man who pulls the trigger. One kills the body, the other the soul.'

"Rachel slept for two days and two nights. It was nearly lunchtime when she showed her sleepy, but by then smiling face in the kitchen. 'Good morning, Margaret, would you show me the shower, please?' Rachel approached my wife politely.

" 'The truth of the matter,' my wife replied with a touch of embarrassment, 'is that we don't have a shower here. We wash in a washbasin in a room we call the "bathroom" because we bathe there, but we don't have the modern facilities you must be used to. It does the trick for us; I hope you'll get used to it soon, too.'

The Farm on the Dyke

" 'Well, all right,' she said. 'While the water heats up, can I have my breakfast?'

"At that comment my wife's ears perked up like those of a rabbit in the field listening for the hunter's steps. Margaret invited the young girl to sit for a second with us.

" 'Look, Rachel, it's best that we get a few things out in the open for everyone's sake. We had a Jewish lady here with us until the day we picked you up. She spent a long time with us and she became our friend; in fact, by the time we parted, we all felt we had left a family member behind. How did this happen? Mostly because we had very clear expectations from each other. She never worked for me, but she never expected to be waited on, either. Do you understand what I am trying to tell you?'

" 'Fine, I just won't have breakfast, if it's such a hardship for you people to be properly hospitable. In our house, any visitor who stayed overnight would be served breakfast in bed, if that was his heart's desire.' Rachel stormed out of the kitchen, leaving us behind with our mouths open. We had never been addressed in such an insolent manner by anyone.

"We feared for the future of this association. But the worst was yet to come. My helper, Wilto, saw Rachel on the road to the village. When he asked her where she was headed, she snapped at him: 'I'm going to check out this hole-in-the-wall for some fun. Do you have any objections?' He insisted that she return to the house at once. Rachel just shrugged her shoulders and continued on her way to Ternaard, wiggling her posterior. I had to have a stern chat with that snooty brat.

"Rachel could not be contained. In spite of admonishments and blatant orders to refrain from showing herself in public, she continued to sneak off to wherever her fancy would take her.

" 'Is she determined to get apprehended, or is she too dumb to understand the danger she is in? Why does she think we are hiding her?' Margaret would ask me, time after time. Every day she grew more anxious that the girl's recklessness would lead to our destruction. Once again, I sat down with Rachel to impress upon her the irrevocable consequences of her being denounced or caught by a German patrol.

" 'Don't you worry your potato head for me, cousin Bill,' Rachel reassured me in such a flippant manner that I could not control my welling anger.

" 'Now you listen to me, and listen good. I know that this underground life is no life for a young person, but that's the way it has to be if you want to stay alive. I want you to hide, and that's an order.' I had not given such an explicit command since my artillery days. 'You owe us no gratitude for hiding you—that's our duty, and we do it without hesitation. But we do expect you to take all the necessary precautions so that our lives will not be in jeopardy. Our children have as much right to live as you do. This stinking war can't last for ever. Then you can go back to Amsterdam and party every night if that's what makes you happy. Until then, you stay away from the village. You can go on the dyke and watch the sea; it'll fill you with excitement if that's what you need, or it will give you a sense of peace. But that's it. Is that clear?'

" 'Just who do you think I am?' She looked at me as if I was a toad. 'A bubble-headed, starry-eyed goose? I can talk myself out of any situation. I speak German and French fluently. This is the boonies; there are no German troops stationed here to conduct searches. And I can disarm the odd patrol with the flash of a smile or a turn of my skirt, and I can lead them on with a dirty joke in German. As for the townsfolk, they mind their business—you told me that yourself. Live and let live, for goodness sake!'

"I decided to find another hiding place for Rachel. I was not the man to re-educate her. She was a young animal who was bucking all attempts to dull the call of the wild. Live and let live—she had hit the nail on the head—but her avid thirst for adventure undermined our chances to live. 'She's got to go, and go fast,' I resolved.

"That night I came home past midnight, exhausted and defeated. None of my contact people had a place for her. They all sensed trouble. I spent days searching for a hospitable Frisian to take her. Finally, I found a young family in nearby Anjum willing to rise to the task. They were already sheltering another Jewish adolescent who was just as lonely and disoriented as Rachel. I could hardly wait to let Margaret know the good news. When I opened the kitchen door, my stomach jumped to my throat: Margaret was sitting in the kitchen in her nightgown, her hair dishevelled as if she had just been woken from a deep sleep by Satan himself.

" 'Oh, my God, Bill, thank heaven you're here; Rachel has been shot to death,' she blurted out in a fit of tears. 'Old man de Jong passed by half an hour ago to warn me that earlier this evening that good-for-nothing NSB-er and his accomplice accosted her as she was riding the bike into town. They sandwiched the unsuspecting kid. Then suddenly, one of the bastards pulled a revolver out of his coat pocket, ordering her to turn her back to the wall with her hands raised high. The other proceeded to pretend to search her, but in the process, he took advantage of her. Rachel turned around and kicked the degenerate in the groin. She jumped on her bike and wheeled away breathlessly. The other one shot her in the back. That poor child, that poor restless child...what have they done to her? What have we done to her? God have pity on us.'

"I held my wife silently. I wanted revenge—blood for blood. This must not go unpunished. I wanted to run into town and strangle the sons-of-bitches with my bare hands. But reality cooled my anger fast. Before anything else, I had to take protective steps in case of a raid. Then I would deal with the bastard.

"I took the kids to my brother Ian's place in Bergum. Then I hugged my wife, thinking that might be the last time I would ever see her. 'I'll try something that may work,' I told Margaret. I stormed out of the house on my bike, peddling for my life towards Ternaard. I went to the NSB-er's. I heard loud voices inside and I entered without knocking. The small room was filled with smoke. The three men around the kitchen table were stunned when they saw me fill the door frame. One of them reached into his pocket and left his hand there. It was obvious to all that my visit was not of a social nature.

"'To what do I owe this unprecedented honour, Mr. Bouwma?' The host spoke with thinly veiled sarcasm. But he didn't fool me: his voice was shaking. 'I want to talk to you, Pieter, alone,' I said. The two others seemed only too happy to clear out fast.

"'Listen, Zwarte Pieter'—I cut right to the matter, using the derogatory name the Dutch reserve for evil-doers—'you shot a young woman this afternoon.'

"'What's it to you? She was a Jewish bitch. Unless you were the one hiding her.' The NSB-er launched a weak counter-attack.

"'Perhaps I was, perhaps I wasn't.' I was determined to stay with the text I had rehearsed in my head. 'That's not important, not now, not tomorrow. Nor does it make any difference whether she was or was not Jewish. She was a kid. And you bastards made her the object of your filthy games. You have a choice now. Get out of Ternaard on the first bus, disappear. Or stay put, and within the week you'll die in a ditch like a dog. I give you my word that if you don't vanish, your days will end within one week. This is the will of your neighbours;

I'm only their spokesman. And one more thing: should you run to the Germans for help, they'll give it to you. But know this: if suddenly we should have a raid, for each person arrested you will suffer torture of your body and mind that you have never even imagined, not in your worst nightmares. Am I making myself clear?'

"The NSB-er's face had turned to chalk. My words had had an effect. The murderer was terrified for his life.

"I turned around without a word. Before I closed the door behind me, I looked at the petrified louse and reminded him with ice in my voice: 'Tomorrow morning, the first bus, or else...'

"The news of the first casualty of the war in Ternaard blanketed our community in sorrow. No one spoke of it; no one asked questions about anything relating to the NSB-er who, in fact, had disappeared without a trace. No one knew what had happened to the victim's body. Margaret and I scarcely spoke to each other. Cousin Edith vanished one day, then Cousin Rachel. The young ones learned, without being told, about vulnerability. They began to fear for their mother and for their grandmother, who was still sheltering Sonja. I decided to spend more time at home in the evenings. While most evenings I was reading, it was reassuring for them to have me around. Margaret grew unusually quiet. The children missed her soothing words, but they knew that their mother was consumed by a deep sadness. Silence was not their companion, it was their guardian angel."

"What would you have done had your bluff failed to have the desired effect on the NSB-er?" I questioned Bill.

"Who knows?" The answer was clear. "I would've thought of something else.

"A week after Rachel's death, at bedtime, someone knocked on the back door. 'I need to talk to you urgently. Come out for a minute.' The stranger did not introduce himself. Margaret's furrowed brow accompanied me to the door and beyond. She knew what these nameless visits were about. We had not come to any kind of decision about our continued rescue activities. And somehow, as if the underground knew that we were navigating treacherous waters in the dark, they were allowing us the time to reach some kind of a harbour. But Margaret realized without discussion that I would extend my assistance — our assistance — to another Jew in need. Our pain was nothing compared to what a Jew had to endure in those days — deportations, torture, execution.

The Farm on the Dyke

"We all grew more brittle in the grip of famine as the country endured its fifth winter under Nazi domination. Jews were disappearing from the land faster than people imagined possible. Frisian farmland became the haven for an increasing number of desperate Jews. The resistance could no longer afford to respect our grief. So, when the stranger appeared at our door, we were both ready to get involved again. Once more, it was a young woman who needed to be hidden at once. She was already in Ternaard, with Dr. Dykstra, but he had a full house. Without hesitating, I offered to fetch her and place her with the woman who had agreed to take in Rachel. By the time I returned, Margaret was fast asleep. When my aching body sank into the bed, she opened her eyes.

" 'Her name is Irma Bloch. The Ypmas were happy to have her.' Margaret heard what she wanted to hear. A person in need was taken care of, and thank God, not in her house. She was not quite ready for that.

"One Sunday morning, after service, a kid slipped a piece of paper into my hand. On the way out of the village, I read the note: 'Come to see us. We have some important news for you concerning our young friend. The Ypmas.'

"That evening I found out that Irma was pregnant. I told them I needed a day to see what could be done. Pregnant women were the hardest to place. The next evening, I returned to Anjum with an outlandish proposition. One had to be inventive those days, you know. Luckily, the Ypmas took their underground work very seriously. I asked them to have the two Jewish women join us.

" 'Do you have full trust in your doctor?' I asked the Ypmas.

" 'Dr. Hogeterp delivered both of us. He has been like a member of the family.'

" 'Here is my plan, then. Louisa, you'll pretend to be pregnant. Irma will keep out of sight as soon as her condition begins to show. From then on, you, Louisa, will start padding your...hmm...you know what I mean. Your doctor must be in on the secret; obviously without his and the midwife's participation, we can't pull it off. They'll have to call on you and not you on them. When the time comes, she'll deliver the baby and you'll claim that it is yours. Of course, you'll have to give the baby your name.' "

"Were you always so clever in inventing schemes?" Vicki asked.

"No, not at all. I had never needed to scheme, so I never bothered. Before the war, my life was an open book. Once we started hiding Jews, I had to get myself a new book and keep it closed," Bill replied.

"Scheming is not a Frisian habit, in general," Margaret added.

"I stole a glance at Irma," Bill said, continuing his story. "Her face was ashen. Even from a distance I could see her lips quiver, but she remained silent. Her eyes were glistening with barely hidden tears. 'The war can't last for ever,' I said, turning towards her. 'Once we are free, you'll change the birth certificate.' She shed silent tears.

" 'My husband and I accept the challenge without hesitation.' Louisa seemed frightened to hear what she was saying. Owen approved with a nod.

"Over the next few weeks, I placed eight more Jewish kids. I was beginning to tire. One night, just after I collapsed in bed, we heard a knock on the back door. A man I had seen only once in my life stood there, visibly shaken.

" 'I've got someone on my tricycle who wants to kill herself. Help me, please!'

" 'Come in, for goodness sake. No one is going to kill herself at *my* back door.' My wife spoke with anger in her voice. She was standing behind me in her nightgown. The man reappeared in the doorway, pushing his tricycle.

"We witnessed a most peculiar spectacle. On the back of the tricycle there was a large blanket-covered package tied to the frame of the luggage carrier with a length of rope. This shapeless bundle was crowned with a large heap of lampshades. Margaret and I looked at each other to make sure we were not dreaming. When the man took off the outlandish wrapping, we saw a frail young girl, curled in the fetal position. Her bright red hair and her chalky white face glowed in the dark night. The man carried her into the house. She could not have been more than twelve years old—a starved young girl with pallid cheeks and flat green eyes. She was clad in dirty rags, but she did not seem to care about what was happening to her.

" 'Her name is Ko. Old lady Zwaan was hiding her, then she threw her out. She's got a couple of young lads as paying guests as well, if you know what I mean. According to her, this child and the boys were up to no good. When she caught her half naked, between the two in the back of her stable, she picked up the pitchfork and chased her off her property. A neighbour found the kid half-dead by the road. He fed her, gave her these rags, and sent her on her way. My brother found her unconscious in the pigsty. We have our hands full from sun up to sun down with...well, let's just say we're busy.'

" 'Say no more,' I interrupted him. 'We'll keep her, of course.'

" 'We'll fatten you up, dear, and give you some decent clothing. You'll rest up and recover here. And you'll stay with us until it's safe for you to go home,' Margaret said to the young person. 'Come with me, Ko. Let's get you settled.' Margaret reached for the girl's hand.

" 'Don't touch me! I've got a cyanide tablet. I'll swallow it right in front of your eyes,' Ko screamed with a weird fire in her voice, as she recoiled from Margaret. She looked like a trapped wild creature.

" 'Don't be scared, Ko. We're good people; we want you to live with us. We have three kids, plenty of food. The farm is large, when the fog rolls in you can't even see the nearest farmhouse, and the farmer is a good man, so let's not speak about cyanide. Come on, Ko, how about some sturdy potato soup and a nice chunk of cheese?' Once more Margaret attempted to get close to the bewildered young woman. But the girl met this second approach with the same violent rebuttal as the first one. 'See my pill? It's cyanide. I swear I'll take it if anyone comes near me,' Ko hissed with her bony arm stretched out to display in her dirty palm the lethal white tablet.

" 'Look, miss,' I began, trying another approach, 'you're not the first Jew we've had in this house. We had a lady from Amsterdam, then a young girl, also from the capital, and we've placed about twenty Jewish kids all around the region. So you see, we're not the enemy, we are friends. You may be the chosen people, but this time around, the Almighty has chosen us to save His people. So don't insult Him by threatening to throw away the life He gave you.'

"Ko remained silent. She pulled her arm close to herself and held the fist with the pill tightly against her chest. She just stared into the night.

" 'Where are the women you claim to have been hiding? Are they still alive? Are they still here?' Ko asked finally with distrust in her voice.

" 'One of them, Edith Cohen, had to be taken to Amstelveen for surgery,' I revealed to her. It wasn't smart to say that much in front of this stranger. I was breaking the sacred rule of the resistance: secrecy. The doctor could be traced and, fearing for his life, could be forced to talk. But I was faced with a crisis. I had to give concrete proof to Ko that we were on her side.

" 'Edith Cohen may be a relative of mine. My Uncle Simon was married to an Edith,' Ko said, more for herself than for us.

" 'That's our Edith,' I said with a sigh of relief. We had made contact with her.

" 'I remember you now.' Margaret was excited. 'When Sonja came to Mother, she told Edith that a member of Simon's family named Ko survived and was being hidden in Friesland. That's you! Well, isn't this a small world. The good Lord scatters His people, then gathers them again in small circles.' This time Margaret didn't try to touch Ko. I shook hands with the man, closed the door, and signalled to my wife to follow me to the bedroom.

"The next morning, we found Ko sitting at the kitchen table, scrubbed shiny, her bright red hair groomed as well as was possible. The dirty plate in front of her indicated that she had not waited for us to serve her. She had eaten the potato soup offered to her last night, cold, for fear of waking us.

" 'Good morning, madam, good morning, sir. My name is Ko. Forgive me for disturbing the calm of your home; it won't happen again. If you keep me, I'll do all the housework to pay you for my room and board. I am not a beggar and I don't take charity. I am a person, you know.' She sounded humiliated, violated, and wrung out. 'I'm not a whore, a slut, a tart, a devil, a witch, or any of the other horrible things old lady Zwaan accused me of.... I'm just a human being.... I'm a person even though I'm Jewish.... I'm nothing but a person.... I'm a person...you know....' By then her emaciated body was hunched under the weight of her shame.

"The children stood there in their nightshirts, dumbfounded. They had never seen such a curious scene, such an extraordinary person. But they already knew that every now and then the war would sweep unusual people onto their threshold and that, eventually, it would all calm down. Margaret and I were silently weeping, undone by so much human suffering.

" 'There was once another innocent child born to a Jewish mother, tormented and tortured by cruel people. He turned out to be our Saviour,' I whispered more as a consoling lament for myself than as an encouragement for Ko.

"She settled into our life little by little. She had horrible nightmares every time she closed her eyes. And each time she woke up the whole household with her blood-chilling, inarticulate screaming. No one ever raised a word of reproach to her. Margaret's fine intuition led her to allow Ko to help with the chores. The girl had to do her share to feel like an ordinary person. She needed it as much as a sick person needs medication.

" 'Old lady Zwaan was wrong, all wrong,' she opened up to Margaret without preamble one morning while they were cleaning up after breakfast. It appears that when the old woman saw her with those brutes, with her clothes undone, she just jumped to the wrong conclusion. They had dragged Ko into the back of the stable, ripped her clothes off, and abused her. She hadn't had a chance to jump to her feet before they fell on top of her, ripping at her blouse and skirt. That's when old lady Zwaan came in and chased her away with the pitchfork.

"Later that week, we had a disturbing visit from Mr. Huizinga, the notary. 'Look, Bill and Margaret, I'm risking a great deal just by coming here, but I have to warn you. You are in grave danger here. Not that anyone wants to harm you, you enjoy everyone's respect. We also know how much you have done for the Jews. Even your mother is involved. I don't think any harm will come to her, but these are unpredictable times. As notary I see a lot of people and I hear a lot of things. And one of the things I have been hearing lately is about you hiding Jews. Understand me, nobody wants to do you in. The good people in town, without intending to do so, started a snowball. One man says to his friend: "Bill Bouwma has Jews, but don't tell the wife, you know how women gossip." But he does tell his wife, because he has no secrets from her. The wife has a best friend who knows how to keep a secret, so she tells the friend. And soon enough a whole circle of friends and acquaintances know everything that you have done, and perhaps even more. There are rumours about you and Zwarte Pieter's disappearance and about the shooting of that Jewish girl. You see what I am getting at? Your name comes up too often. In fact, I have been told by someone who works at the German garrison in Holwerd that your name has already reached certain hostile ears. Bill and Margaret, be careful.'

"We were on the edge of panic that night. What were they going to do? Ko would take her cyanide pill if she were to be moved again. But how could we not move her? We had no real hiding place to speak of. There was a large buffet in the corner of the kitchen with a chair behind it. When neighbours, or friends dropped in, our Jewish guest would climb in behind. No one could see in, but the person hiding could hear everything. When the visitor left, she would climb out. We

had never given a thought to the possibility that we might be raided.
And we had been so cautious. During Rachel's short stay no one had
denounced us, despite her indiscretions. Even Zwarte Pieter had not
set the Germans on us. How ironic it seemed that it was the good
people of Ternaard who posed the greatest danger to us with their
idle chitchat. That's what happens when people talk without having
anything important to say. I thought we Frisians were smarter than
that.

" 'Two things must be done: Ko must go to my brother Piet's
house; as much as he refuses to get involved, he won't let us down.'
I had decided to tackle the crisis head on.

"I never questioned my brother's passivity. Piet did not want to
be involved with the Jews; that was his choice. It was also common
knowledge that Piet Bouwma minded his own onions and that was
that. He didn't participate in anything—not before the war, not during
it. He was a truly solitary man. I went to see Piet immediately and
told him about the crisis. He remained silent for several minutes.
The wheels were turning slowly in my brother's brain, but they *were*
turning.

" 'Send her over,' he said finally. 'We'll keep her for a while. Let's
hope some s.o.b. doesn't put two and two together and come up with
four. I'll take care of the wife. But don't leave the girl here longer
than necessary.'

"The other matter was to provide Sonja with a counterfeit past and
papers to legally support it. Removing her from the community would
have aroused curiosity among the kids and even their parents. The
school could get involved. The local police gave us much leeway, but
they would be forced to investigate the disappearance of a child. We
needed papers for her, and we needed them fast. In the meantime, I
sent her to visit the Ypmas.

"When I went home, Ko and the kids were singing. 'We made
cookies and we're having a party, right kids?' She looked as proud
as the little ones. I was delighted that the young woman was back
to enjoying the simple pleasures of life. Even her nightmares were
no longer so violent. Margaret had definitely snuck into her heart.
Ko had adopted Margaret as her substitute mother. I shuddered at the
thought of having to uproot this vulnerable creature again.

"But that night, the three of us sat down around the kitchen table
and I jumped into the story with both feet. 'Ko, you're going on
a visit to my brother's for a while. Because so many people wag

their tongues uselessly, we are expecting to be raided. If they catch you here, that's it for all of us. Even Hendrik, Aafke, and the baby.' I looked Ko straight in the eye. I felt like I was pleading for my children's lives.

" 'For how long?' Ko asked in a whisper, seemingly absorbed by the intricate pattern of grooves in the old kitchen table.

" 'Just for a few days. I'll work out something for you in the meantime. My brother and his wife are good people. They look scary, because they don't have much to smile about, but Piet and I had the same mother and father.' "

"Excuse me for digressing for a moment," I said, interrupting Bill's story. "As I listen to you describe the difference between your behaviour and that of your brother, I wonder if you can shed some light on how it was that the two of you came from the same home and yet reacted in such different ways to the plight of the Jews. How was that possible?"

"Piet was Piet and I was I," Bill responded laconically. "That's all I know.

" 'All right, let's go then, the sooner, the better.' " Bill picked up his story again. "She had no belongings to pack, except for a nightshirt, a couple of undergarments, an old sweater of Margaret's, and some personal hygiene items, symbols of her re-entry into the company of civilized folks. Margaret hugged her warmly, perhaps more effusively than she had ever embraced our own kids. I took Ko to Piet's that very night.

"The next day, I went to Leeuwarden to secure documents for Sonja. When I got back, I fell into bed exhausted. A bit after midnight, we were awakened by loud banging on the front door. Obviously we were not swift enough for the intruders' taste, because they began to kick the door, as well. I was not going to receive whoever was out there in my nightshirt and bare feet—that would have been undignified. My concern for dignity led to our front door being kicked in. By the time we got to the front room it was full of Germans and Dutch stormtroopers. There were ten of them in the raiding party.

" 'Do you have to make such a ruckus?' I whispered in anger. 'First you break my door, then you wake the kids and scare them out of their wits, you brave heroes!'

" 'We have reason to believe that you're hiding Jews in the house,' said one of the Dutch soldiers while the others were sniffing around.

" 'If you'll excuse me, I've been having cramps all evening, and I'm afraid nature's calling again.' Without waiting for permission, my wife dashed out of the room. When the buzzards left, she told me what it was all about. The day before, when I had dropped off Sonja's papers, my mother had given me a bundle of resistance literature. I had left the papers on the kitchen table. Margaret remembered the leaflets and that's what caused her sudden cramps. She grabbed the bundle and dashed into the bathroom, locking the door behind her. With an immense sigh of relief, she began to shred paper feverishly. But before Margaret could dispose of them all, a couple of troopers began to kick the bathroom door. She stuffed the rest in her underwear and opened the door in a huff. 'There you are, victorious soldiers of the Reich, you can have the toilet all to yourselves, the both of you,' and she walked past them.

"They searched the house from top to bottom, but found nothing that gave them an excuse to arrest us. They did, however, take Wilto, the fellow who helped me in the fields, and questioned him about the Jewess. He insisted that he had never seen a Jewess on my property. They loaded Wilto into the back of a truck already full of people less fortunate than us. Wilto was young; they could always use him in one of those forced labour camps. We never learned what happened to the poor lad in return for his silence.

"Three days after the raid, I had arranged to remove Ko from Piet's house. Nothing seemed simple in this cat-and-mouse game but every once in a while things snapped together like two pieces of a puzzle. I had sought out Dr. Dykstra for advice about where to place Ko.

" 'Take her where they'd expect her the least—back to Amsterdam. Here you can't be of much use to her anymore. You are a marked man. You have to get out of this business.' You'd never guess where he sent me: to Dr. Gerrits, in Amstelveen, where we left Edith!

" 'Are you sure it's okay?' I asked in awe.

" 'Young man, I never thought I'd see the day when I'd have to tell you that you talk too much. Mostly you ask too many useless questions instead of being on your way to fetch the girl. About face, and out you go.' The old crusty doctor was furious. But as I was leaving, he called out after me: 'Do you really think I would send you all the way to Amsterdam if I wasn't a hundred per cent sure that it's okay?'

"Ko was terrified at the idea of having to board a train. And we had to board several. She was not sporting the yellow star, nor did she have any fake papers. She was naked in a world full of Jew hunters. But it had to be done.

" 'Here is the plan,' I said. 'We board the same car but not together. You sit on one side; I, on the other. You never know what might happen: somebody may recognize you, or someone may want to get me. This way they won't get both of us. In any event, you don't know me, I don't know you.' We boarded the train without incident. Fortunately, there were no Germans in our car. But we could hear them singing in the next car. When we reached our destination, we had to make our way to the doctor's house on foot, at times, to be on the safe side, through backyards. At one point, I jumped across a fence and fell head first into a large, full garbage bin. When I climbed out like a ridiculous puppet, Ko could not stifle her laughter, but we both ducked instantly. This was not the time for levity.

"Finally, we made it to the doctor's house. Once again, it was Mrs. Gerrits who opened the door, and once again, she ushered us in with hospitality. 'Please come in, we have been expecting you.' Behind the white door, the doctor was dozing when his wife ushered us into his office.

" 'Come, come, how nice to see you again. I see you're still a smuggler of contraband lives, aren't you? Well, I hope the good Lord will reward you one day, because you can't expect any reward in this life.'

" 'I don't expect anything, doctor, just to make sure that these people see the end of the war in the best possible health.'

" 'Well, you'll be pleased to know that our mutual friend here'— the doctor acknowledged Ko for the first time, with a grandfatherly smile—'will be in good company. She will be taken tomorrow morning to the same barn where Edith is spending her extended holiday. The owners are marvellous people: our son and daughter-in-law.'

"Ko nearly fainted in her relief. Sometimes things do work out. I beat a hasty retreat after wishing Ko God's blessings and I headed back to Ternaard."

"That's the closest to a happy ending so far in your story," Vicki said with a sigh of relief.

"Let's stretch our legs for a few moments, shall we?" Bill suggested. "My joints are beginning to feel a little rusty."

"When were you liberated?" I asked our hosts, after a brief break in the interview.

"Freedom shone upon Ternaard for the first time in five years on a crisp late April day in 1945. As if nature wanted to do its share to celebrate this rebirth, the familiar fog kept its distance from the jubilant village. Less than twenty-four hours before, German troops and equipment had swept through the main street with silent fervour. The arrogance usually etched into those stony faces had given way to worry. They were running home to Papa Adolf like so many mischievous brats. Except this time Papa Adolf had to disappear also. I can't say I felt sorry for any of them.

"There had never been so many people in the streets of Ternaard. There was no trace of the habitual Frisian reserve. Joy flowed freely throughout the village. There were orange ribbons dancing in the brand-new breeze. It was contagious, intoxicating, and feverish. You had to be there, what can I say?

" 'The reign of fear is over!' Margaret exclaimed. 'No more hiding people, no more trembling in the night, no more raids! I only wish we could share this day with our Jewish friends. This is their day, the day none of us were sure we would ever see with our own eyes.'

"At first I didn't want to go into town. I feared the powerful feelings exploding inside me and I didn't want to be a spoil-sport. I wanted to stay home and blow my bugle, which I hadn't touched for five years. But the children wanted to be free that day. So we all rode our bikes into town to celebrate with Grandma and Sonja. They, too, were in the street. Mother hugged every member of the family, planting a teary kiss on every cheek. Indeed an extraordinary day, for she was not given to such demonstrations of affection, especially in public.

" 'Today, I love everyone,' she shouted, bursting with happiness. 'Even the Germans. I love them for having left, and I'll continue to love them at a distance.' We all laughed. Sonja was sporting an orange kerchief and orange ribbons in her pigtails.

" 'I can go home soon. I can see my parents. I'll miss you, Grandma, but I've got to go home and be with my family, my Jewish family....' She was running around like a mischievous puppy. She ran up to neighbours and exclaimed: 'I'm Jewish, I'm Jewish. I bet you didn't know I'm Jewish.' She discovered the taste of freedom, the joy of pride in being openly Jewish.

The Farm on the Dyke

"The next day I went over to shake hands with the Ypmas and to salute Irma Bloch. They were all celebrating. Irma had just delivered a baby boy. What can I say, I was once more moved to tears. It had to be a sign, a peace offering by a God to His people who, once more, had lost His protection.

" 'The first child of freedom will be a leader of men,' I said to all with a smile and a tear in my eye. 'It's a good thing this miserable war is over. I haven't shed as many tears in more than thirty years as I have in these past twelve months.' I shook Owen Ypma's square hand and said: 'Brother, you're a good man, you and I have a friendship to build. What we shared together is a blood bond, and this baby is the proof of what people can do to fight even the most powerful army without shooting one single bullet. One of these days, we'll go fishing.'

" 'If anyone deserves any credit,' Owen said with a grin, 'it's my wife. She bore the brunt of the extra work and worry. I was hardly any help at all.'

"Irma was in the bedroom, radiant, with her son beside her, on this day when everything smelled of spring. Even the exhaustion of labour could not clip the wings of her happiness and her gratitude.

" 'You people are saints. You'll go down in history as holy men and women,' she said between bursts of laughter. 'I will name my boy Louis Owen Wilhelm in honour of all of you people without whom he would never have been born. If only Maurice could be here to see, to hold his son.' It was as if someone had turned the sunlight off in the sky. Mourning settled into her dark eyes.

"I placed a hesitant hand on the grieving woman's shoulder. I was not sure if it was decent for me to touch her, but it was a unique day, with unique rules.

" 'God will look after Maurice so that you may look after your child without worry. No one can replace a lost life but you didn't really lose him; obviously God needed him. As for little Louis, he will always have at least two fathers, right neighbour?'

" 'Uhmm,' the other agreed in a scarcely audible voice.

"A week later, close to supper time, a lady showed up at our door. She looked tired and dusty, but her pale face was animated with a peculiar light.

" 'My name is Mrs. van Eyck,' she said when I appeared on the threshold. 'I've come for my daughter.'

" 'Your daughter?' I repeated. 'There must be some mistake. We don't have anyone's daughter here except our own.'

" 'You must have her. The people in the underground in Utrecht told me you had my Sonja and you say you don't know her.... What does all this mean?' She was on the edge of hysterics. 'Are you saying that you don't know anything about my Sonja?'

" 'Sonja is your daughter? Why didn't you say so in the first place? She's just fine, but not here. She is at my mother's place in town. Are you all right, Mrs. van Eyck? You don't look so good.... Come on inside, have a bite to eat. We're about to have supper....'

" 'Oh, no, I just want to pick up my Sonja.' She stopped suddenly as if she couldn't believe her own words.

" 'Margaret, set another place. We have an honoured guest— Sonja's mother has come to fetch her.' Margaret jumped as if she had been pinched. 'Oh my God, you're Gerda, Edith's sister, aren't you?'

" 'You know Edith? Is she here, too?' She could hardly speak. We told her the story of Edith and Ko. As she was listening, her face looked like the sky during a sunshower.

"With Sonja gone, life returned to normal in a couple of months for all of us. It had a new face, not entirely unknown but with a few more wrinkles on it, each one commemorating a crisis, a loss, a betrayal. It was the portrait of a family that had survived shame and humiliation, torment and fear. Most importantly, it had a great deal of vigour in it. There would be no more cloak-and-dagger adventures, no more faceless encounters to organize and to manage. In the still of the evening, or in my solitary labour in the field, I had the time and the inclination to pose some questions about my people. Why had this all been necessary? Why had it all been possible? Every Dutch man and woman was responsible for each lost life, and in my heart, I convicted the whole nation of Rachel's murder. The man who pointed the gun acted with the permission of his country. No one raised a voice to prevent him from pulling the trigger. Sure, the day of reckoning would come sooner or later, but people were fools if they believed that it was possible to pay for a child's murder by jailing or even hanging her assassin. Taking one life would never bring back another one.

"So what then? I was not about to set myself up either as a judge or as an example. But still, so many Christians whose lives revolved around the teachings of Christ, for whom the word of the *dominee* was their spiritual law, let so many people die under their empty gaze. So many homes had empty beds, so many people had empty moments, so many farms had plenty of food. Everyone had eyes, but some chose not to see. Where was their heart, where was their pastor, where was their soul?

" 'How can we go on living in a community of dead souls?' I reflected aloud one night in bed. 'Europe has become a cemetery pretending to come alive.'

" 'Do you think it would be different anywhere else?' Margaret asked.

" 'Perhaps...perhaps not. In the New World, at least the air is clean and guiltless. Here everything is saturated with violence, with silent shame. Corruption thrives in high places. The administration is too infected to be able to cleanse itself. For me, every cobble-stone touched by a German boot is a tombstone. So many good Dutch Christians fought not only for the idea of freedom but for freedom itself. And so many had to die because there were not enough of them. How can we ever meet the eyes of a Jew when we know that others died because not enough Christians cared about what would happen to them? What we did was miserably insignificant.'

" 'As far as we are concerned it was miserably insignificant,' Margaret interrupted me, 'but it meant the difference between life and death for Edith, Ko, Irma, and the twenty or so other people you helped to place. Ask them if what we did was meaningless.'

" 'Are you saying that we deserve to be praised or rewarded because we made a gesture on the side of decency?'

" 'No Bill, not at all,' Margaret answered in haste, but I could see that her thoughts were elsewhere. 'Bill, I want another baby, I want a new life in this house.' "

"Two months later, on a Sunday evening, there was a knock on the kitchen door. We had not yet gotten over expecting someone from the underground every time a knock on that door interrupted the silence of evening. After a moment's hesitation I let out a sigh of relief.

" 'Those days are over, mother,' I said as I walked towards the back door. 'Well, well, look what the cat dragged in, all the way from the fancy capital down south! Come in, for goodness sake. Don't stand on formality. This is your home, so don't expect a written invitation.'

"Margaret jumped like a grasshopper. She knew it had to be one of our Jewish friends. What she didn't know was that it was all of them together: Edith, Ko, Sonja, and Gerda van Eyck. The women lost their composure; they hugged and kissed, spun and jumped. I felt out of place and awkward. But I was delighted to see these unexpected visitors.

"Edith had spent all of her time since the liberation trying to track down Simon. Her efforts were crowned in black thorns: he had been shot while trying to escape from Westerbork. She was now keeping company with the man who had brought her the news. Ko's attempts to find her family met with the same dark fate: they had been swallowed by the mud of Auschwitz. The aunt was working for the butcher she had helped before the war. The niece was unable to cope with the graveless deaths of her family: she had requested permission to enter Australia, as far from the theatre of death as possible. What would she do there? Something, it didn't really matter, as long as it did not remind her of her losses.

"A few nights later, I stunned my wife with the statement: 'Let's go to Brazil.'

" 'Brazil...why should we go to Brazil?' Margaret thought she hadn't heard right. I spoke to her about the vast South American wilderness, about how people are people there, white and black, Christian and Jew, all live in peace, and about how far it is from memories. 'That little Ko, she has the right idea,' I told her. 'There is too much guilt to rise above here, too many angry questions to swallow each time you meet a stranger, too many traitors riding with their heads high. This place is stifling us.'

" 'But for better or worse, this is our home, this is where our families are, this is where our dead are buried. This is where we have a roof over our heads. I have seen during the war what it is like being on someone else's land. I don't want to be a stranger. I don't want our children to grow up with a language I will probably never learn. Our baby will be Frisian wherever we are, but I want him to be a Dutch citizen, too.'

"That's how I learned that I was about to be a father for the fourth time. I was not about to push my travelling urge on my pregnant wife. But as time wore on, I felt more and more hemmed in in my own country. New regulations dictated more and more intrusively how I had to conduct my household. I hadn't obeyed many of the rules of the oppressor for they deprived me of my final say over my own property. Now that we were free again, I deeply resented that I was being treated by my own government as a child. I had to give up half

of a calf, for I had no right to hold onto the other. I had to slaughter
good dairy cows because I was told to do so.

" 'Do this, don't do that,' I kept complaining. 'A man is no longer
a man in this country. NSB traitors are again in power and are telling
decent citizens what's right and what's wrong. Not only are there too
many rules but too many of them just don't make sense. I am sick
of it all. This world is too small for them and me to share in peace.'
But my baby was growing in my wife's belly and she could not be
disturbed. 'There is nothing more important than letting a life grow
in peace,' I thought. But my soul was not quiet.

"Emily was born in the middle of a starry Sunday night, in the
autumn of 1946. Whether she just didn't find her mother's womb a
peaceful-enough nest or she wasn't meant to follow nature's plans,
she came into the world two months sooner than expected. Her
precarious little life absorbed all of Margaret's waking hours. In spite
of all the cajoling, all the lullabies, all the sunshine in her mother's
milk, Emily did not live long enough to greet the new year.

"Darkness claimed Margaret's body and soul. I could not stay in
the house where my child had failed to wake up one morning. I
roamed the fields during the day, paced on the dyke at night. I lost my
sense of direction; nothing seemed to hold meaning for me. Bitterness
infused me and, now and again, I would rebel against God, against
man, and even against my wife.

" 'If we had resettled in the free air of the New World, the baby
would have had a better chance to thrive. All the death and dying that
lingers in the air of this corrupt old continent has robbed my baby of
her breath,' I thought. Sometimes, when I was in a more settled mood,
I was embarrassed at having allowed myself to be guided by blind
anger. On other days, when the dirt under me was burning my feet,
I let my imagination build boisterous arguments against a possible
future in my homeland.

" 'If you are still eager to turn your back on this farm, I won't
object,' my wife said to me one day. Her colourless words surprised
me. Once she had buried our baby in the land that had seen her birth,
she no longer felt the need to stay. 'This land has exacted from me the
ultimate toll. I have nothing else to give it. I'm ready to go wherever
and whenever you want.'

"Canada appealed to me the most, with its vast frontier and endless
farms. I also had admiration and gratitude for these people who had
selflessly liberated my country. I had heard of some organization that

arranged employment for Dutch farmers in Canada. Without saying a word to the family, I went into Leeuwarden to investigate the matter. I found all the answers I needed in a few hours. Choosing Canada proved to be practical and timely: it was a most readily accessible country for farmers. I filled out the application with as much thought to what I was doing as if I were writing a greeting card.

"Three weeks later, I was hoeing sugar beets when my son Hendrik came to inform me that in five weeks' time our ship was sailing for Canada. I took a long look at my beets before I put my hoe down. I turned around and walked back to the house. I never saw my sugar beets again.

"The family did not applaud the news of the departure. Margaret's sister was outraged that we were breaking up the family and that we were robbing our kids of their roots. But by then even Margaret had begun to feel stifled. Everything seemed swollen with bad memories. She was ready to put behind us all that belonged to the long and troubled night.

"The end of the next month found us on a train, cutting through the Canadian East towards Ontario. Everything we owned was on that train."

Bill and Margaret recently celebrated their fiftieth wedding anniversary, surrounded by their three children and their spouses and their fourteen grandchildren. The homey festivities took place in the senior Bouwmas' splendid flower garden behind their modest home near Kingston.

"To Mum and Dad. May they live to be a hundred together, in good health and peace," Hank toasted his parents, who were at once delighted to be in the middle of this family circle, and yearning for a more modest place on the edge of it. What is praiseworthy about having lived this long with each other? What else could they have done? They did what came as a matter of course to them. After all, they loved each other, naturally....

Rebels in the Manse:

Pieter and Joekje Miedema

"My husband has always refused to tell the story of his war-time antics to anyone outside the immediate family," Mrs. Miedema informed me during our first telephone conversation after she had received my letter. "But this time, he's agreed to your request. The children worked on him, and so did I. Please, Dr. Stein, don't misunderstand me. I don't want to brag. All we did—and I should really say, 'he' and not 'we'—was to respond the decent way to threats against the lives of innocent people."

"But the decent way to respond could have cost him his life," I interjected. "As a minister, I imagine he got involved regardless of the risks."

"Don't let that fool you." There was a sudden conspiratorial tone to her voice. "Sure, he has always been a good Christian. But there was another side to Pieter that you should know about: he thrived on excitement. Between his love of adventure and his respect for life, you couldn't have tied him down."

"Why do you think he agreed to tell his story this time?"

"Well, it's hard to pinpoint exactly. But the children and I have been after him. We thought that it would be good for him to recall those days when he was so vital. And then there are the grandchildren.

They should learn what kind of man their grandfather was so that they can hand down to their kids his way of life. Mind you, we have said these things to him before and his response has always been negative. I believe this time, you made the difference. When you sent us your book, *Broken Silence* , he read it. 'It's okay.' That's all he said. Then I read your book and I understood what he meant. You earned his trust with your story. And one more thing: I believe your book might have challenged him to tell *his* story. That would be typical of old Pieter Miedema."

Mrs. Miedema and I spoke a few more times before Vicki and I set out to meet them in their Bowmanville, Ontario bungalow. Each time, it was she who called me. I welcomed her friendly voice. It became clear that for reasons yet unknown the interview was to be a real event in their family. And each time we spoke, she revealed more information about herself and her husband. I was not only touched by her eagerness but also quite grateful. All previous telephone contacts with rescuers were reserved, matter-of-fact, hesitant.

"By the time we all shake hands, we'll be old friends," I told Mrs. Miedema a week before we were to meet.

"Well, there is one thing that you should know," she said with none of her habitual cheeriness. "My husband cannot really speak. He had a stroke a few years ago. He can manage a few words, but that's all. I'll have to speak for him most of the time. And he'll let me know if he's unhappy with what I say. Is that all right with you and your wife?"

"Under such circumstances, we're even more grateful to you and your husband for letting us come into your home," I reassured her. I had a fleeting moment of concern about the format of the interview but I was not about to let her know that.

"There is one more thing." For the first time, I heard an anxious quiver in her voice. "Pieter will be operated on the day after the interview. He'll be in the hospital for a couple of days prior to his surgery. If you want to meet him, you'll have to see him in Oshawa General Hospital. If not, we'll have to postpone the interview until he comes home. But to tell you the truth, I hope you'll come. This is just what he needs to pick up his morale."

"We'll be there, Mrs. Miedema. It's the least we can do."

A week later, Vicki and I turned the corner onto the Miedemas' street in Bowmanville, a small town in southern Ontario. When we got out of our car, a tall, sturdy woman dressed in various shades of grey was waiting for us on her tiny porch. Her face was radiant, and her handshake strong. She ushered us into her home.

The Miedemas' well-worn living room gave evidence that it had seen a great deal of living. The numerous faded embroideries and the piles of magazines and books in Frisian made it clear that our hosts still hovered between two worlds.

"Please, call me Joyce," she requested with a touch of shyness in her voice when she returned with the refreshments. "My real name is 'Joekje', but it sounded too foreign, so I changed it. And so did my oldest daughter, 'Sietske'. She is now called 'Sylvia'. When you live among Canadians, you might as well have names they can pronounce, right?"

We chatted at length about Pieter's health, about the children—theirs and ours—and about our project. It just seemed more natural to visit than to interview.

I felt relaxed in this simple home. Usually, I needed time to let the awkwardness pass, but Joyce made me feel so at ease that the interview began naturally.

"It all began with the ministers' meeting," Joyce related. "Until then, the fate of the Jews was only an abstract matter of compassion and concern. Pieter had been constantly preoccupied with working out some plan of action. Then he called the meeting, making sure that the topic would surface. I can tell you, my friends, even though I wasn't present, it was an explosive meeting of minds.

" 'And now, there's one more item that requires our attention,' Dr. Sybrandy announced in a detached tone. 'As awkward as it might be for all of us, we can't avoid dealing with the Jewish question. We need to come up with a common position regarding the eventual wave of refugees. None of us believes, I am sure, that the relocation of Dutch Jewry can be avoided.'

" 'Deportation, not relocation,' Pieter interjected laconically, locking his gaze on his senior colleague. Sybrandy was visibly disturbed.

" 'He's stalling for time. He doesn't have the vaguest notion about how to deal with this thorny issue,' Pieter observed silently.

"Pieter had been recently ordained, but already had a reputation as a rather hot-headed champion of the poor and distressed, and his confrontational outbursts on these subjects were not tempered by respect for his elders or his superiors. That's why he was offered the congregation in Drachtstercompanie.

"But, you see, Pieter didn't consider himself a trouble-maker. 'The Church, not unlike other ancient institutions, is similar to a precious library,' Pieter used to explain to me. 'Each book remains intact from one generation to the next; once in a while, though, it's essential that someone come along and dust the collection. Such a man is never popular because he makes breathing difficult for other people. I am willing to take upon myself this unpopular task.'

" 'The Germans will herd together the Jews and deport them to heaven knows where, and I have no doubt that the Germans intend to do away with every single one of them—man, woman, child; young and old. It's that simple.' My husband laid his thoughts on the table as if they were a deck of cards with which he was going to convey God's truth to non-believers. 'They have already deported massive numbers of Jews from other occupied countries; why would they spare our Jews? I have no doubt about what is ahead.'

" 'If you don't mind my interruption, Pieter, aren't you being a tad too pessimistic, and perhaps just a tad too dramatic?' Dr. Vissers' unctuous smile and measured delivery fuelled the fire of Pieter's impatience.

" 'I don't think so, Dominee,' Pieter said to his elder. His words were as forceful as the other's had been facile. 'We have all read our moderator's pastoral letter, and I made sure that our Mennonite colleagues had a chance to read it, too: "The Germans have already started, and will continue, to remove the Jewish population of Holland." There can be only one interpretation of the moderator's words. That's why he instructed us to share them with our congregations.'

" 'I certainly didn't hesitate,' Dominee Boersma hastened to proclaim. 'The problem arose when members of my congregation started to inquire about what action to take if the turbulence spreads to our community. Can there be any doubt that some Jews want to hide in Friesland? For one thing, there is no Jewish population to speak of outside of Leeuwarden, and, for another, the farmlands afford considerable invisibility. And I have no answer to give to my flock. Therein lies the heart of the problem. When the pastor doesn't know which way to go the flock grows anxious. And that can lead to chaos. We must come to an agreement for the sake of our people's peace of mind.'

" 'I want to tell you a story'—Pieter paused for a second to gather his strength—'I don't know what each of you remembers about the day we surrendered to the occupying forces. I have two memories.

It was a glorious spring day, our land was awash with sunshine. And I thought: "The Lord has blessed us with a perfect day." And as a counterpoint to this inspiring harmony, I had to remind myself: "And our country has just been overrun by an aggressor. Slavery is upon us." '

" 'The other memory has to do with a man named Grondsma, a decent lad from our congregation. He came to inform me that he was signing up with the NSB. He thought I would be happy to learn the news, because he had heard me say on several occasions that Hitler's Fascists and we Frisians had a lot in common: we all stand for stamping out poverty and for reclaiming the power usurped by the rich. My eyes clouded as I heard this man bring me his gruesome news. He was proud of himself, like a small child boasting to his parents about a great deed.'

" 'You have been misguided, Grondsma,' Pieter told him. 'You recall correctly that I—like many other well-intentioned but misinformed people—used to support Hitler in his efforts to uplift the needy and the downtrodden. But when he started to persecute the Jews and when he invaded Poland he showed his true colours. We severed our loose links to the Nazi. So you see, my friend, your joining the NSB is a grave mistake.' He left even more confused than he had been when he came. I felt guilt for having misled that man. It was a powerful lesson for me. I don't ever want to repeat the mistake of ill preparing my people to face moral crises with a clear conscience. There is only one relevant question right now: What will we do when a Jewish refugee knocks on our door?'

" 'There's no simple way to expedite this matter,' Sybrandy replied. 'We must tell our congregations to protect their homes at all cost. That much is clear, the rest...'

" 'I'd like to voice yet another concern,' Reverend de Jong said, joining the debate. 'If we advise our congregations to act in a manner that could be seen as breaking the law, wouldn't we be liable to charges of sedition? And yet, I see Pieter Miedema's concern for the miserable refugees for whom we might be the last hope. This is a complex question with no simple answer.'

" 'When a Jew knocks on your door, open it and do your best to save the fugitive and your own household.' Pieter stood up to give more weight to his words. 'Is this palatable for you, Dominee?'

"With those words the meeting came to an end. Some uttered words of caution trying to mask their fright. Even those who supported Pieter tactfully retired behind a screen of silence. They planned to show their support for him later, when it was safer.

"So, with one sentence, Pieter committed us to an often solitary task. The choice was his. I shared it with conviction and loyalty. And with anguish."

" 'We'll have to find our own ways to help the Jews when they reach us,' he told me that night. 'Most of the others are just too scared. No wonder they think of me as a rebel. I advocate change—and there's no two ways about it. Our church cannot opt for apathy when we might be deluged with desperate refugees. I, for one, have to take a stance against isolationism. I will find a way—don't worry, Joekje—I will help the Jews even if I lose my congregation. If Church and politics are spouses in Friesland, I want to decide if I will wed a brunette or a redhead. Our people's interest demands that I choose a redhead.' And that's how Pieter came to be known as 'the Red Dominee'.

"The next Sunday, after a sermon full of compassion for the hunted, he reread the relevant passages of the moderator's letter. In closing, he looked around to catch as many glances as possible. He spoke with the voice of a concerned, frightened father cautioning his son before a great adventure.

" 'Don't make hasty decisions right here, while you're under the influence of your excitable minister. Allow yourselves to cool off in the darkness of your bedroom after you've said good-night to your mate. Just before you address your final words of humility and gratitude to the Lord for another fine day, though, imagine how replenished you will feel tomorrow morning after a night blessed with the sleep of the just. Then imagine that someone knocks on your door. And that someone is a mother with a small child, both sporting the yellow badge of shame. They are seeking shelter from the sharp teeth of the Nazi wolf. Look deeply into the panic-inflamed eyes of the mother, and then imagine the wolf carrying off the child. Then decide: Will I shut my door to these creatures, or will I usher them into my home, and if need be, share with them my bed? Once you come to a decision, go to sleep. If you wake up happy and refreshed, you have made the same decision I have. If you have a disturbed, restless night, possibly even a nightmare, you chose the worst solitude a man can discover: his own exclusion from the family of man. Because if you opt against opening your home and heart to an innocent fugitive, you have no place in the community of the just.' You know, I may live to be a hundred but that sermon will always stay in my mind, word for word. Such is Pieter's magic."

"'Dominee, do you have a moment for me? It's quite urgent.' Pieter opened the door wide. A breeze of fresh air entered with the agitated visitor.

"'Come in, Grondsma, catch your breath, and let's hear what's so urgent.' His voice was warm but I could detect a note of caution in it. When you are married, you learn to hear secret sounds. I'm sure you know what I mean.

"'Please, Dominee, may I have a sheet of paper and a pen? I want to send a letter and it can't wait any longer. And I must write it in your presence.' Without a word, Pieter left the room and returned with the requested stationery. The man wrote faster than one would expect for a young farmer. It took him but thirty seconds to dash off his missive.

"'Here, Dominee. After today's sermon, I did just what you said. And when I thought of defenseless people being driven from their homes, I could not close my eyes. I have never met a Jew, so why would I participate in killing one? So this is what I came up with.' He handed the sheet of paper to Pieter, who read the clumsy writing aloud. I could hear tears in his voice: 'I, Jan Grondsma, withdraw my membership in the NSB. I no longer share the ideals of the party. Respectfully yours, J. Grondsma. P.S. Please, save your souls and don't hurt innocent Jews.'

"'I shake your hand with humility and respect, my friend. No one deserves greater admiration than the one who not only recognizes that he has done wrong but also hurries to undo the harm. But it's one thing to recant, and it's another to point the gun of the angry enemy at your own chest. What if you rewrite this letter and state only that which is true: "Due to circumstances beyond my control, I can no longer participate in the activities of the party; therefore, the only honourable choice left to me is to cancel my membership. Trusting in the victory of the just, I remain sincerely yours."'

"'Pieter, you know that you can always count on me,' I told him that night right after he turned out the lights, 'even if it means breaking the law. I'm your wife and I believe in your cause. But don't be surprised if now and then you see me on the edge of my seat with my nails digging into my palms. I know what's waiting for us. We'll be involved in activities that will arouse the fury of the authorities and we'll be likely targets for the same bullet or the same rifle butt as the Jew. I have never been hit in my life, Pieter. I have never been hurt by anyone. I can't even imagine the horror that rips through your whole being when another human being strikes you. My teeth chatter even as I speak these words.

" 'I will do my share of your work, of our work. Just don't expect me to be joyous and carefree along the road. It's one thing to do what must be done, and it's quite another to remain sane when what must be done is madness. I'm very scared, Pieter, for you and for me. And most of all, for that tiny life that's growing inside me. We're so young to die, Pieter! I want us to raise a family. I want a life rich with experience and service—and joy. I want a house full of kids and lots of laughter between meals and prayer. If need be, I'll give up my bed for an unwell Jew. But tell me Pieter, is it wrong to fear those moments of hardship? Is it a flaw to begrudge the fact that I might have to make these sacrifices?'

" 'I, too, am frightened as I think of the struggle ahead of us,' Pieter answered. 'But I fear even more for the souls of those who don't take their places on the hidden barricades. You and I, with some help from the "Boss", will see better days. We take care of the Jews and, I hope, He will take care of us. I have nothing to offer you but my love and the vow I took on the day of our wedding. And a tremendous amount of fear. Some trousseau! My poor Joekje, you thought it would be peaceful to be the minister's wife. I'm afraid that you've got yourself the wrong minister. Our child will see the world in its worst light, alas, but we don't have much control over these things. If He and I are going to continue to work together, He must correct some of His ways, so that we can correct a lot of ours.'

"After that life put on its habitual grey overalls in our manse. 'Perhaps the whole upheaval was quite premature,' I thought. But my husband knew better. The news from Amsterdam was as frightening as he had expected it to be. The Germans and their Dutch underlings herded all Jews into a crammed section of old Amsterdam, between the shadows of two old synagogues. They put forth laws by the bushel that would make a Jew's life not only tainted, but also impossible to live. Rumours of suicides were as frequent as the sunset.

Rebels in the Manse

"'Why are they waiting to the last minute?' I asked Pieter one night after we had listened to an illegal broadcast from England. 'Why can't the Jews get out of town right now, before the rush is on?'

"'Because the unlikely pair of fear and hope paralyses them. They still believe in miracles. It's one of the mysteries of human life: as long as you don't see the flames of fire that threaten your own roof, you're not moved to abandon your home, neighbours, and, in many cases, your helpless parents. Who knows when the moment is right to turn your back on your entire life and rush to safety? If you stay put the shrinking sky seems to howl in madness. If you run, the uncertainty that you see in every stranger's eye can only set your insides on fire.'"

"The winter of '42 was ending when, out of the last reaches of the unfriendly cold, a visitor appeared on the manse's threshold.

"'Joekje, is the Dominee home?' Terpstra, the town policeman, spoke in an ominous tone, as if he had just seen the face of the devil. 'I need to speak to him in private,' he added when he saw my affirmative nod.

"'Dominee, I'm afraid I have bad news for you. Your presence is requested at a hearing by the security services at Nazi headquarters in Leeuwarden first thing tomorrow morning. Beware, Dominee, these people are not on your side.'

"We spent the night saying farewell and planning for a life without Pieter in the manse. I could sense that his mind was racing in the darkness. How do you cram a whole life's worth of living into one night?

"'What could I have done that would attract their attention? It can't just be my stance on the Jews,' Pieter wondered distractedly.

"'I will plant a vegetable garden.' My mind was on maternal concerns, on the need to nourish the survivors. I had to focus on them or I would have lost my good sense. 'Just as I did when my mother stopped working, I will plant leafy greens, peas, beans, and lots of potatoes. Yes, that's what I'll do.'

"'I've got to be able to speak to those Nazis so that they don't see my fear.'

"'Fortunately, the worst of the winter is behind us. We don't have to worry too much about heating. Oh, Pieter...what are we doing? We're already assuming the worst. Whatever happened to our faith?

Quiet Heroes

Let's talk about the baby.... Let's talk about how we'll raise her—
I'm convinced it's a girl, a mother has inside information about these
things....' No matter how many times we tried to distract ourselves
from thinking about the looming dawn, our thoughts seemed to run
on a circular track.

"The drizzle of the unfriendly morning found Pieter on his bicycle
headed for Drachten, where he could catch a tram for the provincial
capital. He didn't know whether it was the freezing rain or the bone-
chilling terror that prevented him from getting hold of himself. 'What
if I panic and I lose control? What if they succeed in making me say
things I don't want to say? I must behave as they do. If they are polite
and measured, I'll reciprocate. If they get abusive, I'll dish it back to
them. This is all fine, sitting here in the empty tram, but will I be able
to act wisely when the time comes?'

"They made him wait four hours in the corridors of the headquarters filled with the hateful foreign uniforms and servile but haughty
Dutch collaborators. 'Why did they have to order me to appear before
the roosters rise? It's part of the process, an attempt to wear down the
suspect's will to resist, I suppose.'

"'Reverend Miedema, it was good of you to respond to our
request so promptly.' An SS officer entered the room, followed by
a small entourage. 'Forgive our tardiness, but you people keep us
hopping—I guess that's to be expected. I certainly have no grudge
against you. You're just doing what comes naturally to you, and
we do what comes naturally to us as security officers. Now shall
we come to the heart of the matter without further ado? I wish to
finish this...interview...before lunch. It's entirely up to you when we
sit down to eat. I am counting on your co-operation, Reverend. It's
quite refreshing to be able to conduct our meeting in German. I
understand you're quite a linguist, Reverend Miedema. You even
know Hebrew....' The officer sat down behind the large desk, and
looked at a thin file.

"Pieter was disconcerted by the German's high-handed manner.
His command of German was adequate, but not sufficient for a
cat-and-mouse game.

"'My proficiency in German is limited to reading. I would prefer
to avail myself of the services of an interpreter.'

"'What do you have against the Third Reich, specifically and
in general?' The German completely ignored Pieter's request. 'And
spare me the cheap words of protest—I've heard them all. Just the

truth. The more you lie, the greater the consequences for you. Now you know the rules, you can start playing."

" 'I refuse to be treated like this,' Pieter protested in indignation. 'I——'

" 'Just what did you mean by accusing the Führer of enslaving eighty million people?' The German interrupted Pieter's outburst.

" 'I never said anything of the sort. And anyone claiming the contrary is a liar. I want him to say it to my face if he has the courage. This is not justice; this is a kangaroo court, and I won't participate in such illegal proceedings.' To give more weight to his counter-attack Pieter jumped to his feet while he was addressing his interrogator.

" 'Perhaps I didn't make it clear enough for you, Miedema.' The German changed tack and now sounded respectful. 'I will put all my cards on the table. Fact: I know that you did make a highly derogatory statement about the Führer. Fact: Since we are living under statutory law, such charges need not have a very high standard of proof, nor a full-fledged trial to bring down a verdict of guilty. Fact: On the strength of my recommendation, you will endure a life sentence of forced labour. Fact: By the time you are brought before me, we already have a lot more on you than just a neighbour's petty complaint or some opportunist's anonymous denunciation. And one more fact: Contrary to malicious rumours, we need not resort to torture to get through to saboteurs and shit-disturbers. We reserve that for particularly vicious traitors who think we are boy-scouts. Now, one more time, what did you mean by accusing the Führer of enslaving eighty million people?'

" 'Your *facts* are drivel as far as I'm concerned,' Pieter responded. 'I, too, conduct myself according to certain facts. Such as: I never get involved with politics. My mandate is to guide people's consciences according to the tenets of our faith. My words are always directed to the soul of the congregation. The rest is a private matter. I don't stick my nose into anyone's business. I would never make a statement about your Führer as long as he doesn't make a statement about me. And just one more thing. Your veiled threats are meaningless, because no pain can force me to own up to something that I haven't done.'

"The confrontation continued in this vein for four hours. The tide of violent outbursts waned and waxed without pause. The German seemed stumped. Finally, he opted for lunch. 'To show that we're in fact fair and mindful of people's fallibility, I'm going to let you go this time.'

"Pieter had won. The interrogator knew it, and he was not at all pleased. 'It's possible that you're telling the truth. This time I will give you the benefit of the doubt. But there won't be a second time. If your name appears once more on my desk you'll be on the way to the quarries of Mauthausen faster than I can say grace before dinner. And once you're there, you'll live as long as you can be productive. We have no use for parasites. The minute you stop earning your keep, you'll be shot. And just to expedite matters, I want you to sign this simple statement. A mere formality. It's your death warrant. Good, now go. Just keep in mind that from here on in you will be under closer scrutiny than if we had planted a microphone under your skin. By the way, I never say grace before dinner.'

"By the time our phone rang, it was nearly four o'clock in the afternoon. 'Joekje, I'm free. I'm coming home tonight.' Pieter's voice bore the marks of exhaustion and elation.

" 'There's a spineless informer in my youth group.' Pieter recounted the events of the day as he wolfed down his food. 'I must find out who wants to get rid of me. Otherwise, I'm as good as dead. In any event, from here on in we're involved, Joekje. Our feet are wet. Let's pray that the puddle in which we stand will not turn to blood.' "

"A month later, Sietske was born amid hope and anguish. How could we fully rejoice in bringing her into a violence- and fear-riddled landscape? And yet, how could we not rejoice in the spectacle of that little girl, oblivious to all the noise in the world?

"I was in my own world, a world in which only the three of us existed. Pieter, on the other hand, was absent more and more often. 'It's just matter of a short time. There will be Jews who'll go into hiding rather than allow the Nazis to treat them worse than cattle.'

"Then, one night in early April Reverend Wiersma called at the manse. Little Sietske was exactly a month old that night.

" 'Pieter, we've got company,' he said. The senior minister, Pieter's immediate superior and friend, never lost his composure. Together, the two of them made a fine team: Dr. Wiersma had an intricate knowledge of the system and Pieter had a boundless supply of cunning.

" 'We have to find a home for a young boy who needs to vanish. We have only thirty-six hours. And it's too risky to transport him.'

" 'I don't have an address right around here at the moment, but I think I can come up with one. I will pay a visit tonight to a neighbour. As president of the local agrarian association, he certainly could be a rich source of generous addresses.

"Later that night, Pieter returned, tired, frustrated, and angry. 'I went to see Klaas Rekker. Greasy in his smugness, he announced to me that the agrarian association is fully committed to the NSB's political and racial program. And I was going to ask him to hide a Jew! I could have landed all of us in the bottom of a ditch or in Mauthausen. Now, I still don't have a place for the fugitive. I must somehow get hold of their membership list and circulate it among my colleagues. But for now, I'm going to try my luck at your father's house. He has plenty of space. While he might be a touch sour on the project and not particularly generously disposed towards strangers, underneath that thick layer of gravel, there runs a clear river of pure Christian blood. He'll grunt and groan but he'll do it.'

"This time, Pieter returned quickly and looked totally undone.

" 'Your father said he thinks I'm being irresponsible. As expected, he didn't jump for joy at the thought of harbouring a Jewish refugee.' Pieter was on the edge of tears. ' "You have a child now; you owe all your responsibility to her and to her mother. You can't get involved with the lives of every little Jew. What are those people to us anyway? Why should I risk my peace and tranquillity for someone who means nothing to me?"

" ' "What if Christ himself came knocking on your door, father?" I was disheartened. I anticipated vigorous resistance, but not the cold, impassible wall of refusal. "Would you send Him away, too?"

" ' "Of course not," your father barked at me. "How can you compare the two? One is our Saviour; the other is just a nobody. I don't see the connection at all. You as a minister, you should be the first one to know that, Pieter."

" ' "And you, father, as a Christian and an elder in our Church, you should be more familiar with the words of Jesus Christ: 'The things that you do to the least of my friends, you do to me.' Do you recall that Jesus was nothing more than a little Jew?"

" ' "It's still different." Your father dug his chin into his chest. He avoided my eyes, but his obstinance was not a subject for discussion. "I will risk nothing for a stranger," he said.

" 'I told him that if we fear strangers and because of our fear we don't even try to befriend them, we'll all become strangers to ourselves and then we'll have real cause for fear. Resigned to another failure, I left him. And the bottom line is that we still have no place for the boy.'

"Pieter learned the taste of bitterness. But there was no time to savour it, because the youngster was coming.

" 'Joekje, the boy must be hidden, and to my great consternation I can't find anyone to take him. We will have to keep him with us, at least until we can find him a more suitable residence. What do you say?'

" 'I say whatever you say,' I answered automatically. 'You know how frightened I am of this whole enterprise. But I shall learn either to master my anxiety or at least to hide it. To be quite practical, though, I would have thought that our home would be the first to be searched, because of your reputation. And we can't forget about your signing your own death warrant. How secure would we be with a Jew in the manse if it were subjected to a search?'

" 'I can't worry about that now.' Pieter always got impatient when he had no immediate answers to questions of importance. As his wife, I realized that the impatience was directed at himself: he tolerated the human limitations of others, but not his own. 'He must be saved, and that's all that matters,' he said, kissing me tenderly on the cheek and giving me a one-armed embrace. That always worked when my spirits needed lifting.

" 'I have to go on an errand,' Pieter announced the next evening, just after supper. He had a mysterious air about him, as if those were not the words he really meant to speak. And I knew. I replied with silence and continued to tend to my household chores. Later I learned that he rode his bicycle to a cluster of birch trees outside of town. Wiersma was waiting there for him with the boy.

"When I met Juul deWitt that night, I took one long look at his loud mustard-and-orange checkered cap and matching necktie, felt a total lack of warmth about him, and disliked him at once. But then I thought: 'Where does it say that I have to like the people I must help in times of distress? We'll all exercise patience and tolerance. And if he proves to be too much of an irritant, I'll just lock myself in an empty room and scream until I blow my frustration out through my ears.'

"My initial reaction to him proved to be right on the button. It irked me no end that this fine physical specimen was chronically lazy. Not that I expected help from him; after all, I had managed quite well before his arrival and one extra person certainly didn't add much to my workload. It was something else. I wanted him to help out with the simple tasks of daily living to occupy his mind and to make him feel useful and not demoralized. You see, I would feel punished if I had to remain idle. Work gives life meaning to many Frisians.

" 'Juul is moving on to a more suitable place on a farm, where he will be out of sight and out of danger,' Pieter informed me about three months after the boy's arrival. 'In his place we'll receive his older brother, Louis. A little birdie told me that we are coming out winners on this exchange. Juul is a young bull who can't cope with being dependent on a mere Frisian country minister's wife. He needs a robust man to challenge him to heavy physical work. Louis, on the other hand, so I was told, is more tame, more his mother's son. I think he'll be a better companion for you; after all you're the one who spends the most time with our guest.'

"Juul went to the farmer the same day Louis settled into the large manse, inheriting his brother's room.

" 'We have to find three more places for their younger brothers and one more for the mother. Where they are right now is not at all safe because the arrangement is based on extortion,' Wiersma told my husband. 'The greedy pigs want three thousand guilders per person for papers alone and an additional fifteen hundred for room and board. It's highway robbery in the first place, and it's blood money in the second.'

" 'And in the third place,' Pieter added, 'should the family run out of money or should someone offer the farmer more, he would throw the mother and her three sons out like four squeezed lemons. We'll have to find them a place—preferably a separate place for each one. What madness this world of ours is experiencing, my friend. Now we are in the business of splitting up families. How absurd, and yet, it must be done.'

"Well, would you believe it: Louis didn't prove to be a more pleasant house guest than his brother. He, too, was restless and, at times, impolite.

" 'I want you to fix it so that I can see my girlfriend,' he stated one day.

" 'Louis, you can't go to the city,' Pieter said. 'It would amount to suicide.'

" 'Who is speaking of me going to the city?' He spoke with the cigarette still in the corner of his mouth. 'I want her to move in with me. I don't see why not.'

" 'I'll tell you why not. This is a respectable Christian house, a minister's house, to which the community looks as an example of propriety. I will not tolerate that kind of libertine living under my roof. Besides, since the birth of our baby, there is a constant procession of visitors. Look, if you're lonesome, I'd be glad to take you on a walk now and then. At night, when the neighbours have already retired, it would be safe, I'm quite sure.'

"That night the two men snuck out for a stroll through the field stretching behind the village.

" 'The kid is demoralized, there's no doubt about that,' Pieter told me when they came back. 'We can't even begin to imagine how tediously boring and depressing it is for someone like him to look at the four walls all day and—for excitement and exercise—to look forward to kitchen duties.'

" ' "You people are not a great deal freer than I, but then again you have each other." ' Pieter was quoting Louis's words. ' "Besides, you chose this life. I didn't. How would you know what it is like being alive thanks to charity? There's nothing wrong with you people, but we are fundamentally different. You could never understand my life. I am an eighteen-year-old Jew from an affluent, urban family. I've many ties with artists and bohemians. I lost my virginity at fourteen. I know it's not your fault, but it's not mine, either, that my survival requires that your world be imposed on mine. And one more thing: my insistence on bringing my Christian girlfriend here wasn't frivolous. She is my lifeline to the normal world." '

" 'I seriously wonder if I wouldn't be better off joining the underground and living my life to the fullest,' he confided in me one day. 'I'd rather live for a brief, intense moment that sizzles with action than gather dust in a provincial manse.'

" 'So, what's holding you back?' I asked him.

" 'When a letter from my mother reaches me and I read her words of caution, I say to myself that I owe it to her to take the best possible care to survive for her. "Stay away from the window at all times, my little Louis, because the windows are the eyes of the street and the street is the feeding-ground of the monster that swallows up careless Jews." How can I not heed such loving words? I wish I were less confused. If we all have to die, well, let's get it over with. But I can't bare lingering between life and death.'

"I had tears in my eyes listening to these pitiful words. And I felt guilty. It's so easy to judge others, isn't it?

" 'You may be a very mature eighteen-year-old, Louis, but you still speak with the words of a child,' Pieter said to him one evening. 'There is nothing rational about war or warriors. Does it make sense to kill someone because of an accident of birth? Does it make any more sense to risk your life in a foreign land, pitted against people whose dreams in life are carbon copies of your dreams? To stop the war just like that because it's not rational to kill is not a reasonable expectation. If you set out to stop the war altogether, you might as well say farewell to life.

" 'But if you say: "I am going to save the life of one person in addition to my own", or "I'm going to hide one family", or "I'm going to blow up one little bridge, that's all", then you have a chance for a victory that makes sense, because that is something you can actually do, something you can see with your own eyes and smell with your own nose. You have to cut the war down to size. That's what we are trying to do, Louis. Should I lose my life in this struggle, I will have registered a human victory if you or your brother or someone like you survives.'

"The following week, Pieter presented identification papers to Louis in the name of a travelling cosmetics salesman from Rotterdam. Louis was ecstatic.

" 'Not so fast, Louis,' Pieter cautioned the boy. 'As a travelling salesman you can't show your face a great deal. You may walk the streets once every two weeks. And even then, you're a healthy young lad, just the kind the Germans love to deport. So act with judgement, not impulse.'

"Louis calmed down considerably during the weeks that followed. It seemed that his 'pass' gave him a purpose that was within his reach. When he could walk freely and even engage people in casual conversation, he had the illusion that he, too, was a normal human being.

"And then, one day, Pieter was warned by his policeman friend, Terpstra, that rumour was afoot that young Dominee Miedema had a Jew in the manse.

"Louis had to disappear. And so he did—as fast as he had come. Without a trace, but not without a friend."

Quiet Heroes

As Mrs. Miedema finished that sentence, a grey-haired young woman soundlessly entered the living room, as if on cue. "I'm Sylvia, the first-born of the Miedema children. I hope you don't mind my coming. I've heard these stories all my life. Each time, I feel renewed by my parents' courage. They hate the thought of speaking about it, especially my dad, but we children believe that what they did should not disappear with them. Please, don't pay any attention to me. I'll just blend into the background and listen."

"The very night Louis was placed, our phone rang," Joyce continued. "It was Dr. Touw, one of Pieter's colleagues from nearby Veenwouden.

" 'Pieter, I'm coming over right away. I have to consult with you at once.'

" 'Do you have any new books for me by any chance?' Pieter asked obliquely about the purpose of his visit.

" 'No, I've got nothing to bring to you right now; perhaps in the near future. I've heard about a whole library being made available to ministers of our area. Perhaps you'll be able to put your hands on a volume or two. We can talk about that over coffee.'

" 'There is a Jewish children's TB sanatorium down south, in Kootwijk-ann-Zee.' Dr. Touw got right to the story that brought him to our manse at such a late hour. 'The Germans are planning to flood the whole area. We have to rescue all the children. A local contact down there called me to see if we could place fourteen of their forty-two young patients in our community. We have one week to act.'

" 'Fourteen places in a week!' Pieter couldn't believe his ears. 'Well, if that's what's required, that's what we'll do. It's that simple— in principle. In practice..., well, that's another story.'

"The word spread in the community like a brush fire. How it was not discovered is one of the many mysteries of those timeless days and nights. 'One of these days, we'll hear a knock on the door and it will be the SS,' I thought to myself. I said nothing: some things take on a different dimension when they are mentioned aloud. Fear is more manageable when only you know about it.

"Pieter's early sermons about opening doors to the homeless grew sturdy roots. One day, one of the oldest members of the congregation, Willie Trukstra, knocked on our door, asking to speak to my husband.

70

Rebels in the Manse

" 'Dominee, I'm in a real dilemma. I've heard that you need hiding places for Jewish children. As you suggested, my door is open day and night. The only problem is that I am more dead than alive. I have a bad heart and, as you know, all my life I've been infirm. My sister says she could help, but my husband still fears for my health. What should I do? I'm afraid to do the wrong thing, but I don't know what the right thing is.'

" 'Go home, Willie,' Pieter said, with a lump in his throat. 'You did your share in your younger years. Your heart may give you some trouble here and there, but it's still in the right place. You're exempt from any responsibility in this undertaking. You can rest in peace.'

"Shortly after Willie's visit, there was another knock on the door. With an exhausted sigh, Pieter rose from the world of his thoughts to open it.

" 'Can I come in at this late hour of the evening?' asked a man with a vaguely familiar face. 'I thought it would be safer to come now, at an hour when fewer eyes spy on their neighbours' visitors.'

" 'The door is open.' Pieter's work had no schedule.

" 'I understand you need a few extra hands to help you transport forbidden cargo through the night.' The man spoke with hesitation. 'I just wanted you to know that I'm available.'

" 'That's quite inspiring, my friend,' Pieter responded with guarded warmth, 'but I'm ashamed to admit that I can't quite pin a name to your face. Are you in my congregation?'

" 'Well, I am, but with all the work and everything else...you know....'

" 'That's quite all right. You're not here to account for your conduct. And I am not your judge. As for your offer, we'll have to see. Do you know where a sickly child can be hidden until the sunshine becomes safe once again?'

" 'I can help in many different ways and I am not afraid to do anything. I am a poor man with a large family that must be fed. My services are available, if you could compensate me for my trouble. And then there are some neighbours whose discretion must be secured with the occasional gift....'

" 'And just what is the tariff for each of your services?' Pieter's voice was edged with sarcasm. 'Help is always welcome; fees, however, are hard to raise,' he added in a more diplomatic tone. 'As you may know my services are free for the asking.'

" 'Well, there is nothing magic about the formula, Dominee,' the man said; he was on firmer ground once he had been asked to quote figures. 'A pick-up is the most dangerous part of the whole transaction. The price varies with the level of risk involved. If I lose my hide in the deal, I don't have a spare one, yet somehow I have to provide for my family. It's two thousand guilders for each pick-up. And it's two thousand guilders for each hiding place.'

" 'Well, we'll have to see. Our coffers are bare. And I'll also have to check into your reliability. After all, we are speaking about lives, not potatoes. What's your name, my friend?' That was the only thing Pieter really wanted to know; the underground would take care of the rest. He was repelled by this encounter with a merchant of human lives.

" 'Rimmer Bandsma—I'll never forget his name.' Pieter told me just as we were retiring. 'I never realized how ugly a man is whose soul is rotten.'

"And the children came, one at a time, all fourteen of them, each with a curse on his head, each with fear painted on his face, each dull-eyed and hanging onto Pieter's hand. You see, even these disowned children had a shred of faith left that a Messiah would appear. And why not? Children were created to be immortal.

"So, on fourteen consecutive nights Pieter left the manse, never being sure that he would see the dawn. But as the nights rolled by silently, he grew more and more confused. His conscience was weighed down for he had begun to question the power of his faith. What kind of a Church is it that fails to see in the eyes of children the obvious—that they are children at risk—my husband wondered. Where are the soldiers of God? In their beds sleeping the greedy sleep of the indifferent. Is this is my flock? Is this all I can inspire in a whole congregation of Christians? What does it say about my leadership?

"Pieter's queries remained without answer, and he was not surprised. But at the end of the fourteenth night, all the Kootwijk kids were settled in a safe nest. And in those days, that was the only thing that really mattered.

"Shortly after the arrival of 1943, another face appeared in the manse. It, too, needed the quiet anonymity of Drachtstercompanie. Douwe Zegerius, a theologian from Utrecht, had been Pieter's friend, chess opponent, and spiritual sparring partner for many years. The two had been inseparable in their student days. They were perfectly matched—both explosive, given to quick changes of mood, and profoundly rooted in their idealism.

" 'No, we can't save mankind,' the two used to state, with mock solemnity, 'at least not yet.'

" 'There is precious little we can't overcome together,' Pieter pronounced once without modesty, 'if only we could master our sense of inferiority.'

"Other times, they would abandon themselves to the depths of despair. 'There is so much to be done, and so few of us are willing to really make a difference,' Pieter whispered, close to tears.

"They were reconciled—no, challenged—to committing their lives to bringing a new meaning to the word 'reform'.

" 'Pieter, old friend, I *must* come to see you. How soon can I come?'

" 'If you need a red carpet and a choir of virgins, give me a couple of weeks.' Pieter's voice resounded richly with excitement. It was the best news my husband had heard in a long time. 'But if you're willing to settle for something a trifle more modest, what's wrong with tonight?'

" 'I'm withering in the desert and the Lord sends me Douwe.' Pieter seemed overwhelmed with gratitude after the call. 'I'm definitely not alone.'

" 'As you see, I'm a marked man. I can no longer even pretend to get lost in a crowd. That's why I have to find shelter away from the crowd,' Douwe told us after the first wave of exuberant hugs and kisses. 'I have been cursed with eczema all over my body. Now I'm burning from inside and out. And the NSB is hot on my trail. I went one step too far for their taste. Utrecht is crawling with traitors. They seem to grow like weeds after the rain.

" 'I have made too many waves in Fascist circles. I organized a group of young scholars to sabotage the alien-registration scheme. By the time we were done, they were not any clearer about who was a Jew and who wasn't. That was the first blow. But they could pin nothing on me. I can't even remember how many false IDs and food coupons went through my hands. I was questioned a half-dozen times. Each time they had to let me go. A couple of days ago, however, they outfoxed the fox. An informant fingered me as the master-mind behind a counterfeit operation. Thanks to this cursed eczema a positive identification was child's play. The slimy traitor who sold me out will get his just dessert. Fortunately, we, too, have our informants, and one of them slipped me the message to make myself scarce.'

" 'They can look until the day after doomsday, as long as you stay with us,' Pieter said with a self-satisfied grin on his face.

"Pieter's spirits were recharged by his friend's sojourn on our top floor, even though he had hardly any leisure time to spend with Douwe. The telephone kept ringing. And most calls were pleas for help.

" 'I have two more books for your collection, Pieter. You'd better come to pick them up because I can't hold onto them for long.' That's all my husband needed to hear. He got on his bicycle and rode without stopping to Veenwouden, to Dr. Touw's manse.

"Once more, it was not a pretty story. It had to do with a nine-year-old boy and his fourteen-year-old sister. These two kids had been sent to Veenwouden by their parents for safekeeping. As far as the parents knew, the children were in good hands. When the air got a touch too thin for the parents down south, they decided to join their children. A shabby spectacle greeted them. They had been cruelly duped. The children were haggard, clad in dirty rags. And for this they had been paying three thousand guilders a month. When the father demanded an explanation, the peasant snapped at them: 'They are alive, your brats, aren't they? Well, then, what are you complaining about? If you aren't satisfied, take your brats and get out of here right now! And don't forget to resew the yellow star on their chests! They could be shot in the head for less than that!'

"Mr. Lezer, the father, hastened to befriend the grumpy farmer. 'You are absolutely right. Our children are alive and healthy thanks to you and we wouldn't want to change a thing about the present arrangement. In fact, I'd like you to shelter us, too.'

" 'That will be another five thousand guilders, payable in advance,' the farmer said, without looking at them. As far as he was concerned, these people mattered only as a source of income. He didn't care what happened to them. It was a rare opportunity to make a lot of money, and he knew such opportunities had to be taken immediately.

"I wish I could throw my hands in the air and exclaim 'this is not possible, a Frisian Christian would never behave in such a fashion,' but, alas, my friends, we had our share of leeches. I'm ashamed of them to this day. But, you know what? After all these years, I'm better off just sticking with the facts. Don't you agree?

"Mr. Lezer, a man blessed with a keen mind, sought out Dr. Touw. The good pastor promised the desperate man that within a week he would find another place for them. And then, he called Pieter.

" 'I'll do my best, but miracles are in short supply these days,' my husband told him. 'I don't know how long it will take, but I'll work out something for them. You can tell them that much.'

"A few days later, Pieter sent van Emst, the forest ranger, to Touw with a message. 'Instruct L. to take his family on a short walk tomorrow after supper. They will be met by a friend at your manse at exactly 8:00 p.m. He'll bring them to Quatrebras. God bless.'

"Van Emst was a personal friend of Pieter's. Together with Oosting, his assistant, they were principal partners in creating an extraordinary hiding place for the four Lezers.

"As planned, van Emst's range truck pulled up to Dr. Touw's door. These operations had to be orchestrated with the precision of complex surgery. Most of the time they involved several stops in which the live cargo was handed over to another comrade, in relay fashion. A one-minute delay at the first pick-up point could amount to four or five minutes' delay in reaching the last stop. That was enough time for the whole mission to be undermined.

"One after the other, the four Jews filed into the truck. Van Emst had filled the vehicle with crates of tools, plants, and all sorts of debris, leaving just enough room for the four people to hide in the back. Once he was on the open road, he pulled over under a shady tree to re-stack the crates so that even if they were intercepted by a floating patrol, the fugitives couldn't be seen without unloading the truck completely.

"They had been riding for nearly an hour when they reached the edge of the conservation area."

"Perhaps this would be a good point to stop," Sylvia interjected. "I think my father would love to be present as Mom tells you the rest of the story."

"You're right, Sylvia," Joyce hastily agreed with her daughter. "Besides, he must be waiting for us. And patience has never been one of Pieter's virtues. But let me ask you a delicate question, Vicki and André. Are you sure you want to meet him in his present condition? With all the tubes and the IV and all, he isn't a pretty sight...."

"Don't worry about me," Vicki reassured the anxious woman. "I work in a hospital so I'm used to illness and the medical paraphernalia that goes along with it."

"I'm more worried about him finding the journey into the past too heavy a burden to pick up now—especially on the eve of his surgery," I said, concerned.

"Don't fret about Pieter." There was a note of pride and trust in her voice. "He's ready for you. Rather than undermining his strength, the project will invigorate him. You'll see—my Pieter may be a bit rusty, but he can still be a pretty tough nail."

"It'll take his mind off tomorrow's surgery," Sylvia added. "Just remember that he can't really speak since his stroke. He tries, God knows how he tries, but without much success. You'll have to be patient with his frustration and his anger."

When we arrived at the hospital, we met the rest of the Miedema family: Jekke, the youngest daughter; Jalda, her brother; and Pamela, Jalda's wife. They had their two teenage boys with them. We set up our headquarters in a small conference room made available to us by the hospital staff.

"This is Reverend Pieter Miedema, my husband." Despite the sturdy front Joyce presented there was a faint flutter in her delivery. She, too, was a touch unnerved by the encounter.

The minister and I looked at each other. His face betrayed no emotion. In his pale grey eyes, a flicker of a smile greeted us. We shook hands. He offered me his left, the one that still had life in it. It was warm and reassuring.

"I can't tell you how grateful I am to you for consenting to tell us your story, after all these years of silence," I said by way of a greeting.

Pieter's eyes flashed another smile. "You, too," he said laconically. I looked at Joyce in confusion.

"Pieter has read your book. Your courage to revisit the past inspired him to do the same."

"Go!" Pieter seemed to grow impatient.

"Father wishes to get rolling," Joyce explained. "The stroke hasn't changed his distaste for idleness."

" 'This is as far as we can go by vehicle; the rest we'll have to tackle on foot,' you informed the four silent passengers. They staggered out of the truck with stiff muscles and joints. Mia, the older of the two Lezer children, was shivering in the dark. Flip, the nine-year-old, held on tightly to his father's hand as if he expected to see phantoms, skeletons, goblins, and other terrifying creatures. You'll stop me if I am not telling it right, won't you?"

Pieter nodded.

"Oosting had been waiting for the group to guide them through the forest. He knew and loved the conservation area as if he had been born there. Every tree was a friend; every bush knew the gentle touch of his hands.

" 'You have to follow us in single file,' he whispered to the Lezers. 'There are no roads leading into the bush. If you get lost, I won't be able to retrieve you.'

" 'I'll stay behind to make sure that nobody strays or is eaten by a bear,' van Emst added.

"You elbowed your way through the dense bush until, about forty minutes later, Oosting stopped at the head of the line. Everyone huddled around a scarcely perceptible hump surrounded by thick, untamed growth.

" 'A bunker! My God, how in the world...' Harri Lezer couldn't believe his eyes. How could anyone have constructed a bunker in a forest without roads or paths? He leaned down to touch the roof of the bunker. 'I just can't believe this. How could anyone transport and heat tar here? And apparently without disturbing the vegetation. You people are magicians.' Mrs. Lezer and the children were speechless.

" 'Go on, inspect it inside,' you suggested. 'You'll be quite surprised. Once you are all inside, close the door behind you and turn on the light.' You handed Lezer a large flashlight.

" 'This is simply incredible,' the father said when he reappeared. 'I have seen a few cleverly built edifices in my life, but this one is extraordinary.'

" 'It'll take some getting used to, but we'll be fine in there,' the mother added without conviction. 'The inside is so big! And you've totally furnished it! A bed for Harri and me and one for the children—complete with warm blankets and pillows. Where did you get those beautiful flowered curtains? And how did you manage to equip an entire underground kitchen? I haven't seen so much food for ages. You wonderful people have thought of everything. The least we can do to show our gratitude is to give the home you built for us a chance. And with good cheer.'

" 'From here on, this is your home. I'll be coming by at least once a week to bring you food. Jurgen will drop by once a week at least. He practically lives in the forest, perhaps on the order of his wife. And our master engineer, the ranger, is your official concierge. He, too, is likely to drop in on you occasionally. If anybody else shows up, you're not in. In all seriousness, no one will ever disturb you in this corner of the woods. I alone have the right to hunt in here by law. I will explain that another time. You are absolutely safe here. We still have to devise a way you can cook without smoke. That's the only puzzle we have not yet been able to solve.'

" 'Just one minute, please,' Lezer called out as you were leaving. 'Just who are you? What's your name and why are you so kind to us? Nobody is this good. You must want something in exchange. What is it? Money? How can anything like this be given a monetary value? So, what is it?'

" 'Oh, who am I? I'm an ordinary man. The only thing I expect is that you do your best to survive. The Germans want to strip us of our Jewish friends, but we have our own ideas about that. I don't want your money. Whatever this bunker cost us, we requisitioned from the enemy. Ah, by the way, I am the junior minister of a nearby reformed church. And my name is Pieter.'

"By the time you paid your next visit to the Lezers, Harri had thought of a way to cook without smoke. But you know, if my life depended on it, I couldn't describe it. All I remember is that you were very impressed with it.

"One day, when you took the Lezers a couple of rabbits, they wanted to hear about your hunting privileges. 'I have a little arrangement with a noble hunter who is a member of the NSB. I enjoy the reputation in this neck of the woods of being a responsible hunter, one who is more committed to preserving wildlife than to hunting. The NSB man pulled some strings with his buddies and came up with two permits, one for him and one for me. There are fewer than thirty such permits issued for the whole province. We have an agreement never to poach on each other's territory.'

" 'I certainly hope he abides by the contract.' Harri wasn't convinced of the safety of the arrangement. 'Do you trust the word of a traitor?'

" 'We don't have much of a choice, my friend,' you reassured him lamely. 'I do suspect, however, that you may not be the only Jews enjoying the quiet hospitality of the woods. That, in time, may be a greater cause for concern than my hunting NSB neighbour.'

"Life in the bunker became routine. It even included school work for the two Lezer youngsters. 'One of these days, you will return to your studies. There is no reason in the world why you should fall behind. We may be living in the woods, with animals as our next-door neighbours, but that doesn't mean we should stop being civilized creatures.' Mrs. Lezer was forever scheming to spare the children demoralizing boredom.

" 'That's what I like to see, children hard at work over school books,' you complimented the Lezer children on one of your bi-monthly visits to the bunker. 'In fact, I believe I can be of help to the young lady who, by now, should be in her third year of gymnasium, am I right? Well, with only one year before graduation regular tutoring in Greek and Latin is in order. From here on, as far as my other duties permit, I will come to see you every Thursday for a lesson.'

"The mother had silent tears in her eyes. 'What can I do for you, Pieter? How can we be of some use in your life? It can't all be one-sided. Let me do something for you.'

" 'So be it. Last time I was here you made a fabulous caramel pudding. It was perfect. Make me some caramel pudding one day.'

" 'Would you accept a dinner invitation for you and your wife for next week?' Mrs. Lezer asked boldly. 'It would be a splendid occasion to commemorate the fourth month of our wilderness adventure.'

" 'You've got yourself a dinner party. Next Thursday, after Mia's lesson, we'll celebrate.' "

" 'This is a veritable jungle,' I said as we made our way to the Lezers' hideaway the following week. I had never been in the conservation area before. 'I hope I'm not going to go into labour in here, or I may never get out in time to deliver in my own bed.' You were doing your best to break a path through the thick bushy growth for me. I was in my last month of pregnancy with our second child. But the bush was tenaciously dense; it refused to open for me. We had to use our hands, elbows, and shoulders to break through the virgin forest and it closed behind as we advanced.

" 'I feel like a bush pioneer,' I said with a nervous laugh. 'I don't see how we'll ever find the path again.'

" 'What path?' You laughed smugly. 'A pretty safe hide-out, wouldn't you say, my dear?'

"The meal was a success. I don't know how she did it. 'I hope that soon we will be able to return the favour in our home,' I said in parting.

" 'It's a deal.' Harri raised his glass of apple cider. 'Next year in Drachtstercompanie, the Jerusalem of Friesland.' "

"The Nazis were getting more desperate for prisoners. As the war depleted their human resources, they began to round up young Dutchmen, dragging them off to forced-labour sites where our boys worked as beasts of burden. This meant, of course that hiding places were harder and harder to come by. And you found it increasingly more difficult to place your charges.

" 'I have a nasty situation on my hands,' Dr. deGroot said to you one evening. 'A young tailor must go under. An informer ratted on the family who was hiding him and I had to get him out of there before the NSB could find him. But I can't keep him in my house. Between my patients and my family, it's like a marketplace. I'm counting on you, Pieter, for a solution for Joseph.'

" 'I'm fresh out of resources, Doctor.' You were half asleep as you spoke. 'I can't keep on top of recruitment and placement in addition to my regular duties. I'm sure if anyone understands that, it's you, Doctor. After all, we are in the same business; we even have the same clientele. You heal the body, I look after the soul. But I will try to come up with something.'

" 'I have a tentative solution to Joseph's problem,' you told the doctor the following evening. 'I'll take him into the forest where he can join a family. I hope they'll get along. If they don't, I'll strangle them all.'

"The next evening, you stopped the borrowed car in front of Dr. deGroot's house. 'Dominee?' a timid male voice inquired.

" 'Joseph?'

" 'I'm from Amsterdam originally,' the tailor began his story. I don't remember the details. But I recall that he was full of hatred and lusted for bloody revenge. He said to you: 'Many of my people are scared to die, that's why they hide. Not me. I hide because I want to live. I have to bring about justice. I have never known the meaning of the word hatred. Now all I can think of is hatred. It's like a poison.'

" 'You're right,' you replied. 'Hatred is a poison. And no one is immune to its effects. Your hatred will end up choking you to death. The moment will come when you will no longer be able to recognize the sweetness of an age-old melody. You'll hear only a monotonous chant: "I hate, I hate, I hate." My fondest wish for you is that when the moment of freedom comes, you'll be inclined to convert "I hate" into "I am alive".'

"Joseph's arrival was not welcomed with enthusiasm. To be sure, there was enough space for him and food was of no concern, but he was a stranger, an outsider. The family felt that its privacy was being violated. And Joseph did his share to poison their cohabitation.

" 'You eat meat and dairy in the same dish? And you want me to soil my mouth with such forbidden fare?' Joseph was outraged as the five of them sat around the table for their first meal. Hanna and her family were delighted with whatever foodstuffs you provided them. They were totally assimilated into Dutch secular society and didn't observe Jewish dietary laws.

" 'Joseph, we are not religious people, but we are Jews.' Harri threw up a conciliatory bridge between the family and the offended newcomer. 'We have to make the best of it in the wilderness. Our ancestors did the same. How about being friends?'

"But he failed. 'We are growing more intolerant of each other by the day,' Harri informed you on your next visit. 'During these two weeks the atmosphere has been so full of poison that it will end up killing us. Can you do something?'

" 'They are determined to make life repulsive to me,' Joseph whispered to you the first chance he had. 'They want me to run into the forest. But I will not commit suicide just to make life more comfortable for them. Can you do something, Dominee, to get me out of here? Please!'

" 'Pack your things, Joseph. You're moving in with us.' You didn't usually make decisions alone that directly involved me, but you realized that the situation was explosive among your five protégés. 'Our manse is so spacious that if you don't want to commune with anyone, you are free to enjoy the comfort of your solitude. Your devotion to your faith inspires me with humility and with a touch of awe. We can't provide you with kosher food, but my wife will do whatever she can to offend you as little as possible.'

"Douwe moved down to the second floor to leave Joseph a whole kingdom of silence. And the tailor was happy in his solitude. He borrowed my sewing machine so that he could volunteer his services to the family. Textiles were rationed in those days, you know, as food was, making it virtually impossible to acquire new items of clothing. I proposed to my father that my 'friend' rebuild his overcoat for the next winter. The garment impressed its owner beyond expectation. In a matter of five days, Joseph had a dozen coats to make over. He was a man with a mission and the peaceful realm in which to carry it out.

"Then Dirk Thysse came. His arrival shattered Joseph's peace. He was a medical student at the University of Groningen. When he repeatedly refused to sign various oaths of allegiance to the new rulers of the land, he became open to deportation to Germany. He was a relative of Dr. deGroot. Thus, from Groningen to our doctor's door and from there to our third floor, the road was straight.

" 'The two of you will have ample room up here for as much or as little contact as you wish,' you reassured the cohabitants of the third floor. There was only one room to share, but it was spacious enough for a family.

" 'I can't believe I'm not dreaming,' you shared your surprise with me a week after Dirk's arrival. 'The odd couple of Drachtstercompanie has become inseparable. The Lord plays with a different deck of cards every day. He just keeps us guessing and we are seldom right. But who is complaining?'

"All the rooms were occupied, and yet, our hospitality had to be extended to one more Jew. Jan Gans was not only Jewish, but he was also a member of the resistance group credited with blowing up a bridge while a German ammunitions truck was crossing it. The whole area was awash with soldiers eager for revenge.

" 'We will shelter Jan Gans even if I have to give him my own bed.' Your sombre tone left no room for discussion. 'They will have to string me up before they catch him.'

"Jan Gans joined us on All Saints' Day, 1943, just a couple of minutes before midnight. He came accompanied by a comrade. Both of them were disguised as German soldiers.

" 'I'm staying only for twenty-four hours; a safer place at a widower's dairy farm is being arranged for me. In the meantime, I'm grateful for the chance to sleep in a real bed, to take a bath, and to feast my eyes on friendly people.' After a bite, he retired. Douwe insisted that the young resistance worker take his bed.

" 'I will sleep on the floor. It'll give me the illusion of still being actively involved,' he said.

"Jan Gans was shot to death before he left the village the next night. It took only one day of checking around for you to find out that his subsequent hiding plans were nothing but a trap. I could see anger tense your body and I thought of Joseph's constant companion—hatred.

" 'If I ever held the assassin of Jan Gans in my hands, I would have no difficulty in strangling him and I'd worry about my salvation later.' It was your first failure. Poor Pieter, you were not well equipped for the senseless death of a young comrade. But before you had a chance to settle into your grief, evil winds blew more dark clouds in our direction.

" 'We have to move all of our friends out of our home,' you told me that night. 'Can you imagine, Joekje? Because of a lousy traitor, we have to move Douwe, Joseph, and Dirk into that jungle out there. Who knows how long it will take the security forces to trace Jan's last resting place? We can't just pretend nothing happened.'

"We were all relieved when Joseph was received by the tailor in Veenwouden. Douwe was harder to settle. In fact, no one cared to take in a man marked by eczema. Finally the local notary public took pity on him, but first Dr. deGroot had to guarantee that he was not going to catch the man's skin disease. Dirk spent the night at the doctor's place and then disappeared. No one ever heard from him again.

" 'Why don't you pack up the baby and go stay with your brother for a while?' You wanted us out of that house. You were too busy yourself to spend any time in the manse. In fact, you were sorely neglecting your ministerial duties.

"My brother had a flower and vegetable business in nearby Appelscha. It was good to know that all you had to worry about was yourself. And your hidden friends, of course."

At this point, Joyce stopped her tale. She looked perplexed. And so did the rest of the people in the smoke-filled room. We all saw that Pieter grew agitated.

"What's the matter, Father? Did I make a mistake? Did I leave something out? What are you trying to say?"

Pieter's face turned purple in his effort to communicate. His family kept offering him suggestions but each time he shook his head more vigorously in disagreement. With a violent movement of his left hand, he would point at Sylvia.

"Did I say something to offend you, Dad? Do you want me to leave the room?" she asked anxiously.

"Nay, nay, nay, nay!" Pieter's expression was tortured.

To alleviate her stress, Sylvia took a cigarette from the pack in front of her. "Yeah, yeah, yeah!" Pieter's voice was hoarse from all the choked back sounds of anger. But he was also relieved. We finally understood him: he wanted a cigarette.

General levity followed. All the Miedemas were off the hook. None of them had done anything to offend the silenced patriarch.

I kept looking into Pieter's eyes. And I remained shaken by the sight of unexpressable anger that persisted even after he lit his cigarette. He took a puff, then motioned to his wife to go on.

" 'What in the world is happening out there at this hour of the night? It sounds like the earth is shaking.' I was awakened in my brother's house around two o'clock in the morning. The night was sultry and oppressive. I left the window open for more comfort. 'German soldiers by the hundreds—my God what do they want at this hour? There are enough soldiers out there to conduct a small war.'

" 'Just stay in your room and go back to your bed, that's the best thing you can do if they are making a door-to-door search,' my brother suggested. 'I have to get Henk and Tinie out of sight or we'll all be thrown into the boiling soup.' He, too, was sheltering a Jewish couple. An hour later, they came. Several German soldiers invaded my room with their guns in combat readiness. They looked around and left without a word. What were they after? I found out soon enough. By seven o'clock heavy trucks loaded with human cargo were leaving the town.

" 'They've got the hotelkeeper, the notary, and the junior minister!' My brother couldn't believe his eyes. 'They are taking all the prominent people of Appelscha.'

" 'I must go home immediately,' I told my brother. 'Pieter may be in danger. I can't stay here as long as he may need some assistance.'

" 'They are all over the area, searching every house, looking behind every tree, under every bridge, in the bottom of every ditch.' That was the feverish rumour that greeted me on my return to Drachtstercompanie.

" 'The Lezers, they will find the Lezers in the forest.' I panicked as if they were my own flesh and blood. 'Pieter must be trying to relocate them. He must be informed about what's happening. Van Emst and Oosting, too.'

"First, I sat by the telephone hoping it would ring and provide me with an appeasing message. Then I became itchy, as if I had a bad case of hives. I went for a stroll with the baby.

" 'You look like you have just seen death in person, Gijs,' I greeted van der Welde, our next-door neighbour, the only taxi-driver in town. 'Are you all right? You look green.'

" 'Joekje, you hit the nail on the head.' The robust man was shaking as if he had a chill. 'I have indeed just seen death in person. An hour ago, I got a note to pick up a fare near Quatrebras. I can't describe to you what was waiting for me. My fare was dead. Killed. Not shot or hanged — clubbed to death. It used to be the forest ranger, van Emst; now it's just shapeless pulp.'

" 'Van Emst has been clubbed to death!' My heart was beating in my temples, racing to the rhythm of madness. 'Pieter might be next, if not already done in. I've got to do something or I'll lose my mind.'

" 'Gijs, take me to Oosting's house. Perhaps he knows something about his whereabouts.' Gijs van der Welde asked no questions.

" 'Jurgen and my son Arend were taken to Groningen for questioning.' Oosting's wife's pupils were dilated with terror. 'There's nothing we can do. You know what they did to my brother. Why should they spare my husband and son. The wretched man kept saying, "One of these days, this madness is going to cost me my head." And he was right. But not like this.... Who would have thought a strong, decent man could be clubbed to death for trying to save lives. And now my husband and my boy are gone, too. And your poor husband is probably in the same boat as my men.'

" 'Let's go home, Joekje. There is nothing to gain from roaming the countryside hoping to find a mouse in the field.' The taxi-driver was trying to be solicitous. 'You and the baby can stay with me and my wife as long as you wish.' I let the man lead me to his home. I was in another world. A world without Pieter."

"Would you like to stop here, Joyce?" Vicki asked, noticing the old woman's lips quiver. There were discreetly hidden tears in my wife's voice. "I thought that the rescuers' stories would uncover the good news about the Holocaust."

"There is no good news about the Holocaust," Joyce replied quietly. She was in control again. She turned towards her husband, signalling that she wanted to go on.

"All this time, you were in the bush, right, Father? You knew that your comrades had been picked up. Not having time to recruit helpers, you took upon yourself the relocation of the Lezers deeper into the forest.

" 'Pieter, it's you? Thank heavens! We heard footsteps and were sure we were doomed,' Harri sighed, tears choking him.

" 'I was ready for the worst,' Hanna added. The two kids returned to bed: the danger was over and for now there was nothing to worry about. It was the middle of the night—what's more natural than sleeping?

"You told them about the merciless hunt for all kinds of fugitives. 'They got van Emst, and probably Oosting, as well. They may extend their search all the way to the conservation area.

" 'Let's not be careless. If they aren't coming tonight, they might be here by tomorrow or the day after. I'll have to spend the night here because of the curfew. At daybreak, we will move you deeper into the forest. I'm alone. I'll have to depend on all of you for help.' Then, to change the subject, you said, 'As long as I'm here, how about some of that caramel pudding, Hanna?'—Ever since you had revealed your craving for her dessert, she'd kept some for you in her cooler, hadn't she?—Then, pudding in hand, you retired into the 'parsonage'.

"The parsonage was a shelter Harri made for you out of straw. Indeed, you were severely allergic to mosquito venom and the conservation area was a fertile paradise for them.

"But that night the mosquitoes found you even in the parsonage. 'Well, if I'm not able to sleep, I might as well have some more caramel pudding in my stomach. Perhaps if I move around a bit I'll find another spot less well frequented by the bloodsuckers,' you thought. You set out for a stroll through the still darkness of the forest. Is this how it happened, Father? Shall I go on?"

The question was obviously an attempt to involve the silenced minister in the telling of his own story. Joyce knew every detail as well as if she had lived through it herself. Over the years, his war-time memories had become the family's common property.

Pieter Miedema nodded with his eyes, without moving a muscle. That was enough for his wife.

" 'The Germans!' Your insides twisted into a gigantic knot as the sharp beams of flashlights lacerated the darkness of the forest. 'That's the end for us and there is not a thing I can do about it.' You dared not move. The Germans were a few steps from you.

"The search party passed by the Lezers without discovering them. 'Now I know that in addition to the Lord loving us all, we are also in possession of an astronomical chunk of luck.' You revealed to the unsuspecting family how close they had come to being apprehended while they were sleeping. 'Let's not waste a minute. Who knows when they may come back.'

"Two days later the bunker's contents were relocated to the new site. Suddenly, out of the blue, the two kids exploded in a torrent of verbal abuse. And the parents let them hurl the worst kind of insults at each other. 'You must let them vent their fears, frustrations, and bottled-up hostility or else they choke to death,' Hanna said, having noticed the bewildered expression on your face. 'Every once in a while they tear each other to shreds with the most cruel words. But after the storm they become their usual loving selves.' 'You should hear Hanna and me go at each other sometimes,' Harri added.

"You spent the night in the new parsonage. Mia even made a sign for your private shelter. At four o'clock the next morning you set out for your mother's place. By then, no one had heard from you for almost five days. 'I'll be back Thursday. Mia, you'll have a Latin and Greek test, so bone up, you lazy bum.'

"You were devastated when your mother told you of van Emst's horrible death. There was still no trace of Oosting and his son. 'Jan Gans, van Emst, perhaps the Oostings, and so many more. Do all the good men have to be killed before the bloodshed ends? If only there was a way to get word to Joekje. I can't even imagine what she must be going through, left alone with two small kids.'

"As for me, I did everything to avoid dwelling on your absence. I was determined to go on, with or without you. That very day I hired a young woman to help me. The nights were more difficult. I was used to the solitude, since so much of resistance work had to be done at night. But fantasies tormented me every night about what might have happened to you."

Joyce stopped again. I looked at her, then at him. His eyes were moist. She put her hand on his ruddy cheek and he moved away awkwardly.

"Go!" he said. And she knew. In spite of the pain, she had to continue.

"On the fourth day of your absence, a woman knocked on my door. 'Mrs. Miedema, Dr. deGroot sent me.' She neither introduced herself, nor sat down. 'I know that you and the *dominee* have done a great deal for those in need. We both know the rules, Mrs. Miedema—never reveal anything to a stranger. All I can tell you is that I need your help.

"'Just a couple of kilometres from here, the underground has placed a detective and his wife. He has done us invaluable service many a time. His wife is about to have a baby and the farmer wants them off his property. He wants no baby crying in case someone drops in for a visit. Dr. deGroot told me that he thought your manse was empty. How about letting her have the baby here?' How could I say no to a mother about to deliver her baby? 'If this is a trap,' I told her, 'you'll have the orphaning of my two tiny children on your conscience. You're a woman; I hope you both know and *feel* what I am risking.'

"That very night, I assisted Dr. deGroot in delivering the detective's wife's newborn girl.

"The next day, however, the new house guests became unpleasant, making comments about the provincialism of the manse and my backward mannerisms. I had expected nothing but quiet respect for me and my home from them. Naturally I felt hurt. 'How would you feel about moving upstairs since you are alone and leaving us the master bedroom? With our newborn baby it would make more sense, wouldn't it?' 'No, it wouldn't. That is my room and my husband's room. It is our private world. I let your wife have her baby in my bed. But now I want you to go upstairs, all of you. If it's a bother, perhaps you'd like to find another place.' They moved upstairs without another word.

"On the sixth day of your absence, another stranger knocked on my door. I opened it a little and slammed it immediately. Dressed in rags and dark glasses, the man looked like he hadn't taken a bath since his mother stopped washing him. I had heard of some itinerant gypsies hiding out in the region. 'I'm alone. I'm scared. What if he's crazy and tries to harm me or the children?' There was another knock on the door and another. As the man outside insisted, I thought I was going to lose my sanity. I went into the kitchen to distract myself.

"The knocking stopped. 'Thank God, he's finally left,' I thought. Then I saw a face in the kitchen window. I almost fainted. Was I hallucinating or was it real? I no longer knew: the man in the rags and dark glasses was you disguised as a vagabond.

"'My God, Pieter, you could have frightened me to death!' I exclaimed as we hugged. 'I would never have recognized you. I'm so glad you're home.' Remember, Father? What a fright you gave me!" There was tender reproach in her voice. "I was so happy to see you that night. And I'm so happy to see you now," her eyes seemed to be saying.

Pieter answered his wife's glance with a faint smile. He knew what she meant.

" 'I'm afraid, my dear it's just a whirlwind visit to tuck the children in and to kiss you goodnight. Then I have to go. My enemies never sleep.'

"Then there was another knock on the door.

" 'Is the *dominee* here?' an old man asked, breathless, as if he had been running for a long while. 'If he's here, make him go away at once. And if he is away, don't let him in. Three Germans and a couple of NSB-ers are on their way to pick up the "young *dominee*".' And he disappeared into the night.

"You took some money and kissed me goodbye; then you were gone once more. 'From tomorrow on I'll be somewhere in Groningen. I don't know any more myself.'

"After you closed the door I got rid of all evidence of our illegal activities. I took the rest of the money, all the gold we had hidden for safekeeping, as well as the illegal ration coupons and rushed over to the doctor's house. 'If they come to ask you about my husband, Doctor, please tell them that he is a sick man so that they'll stop looking for him.'

" 'I have to run over to the farmer to fetch some milk. Mr. van Dijk, would you mind looking after my little ones for thirty minutes or so?' I asked the detective the next evening after I had tucked in my two children.

" 'My wife has gone to call on the other *dominee*. I'm alone with our baby. I might as well keep an ear out for yours,' he said phlegmatically. When I returned thirty minutes later, I was surprised to find the minister from the Christian Reform Church in front of the house. 'The Germans are coming. They're in Uraterp. We're next.' 'Have you seen the van Dijks, Bernaard, the woman was supposed to have gone to see you. Do they know about the Germans?' I asked. 'She was with me when I got the news. I sat her on my cross bar and bicycled her home. She dashed in. Seconds later they made off on foot.'

" 'If they're gone, who's with my children?' I bolted up the steps leading to the children's room. With one arm I scooped up Piet, with the other I picked up Siets and I flew over to the doctor's house. 'Let me leave the kids here until I arrange something. The Germans are on their way to arrest me.' I continued on my quest for a safe place for the three of us. A couple of kilometres out of town I knocked on the door of the Hoekstra brothers. They were involved with the underground one way or another. 'Go, hide in a hurry. They're coming for you.' 'But I'm pregnant, I can't run around like a headless chicken. I can't take it; I'll lose my baby.' 'If you don't go, they'll get your baby out of you before its time.' Jan was in a ghoulish mood.

"Without thinking, I made my way home to pick up a few essentials for the children and myself. Running down the stairs, I froze. The little bridge near the manse was rattling under a crossing car. I collapsed in resignation. 'Nobody can outrun his destiny. What has been decreed for us by the Lord, will have to happen.'

"It was Vellinga, the butcher from Uraterp, coming to take us to safety in his truck. 'Do you have a place to hide?' Joseph inquired. 'Well, I don't really know. My husband knows who is safe but I am not sure....' I was at loss. 'Perhaps...this farmer near us would take us in for a while.'

"The butcher's truck cut through the rye field. 'It's a lot safer this way than on the road,' he explained.

" 'I see a man pedalling right for us,' I exclaimed in fright. 'Where do we go now? We can't even hide the truck anywhere.'

" 'Let's hide in the rye. It's high enough.' The butcher was trying to sound calm but he, too, was shaken by the appearance of the solitary cyclist. 'If he tries something nasty I'll kill him.' And he pulled out a large pocket knife.

" 'It's de Vos. We're safe.' I sighed, relieved. 'We were headed towards his farm. Perhaps he too is in trouble.' I emerged from the rye field to meet him.

" 'So you're running away, too,' he commented without much concern. 'I'm going to your place. I've got the van Dijks in my house. He forgot a piece of damning evidence in their room. I'm going to fetch it for him.' 'Well, I was going to ask you to hide us, but you have a full house already.' 'Go to Boonstra. He's one of your husband's flock.' And he was on his way.

"The Boonstras opened their home and hearts to us. 'We'll always have room for the *dominee's* family.' The farmer sounded solemn. 'We'll be a little tight but we'll be safe and cozy.' With that, we bedded down all the kids right in the Boonstra children's room.

Rebels in the Manse

" 'From the kitchen we can see the windows of the manse when the lights are on,' my hostess told me. 'With these you'll have a better view.' Her man handed me an old pair of binoculars. I zeroed in on my abandoned home.

" 'Well, they're sure there and they seem madder than rabid dogs,' I exclaimed. 'One of them is pointing at the hot kettle on the stove. They realize that we must have been tipped off. I had just warmed water for tea when we had to flee.'

"They turned the contents of the manse upside down. It was past three in the morning when they finally gave up, thoroughly frustrated. And I watched how they were desecrating my home. They sealed our doors. We were officially homeless. I will remember that May first for as long as I live.

"What followed for us was a pilgrimage of nearly a year. During that time I had my third baby, this one in a clinic because of complications. 'You must rest and stop your nomadic existence for a while,' the doctor advised me. So we returned to your mother's place. Every now and then, you would make a brief appearance, as safety and the resistance permitted. By then, your mother had other company, as well. She took in two English pilots whose plane had been shot down in a nearby field. 'We have another comrade out there. We think he's alive but we couldn't find him. His name is Patrick Horn,' one of the pilots told you. 'If he's out there, I'll bring him back here. Don't worry,' you said.

"By then, I was at the end of my rope. So I went to stay with various members of my family to wait until things calmed down.

"Our friends must be wondering about the Lezers. Well, you didn't forget them, did you, Father? You had confided in another forest ranger about them. 'Don't worry, I'll take care of them,' he reassured you. 'Besides, I know all about the family in the bunker. Van Emst had a tragically loose mouth. He couldn't keep a secret even though his life depended on it. Don't worry about me, Dominee. I am a man without a voice.'

"Liberation day found you in your mother's house together with the English pilots. Patrick Horn was among them, thanks to you. Go on, you old fool! It *is* the truth. You don't have to skewer me with your eyes. Look at him, my friends. It was easier for him to risk his life than to take credit for his bravery. What did the pilot tell you? 'We owe our lives to you, Reverend. Without ever firing a shot, you give a new dimension to the term "war hero".'

"And what did you say to that? 'I don't much like the sound of that term. Anyway you twist it, it still glorifies war. What we have done has nothing to do with that at all. It's all a matter of being available, with the right kind of help at the right time. Go home, my friends, and come back to us in peace time and we'll have a big celebration. For now, there are still bodies to bury, wounds to heal, traitors to flush out.'

"You went back to the manse with a vague idea about what to expect. And yet, to see the evidence of insane destruction was an awesome experience for you, not only because your warm and orderly home had been wrecked but also because the wreckage shed new light on the violent nature of ordinary folks like ourselves. 'If they could do this to us, why couldn't I be coerced, convinced, or cajoled into a similar act of hatred? Can a man destroy another man's home and still make claims to having a soul like the rest of us? Or are we all dormant monsters? What does this say about Christ, our Brother? My God, how could you allow such destruction? How many Christs need be crucified to convince You that we need Your intervention?' I believe that was perhaps your greatest ordeal because it raised in you ugly doubts about man and his Creator.

" 'Don't bring your family back just yet,' the *burgemeester* advised you. 'Let things calm down. Wait until the country is rid of the enemy, until the fire of hatred is doused in forgiveness.'

"So, we were reunited the day after all of Holland was liberated. We restored order in the manse. 'We are together, all of us, enriched by three new lives. Most of our friends survived to share in our celebration of life. The land is fertile, we are healthy and our will is strong. We have a lot to be thankful for,' you said in your first grace around the family dinner table.

"The next day, we took the children to Drachten to participate in national liberation day festivities. The town was bursting with enthusiasm. People who hadn't seen one another for months, even years, hugged, slapped each other on the back, toasted their good fortune, shouting their freedom to the sky. It was our first stroll as a family, and we were proud and relieved.

" 'Look, Pieter, it's her, it's the van Dijk woman.' I tugged on your arm. 'I wonder if she'll have the decency to at least say hello.'

" 'So you made it, too,' the detective's wife looked at me with disdain. 'I guess I owe you a word of gratitude. Well, I wish you lots of luck in life. Look me up sometime. I'll give you a few tips on interior decorating and fashion. God knows you can use some.' All of a sudden I felt dirty. And insignificant. Like a cigarette butt that had just been crushed by someone's heel.

" 'Just because you have risked your life for somebody doesn't mean that that person is decent,' you said, trying to console me. And you were furious. 'The world has always had its share of ugliness; after a major storm, much scum floats to the surface. There is a lot of cleansing still waiting for us.'

"The congregation was coming alive again. 'The war years were hell to live through, to be sure,' a man commented one Sunday, in June 1945, 'but it was also exciting. We knew we were alive. We made our presence felt.' Many of our neighbours shared his ambivalence about sinking back into the grey sameness of everyday life.

"And you, Father, you had your work cut out. Many wouldn't forgive you for involving the Church in the resistance. 'The Church is the home of God. There is no room in it for politics,' they said. Or, 'Politics is a pile of garbage men create for one another. Anyone dragging the Church into this mess is committing blasphemy.' Your name was never mentioned, but everyone knew. 'By staying idle at a time when we are the last resort for innocent people condemned to die, we blaspheme against God's commandment against killing.' You pronounced those words from the pulpit deliberately slowly to make sure that they would sink in. 'Every Christian who failed to open his door to a fugitive, failed to remember Christ's example. And without the lessons of Christ foremost in our hearts, how can we call ourselves Christians?' I can still hear your words. Let me tell you, my friends, he was glorious.

"But his opponents fought back. 'There is not one sentence anywhere in our Church's code of ethics that directs us to get involved in saving lives. No one expects us to become saviours,' one of the elders proclaimed. 'Christ showed the way every day in His every action. If one chooses to be blind, one has to be prepared to look into the mirror and to see the face of Barabbas grimace back at him. There is none so blind as he who chooses not to see; there is none so deaf as he who chooses not to hear,' you retorted.

"It would have been lonely for you without the radiant portrait of Harri Lezer, the new commandant of the detention camp for war criminals in Diver, in nearby Drenthe.

"When you first heard that Lezer had been appointed head of the camp, you feared for his soul. 'Just wait until the war is over! Just wait, I'll show these rotten traitors the wrath of man! I'll hound every NSB-er to his grave. He'll be sorry he was ever born, if I get my hands on him,' he'd said.

"You rushed to see him in his new home near the campsite. And you found a changed man. 'We said a lot of things in the forest, Pieter. We needed those violent fantasies of revenge to convince ourselves that we were still human. Now that we are really alive again, we will not soil our hands. The torturers and murderers will pay according to our laws. We will not apply to them their own laws. It's time to let the sunshine in, Pieter.'

"And what did you do? You hugged him and kissed him on the cheek. 'You're a better Christian than most members of my Church.' 'Christian or Jewish, what's the difference as long as you never forget that you're a man, not better and not worse than your next-door neighbour.'

"Your war-time activities didn't go unrecognized, even if in your own town you were less than a hero. First, you received a citation issued by the General Headquarters of the Resistance Movement in Utrecht. Then another one signed by General Eisenhower and Field Marshal Montgomery. And then, you got a note of gratitude from the English pilot Patrick Horn: 'I hope that your courage and dedication to humanity will be rewarded soon. You deserve the best.' 'So it was thanks to him that Eisenhower and Monty found out about my modest adventures,' you said to me with a faint smile. We both cherished his letter the most.

"Then we were uprooted from our town. 'We need you to build morale and community spirit in Dwingelo,' they told you. This transfer changed our lives.

"The first Sunday, your church was overflowing with worshippers. Everyone wanted to hear the maverick. You were on trial and your judges—the influential members of the congregation—came harbouring prejudice and apprehension. 'My first sermon to you deals with the consequences of closing our hearts to the teachings of Christ.' Some of the elders frowned. 'There are times when it's frightening to open one's eyes to see the path He has cut for us. One's heart is filled with fear that if one allows that spectacle to enter one's eyes, a terrifying panorama will unfold in one's soul. In the centre of that desolate landscape one can't fail to discover the shadow of the cross on one's own grave. But, my friends, consider the alternative. If we allow our fear to dominate our moral horizons, we will in fact bring upon ourselves an era of inner darkness illuminated only by flashes of bad conscience. "Am I my brother's keeper?" generations of Cains have asked with irate indifference towards the plight of others. There are countless ways to answer this simple question. But there is only one that makes sense to me: "Not only am I my brother's keeper, my brother is *my* keeper." Without this tacit contract, I am as vulnerable as he is without me.'

" 'Dominee, your sermon was powerful and to the point.' Gerrits, one of the richest elders came to seek you out after the service. 'This community, however, faces more burning issues than who must save whom.'

" 'If you forgive my presumption,' Hogeterp, another wealthy elder chimed in, 'we know this community better than you. We have been taking its pulse ever since we grew out of short pants. We are responsible for its welfare in that we rent the people the land on which they earn their daily bread. We know what they need to hear. To put it bluntly, we would much appreciate it if you would consult with the elders concerning the topics of your sermons. All your predecessors saw the wisdom of this collaboration.'

" 'And I believe, my friends, that it would serve the best interest of the entire congregation if we all busied ourselves with what we know best. I give you my word that I'll never interfere with your land leasing or your cattle marketing. In exchange all I am asking is that you leave preaching and the other ministerial duties to me. Your thoughts are always welcome, but I'll retain for myself the judgement required to carry on with my ministry.'

"The following Sunday the church was empty. And the Sunday after was the same. But your Wednesday Bible study groups were filled to capacity. 'What is happening, my friends? I am profoundly confused,' you addressed one group. 'Why is my church empty on Sundays? Today you're all here, but none of you attended services the last two Sundays. What's going on?'

" 'We want to feed and shelter our families,' one of them said in a whisper.

" 'We rent our lands from the owners,' another one spoke out. 'We were all warned: "You go to hear Miedema and I won't rent to you any longer." '

" 'So the rich are still squeezing the poor!' you shouted, with your eyes bulging like those of a frog. I can tell you, Vicki and André, when Father used to shout, he was a frightening sight. His face turned purple with rage. 'Five years of slavery taught them nothing. Well, I'll put an end to the reign of leeches. Come to services Sunday and I shall protect your lands and homes.'

"The next Sunday the church was again empty. 'Fear is sweeping our town like leprosy. People have shut their hearts to the Lord and to each other. We might as well be dead,' you told me.

" 'Do you really need this struggle, Pieter?' your friend Jan Dijkstra asked you that evening. 'You have fought for years with all sorts of enemies, don't you think it's time to pack it in and devote some time to the peaceful enjoyment of your family? Come, join us in Canada. We're sailing in three weeks, you know that. They need ministers in the new immigrant communities.'

" 'I'm not a quitter. Those Godless parasites won't chase me out of town,' you kept repeating stubbornly."

" 'Wanted: Reformed Ministers. Come to Canada; our Dutch brethren need you. For information, call Dr. McFarlane, representing the Presbyterian Church of Quebec in The Hague.'

" 'There could be no harm in listening to the man,' you told me hesitantly.

" 'Our Church will provide you with a congregation upon your arrival either in Quebec or in Ontario. We will, of course, have suitable quarters waiting for you. Come, Pieter, this will be the challenge of your life.'

" 'Let's give the New World a chance, Joekje.' You were ready for a new adventure, one that sounded so rewarding and so safe. By the spring of 1952, you were a father of five children. It had to be safe and sound. 'With a ministry and a home waiting for us, the risk is quite manageable,' we agreed.

"After liquidating our assets we still didn't have enough cash to pay for seven passages and leave us some change in our pockets upon setting foot in Canada. We applied to the government for a relocation subsidy. They approved twenty-five hundred guilders for us. A month before departure, we got a letter from the government: according to some new information they'd received, the authorities deemed that we had the means to bear the costs of emigration. Thus, we lost the subsidy.

" 'One of our "friends" in Dwingelo chose this roundabout way to let us know that they hated to see us go.' Boy, you were hurt. 'No matter, it just makes turning my back on them that much easier.'

"We had already cashed in all the savings we had put away for the children's education. There was nothing left to sell. I hated the thought of asking her for a loan, or even disturbing her in her grief, but Hanna was the only person I knew who would be able to loan us that amount. I forgot to mention that Harri Lezer had just passed away during the winter. It was an unexpected blow to us all. He was felled by a heart attack at the age of fifty.

"Hanna handed you a cheque for twenty-five hundred guilders. 'And consider it our "bon voyage" gift. I know that's what Harri would have wanted.'

"On September 24, 1952, we landed on Canadian soil. We were tired but alive with anticipation.

"Well, there you have it. Oh, there is a lot more that happened to us. We had good times and we had not so good ones. In Canada, we lived quietly; we were more often poor than not, but our family grew very strong and that made us rich."

On June 20, 1979, the sun decided not to rise on the Miedema family. Pieter suffered a devastating stroke, robbing him of his ability to speak. The long road to recovery was sinuous. Frustration and silence became his constant companions—and a forever devoted Joekje.

"Just one more thing," Sylvia said as Vicki was about to unplug the tape-recorder. "My son's grade-four teacher gave the class the assignment of recounting an adventure that happened to somebody they knew. So he told the story of how mosquitoes saved his grandpa's life in the woods during the Second World War. And you know what, the teacher rejected his contribution! 'It couldn't have happened the way you tell it, it's too incredible,' she said. Sometimes people, even teachers, have a hard time dealing with reality if it isn't trimmed to the dimensions of their own experience. With one simple sentence, George's teacher wiped out part of our existence. We don't fit into her Canadian panorama. That sums it all up for me and Dad, right, Dad?"

"Well, I'd like to propose one more story. In a way, it is an epilogue to my parents' war-time antics." Jekke, Sylvia's younger sister, had a smile on her face as she looked at her father, then at her mother's tears lingering in the corner of her tired eyes. "We might have had a very hard life as children, but we always knew who father was, who mother was, who was the boss, what were the rules, and most of all that we had their unconditional love. We might have had to do our homework by candlelight, and we might have had to dry out our clothes by the oil burner as we stood in them because we had no other clothes to change in to. But for us that was the only life we knew; all the other kids lived the same way we did, and we had fun. When, much later, I visited a couple of elderly ladies from our church to keep them company, I told them about Mom and Dad's involvement with rescuing, and about our lives in the Great White North. When I finished, both of them were weeping. That's when I discovered that according to Canadian standards we had an unhappy childhood. But as far as we were concerned, we were happy. Weren't we, Father? You had a great adventure in the forest, hunting, trying to outfox the fox; sometimes you won and sometimes the fox had the better of you. And, yes, Mom, you endured beyond your limit. You bore in your body and your soul all the pain that the rest of us didn't feel."

"We have good memories and we have some not so good ones." Joyce flashed a thankful but tired smile at her daughter. "But when all is said and done, what matters really is that we did the best we could and we are all alive to tell the story."

The House on the Hereweg:

Lidia Feenstra

Mrs. Feenstra's apartment house is a drab, lime green, four-storey building on a quiet residential street in Niagara Falls. Nothing suggests that the town is one of the world's most glamorous tourist attractions. It's the middle of May and one would expect colourful flowers, or at least lush green vegetation. And yet, there isn't even a tree next to the lacklustre edifice. I'm disappointed. Somehow I imagined Mrs. Feenstra surrounded with dense green lawns and centuries-old trees, reminders of her native Netherlands. Her voice had been so full of excitement on the phone that I had a mental image of her as a woman of fine taste who would surround herself with things of beauty, with objects that evoke deep feelings and cherished memories.

I rang the bell downstairs with some trepidation. I didn't quite know what to expect, except, very likely, a brittle elderly lady for whom going back into the past might be strenuous exercise. She was a widow; there was no one to give her moral support should the road we were about to take get too bumpy— except me. And *I* was a stranger. And *I* was an hour late.

"I began to think you were not coming." This was her first sentence to me. There was no reproach in her words. It was a statement of fact. I told Mrs. Feenstra about getting lost.

"Well, there's no harm. It's not like I have to hurry anywhere. Go ahead, make yourself comfortable. I'll bring us some refreshments." And she disappeared to the kitchen.

Her spacious living room was furnished with old-world charm, partially confirming my fantasy about this lady. Every object seemed to have been selected because it connected her to distant places and times. Much of it had probably been transplanted from her previous home in Northern Holland: lots of china knick-knacks, including several Hummel figurines; photographs; embroidered cushions; lace doilies — each linked to a memory, I was certain. And plants, lots of them—nothing fragile that would require delicate care, but many different cactuses. Symbols of ruggedness and survival? An impressive Philips radio, with a hypnotically glowing magic green eye, in a shining walnut cabinet—at least forty years old — dominated Lidia Feenstra's living room. There was no doubt in my mind, I was in the presence of a strong personality—a woman who was as enduring as that radio and as complex as the various components of her domestic landscape.

"I see you're taking inventory," she commented with a benign smile. "Go ahead, everything is there. I shipped my entire household when I moved from Groningen to Canada in 1961. What can I say? I am sentimental. The past is all I have. Not that it has been so glorious, but, as I've just said, it's all I have left. I carry the bad memories with me wherever I go, whether I like it or not. So I might as well surround myself with the reminders of happy moments as well. It's all a matter of balance: something has always tried to elude me, but that, here and there, I manage to catch by the tail. I've always been a very emotional person; some people avoid me for that very reason, some others like me for it. In the long run, it all averages out. As I said, it's a matter of balance. Look at me now, I just keep babbling on as if that's what you had come for."

She looked profoundly embarrassed, like a schoolgirl caught cheating on an assignment. That, too, seemed to be part of who Lidia was in her seventh decade of life. She had a matronly bearing but it was impossible not to detect the impish youngster in her bright blue eyes and around her lips.

"I am ready to begin." She announced in a very business-like manner.

"I thought you could just go ahead and talk about your life, as the memories pop into your mind," I prompted her. She looked perplexed.

"But where do I begin? How do I know what's important? I would much prefer if you asked me questions, then I'll answer to the best of my recollection. I'm an old woman, you know, even if I don't look it."

"Well, Mrs. Feenstra, how about beginning with your most vivid recollection of your involvement with rescuing Jews during the war?"

She seemed lost and embarrassed, then I saw the light in her bright eyes dim.

" 'It's not lady-like to peek into somebody else's soup pot,' Lexie scolded old Mrs. Takens. This casual lesson in etiquette cost Lexie, a twenty-six-year-old Jew, his life. A few minutes after he was killed, his protector—my husband, Willem—was summarily executed in our own home.' There you have it. As far as I am concerned we could stop right there. There is nothing of any significance to add. When the life was taken from my husband and my friend, nothing else really mattered—not then, not since, and not now. Except for Lizzie, my daughter, of course. Without her I wouldn't be here today."

Mrs. Feenstra grew silent. I looked at her with anxious anticipation. Her body was limp in her armchair, her gaze unfocused. She seemed to be elsewhere. But then she raised her eyes to look at me and shook her head with a scarcely perceptible motion. She was in control again. Only the brisk wringing of her hands gave a sign that her agitation persisted.

"Lexie was a Dutch Jew and Willem, a Dutch Christian, hiding him from the Nazis. The calendar read January 21, 1945, not quite four months before Canadian soldiers would rid the northern Dutch city of Groningen of the Fascist plague. I lost my husband, Willem, and, with him, the perfection of my family circle. There has not been a man in my life since. What an absurd waste of so many lives! What does kitchen protocol have to do with murder? I cannot explain it. All I can do is recount a story born on a dark January night, a story that has kept me loyal company but refuses to grow old with me. So ask away, Mr. Stein, what else do you need to know?"

Quiet Heroes

"What was your life like prior to your involvement with the resistance?" I asked.

"Willem and I had planned to have a comfortable existence in the medieval city of Groningen. Willem managed a small winery, without ever sampling its products. He had no worries, no vices, no particular hobbies to distract him from his only joy: his tiny family. I was the perfect mate for him, happy to build a modestly elegant nest for my husband and daughter, Lizzie. We had a home on the Hereweg, one of Groningen's busy commercial streets. It was more imposing for its size than for its opulence. The rest is of no interest to you. Unless you want me to tell you insignificant details about my youth."

"Well, then, how about sharing with me the story of how you came to be involved with the rescuing?"

"During the occupation, Willem was heading a group of twenty-one young men, while I remained on the sidelines. I knew virtually nothing about what really went on during those furtive encounters. I asked no questions and no information was volunteered to me.

"I was, however, keenly aware of the war. Stringent laws aimed to break the rebellious spirit of my pacifist country. One of these laws required that everyone turn in his radio to the authorities. It would have amounted to cutting off our ears. We obeyed the law, like most people: we handed in one cheap set and hid a powerful Philips under some loosened planks in the kitchen floor. Every night, at the stroke of midnight, we listened to the BBC to learn the latest developments. Many a night I shed tears of anguish. I had nothing but contempt for the Germans and their local lackeys.

"We could have avoided most hardships caused by the occupation other than the humiliation of being vanquished. Neither one of us could remain insensitive, however, to the anti-Jewish measures that pushed our friends towards an ominous fate.

" 'They are no longer permitted in restaurants, parks, libraries, laundries, or grocery stores,' I lamented, wringing my hands—a sure sign of my agitation. (By the way, to this day I have never lost this habit.) 'Now they are branded like cattle. How long can this go on?'

" 'There's worse, Lidia; they have been taking them to Germany and Poland. They claim that the Jews are being used in constructive labour—hard, but they're being fairly remunerated. But we know the truth. Over four hundred Jews were taken to the quarries of Mauthausen after the February Strike in 1941. Not one of them is alive. Since then more and more of them disappear. "Reprisals for sabotage activities," the bastards claim, with a cynical shrug of their shoulders.' Willem was outraged over the fate of our Jewish compatriots.

" 'We have to do something, Willem. I don't know what, but we can't just watch them disappear in those camps. How can I remain uninvolved and live at peace with myself? "What can one person do, anyway?" Emma van Wijk asked me yesterday when I proposed that we do something to help the Jews. "Nothing except get caught and be taken to Westerbork with the Jews or get shot in the back." "No, absolutely not," I disagreed with her. "If we all saved just one Jew, the Germans wouldn't find a soul to deport. Even they can't wipe out a whole nation of sixteen million." '

"A few days later, Willem called me from the winery. 'Lidia, tonight I'll bring home a little doggie. I'm sure you'll like him. Can you make some preparations for him on the third floor?'

"My heart was pounding when I hung up. I began to pace back and forth in the living room, wringing my hands. Of course, there was no question of any dog. I was allergic to furry animals. He was bringing home a Jewish fugitive! This was the opportunity I had been waiting for—finally to do something in order to save a life.

" 'My God, I'm scared out of my wits. This is a dangerous business. We can all be killed. I never thought I would be so frightened when the moment came for action. But it's too late; he's coming tonight and from now until liberation we will have to live in the constant company of fear. The same fear the Jews have had to cope with ever since the Germans decided to do God's work and decree who will live and who will die. Well, that does it, enough is enough. At least one Jew will not go to his fate, because Willem and I won't let it happen...unless we are all betrayed, and then we will all disappear....'

"I went upstairs to the third floor to prepare the room. The most important thing was to make sure the window was blacked out completely, not to allow one single ray of light to attract the attention of the police. The room was large but sparsely furnished: a single bed, a chest of drawers, a small table, and a student chair. I brought up linen for the bed. I even dug up a nice throw rug, covering half of the creaking old parquet floor. My mind was absorbed by the task, but my ambivalent feelings didn't leave me for a moment. I went up and down the stairs at least a dozen times: I was so taken with the upcoming change in our lives that I no longer knew what I was doing. On my last trip to the newly appointed shelter I left a small ficus plant in the corner. 'At least he'll have some evidence of life in this minuscule universe,' I thought.

"That evening, however, Willem came home alone. He collapsed into the nearest kitchen chair without a word. 'I saw naked terror today, Lidia, I saw it with my own eyes. I'll never be able to close them again without it haunting me.' His voice conveyed a kind of raw pain that could only be echoed by tonelessness. With trembling fingers, I caressed the back of his head.

" 'I was going over some order forms when one of the lads burst through the door: "Mijnheer Feenstra, come at once, come into the street...." I ran after him and my feet froze to the cobble-stones as my eyes fell on the body of a young man. The only thing covering his back was blood. No skin, no flesh: just blood. A yellow star soiled with his own blood lay next to his head, completing the story with tragic finality. I didn't dare to go any closer. But I had to know. Sure enough, it was Gerrit—the very same person I was going to bring home tonight. Just a few more steps, and he would have made it to the winery. He had been skinned alive, crucified in the street, with his face smashed in the dirt.'

"I fell on my knees to hug my husband as tightly as I could, hoping to exorcise with love the horrible memory. Then we both sat there weeping.

" 'It's not tears that we need,' Willem said in a resolute whisper. 'We need to be prepared; we need to seek out people in need; we need to act, not react.'

" 'Whatever you think we can do, I'm with you. This can't go on.' I needed to pledge my commitment aloud.

"For the next few days, Willem brought home construction material, a little bit every evening. Then, on Sunday, he built a hiding place in the largest of the three upstairs rooms. It had a large closet, extending deeply into the cavern of a gable. Willem walled off most of it, leaving only a shallow front. The hidden chamber afforded modest seclusion for up to three people, lying on mattresses. For the front of the closet we gathered all the old clothes we had. I canvassed all of my trustworthy friends for old suits, dresses, and coats. 'I'm collecting them for the evacuees,' I told them. It made sense because thousands of people had lost everything in the bombing of Rotterdam."

"Do you recall the day Rotterdam was bombed?" I interjected.

"And how! Certain things you just never forget, no matter how hard you try. Besides, as painful as those memories are, I want to remember them. They are part of me. It was on May 10, 1940. It seemed to me that the white puffy clouds had been turned into steel birds by the evil whim of a sorcerer. 'How could a human being create something that ugly and that threatening?' I wondered as I looked at the sky darkened by warplanes rushing towards the condemned city. Willem turned on the radio at once: we were at war, indeed, and the city of Rotterdam was on its way to destruction.

" 'I have always been on the side of life, but these degenerates don't deserve anything better than what they perpetrate on us,' I told Willem. 'I want them to know the same suffering they afflict on our peaceful little nation. Whom did the mothers of Rotterdam hurt to merit this?' No, indeed, I am not about to forget Rotterdam and the endless procession of evacuees.

"But to come back to my story, the hiding place was inaugurated five days after Willem put the finishing touches to it. He had ample connections in the underground. That evening, soon after Lizzie had been tucked in for the night, the downstair's doorbell rang with three rapid bursts followed by one long one. Willem and I locked glances: the code of the resistance. A nameless man stood silhouetted in the doorway. This is how Sammy van Hassel first entered the life of our family.

"He was a quiet boy of twenty-one from Utrecht where he was a student until the new masters of the country closed the gates of learning to Jews. He had been on the run for years. We were his thirty-seventh or possibly thirty-eighth hosts. After a while it was hard to keep track. There was nothing more dangerous than hiding a young Jewish male. To further complicate matters, during the first year of hiding, Sammy would rather have died than violate the sacred laws of his faith. Then one day just before Passover in 1942, his host got arrested for black-marketeering: he was trying to secure some illegally slaughtered kosher beef in trade for a piece of jewellery. He was freed by a compassionate police officer. For Sammy, on that Passover more than the herbs were bitter. He thanked his host for the sacrifice and he announced that from that day on he would not consider himself bound by any of the Jewish dietary laws.

"His host held himself responsible for what he considered to be Sammy's loss of faith. Life in hiding had its own logic, its own peculiar tension: the incident undermined their rapport to the extent that they could not get along without quarrelling. Shortly after, Sammy was taken to another hiding place. By then, the young man had sunk into a deep silence from which nothing could move him. He spoke only when it was essential and observed only minimal civilities.

" 'Is there anything special you'd like me to prepare for you tomorrow, Sammy?' I would ask him, hoping to cheer him up. 'My Willem can produce some astonishing morsels. You see, he manages the winery. We never touch alcohol, but he knows many a farmer who would gladly part with a chicken or two, a piece of pork, a dozen eggs, or the like, for the pleasures of a few bottles of wine. So what will it be, young man?'

" 'Whatever you have in the house is my preference. I would very much appreciate it if you and Mr. Feenstra didn't go to any trouble whatsoever on my account.'

" 'Hiding a Jew is really not a big deal. One has to be discreet, of course. But then again, one is always better off keeping private what's private. Sammy eats like a bird; he would do his own dishes and laundry if I'd allow him to, and he never intrudes on our family life. Most of the time I don't even know that he is upstairs,' I told Willy about six weeks after Sammy joined us.

" 'Are you willing to accept more?' Willem asked, with a wink.

" 'Why not?' I answered without even giving it a second thought. 'You know, Willy, my mother had nine children of her own, all living at home during the Great War. There were a couple of young Hungarians in town who had had enough of fighting and took English leave of the front and of their country. "Well," my mother said, "I don't see why I can't take them in." If she could cope with two refugees on top of the nine of us, I don't see why I can't cope with another Jew.'

" 'How about two? Two brothers, relations of a friend from down under....' Willy winked once again.

" 'Have them come, this pair of bookends, by all means. They may have to squeeze in a bit, and if the farmers become less thirsty, we may all have to eat a little less. No need to make a big fuss about one more person.'

"And you know, Mr. Stein, what my husband did? He shook my hand as if we were comrades, fancy that. Willy was proud of me, I am not ashamed to tell you. There were not many women with my kind of courage."

The House on the Hereweg

"I'm glad to hear that you give credit to yourself for your courage," I said.

"Why shouldn't I? It's the truth. Anyway, Lexie and Dolph arrived the next evening. They had one small bag between them.

" '*Mevrouw, Mijnheer*, I am Alexander Brenner.' One of the lads came forth and took a deep bow. It was hard to know if he was a bit of a clown, a bit gauche, or just plain exuberant. I liked him instantly. A young man of spirit: just what Sammy and I needed.

" 'And this unimpressive rogue is my brother, Adolph, the shame of the family. Not being excessively proud of his namesake, he responds to Dolph, if you please.' And he took another theatrical bow.

" 'Are we supposed to applaud or what?' I entered into the game happily. 'It's been some time since I've been to the circus, so naturally I welcome a couple of clowns under my own roof.'

" 'Just one, lady, just one, if you pardon the disappointment.' Dolph entered the conversation for the first time. 'My brother Lexie is the buffoon of the team; I'm the worrier. He can forget that any day may be our last; I can't. He sees danger nowhere; I see it for both of us, everywhere.'

" 'Well, my friends,' Willy chimed in cordially, 'you're in good hands here. We have what it takes to keep you safe. Except for my wife, Lizzie, our three-year-old, and Sammy there is no one in this castle and we are not in the habit of receiving guests these days. And if some unexpected visitors do happen to come, we have a smart little shelter for our honoured guests on the third floor.

" 'Just in case you wonder, Sammy is another Jewish lad sharing our household,' Willy said. 'He is discretion personified, eats shadows and tears, walks on feathers. Sometimes I wonder if he ever learned to smile.'

" 'A Jew in hiding nowadays doesn't have a great deal to smile about,' Dolph mused in his low baritone.

" 'Except that he is alive and not behind barbed wires.' Lexie pronounced his assessment of their predicament.

" 'Did he say "Brenner", Willy?' I asked my husband once we had all settled down.

" 'He sure did,' he answered with the same expression on his face as the day before, when he had asked me if two were just as welcome as one.

" 'Are they related to Karel and Annemarie by any chance?' I was beginning to catch on.

" 'None other than.'

" 'And you knew it, didn't you, you good-for-nothing?'

" 'I sure did.' Willy had a big playful grin on his face as if he had just been unmasked."

"Who are Karel and Annemarie?" I interrupted her.

"Karel was the oldest of the three Brenner brothers and Annemarie was his wife. I'll tell you in a moment how I got to know them. It's quite a story, I promise you. But at that moment, talking with Willy, I started to put the pieces together. Alexander and Adolph Brenner had been under since the beginning."

"You mean they'd been in hiding?" I wanted to clarify the term "under".

"Or joined the resistance," she replied. "It means that they chose to vanish. Lexie got caught, and was sent to Westerbork. But he escaped through the bushes when it was still possible to escape. That was before my time. I was beside myself with excitement. What memories these two boys stirred up in me! 'My God, Lizzie was just a toddler,' I recalled. 'She could have lost her mother before she turned two years old. How insanely reckless of me!'

" 'Reckless, definitely,' Willem commented. 'Mad, without a doubt; insane and out of the question.' There was not a wisp of resentment or criticism in his words. Living through those thirty-six hours was for him like being locked up in a leper colony with little hope of escaping. But, in fact, it was I who entered the 'transit camp' in the sanitized jargon of its masters, a desert of anguish and a frosty last station before death for most of its Jewish inmates."

"You chose to enter Westerbork?" I couldn't believe my ears.

"I told you this is quite story. You're in for a treat, Mr. Stein. Nearly two years had passed since I had agreed to help out an old school friend of mine by taking over her babysitting engagement. I had to look after a pair of Jewish twins whose father was already in Westerbork and the mother needed to take care of some urgent matter.

"As agreed, I showed up at the Brenner residence at eight o'clock. The young woman did her best to hide her agitation. 'Oh, it's so kind of you to help us out, total strangers, and on such short notice,' she said. Her name was Annemarie. 'I have some urgent packing to do which I don't want the kids to see; they ask too many questions. After that, I have to run out for a short while. I won't be very long, I promise. I can't thank you enough, after all there is a law against you being here.'

" 'You just do what you have to do. As for that ridiculous law, I go where I please; I visit whom I please; there is no law that can change that.' I had scarcely settled in with the two five-year-olds when I heard forceful banging on the front door.

" 'You must come with us at once!' A Dutch policeman snapped at Annemarie, who stood there in silence and showed not the slightest sign of surprise. An ominous-looking SS man stood next to the SD man. That's why she was packing so feverishly. She was planning on going under later that night....

" 'You must come with us at once!'

"Annemarie lost her composure and she broke into a fit of hysterics. 'Oh no, not that, I can't go.... I'm scared.... Don't make me please, anything but that....'

"In a flash, I grabbed the boys by the hand, dragged them down the steps, and casually, as if the two scarecrows were air, I said to Annemarie: 'Well, my dear, me and the boys have just got to go. My husband will give me hell for keeping the kids out so late. Let's keep in touch, all right? I so enjoyed our chat. Come, my boys, say good night to Mrs. Brenner. Daddy's waiting for us.'

"I couldn't believe what came out of my mouth. I had done a lot of impulsive things in my life, but this staggered even me. But I knew that these people were destined for Westerbork and for unknown places beyond. At least the children had to be saved. The kids seemed confused and I was afraid they would say something disastrous. 'Well, don't mind them. They're so dopey, they may fall on their faces if I don't get them home in a jiffy.' And I made a beeline for the door.

" 'Halt!' The German stopped me cold. He whispered something to the SD man who, in turn, after a moment's scrutiny, came nose to nose with me. I was shivering. 'Are those your children?'

" 'They most certainly are. I'm not in the habit of walking about town with rented or borrowed kids. Just what are you insinuating, officer?'

"Without another word, he squatted in front of Martijn and with a brutal yank he opened the child's shorts. The horrified boy recoiled instinctively, protecting his manhood, that unequivocal evidence of his Judaism.

" 'I thought so, you miserable traitor.' He spat his jubilant anger into my face. 'Now you won't have to worry about leaving them behind because soon you'll be with your beloved Jews, you degenerate whore.'

"The three Brenners were swallowed by the SS truck. 'You will come with me,' the SD man ordered. There was bile in his voice.

" 'I can't understand you, you fine Dutch specimen.' I tried to occupy my mind out of fear that I might faint. 'The German goes about his macabre business without a word, without feeling. For him it's a job. After all, he's just a stranger, a soldier following orders. But you, you act out of hatred against your compatriots. You are just as much subjugated as the rest of us. Do you think for a second that the German thinks more of you for licking his boots than he thinks of those of us who resist him? We are perhaps more of a nuisance to him, but he would shoot you without blinking an eye if those were his orders. He is not your ally, nor am I, or for that matter any decent Dutch citizen. You shuttle between two spiteful faces. Where does that leave you? What will wait for you when this is all over?'

"I wouldn't have been surprised if the traitor had stopped the car and shot me on the spot. But instead, he continued driving without a word. When he stopped the car in front of Police Headquarters, he grabbed me by the arm and stared into my face from so close that I was afraid to breathe.

" 'One day, you yellow-bellied Jew-lovers will be sorry. We will win; there is no doubt about it. And when we do, not one of you will be forgotten. This country will be rid of Jews and Jew-lovers. I have a vision that's shared by the Führer and with all those Germanic people who have had more than their fill of being under the patent-leather boots of Jewish bankers and snivelling liberal ass-lickers. The world belongs to the mighty, to the one who dares to take the ultimate risks. We will do things that the next ten generations won't be able to imagine or understand. But the eleventh will canonize us for the selfless holy work we have undertaken in this gutless century. Yes, I hate you and your kind, for you have no vision and you want to rob me of mine with your sentimental drivel about patriotism. Now, get out of my car before I spit on you.'

" 'You wait here until we take care of you,' he shoved me against a wall inside the busy police building. There were as many people waiting to be interrogated as there were detectives and uniformed officers. My pulse throbbed in my temples.

" 'You shouldn't have been in a Jewish house, you know that, don't you?' The detective levelled the question at me in the interrogation room. It wasn't the same man who had brought me in. This one had no hatred in his face. There was a note of regret in his voice, as if he wanted to say: 'I wish neither one of us was here now.'

" 'Of course, I know the law, but that doesn't mean I wasn't supposed to be there. Perhaps there is a difference these days between what the law says and what people are supposed to do,' I said without energy. I was so exhausted by this time that I didn't have it in me to play games.

" 'Well, I don't know if I can do anything for you at this point. If only you hadn't tried to pull that idiotic trick with the kids.... Did you think for a second that those olive-skinned, dark-haired kids could be passed off as truly Dutch? Did you think that?'

" 'I didn't think anything. I just wanted to save those kids from deportation. They're only five years old,' I said amid tears. The detective brought me a cup of coffee. And he disappeared again, leaving the door open.

" 'Lidia, what in the world are you doing here?' an old school chum of Willem's exclaimed, noticing me as he rushed by the open door. 'Where are Willem and the baby? Are you all right?'

"I told him the highlights of the night's events.

" 'I'll see what I can do. Maybe I can get you out of here. Just have a bit of patience and don't antagonize anyone. I'll be back as soon as possible.'

"It was nearly 5:00 a.m. when I glanced at my watch, before I dozed off. When I woke up a couple of hours later, the door of my cubicle was closed. I feared that they would forget about me behind that closed door. And yet, I couldn't open it because Willem's friend had said to stay put and not to call attention to myself. It was nearly noon when he came back.

" 'It took a lot of doing to get you off, Lidia. Your antics with the kids made the rounds of the office. Promise me that there won't be a second time.'

" 'I promise you that I won't be here ever again.' We both knew that was not what the detective had wanted to hear.

"Our reunion was loud and boisterous. Willem didn't know what to do first—hug and kiss and hold me or yell at me for doing something so incredibly reckless and unrealistic. Lizzie didn't want to let go of my skirt. And I was speechless. I collapsed in the bedroom and fell asleep in a second.

"By dinner time, I was faithfully at my post in the kitchen, looking after my family. 'This is where I belong—enough heroics.' I promised myself never to stray.

"During dinner someone rang the doorbell. A frightened elderly lady in a somewhat worn fur coat appeared on the threshold of the kitchen, followed by a puzzled Willem.

" 'I'm Sarah Novak, Annemarie Brenner's mother. I learned this morning what happened to my poor family from my daughter's neighbour. She also told me about you being there and being taken away by the SD. Please, don't think I'm crazy or ungrateful but I have no one to turn to. It's just a matter of days, perhaps hours before it's my turn. Help those children, please, I beg of you. I have jewellery I can give you. Just help us...I beg of you.'

" 'Mrs. Novak, I assure you that I would do anything in my power to help your grandchildren, but what can I do? I have just been released by the police by a miraculous stroke of luck. How could I do anything at all? I don't see how anyone in my position could help Jews in Westerbork.'

" 'The children were taken without any warm clothes, not even a coat. The cold will kill them before the Nazis get to them. You must get some warm clothes to them....' She sat down and buried her tear-swept face in her lap and her fur coat parted just enough to allow me a glimpse of her yellow star.

" 'Mrs. Novak, I'll do it. I don't know how, but I promise you, I will do my best to get those clothes to the little ones.'

" 'Don't say anything, Willem, please. I know what you must be thinking. I'm thinking the same thing. I have done some stupid things in my life, but this qualifies me for the crown of the queen of idiots.' Willem remained speechless for a few minutes.

" 'Lidia, you have an anonymous guardian angel. I'm sure of that. Otherwise I'd lock you in the house. But you have had such incredible luck so far that it must be your fairy godmother who is keeping you out of the fire. If anyone can do it, you can. I would go in your place, but I wouldn't recognize those people amid thousands of faces. Besides, I believe a woman has a better chance than a man. Just be careful, Lidia, use your heart, but don't forget about your brain.'

"The next afternoon, I presented myself at Police Headquarters. I had put up my long blonde hair in a French roll and for the first time since my last anniversary, I had dabbed a touch of rouge on my cheeks. I was not unpleasant to look at, even if I say so myself.

"At the back of the central hall of the SD headquarters, I caught a glimpse of the brute who had arrested me the other night. 'My God, don't abandon me now.' I wasn't a religious person; I invoked a rapport with God only when I found myself in trouble.

" 'May I have a word with you, Captain?' I whispered to the police officer. I had no idea what his grade was but 'captain' always seemed to sound flattering.

" 'You... I know you...from the other night...with the Jewish kids.... How is it that you are still loose and not behind barbed wire?' He certainly seemed interested in me, but not in the way I was counting on. I came closer to him, so that he could not escape the sweet message of my French perfume.

" 'Could we have some privacy for just five minutes?' Even this brute couldn't remain insensitive to an attractive woman whom he had been determined to send to Westerbork and who now was seeking him out, putting her life in jeopardy.

" 'You want five minutes, you have three,' he informed me in an official monotone.

" 'Captain, I need a favour from you, one that may make no sense to you because I don't think you are a parent, but, on the other hand, it may because under that powerful manly exterior I can sense a sensitive heart. One seldom finds such a fine soul, especially in a military man.' As I sat down, I lazily removed my shawl, revealing my finest, creamy silk blouse. 'I've got the bastard where I want him,' I thought as I noticed him blush.

" 'No man is really a man without a heart,' he said with much less self-assurance than he had shown a few minutes before. He nonchalantly shook a cigarette from his case. 'What can I do for you?'

"You should have heard me, Mr. Stein. I wondered where I found those dramatic words but I made a speech worthy of the best soap opera. I told him about the poor kids freezing to death. And how their survival rested in my getting permission to take warm clothes to them in Westerbork. But I wrapped the facts in the most sugary and the most pathetic coating. I should have been on stage, I tell you. But, most important, it worked. Because this unflinching disciple of Adolf Hitler, this builder of the thousand-year Reich, was undone by his own lust for a provincial woman.

" 'All right,' he said. 'Tonight you meet me at the Jew's house at nine o'clock sharp. I'll let you in. You pack the children's warm clothes, nothing for the mother, understand, just for the children. I'll have a document prepared for you that will allow you into the camp and that will guarantee your safe exit within six hours. And then you come back right away to Groningen. And then...'

" 'And then...' I jumped to my feet in obvious excitement. He probably interpreted it as unbridled passion, but what I felt was the energy of victory: not mine—the Brenner twins'.

"Everything went as planned. I packed two suitcases full of winter clothes in a matter of ten minutes. He was nervously pacing downstairs. It could be highly compromising for his career if he were seen in this Jew's house. When I came down, he grabbed my shoulders with the tenderness of a vice grip. He drew my body against his.

" 'Not now, darling, not here. It could be ruinous for you. Your car is out front! There is time, you big brute, there is plenty of time....' I whispered naughtily. 'You're right,' he grunted with frustration. 'Even you're not worth getting kicked off the force for. But I'll get you soon, won't I?'

" 'Who knows, a smart woman always leaves them guessing.' I had read this coquettish line in one of those pink-covered love stories my mother had forbidden me to touch. He handed me the document signed by none other than the commanding SS officer of Groningen.

" 'In all this cloak-and-dagger drama, I never found out your name,' he said.

" 'Lili van Mansum.' What a wonderful opportunity. He would have a hard time locating me without a name. Willem's friend, the detective, will erase my tracks to and from Police Headquarters.

"He filled in the name on the permit. Then he stopped. 'Any relation to Judge van Mansum?'

" 'Judge Karel-Johan van Mansum is my husband,' I lied, remembering the name of a magistrate whom Willem said had joined the resistance.

" 'A magistrate, no less.' His passion cooled by several degrees. 'Well, let's just put the address of the Provincial Court.'

"The next day, I stepped off the bus in the town of Westerbork. Nothing distinguished it from any other town in the north-eastern province of Drenthe. The camp was well hidden in a small forest. From the bus stop I had a thirty-minute walk. Burdened by the two heavy suitcases, I was exhausted by the time I reached the guardhouse.

" 'Where do you think you're going?' A woman's coarse voice challenged me from the window.

" 'I have a permit to take these cases into the camp for two children,' I said, not too sure of the power of my paper. 'Well, it looks all right to me.' The woman wasn't really interested in me. 'It has an SS stamp, that's all I care.' Then she took a lazy look at me. 'You're a rare bird around here. No one has ever come here with an SS permit and suitcases to boot, asking for the special privilege of going in there. If I was you, I'd leave those cases here and run back to where I came from. You can never be sure of being able to come out of there, on your feet, that is.... '

" 'But I've got...'

" 'In there you can wipe your rear end with your paper if a guard takes a fancy to you, or if he needs to set an example, or if he didn't get it last night from his wife, or who knows what else.... But, it's your hide. You cover it whichever way you want to.'

"I took a deep breath and I entered the camp. I never imagined what was waiting for me. I wanted to look but I was scared of what I might see. I entered a big hall. What opened before me was a spectacle of human degradation. It assaulted all my senses. I had to concentrate on my breathing in order to avoid vomiting or breaking into hysterical screaming. The massive space was filled to the ceiling with constant groans, occasionally pierced by shrill cries. 'Perhaps, I should ask a guard to guide me to the Brenners. After all, I've a permit from a high-ranking SS officer,' I thought. But when I looked around, I abandoned the idea at once: the prison guards, Dutch and German, were lost in a mechanical howling that seemed to be their version of breathing.

" 'Lidia, is that you? Lidia, it's Hendrik van Gelder. Your mother and I used to be neighbours. I even made a suit for your father of blessed memory. You here, I can't believe it. I have a hard enough time figuring out why I am here, but you, a Christian, what could you be here for?'

" 'Do you know Karel and Annemarie Brenner? They're from Groningen, too. Can you help me find them? I have a six-hour permit to take clothing to their kids. I don't have a prayer locating these people before my permit expires. Would you help me search for them, please?'

" 'Sure, searching is a way of life here. We're all searching for something. One searches for his wife, another for his son; one searches for a mother, the other for a brother; one searches for God, the other for a way to shed Him; one searches for a peaceful spot to live in, another for a quiet corner to die in; one searches for the meaning of suffering, the other searches for the way to forget all meaning; one searches for a piece of bread, the other...'

" 'Please, Mr. van Gelder. Let's get going. I don't have the time.'

" 'Oh, how I long to be able to say that once again: let's hurry, I don't have the time, I've got to go...the mark of a free human being. I have the time, and when I run out of time, I'll have only one place to go....' He looked up at the ceiling enigmatically.

"I walked away from this seemingly demented old man.

" 'I'll help you, my dear, of course I'll help you.' Like an ice-breaker he parted the waves of the sea of enchained people. After two hours of hopeless search, we found the Brenners. I collapsed on the edge of a bench.

" 'Your mother begged me to bring warm clothes for your children. Well, here they are. Don't thank me, I just want to get out of here before I lose my mind.' I wanted to spring to my feet, but my muscles were in a trance.

" 'Lidia, Lidia, you've got to go,' the old tailor, my personal Virgil in this hell, reminded me of the passing time. 'You don't want to overstay your welcome in *this* place.' But even that didn't propel me into motion. Karel and Annemarie shook me vigorously and began to shout at me: 'Get out of here, for God's sake, you've got to go before it's too late. Think of your little girl.'

"Van Gelder grabbed me by the arm and dragged my limp body towards the exit, navigating the troubled waters of the unruly mob. 'I'm afraid the rules of hospitality set by my hosts don't permit me to continue on in your company. You're a good girl, Lidia, to risk your life for worthless Jews. Be well, and remember what you have seen here today because if you don't, there may not be one credible witness left to convince an incredulous world that this, too, is a version of human life.'

"When I stepped into the biting winter brightness, I felt like falling on my knees to pray. It really was the work of magic: one minute I was in the bowels of the universe, and the next second, presto, at the stroke of an invisible wand, I was as free as the sky. I'll never forget what I lived through in there. And I'll never be the same again in the company of that memory. I am over seventy years old and each time I think of my visit to Westerbork, I shake and shiver.

"Some few hours later, I was asleep in my bed, sandwiched between my husband and my daughter. I needed to be surrounded with their warmth, their familiar scents. Night after night, for several months, I kept returning to the camp of the condemned, caught in the same hallucinatory madness: each time, I was denied exit. And each time, I'd wake up screaming.

"It was then that our family doctor ordered me to lead a tranquil life. Without an explicit agreement, we shrouded this malignant adventure in silence. I limited my sphere of activity to taking care of my family. I clad myself in my plainest clothing. My friend Evelyn cut my hair short, in a severe style. There was very little chance that the 'captain' would recognize me should we pass each other in the street."

"Would you like to pause for a while, Mrs. Feenstra? You have covered an immense territory. Perhaps, you could use a few moments' distance from those powerful memories." I was deeply moved by what I had just heard and I was worried about how much more pain she could cope with remembering.

"I'm fine. Once I get going, I prefer to go to the end. That's how I survived. You'll see." She took a big breath and recommenced her story. "So two years later, the two Brenner brothers, uncles to the twins, were in our home, sharing our bread, our roof, and our life's security. 'That's all right,' I reassured myself. 'The war is almost over. The German beast has been wounded in so many places that all he needs is the *coup de grâce*. Until then, the boys will be fine here.' That night, however, I was back in Westerbork again.

"Lexie did add a touch of life to the quiet atmosphere of home. He helped in the kitchen, not because he wanted to work off his indebtedness, but because he enjoyed my company and he hated to be inactive. He would clown for Lizzie, making funny faces, frightening faces, sad faces, angry faces. My little girl was enamoured of her new playmate. Lexie was fast becoming a member of the family. His brother, Dolph, was endlessly working at solving chess challenges. Every now and then, he was even able to entice Sammy to join him in a game. I was delighted to see the faint traces of a smile grace the young man's lips more and more often as he beat Dolph, game after game.

"Three weeks passed in this peaceful fashion when, on a Wednesday, we were informed that, like most people in the north, we had to take in evacuees. How could we object? As far as the authorities knew, only three people inhabited that huge house.

"The Takens arrived with the new year, 1945, our fifth year of German occupation. They were in their late sixties, both of fragile construction, both embittered by five years of nomadic existence at the twilight of their lives. They had lost their home, all of their belongings, and their ability to generate an income on which to subsist. While they were not rabid anti-Semites, they resented the Jews and blamed their ill-fate on their existence.

"The presence of the three young men upstairs had to be explained to them somehow, so we passed them off as Dutch Christian students who didn't want to serve under the Germans. The Takens shook their heads disapprovingly when they heard their story. 'It's not our business, of course, but if all the young men hid rather than collaborating with our government, the Germans would completely dominate us. Besides, it's just not natural for healthy young men to hide in attics, eating up the meagre reserves the country still possesses, depriving those who have no means to provide for themselves.' Inga Takens had one constant preoccupation: was there going to be enough food for her?

" 'The Takens have made some alarming contacts,' Willem whispered to Lexie and me in the kitchen, a few weeks later. 'One of my workers saw them leaving Police Headquarters in the company of an SD man. Philip said they seemed pretty chummy. We've got to do something.'

" 'I'll speak to the boys tonight,' an unusually pensive Lexie replied.

"The next morning, Dolph informed us that he and Sammy were leaving that night. He thanked us for everything and he explained the reasons for their hasty departure.

" 'I can't tell you not to go, boys.' Willem looked unusually nervous. 'I'm not entirely sure that I share your concern. Only you two know what risks you are able to live with and what is beyond your means. Dolph, let me check on your contact today, just to make sure you have a place to go. If you don't, I'll try to arrange something for you. And you, Lexie, you can stay, of course, as long as you feel like it. You are like family now.'

"That night Dolph and Sammy left our dark house after we had seen the Takens retire. A man took them away in a horse-drawn wagon full of junk.

"Saturday, January 20, Willem came home a little later than usual. He had a shapeless package, wrapped in newspaper and tied with coarse string, under his arm.

" 'Rejoice, one and all, the farmers' thirst for wine has paid dividends again. What you see under your very eyes is an appetizing hunk of pork. Need I say, illegally slaughtered, which should make it more flavourful and, I'm afraid to say, more dangerous.'

" 'We'll eat with our mouths closed,' Lexie proposed, 'so no one can catch us salivating suspiciously.'

" 'Not to worry, by tomorrow night it will be transformed into a delicious soup. We'll just have to keep the lid on.' I winked at my two boys.

" 'We'll have to invite the Takens, of course, if for no other reason than to shut their mouths, so to speak.' Willem couldn't chase from his mind the warning about the ominous meeting between our billets and the SD man. 'They wouldn't want to squeal on the pig that yields the bacon.'

" 'Old lady Takens would sell her soul for a piece of meat,' I agreed. 'But what do I tell them if they ask where it came from? After all, famine is ravaging the country. Where could we be procuring meat without doing something illegal?'

" 'Silent meat tells no story,' Lexie philosophized. 'I would keep them mystified. When it comes down to the crunch, they would prefer to have their stomachs satisfied rather than their curiosity.'

"Sunday morning, after I had finished tidying up with Lexie's assistance, we put on the soup. Lexie was sitting next to the stove, reading a book as if he were guarding our treasure from some unexpected thief. Willem took Lizzie for a sleigh ride. Around eleven o'clock Lexie heard Mrs. Takens clunking down from upstairs. She was on her way to the only toilet in the house, located right next to the kitchen. Minutes later, the kitchen door opened a crack and through it appeared the old woman's sniffing nose.

" 'Something smells mighty good in here. This old nose hasn't been tickled by such a delicious aroma for years. It reminds me of the good old days.' By then she was in the kitchen, inching her way closer to the stove. The pot was a powerful magnet whose attraction she wasn't about to resist. 'Some people manage to get everything, even in these days of national starvation. I wonder how. Let's just see what's in there that smells so criminally delicious.' With that she lifted the lid, inhaling the steam of the contraband soup through all the pores of her face.

" 'It's not lady-like to peek into somebody else's soup pot,' Lexie commented nonchalantly. He couldn't care less about etiquette of that sort, but this nosy old buzzard rubbed him the wrong way. My heart stopped beating when I heard Lexie's arrogant comment.

" 'And is it gentlemanly to be cheeky with someone who could easily be your grandmother, you good-for-nothing coward!' She slammed the kitchen door behind her, storming upstairs with the grace of an offended queen.

"My forehead was instantly covered with beads of cold sweat. 'You shouldn't have said that to her, Lexie, you shouldn't have. She's going to bring sorrow on this house. I can feel it in my bones. She is spiteful and mean. This might be the occasion she's been waiting for to lash out at us. I don't know what, but we've got to do something.'

" 'Me and my big mouth, now I've brought fear into your home. You've been better to me than anyone else ever has, and look how I pay you back. If it helped, I would vanish this instant, but it's just as criminal to have an illegally slaughtered pig in your house as it is to have a Jew. '

"When Willem and Lizzie came back, I sent her to play while I related to my husband what had just happened. 'Let's just pretend that we attach no importance to the incident,' Willy suggested after a few moments of reflection. He sounded in control of his emotions but he was far from being calm. 'Why don't you knock on their door and invite them for lunch? That may just do the trick of appeasing the hungry beast.'

"No one noticed that the Takens had snuck out without a word. When I went up to knock on their door I found it locked.

" 'I knew it, they went out instead of sticking around for lunch. They always loiter about on Sundays in anticipation of lunch. They must have gone to look for their SD friend. Oh, my God, this pork will kill us all.' Willem didn't like it, either. It was bitterly cold outside, it was snowing, and the sidewalks were slippery. Hardly a day for two brittle elderly people to go on a pleasure promenade, especially at lunchtime. We all lost our appetites, except for Lizzie. We sat around the kitchen table without a word. That Sunday, in our home on the Hereweg, the shadow of death was floating in my golden soup.

"Around six o'clock, the doorbell rang downstairs. 'Lidia, you run up to warn Lexie. I'll go to open the door.' There was a quiver in Willy's voice. Four jack-booted SS men in their ominous black uniforms pushed past him. Two of them were holding Dobermann pinschers on short leashes.

" '*Wo ist der Jüdische Spion?*' One of them cut right to the point. Willy had nothing to say. 'We know for a fact that you're hiding three Jewish spies in your house'— one of the Germans confronted Willem in almost flawless Dutch—'Lexie, Dolph, and Sammy. Where are the Jews?' His voice was calm but threatening. 'You can tell me now or you can tell me later, but you *will* tell me where you keep the Jews hidden.' Willy just stood there, defiantly speechless.

"They let the dogs run free. In a flash, the killer beasts were ripping at Willy's flesh. Three mangled, bloody fingers dangled lifelessly from Willy's right hand—he had used it to protect his face. The dogs were ordered to follow their masters upstairs. Lizzie was screaming in horror. She wanted to run to her father but one of the SS men stopped her with the butt of his pistol. He didn't hurt her; he just froze her with terror. From the third floor we heard the dogs' guttural bark. I stood there, petrified, unable to say a word. The chopped cough of gunshots ripped through the house. One of the SS men ran down the stairs. With a solid yank he grabbed Willy and dragged him upstairs. Now they were all on the third floor, except me and my screaming child who was calling for her daddy. Two more shots. That was all I needed to snap out of my shock and grab my daughter. I ran down the steps with Lizzie in my arms and flew out the open door into the street.

" 'My God, they are killing us. Please save my child. Don't let them kill us,' I was muttering, amid streams of tears. In slippers and housecoat, I ran, stupefied, with my child pressed to my chest, across the wide street. A few minutes later, I was banging on Willy's mother's door.

" 'They've got Lexie and Willy. The house is crawling with SS. Willy is badly hurt, maybe worse.... Mother, take care of Lizzie. I've got to go under...' Witless and numb with horror, I roamed the back streets of my neighbourhood. Not one person's face emerged from the mist of my memory. After an hour of this trance, the fog began to lift from my mind. 'The milk tanker man! Of course!' He was Willy's contact man and he didn't live far from us.

"Minutes later, I was sitting in Jan Nijkamp's kitchen, wearing his wife's housecoat, while my feet soaked in a basin of hot water. I was clutching on to a mug of tea as if my life depended on it.

" 'Oh, my God, it all went terribly wrong at our house; my husband and Lexie may be dead by now, I don't know what happened; I just heard the shots from upstairs. I didn't see anything after the dogs tore off Willy's fingers. Thank God, Lizzie's safe...but my poor man, who knows if he's alive.' I kept repeating my story like a broken record. The Nijkamps didn't interrupt my ravings. Exhausted, I droned myself into a troubled sleep with my feet in the wash basin.

" 'I can't stay here, I've got to disappear, they'll be looking for me, without a doubt. I'll need some clothes to go under.'

"Nijkamp set the network in motion to spirit me out of Groningen where every cobble-stone meant danger and death for me. It was impossible to get any specific information about what had happened in my home on that macabre January evening. Broken threads of murky rumour reached the resistance outposts about a Jew being shot, possibly killed, but no one was speaking with the authority of known fact.

"I spent most of the next two days floating between delirium and oblivion. I couldn't even begin to tell you about the sinister dreams I had, even though I remember them as if all this had happened yesterday. Torturers larger than life looming over my brittle body, shapeless monsters with thousands of teeth ripping at Lizzie's flesh, mocking SD men forcing me to watch my husband being shredded with a chainsaw...."

"Mrs. Feenstra, you need not torment yourself. I get the picture." My heart was racing and my forehead was covered in chilling sweat. I knew those dreams too well.... Mrs. Feenstra had a waxy look in her eyes, staring into the air in front of her as if all those nightmares had materialized on an invisible screen. She seemed possessed by another reality. Feeling hopelessly unable to help, I silently waited for her to return to the present. It was one of those moments when I wished I knew how to pray.

There was a flatness to Mrs. Feenstra's voice when she finally resumed her story. "Juliana Nijkamp didn't quite know what to do. She had never seen anyone in a state of crisis. 'What am I to do? Should I call the doctor over? Maybe he can give you something to calm you down. I just don't know. The neighbours may hear you carrying on like this. You may bring trouble on us all. These days everyone has long ears. I wish he'd come home soon. I don't know what's the right thing to do.' But there was no sign of Nijkamp. He didn't come home that night.

"The two of us were not good company for each other. Juliana resented me for invading her home like this and for putting her husband's life in jeopardy. 'I tell him daily how much I object to his underground activities. But I have to tolerate it because he's not about to sit idly by while the Germans are running the country. But this time he has gone too far. Now he has got me involved.' She kept telling me how she wanted no part of this. And yet, what was she to do, call the police? Sure, she felt sorry for me; no one should have to go through what I had just endured. 'But, you see, Lidia, it is really not my problem. People who get themselves into trouble with the authorities ought to know better: when you play with fire, you're likely to get burned. Is it fair to drag others into the flames? All I want is to be left alone. The Germans are not bothering me. But no, some people, like my husband, had to be heroes. They had to play games with the Germans. Big-shot resistance heroes! All this business about hiding Jews is a really stupid risk to take. Does it make any sense at all to have greater concern for the safety of others than for oneself?' And she never stopped for more than a few minutes. I kept silent. Her drivel left me indifferent. It seemed to me that I was slowly regaining consciousness after major surgery.

"Nijkamp came home shortly after dusk, two days after he ran out to 'take care of business'. 'All right, Lidia, everything is all prepared, we're moving you under.'

" 'What about Willy? Is he alive?' I asked. Two days of delirium had drained me of feeling. From a distant, unfamiliar corner deep inside me, a voice needed to know whether or not I should consider myself a widow.

" 'We don't know anything for sure. Right now you've got to get yourself together, because we have no time to waste. We must be on our way to meet someone. We can't be late. Juliana, help her to get dressed, give her a pair of rainboots, and let's get going. I'll wait by the tanker.'

"When I came out of the house, the milk tanker's engine was already humming. I went to the passenger side of the cabin, and climbed the steep step with considerable effort. I opened the heavy door.

" 'Oh my God, have pity on me!' A scream froze on my lips. A German soldier was sitting in the driver's seat.

" 'Keep it down, for Christ's sake,' the man whispered. 'It's just a disguise. Anyway, you get down, you're not travelling in the passenger seat. You'll have to hide inside the tanker.'

"Even with Nijkamp's help, I didn't have the strength to make it to the top of the vehicle. The bogus German soldier had to push me from behind. He lifted the heavy lid with two hands and with a nod of his head, he urged me to lower myself into the yawning cavern of the empty tanker. As I wasn't in control of my muscles, he had to lower me down into the darkness.

" 'Be careful. The tanker isn't empty,' he warned me. Instead of milk, however, I found six other fugitives squatting in its metal belly. Seconds later, we were on our way towards Friesland where he had orders to fill the tanker with milk.

"I spent the trip in the silent company of shadows. My mind was obsessed with fantasies about Lizzie and Willem. And, of course, Lexie. In this darkness a new feeling was born out of my tormented flesh: hatred for the traitors. I wanted to see those two old vultures die.

" 'If I live to see liberation, I'll avenge the suffering they brought upon us. I swear to God. I don't care what happens to me after, but they will get theirs, the lousy traitors. Oh, how I hate them.... I hate them.'

" 'Shh...' A shadowy voice admonished me. I wasn't aware of having uttered a sound. A coarse hand reached out for mine and squeezed it with firm warmth.

"The tanker came to a stop. Seven hearts stopped for a second within the large truck. We had reached the provincial border between Groningen and Friesland, where a German patrol stopped us. From inside the tanker we could guess rather than really hear the shreds of conversation in German. Nijkamp's mother was from Stuttgart, and he was as fluent in German as he was in Dutch. The underground had provided him with false papers. His 'orders' were to requisition milk in Friesland and bring it back to the German military canteen in Groningen. There were a couple of muffled knocks on the wall of the tanker. The echo was hollow. The guard's curiosity was obviously satisfied, and, seconds later we were rolling peacefully through the Frisian night.

"The tanker stopped one more time. Again, we all held our breath. The clanging sound of boots climbing towards the top of the tanker made it clear to us that the lid was going to be lifted any second.

Whose face was going to appear in the hole? The question was burning in seven throats.

" 'The end of the line,' Nijkamp announced with fatigue in his voice.

" 'Where are we?' someone inquired. 'In Lekkum, near Leeuwarden; you'll be vacationing here for a while,' he said, extending his arm into the cavern to help pull us into the biting, northern January night.

"We followed Nijkamp in silent single file towards the stable door of a large farmhouse. The farmer and his wife were expecting us. They shook hands with each of their faceless guests without a word. Then Mr. Oegema, our host, proceeded to climb the stairs that led to the attic.

"My life in the attic was marked only by my constantly growing anxiety about Lizzie. I had spent over a month in total darkness about my child's fate. It overshadowed my passive mourning for Willy and Lexie. In my soul, I knew they both were dead.

"Then one day, six weeks into my stay in the attic, I burst apart without any restraint. 'I can't stand it anymore!' My words didn't sound like human speech. 'I've got to find my daughter, dead or alive, I've just got to find her. I've got to get to Lizzie....'

"It took four people to hold me down. The Oegemas were at a complete loss. They were not prepared for a crisis of this sort. The group decided to tie me down and to gag me for everyone's safety.

" 'Forgive us, Lidia, for treating you so harshly,' one of the women who was tying me down said. 'We have to do this or else you may bring catastrophe upon all of us.'

"I didn't care one way or another. My energies were concentrated in anguish for my child and hatred for the Takens.

" 'I'm afraid the news is not good, Lidia.' Simon, an old comrade of my husband's was ill at ease in his role of bearer of bad tidings. 'The Germans put in a call to the SD around ten o'clock on that January evening, saying that "There are two bodies ready for pick-up on the third floor on the Hereweg, at number seventeen." They also wanted to know if the Dutch police had anything on a Lidia Feenstra that could lead them to her arrest. When they were offered no usable information, they requested the list of all her relatives. They wanted it by the next day at noon. Two SD men went to your house that same night. According to our man at Police Headquarters, it wasn't a pretty sight....'

" 'Go on, I want to know everything.' My voice was as sharp as a fine blade.

" 'Well, they found your husband with two bullets in his neck and with some of his fingers hanging by a thread. The other body was lying inside a large closet set up as a hiding place. His face was deformed beyond recognition, with his eyes hanging down to where his cheeks used to be. One of the SD men lost his dinner right there. After they removed the bodies, they called your brother-in-law, Gerrit, to have him make funeral arrangements. At the same time, they tried to get out of him where you could possibly be. As for the Jew's body, no one knows what happened to it. These days, there's little value to a live Jew; there is none to a dead one.'

" 'And Lizzie, what about Lizzie?' I was prepared for the worst.

" 'Well, as I said, the hunt was on for you. They banged on the doors of all your relatives. Luckily, we were one step ahead of them. They went first to your sister Laura's. By that time, however, the bastards found nothing. We moved the Jewish couple she had in her house to another safe place. Another pair of goons made it to your mother-in-law's door. They found an elderly lady in mourning but no one else. She wasn't even waiting for our warning. As soon as you dropped little Lizzie off, she bundled her up and took her to a friend's daughter's home. She's still there, and she could stay there for the rest of her life; they take care of her as if she were their own. So you see, you don't have to worry about your little girl.'

" 'I want to bring her here,' I stated irrevocably.

" 'Out of the question,' Simon replied firmly. 'You would never make it. There's a reward out on you. Every German, every SD man, every police dog, is out sniffing after you.'

" 'Then bring her here. I want my daughter to be with me or I'll kill myself tonight. I'm not going to live like this.'

"Poor Simon was not trained for dealing with such an ultimatum. 'Well, I don't know....'

" 'I don't want any more words. You bring her to me or I kill myself. You tell that to the underground. Go on.' I plunged into the darkness of a corner. Simon got back on his bicycle for the sixty-kilometre return trip. He came back the same day, but without Lizzie. 'Your mother-in-law won't even speak to me without a picture of you as evidence that I'm acting on your request.' He spoke in a flat whisper from exhaustion. He produced a camera and he took some snapshots. Once more, he rode back to Groningen. Fortunately, one of the local photographers was a comrade and was able to develop the pictures quickly.

"The next day, shortly before noon, Simon brought Lizzie to the Oegema's attic. Lizzie practically jumped out of her little skin. Joy propelled her into my arms. We melted into one form. I held my child while dry tears burned and soothed my skin simultaneously. That little life cleansed me of the venom that had poisoned my existence for nearly two months.

" 'Where's daddy?' Lizzie enquired without anguish. Silent questions dug deep grooves into my mind. 'Could it be that she banished that bloody spectacle out of her memory? Did God do the decent thing after all and protect her from remembering her father's ordeal? What should I tell her now? If I put off telling her the truth she will shelter herself in a lie. When she learns the truth it may burst on her with a brutality against which she'll have no protection. But how can I tell her now that she will never see her father again? How can a three-year-old carry that much pain in such a tiny, fragile soul without it turning on her? How can I soil the purity of this reunion?'

" 'Mommy, where's my daddy?' Lizzie grew impatient.

"Tilly Cleveringa, one of my hiding mates, answered the child's question. 'Your daddy's gone, little Lizzie. He's gone to a world from which men are not allowed to return. He didn't want to go, but at times even grown-ups can't come and go as they please.' I was grateful to her for rescuing me.

" 'Daddy may not be here, the Allies may not be here; who knows how long we'll have to spend squatting in a dark attic, and yet we're free, you and I, my child.' My scarcely audible words made no impression on my confused daughter. Instead, with the generous fickleness of a small child, Lizzie aimed her turned-up nose in the direction of the kitchen below. 'Something yummy is cooking downstairs and I'm hungry, Mommy.' Life had scored another point." Mrs. Feenstra took a deep cleansing breath. "Now, it's time for some refreshments, Mr. Stein," she said, her voice tired and somewhat tearful.

"Freedom greeted Groningen on May 6, 1945," she continued with partially renewed vigour in her tone. "It was a bright sunny day, I recall. We were liberated by the Canadians. I wasted no time. Five days later, I stood before the Canadian commandant in his headquarters in one of Groningen's hotels. The vile story of treason erupted from inside me with more grief than hatred. Outraged and compassionate, the commandant expedited two men and a Jeep to arrest the culprits. The streets were not yet calm as I was escorted back to my old neighbourhood. Here and there, a desperate German sniper was spending his last cartridges on destruction rather than surrendering.

"I can't tell you how awkward I felt ringing the bell of my own door. It opened timidly after a couple of minutes. The Takens' faces were distorted into counterfeit smiles. Old Mrs. Takens even puckered her splintery lips for a welcoming kiss.

" 'Don't you touch me, you lousy traitors, you murderers!' I launched at them like a starved lion at a much-anticipated prey. The soldiers had to restrain me from tearing into the trembling old couple. 'You'll pay now with your lives for shedding innocent blood. You'll be hanged for what you did to Willy and Lexie.' My rage knew no restraint. How I had been longing for this moment! Nothing was going to bring back what they had frivolously taken from me and my daughter. It soothed the wound, however, to make sure that they would not enjoy a comfortable life of freedom and peace with two murders, a widow, and an orphan left in the wake of their alliance with killers.

"The two Canadian soldiers took the couple into custody. Half an hour later they were in the hands of the liberated Groningen police forces. They were immediately subjected to interrogation to find out who their connection was and who had called the Germans. They offered no resistance; they would have sold their children to save their own hides.

" 'I want the name of your contact in the Dutch authorities, that's all. There's plenty of time for the rest. You're not going anywhere for a long time.' The chief took two men with him and dashed out to arrest the culprit before he had a chance to get away. He was brought in spitting bile at his former colleagues.

"The Canadian commandant allowed me to return home immediately, even in the absence of any documentation substantiating my claims. He obtained from the Dutch authorities special papers for me which entitled me to food-ration coupons. I left Lizzie with Willem's mother.

"My feet moved up the stairs with reluctance. I would have loved to bound up the steps leading to my kitchen and to find that the last three and a half months had never happened: everything would be as

I left it, with the soup on the stove, Lexie nursing it from the kitchen table. Willy and Lizzie would be back in minutes from their romp in the snow. What really was awaiting me was a bare kitchen, devoid of all signs of life, a tomb of a kitchen. I took a deep breath and announced with forced cheer: 'Welcome, home, Lidia Feenstra.' But the worst was waiting for me upstairs. With lead in my legs, I climbed the stairs.

"The fake wall of the hiding place had been crushed. Its remnants littered the rag rug, scantily covering the hardwood floor. Surrounded by a wreath of debris, deep brown stains spoke of the last moments of Lexie Brenner's life on earth. After a long stare at my Jewish friend's blood, I had to close my eyes. I felt faint. When I reopened them I wanted to behold a more tolerable spectacle. It was only then that I discovered that wherever I looked in that room, splatters and spots of blood called out to me. Was I hallucinating? Had I become mad? Was all the blood in the world shed in this one room in my home? I touched the wall facing the closet door. It was punctuated with what must have been arterial blood. My fingers grazed the soiled surface, hoping to discover that it was a mere optical illusion, but my fingers found coagulated blood. With the stiffness of a robot I leaned down to roll up the throw rug to expose the unblemished wood underneath. My gesture was unexpectedly aborted: the thin rug was as stiff as a sheet of plywood, rigid from all the blood it had soaked up on the evening Lexie and Willy were killed.

"Once again, I ran out of that house as fast as my feet would carry me. The first time I left behind the forces of death. This time I fled from an encounter with the dead.

" 'I can't rebuild my life in that house,' I told the Canadian commandant an hour later. 'How can I take my daughter into that tomb, where even the air is saturated with horror and blood? How can I raise a child in there? How can I sleep in there?'

"With compassionate respect, the Canadian asked me to return to my mother-in-law's home until he could have his men look into the matter of finding me a suitable residence.

" 'It might be easier if you dealt with the Dutch authorities directly,' he added, wishing to speed the course of events.

" 'I have more confidence in the Canadian liberators than in the officials of my own country. What guarantee is there that today's masters won't protect their drinking buddies of yesterday?' The commandant had no guarantee to offer. I took his advice and returned to Willy's mother's house, where I waited as I had been told to do. I received several visits from the newly reconstituted police. And each time I had to relive the ordeal of that January day. On one of these painful occasions, the detective revealed that his cousin was one of the SD men sent to the Feenstra home to remove the two corpses.

" 'Even though my cousin was willing to go along with the Germans, he wasn't crazy about them. That night he called me to tell me what he found in your house. He was sick to his stomach. Not just because of the cruelty with which they killed your husband, but also because he found on the kitchen table two freshly emptied wine bottles. The swine had actually toasted their good fortune at having hunted down a Jew and his protector.'

"I felt another wave of hatred well up in my chest. 'I'd love to strangle them with my own hands.' And I felt no shame or guilt for my urge to kill the murderers.

" 'Mrs. Feenstra, you're absolutely right,' the Canadian officer told me after he had had an opportunity to review the file about my bedroom-battlefield. 'The Dutch and Canadian authorities are in agreement that you can't be expected to return to that house. Here's the key to the house of the policeman who tipped off the Germans about the hidden Jew in your home.'

" 'Is that any better?' I asked incredulously. 'Do you really believe that I could close my eyes on the pillow of that monster? Frankly, I don't know how to do that.'

"Without a palatable alternative, I opted for moving into the traitor's house. At least it was furnished; at least there the bloodstains were invisible. I had to face the naked facts of my situation: I didn't have a penny to my name; all of my jewellery had been taken by the murderers; and there was not an object of any value left in the house. Nothing remained from years of gathering, years of building — except Willy's wedding ring, which had miraculously escaped the attention of the vultures. My brother-in-law had slipped it off Willy's finger when he went to identify him at the police morgue.

"Life in the traitor's house was tedious. Inside, I could not forget the previous tenants. Outside, there was not a day the compassionate neigbours wouldn't stop me to commiserate. It was futile to try to escape from the past in that house, haunted by the spectres of the trapper and his victim. I returned to see the chief of detectives with whom I had established a rapport built on trust on my part, compassion and shame on his.

The House on the Hereweg

" 'That house just won't do.' As you must have noticed, Mr. Stein, I tend to be blunt, even with officials. I'm not impressed by titles. 'I need to live somewhere that is not linked to my husband's murder.' At first, my requests fell on deaf ears. 'You're a little excitable, Mrs. Feenstra. You must realize that it hasn't been so long since we've been liberated; things don't return to normal so fast. You're not the only one having to settle into a life populated by ghosts.' But I was relentless. I turned up in every possible office to state my claim.

"Finally, I was offered a house, far from familiar ground, where I could lose my name and begin rebuilding my life. I was willing to sleep on the hard, wood floor in a stark empty house, but I was certainly not about to deprive Lizzie of a bed to sleep in. Once more, she and I had to live apart.

"My daily attempts to sniff out some funds to furnish my home led me to many doors. Opening some resulted in standing face to face with more grief. Crossing the threshold of Philip de Vries, Willem's right-hand man at the winery and his comrade in the resistance, I thought I was looking into a mirror: his widow and orphan received me. He, too, was betrayed, tortured, and finally brutally cut down. With the aid of the bereaved Charlotte de Vries, we tracked down all twenty-one of the employees of the winery. Our efforts were crowned by a cursed panorama: out of the twenty-one young men who comprised Willem's resistance cell, only one had survived to bury and remember the others.

"One morning, early, a new acquaintance dropped by to inform me that a new office was about to be inaugurated to aid those—Jews and Christians—who had lost property during the occupation and who were left without income. Those who had been actively committed to underground activities were guaranteed monthly assistance. I was in tears. Our numbing poverty was over. Lizzie could finally come home. But my tears flowed from another source, as well: this woman, whom I had met only in her capacity as a civil servant, had taken the trouble to seek me out before her working day began, to rush the good news to me. I would have found out about the program in a few days' time, since the government was going to make a public announcement in the newspapers. But this kind person, whose name I never learned, cared enough to act independently. These were tears of relief: after all the corruption, cowardice, and callousness of the past five years, the Dutch government had resumed its task of sheltering its storm-whipped people. The reign of bitter shame was over. The first flower of the summer opened in my heart that morning.

"The reconstruction proceeded in earnest in my home. Yet, there was not a day that I felt free of the tenacious past. But with so much to do to transform that brick shell into a cozy home, would you believe that I forgot about my sworn vengeance. I couldn't attend to today's demands with yesterday's concerns crowding my life. Besides, Lizzie was old enough to want answers that made sense."

"What happened to the Takens?" I inquired.

"They were submitted to countless interrogations before their day in court. They remained faithful to their version of the story: Yes, they did leave the house, hurt and insulted by Lexie's insolence. Yes, Mrs. Takens was profoundly curious as to how the Feenstras had access to meat at a time when slaughtering was strictly against the law. Yes, they were emotionally discomfited by the humiliation of having to depend for their meagre nourishment on the charitable intentions of landlords who seemed to provide that young loafer with everything, when they were lacking the bare necessities. They snuck out of the house to avoid any further humiliating encounter with the other residents of the house. It was after having wandered in the bitter cold streets of Groningen, with no one to turn to for shelter, food, or solace, that they remembered the kind official whom they had met on their one and only previous visit to Police Headquarters. They felt forced to take that awkward step by the inhospitable attitude of the Feenstras. They mentioned to the policeman, just as a measure of comparison, and without the shadow of malice, how the Feenstras favoured the three youngsters who were there illegally whereas they had been billeted in their house on the specific strength of the law. Wasn't that sufficient cause for bitterness? But certainly not for squealing on them. To propose that they had wished to bring harm to the three boys and had revealed their Jewish identity was, of course, preposterous as such behaviour was un-Christian, not to mention inhumane. Yes, it was quite possible that one of them would have casually mentioned that none of the three looked very Dutch, but then again, they were not narrow-minded bigots, they knew that looks weren't everything. Yes, indeed, on their first contact, they did confide in the police official, who was the only friendly voice they had heard addressed to them since they had arrived in Groningen. He did promise to look for a more charitable and generous host for them. And, he said, if they ever saw anything suspicious or worrisome in the Feenstra house, they should feel free to report it to him. Because (and here he lowered his voice to a whisper) he was a member of the resistance. As such, he would know if those people were running any risk of being betrayed just in case they were hiding illegal fugitives. Wasn't it a logical decision to seek out this good man in their moment of gravest need? They told him everything, starting with the disappearance of the two youngsters very soon after their initial visit to the police. At that point, the man casually asked them the names of these people. There certainly couldn't be any harm in that. They ended their story with Lexie's insulting comment in the kitchen. The man reassured them that this would never happen again and that within twenty-four hours they would have accommodations more suitable to their needs and their station in life. He arranged for them to be fed a lavish meal at Headquarters. They spent the night at the officer's mother's home. The next day they were told that they could return to the house on the Hereweg; it was now theirs, just theirs. The Feenstras had gone underground and the fugitive had been apprehended by the Germans. He had put up armed resistance to his lawful arrest, and the SS had had no alternative but to shoot him. They felt very sad for the young man; after all, even though he had atrocious manners, he was still a young man and, moreover, he was a Dutchman. They were as innocent as newborns, and yet they were treated like murderers and traitors. Besides, they had a son, an American citizen, an officer in the armed forces of the United States who was at Pearl Harbor.

"Judge van Mansum dismissed the case against them for lack of sufficient evidence to support the allegations."

"How did you feel about that, Mrs. Feenstra?" I asked.

" 'Let the miserable wretches go on with their guilt-ridden lives,' I decided. 'They know what they did. If they have the shadow of a conscience left, I wouldn't like to have their dreams.' "

"What about their policeman collaborator?"

"His case was short and clear. The Takens irrefutably identified him as the man who took advantage of their vulnerability and betrayed their confidence, leading to the two murders. For his vile treason he was rewarded with the death sentence.

"I didn't find pleasure or even satisfaction in this verdict. And yet how I longed to see the day when it would be pronounced. It no longer affected me that he would be put to death. When the sentence was later commuted to life imprisonment, I experienced a wisp of relief."

"What about Dolph? Did you find out what became of him?" I asked.

"That was the only source of delight for me resulting from the trial. Dolph Brenner wanted to witness the judicial wheels turn. Our reunion was a blend of laughter and silence. I revelled in Dolph's taciturn face. After all, in this tale of horror was not he the attestation of life? The fretful soul of this young man of few words used to inspire compassion and even pity in me. The sweet youth that had animated my friendship with Lexie was absent from our daily contact. Now Lexie was sightless and silent in his anonymous grave, but Dolph was there—suffering, but there. Willy's death and my ordeal were not in vain. One life saved is a window onto the future.

"Dolph, too, was delighted to hug me. But he seemed ill at ease in the presence of my widow's black. 'I am not entirely sure if it was in good taste that I came to flaunt my survival,' he told me. 'Do I have the right to be alive when Willy is dead?' In the lighter moments of our reunion we broke the bread of life-sustaining memories. We might have been in hiding but they were all alive: Lexie, Willy, Lidia, Lizzie, and Dolph. And, of course, the Takens. We recalled their humorous idiosyncrasies, but we meticulously avoided anything that could link our words to January 21. We were both too fragile to confront the tragic images of the blood-bath on the third floor."

"And Karel and Annemarie?"

"Just wait, don't be so impatient, Mr. Stein. I'm getting to them, too. Soon after Dolph's visit, one evening, just after supper, they showed up unannounced at my door. Annemarie and I jumped into each other's arms with the emotion of long-lost sisters. Our bond was a new version of blood relation. Karel's awkward gratitude and timid tongue forced him to keep a decorous distance from me. But I was an exultant woman; my enthusiasm shoved aside the barriers of dusty propriety. I gave Karel a bubbly, effusive hug. We spent a splendid evening together getting reacquainted.

" 'How strange is life. After what you did for us, total strangers, I owe you as much love and affection and respect as I owe my parents, and yet I don't know the first thing about you,' Annemarie said and I blushed.

" 'Don't be silly, you owe me nothing. When you are the mother of one child, you are mother to them all. Besides, somebody had to take a stand against those monsters. Who said only men can be warriors?' I felt somewhat embarrassed by the boundless gratitude of these people. And yet, for the first time since the war, I was able to admit myself that, yes, I was proud of my courage and of my active compassion.

" 'You're not just a warrior, Lidia, you're a hero.' Karel's voice betrayed poorly camouflaged emotion.

" 'I guess I am.' It was a quiet revelation, without fanfare, without joy. It was the summary page of a ledger, with destruction on one side, consolation on the other. A private moment of pride, too. One that did not belong to the curious public eyes and ears. I planned to share it one day with Lizzie and only Lizzie."

The war had scattered Lidia's family. Of them, she alone remained in Groningen with her daughter and with the emptiness of her memories. Four of her siblings had already settled in Canada, land of the liberators of Holland. Lidia's eyes filled with tears of gratitude each and every time she thought of her debt to that country of rescuers. Her meagre financial resources dictated self-denying caution. The ache of her solitude, however, challenged her sensible restraint. Thus, the duel raged for years in her isolated Groningen. The day came when, cut off from her tribe, she was no longer able or willing to resist her family's invitations. What tipped the balance in the end was her curiosity about Canada. Ever since she had begun to take interest in the surviving world of man, that country held a fascination for the widow. So in 1961, Lidia and Lizzie went on an extended visit to Canada that took them from British Columbia to Ontario. It culminated in the two settling permanently in Niagara Falls.

Lidia, however, never really became a Canadian, and she never really stopped being Dutch. She did not have the spirit to embrace a new community or to shed an old one. She has been hovering between two shores in her solitary apartment near the Falls, in which she has recreated the solid, timeless warmth of a Dutch home. She is surrounded with the familiar objects of her post-war struggle against the void and poverty. Her proudest possession, the Philips radio, watches over her with its magic green eye; and a plaque on her wall, awarded to her by Yad Vashem, honours her as one of the "Righteous Among the Nations" for having risked her life to save Jewish lives.

The past no longer bothers her. She lives in a paradoxical blend of peace and moments of effervescence. Her daily routine is not different from that of many septuagenarians. One day, cards, the next lawn bowling or perhaps tea and Dutch cookies with the one

Canadian lady she has befriended. They share a dusk sprinkled with youthful memories, except Lidia's contains more mementoes of suffering than of joy. The others are used to seeing Lidia work herself into a huff over issues that no longer claim their attention.

"It was very wrong of President Reagan to go to Bitburg and honour the murderers," she says. They look at one another knowingly, then one of them changes the topic. They all know Lidia's story. But at their age, all stories lose their piquant energy. What's the difference. It's no longer their world. Who cares?

Lidia does.

Strange Bedfellows:

John and Bertha Datema

We turned into the driveway of a rather imposing property on a main artery of Burlington, Ontario. The lawn in front of the massive red-brick Victorian home of John and Bertha Datema was so large that it seemed inaccurate to call it a front yard. I pulled right up to the door. As we stepped out of our car, we saw that behind the two-storey building an even larger expanse of land stretched all the way to a distant white picket fence. Except for a couple of age-old maple trees, the land was covered with grass. There was no evidence of a real garden.

Before I had a chance to take our equipment out of the trunk, the door opened. A short, timid-looking man appeared on the threshold. He made a few limping steps towards us before risking a smile. I wasn't all that sure that this brittle old man was John Datema. For one thing, I had expected someone tall, sturdy, and self-assured. Instead, there stood a frail, elderly gentleman, looking like quite an unlikely rescuer. Furthermore, his loud purple shirt seemed to contradict everything I had already seen so far of the retiring nature of Frisians of his generation. "Perhaps this is a sickly neighbour of Mr. Datema," I thought.

"Good afternoon, Professor Stein." The man's greeting dispelled any doubt I had about his identity. "So much for pigeon-holing rescuers by their appearance," I concluded silently.

"Welcome to our home. The women are inside. My wife is sweating bullets about this interview." He didn't sound all that calm himself, judging from the faint tremor in his voice.

"Is this the first time you've been interviewed, Mr. Datema?" Vicki asked, as we were making our way into their home.

"Oh, no, this is the third time," he replied. "We had an interview in Washington, and somebody from California came a couple of months ago. But it doesn't seem to get easier. We're just basically shy people, I guess."

"In that case, we are doubly grateful to you for agreeing to the interview," I told him in the hallway cluttered with rough-weather gear. "We'll do everything we can to make this experience as pleasant for you as possible."

That's when I caught a glimpse of his wife, Bertha Datema. She was standing in the living room, awkwardly, as if she were the visitor and we the hosts. "She looks so pale and so fragile. She must be recovering from a grave illness," I thought. Thinking of the interview ahead of us, I felt a few butterflies in my stomach. "The last thing these people need is to be dragged through the rough spots in their lives. I wish I could duck out gracefully."

"Are you sure you feel like going ahead with the interview?" I asked after the introductions.

"This is as good a time as any," our host answered. His voice did sound tired. "If our chalky complexions give you cause for concern, you can put your worries to rest. It's been a long winter and we are not getting any younger. The wife has been a bit under the weather, but when you get to our age, you're under the weather most of the time."

"I'm Tina, the oldest Datema child." A young woman came in from what seemed to be the kitchen. "I was making coffee for us. I hope you don't mind if I listen in. I've heard these stories many times but I still enjoy listening to them. It feels great to hear about my parents in the prime of life."

"So, the two of you are doing this work together?" Mrs. Datema finally ventured a quiet question. The skin on her cheeks seemed transparent. "John and I used to do a lot of things together, also."

"Are you referring to your wartime activities?" Vicki asked her.

"That and everything else," she answered with a bit of colour in her voice and in her cheeks.

"I guess this would be a good time to start talking about the rescue business," John Datema proposed. "You didn't drive out to Burlington to hear about our undistinguished lives."

"Suppose we started with your most vivid memory of the war years," I proposed as Vicki turned on the tape recorder.

"That's an easy one," John replied without hesitation. To my surprise, his voice came alive and his body seemed youthful. He liked the terrain, obviously. He just didn't care for the road that led to it. "It was a tiny episode but I'll never forget it. Why? Well, it sums up what we lived through during the war." He stopped. The lines on his face deepened and he seemed to be dealing with an internal dilemma.

"During the occupation, we had a little Jewish girl, Lise, with us. We also had the local German canteen set up in our home. Some of the soldiers got to know us, including the Jews we were hiding. One of the Germans, Helmut Meissner, befriended Lise. One day, while the two of them were horse-playing, the girl accidentally drew blood. 'You damn little Jew!' he yelled at Lise as he wiped his bloody nose.

"Helmut Meissner, SS corpsman, did not know that Lise was, in fact, Jewish. That eight-year-old sprite had quickly acquired the wisdom of survival: she let the anti-Jewish curse fly by her ears without batting an eye. She knew, without anyone having told her so, that the German intended no malice against her, just as she hadn't intended to hurt him when she punched him in the face. In fact, seconds later, the Nazi was cuddling the feisty child and she was affectionately clinging to his SS uniform.

"By a rather extraordinary twist of fate, the fox and the chicken befriended each other in our modest home in the heart of Noordbergen, a quiet village, indistinguishable from hundreds of others in Friesland.

"Two years after Bertha and I got married in the local Baptist church, we found ourselves in the eye of the storm. We had not planned it that way; you can count on that. The last thing Bertha needed two months before giving birth to our third child was to have our home become a shelter for Jewish fugitives. So when, one night, Jurgen, one of my many brothers, showed up at the house to discuss what to do with a Jewish family, at first she was taken aback when I said without a moment's hesitation: 'You can stop looking, brother; we'll take them in.' "

"What was your reaction to your husband's announcement?" I asked Bertha.

"I felt nauseated as the images of danger rushed past in my mind: 'The house is like a German marketplace, with their cursed kitchen. They are the masters of our home. How can we hide three Jews from them? And even if by some miraculous invention they aren't unmasked by the Germans, there are local NSB traitors who are likely to put two and two together. After all, the village is not only small, it's also tightly knit. Everybody knows everything about everybody. And even if that hurdle is passed, how will we feed them? Where will we make place for them to sleep? What if there is a raid? Where will they hide? What about identification papers? How can two families of strangers get along in a small house? They don't even speak Frisian.... John has done some pretty wild things before, but this really takes the cake.' His heart was in the right place, but he hadn't considered any of the practical issues. I was angry at him for not thinking of his family, especially with the baby practically knocking on the door.

"But what was I going to say: 'No they can't come'? Instead, I swallowed my real feelings and I said: 'Of course, they're welcome here. Just let them come.'

"Deep down, I knew that John was right, of course. The alternative was as clear as the difference between high noon and midnight. If they were scooped up in a raid, their destiny would be sealed: to the camps of death. Nobody in the village had seen them, nobody knew exactly how they worked, but everyone took it for granted that the rumours were true: when picked up, a Jew had only one destination — death.

"How could I let these people go to the camps? It was out of the question! If only there had been another way I would have been prepared to help them. I just did not want to link their destiny to ours. Can you blame me for that?"

"No one can blame you for worrying about your family's safety," Vicki reassured her. "But tell me, how was the contact established between the Jewish family and your brother Jurgen?"

"They were being hidden at my sister Hilda's house," John answered. "But they couldn't stay there any longer; she was beside herself. Her place was tiny, and she was crippled with fear every time someone came to her door. It was Marie, the mother, who finally said to Jurgen, 'I'm not staying here — even if we have to move to a hotel somewhere. Hilda will either get sick with terror or, in her panic, she'll give us away. We've got to go.' Well, we all knew that for three

Strange Bedfellows

Jews to show up at a hotel would be their death sentence. But we also knew that Marie was right. Our sister Hilda was just not made of the stuff this hiding business required. They shouldn't have gone there in the first place.

" 'There's no need to waste time and words,' I said to my brother, 'they'll come here. If we've room for all these Fritzes and Hanses, we'll make sure that they get equal treatment, if not better. These jerks are intruders and they have a damn good life here, whereas those people are Dutch, Jewish or not, they are Dutch. Jurgen, tell the woman that I'll come by tomorrow to discuss a better idea than going to a hotel.' "

"How did you put your wife's worries to rest?" I asked our host.

" 'It'll be all right, Bertha,' I told her. 'Don't worry. We're smarter than the Germans. We'll manage. I've outfoxed the Germans already many times. They are pretty stupid, you know. You just watch— rather than being a threat, they will protect us from outside danger.... As for the neighbours, they'll be taken care of. I know a couple of fellows in the underground. If anybody starts to talk too much, they'll shut them up. But you know people around here — everybody minds his own business. Besides, with all the evacuees, who knows who's who, and what's what. Right?' "

"Was he successful in reassuring you?" I asked his wife.

"I was frozen silent with terror. John was right, he'd always had the better of these bumpkins, but all it would take was one slip, one suspicious Nazi, and it would be goodnight life...."

"Bertha, remember the phoney radio caper?" John turned towards Vicki and me: "I should explain this to you two. We never threw out the old wooden margarine boxes. We stored them in the attic. Well, when the order came to surrender our radio sets, my brother Hendrik and I painted them to look like radio sets and stuck some junky wires and knobs on them. Then we made a deal with a bunch of the guys from the village that I'd take their sets to the school building on my tricycle. Some of them almost wet their pants, they were so scared of getting caught with those phoney sets. Only on the way with the fake ones, I tipped over and went right into the ditch, tricycle, margarine boxes, and all. Before I could get out, the soldiers came by and the police arrived. I asked them to give me a hand reloading all that junk onto the trike. Instead, they took them and handed them in for me! They even gave me receipts for so many radio sets turned in lawfully. Then Hendrik and I sold a bunch of the real radios that some of the

141

yellow-bellies didn't want to keep around the house. We had got away with that scam, so we would do just fine with the Jews."

"Did you know that story?" Vicki asked our hostess.

"I knew it, all right. John had many similar stories. Even before the occupation, he was known as a young lad of many means. But this one was the most prized jewel he had in his crown of tricks. Still, all one needed was one little slip, one German who played it by the book. But you know what he used to say: 'There are times when the right thing to do is to throw away the book. Even the Good Book is full of dirty deeds. More than any book of rules, we need to remember that we are right, and that they are the invaders.' And he was right. They took over our bakery, our home, our country, and turned it all into their pigsty. So what could I do? I had to find a way to build up enough courage to cope with my anxieties, that's all."

"The next day, I went to my sister's house to speak to the mother," Mr. Datema continued. "'Look, Marie, you folks are welcome to move in with us for as long as you need to. We don't have much, but we have enough for all of us. And with the Germans' involuntary contribution, we can make things stretch a bit further.'

"But she was full of all kinds of worries about the presence of the German canteen and the constant traffic of soldiers in my house.

"'There's strength in numbers, Marie,' I tried to convince her. 'For one thing, the village is buzzing with evacuees from the south. And for another, it's not written on your faces that you're Jewish. So you're not a tall blonde; neither is my wife nor my mother and they're no less Christian for it.'

"She was also worried about her son's circumcision.

"'Well, I can't replace what was once taken, if you know what I mean,' I replied. 'What I can do is to keep him with me as much as possible. Rather than hiding him, I will parade him so much that he'll blend in with the decor of the village. He's already making fine progress with Frisian. Who would question a kid who sounds Frisian? Should anyone raise an eyebrow, I'll be there to deal with the situation. There are no guarantees in this stinking business, and you know that. But what I'm offering to you is a hundred shades better than you checking into a hotel.'

"'But what about the Germans?' she asked.

"'I've got that figured out pretty well, too.' I was rather proud of my cunning. 'Don't worry about our "house Germans", the cooks. They eat out of my hand as much as we eat out of their pots. There's

this one cook, Fritz Bohlins, a regular pussycat. He's not only a decent
man, but he also loves kids and making sure that everyone's happy
and well fed. Most of the others are fine people also. They hate the
war and the only weapons they wield are their ladles.'

"'You win,' she said finally. 'God bless you for your care and
courage.'"

"So you didn't harbour a strong anti-German feeling, did you?" I
asked him.

"Definitely not." His answer was unequivocal. "These guys in my
house were living proof that not all Germans were rotten to the core.
There were plenty of good apples, too. Not enough to prevent the
putrefaction caused by the rotten ones, but enough to slow it down a
bit. There were some good eggs among the soldiers who came to the
trough daily too, and I got to know many of them. They did a favour
for us; we did one for them. Many of them didn't want to be there
any more than we wanted them to stay there."

"But what about Germans who passed through?" I asked. "And
you had to have thought about the possibility of being raided...."

"I had thought of that, too. We had two hiding places for our
guests — one outside, one inside. We had a fairly large crawl space
under the kitchen, about a metre high. There was enough space for
three. We left some blankets down there just in case we needed to use
it in the winter. It was covered with a trapdoor, hidden under a throw
rug. As for the outside hiding place, we had a cistern in the back of
the house. It was a drainage pipe that didn't allow water in but was
fully ventilated. There was room enough for ten people. We put down
some pails to sit on. It was covered with tiles so no one would suspect
from above that there was a space below."

"What about you, Mrs. Datema?" Vicki asked. "What was happening with you while John was at his sister's place selling the idea
to Marie?"

"Once I put to rest my overactive imagination, I could tolerate the
constant rumble at the pit of my stomach. 'Of course, we can't let
those people go to their deaths. I would never be able to look at my
kids without thinking that I had bought their security with the lives
of Jewish children.' I don't know how many times I muttered those
words to myself to calm myself down. But I had other concerns, too.
Petty ones, but they gave me a hard time, none the less. I blush as I
think of them. Please, don't judge me for my silliness.

"I worried about sharing my kitchen with another woman, a stranger yet. I'd have to be on my best behaviour constantly. Plus I had this habit of speaking out loud while doing my chores. Now I'd have an audience. She'd think I was weird. But mostly, I'd have to worry about what might come out of my mouth.

"I had no secrets from my husband, but I could not bring myself to confess my 'petty concerns' to John, who was so recklessly brave. When I looked at myself in the mirror on the bedroom wall, I was ashamed of my selfishness. 'What kind of a Christian am I to have these doubts? Every wasted life is another nail in Christ's body. When a child is destroyed, all of us become orphans. How can I forget that?'

"That night, while John and I kept company with a number of half-drunk German soldiers having a melancholy sing-along in our back yard, Jurgen spirited Johanna (alias Marie), Lise, and Jaap van Dijk upstairs.

"'John, I tire easily these days. This baby kicks and tosses and turns like a spinning top. I feel like he wants to stretch his little world beyond the cramped confines of my womb. By noon, I'm winded like a stuffed goose. How will I keep up with looking after all these people?' I whispered to John while the Germans were lost in schnapps, songs, and nostalgia.

"'I already spoke to your parents,' John told me. 'They gave us their blessing and their prayers for our risky undertaking. They also pledged their assistance to both of us. We're not alone, Bertha.'

"The next day, ordinary life began for our two families under the same roof, or at least as ordinary as life could be for anyone sharing a small three-bedroom home and a bakery with a constant flow of German soldiers and SS men."

"What happened to your concerns, Mrs. Datema?" Vicki asked.

"Most of them evaporated after a couple of days. Marie had all the expertise to assess what had to be done and she acted on her own initiative, as if she were in her own home. She also had the sensitivity to know when to retreat discreetly to her room on the second floor. In fact, her presence became a relief for me. In a matter of weeks, we were close friends. She and her kids became natural parts of the hustle and bustle of our household. And I should add that ours was the most bizarre household in the village: an ordinary family sandwiched between Wehrmacht cooks, hungry soldiers, and SS men on the one hand, and Jewish fugitives, on the other.

"The more time I spent with Marie, the more ashamed I felt about my initial petty misgivings. One after another, the naked facts of Marie's ordeal unfolded. I learned of a world built on losses. The more I heard, the sadder I felt.

"They used to have a thriving clothing business in Wierden, not far from John's brother Rudolf's home. Her parents lived in nearby Almelo. God provided them with good health, good hearts, and material comforts. Lise and Jaap were growing like golden tulips.

"Then the Germans shattered this perfect picture. One day her husband went out to make plans about buying their way out of the country through Belgium. He was caught and taken to Germany. And when her brother tried to make it to Marie's house, he fell into an NSB ambush. They beat him senseless. Instead of killing him, they left the poor devil by the roadside. They improvised a sign on which they wrote with his own blood 'Beware, Jewish Mad Dog'. He, too, disappeared.

"If it hadn't been for my brother-in-law, Marie and her kids would have been taken away or perhaps killed. After he had heard what had happened to her brother and her husband, he offered them shelter back home in Friesland.

"I could take only so much at a time of the ghoulish nightmares that made up Marie's world. The more details I heard about my guest's ordeal, the closer I drew to this heroic little woman.

" 'I can't make amends for the sins of others,' I told her one Sunday as we were walking arm in arm after church. 'You and I have a lot more in common than I would ever have thought. You see, Marie, I've never really known any Jews. The only one of your people I ever met was Sammy the butcher who used to come into the bakery every time he and his Frisian wife came to visit her family. He was served with the same neighbourly politeness as anyone else, but we never became friends.

" 'I see nothing in you that I don't recognize in myself. Even your fear for the life of your man; believe me, I have travelled through that dark alley. A few years ago, a truck driver fell asleep at the wheel and he hit John, crushing him against a tree. Every bone in his body was broken. For a couple of months we didn't know whether he was going to make it or whether, if he did, he would ever be on his feet again. He spent ten months in a hospital bed. He endured one kind of hell; I, another. His bones have healed, but he will never be a hundred per cent well. As you see, he still limps, but we have both adapted to this nasty twist of fate and we manage to have as many good moments as bad ones, in spite of everything.'"

"Nothing changed in the public face of our residence." John stepped in once more. "No one said a word about our guests. We didn't make an effort to introduce these 'distant relatives' who, courtesy of the Luftwaffe, had had to evacuate their home, like so many other people billeted in rural Friesland.

"On the one hand, most of the Germans who had expropriated our homes looked right through us. They just came and went as if they owned the place and we, the real owners, were pieces of furniture. Much of the time, that was just fine with us. We Frisians are by nature retiring people who don't like to be noticed under any circumstance. If we had to endure the arrogance of the intruder, it was preferable not to have to suffer his conversation.

"On the other hand, the German cooks had been living in our house long enough to have become rather fond of us. And why not? After all, they came, they shoved aside our living room furniture, scattered straw mattresses all over the floor, and slept there for years. They squeezed me out of my bakery; they took over our yard. They placed their kitchen wagon in the laneway between our home and the house next door under the shade of a couple of trees. And when Allied planes threatened the airfield nine kilometres away from the village, they moved the whole outdoor cooking operation into Bertha's kitchen.

"Just about every house had its German soldiers. But none of them had hosts as pleasant as we were. And they appreciated the hospitality. Our main concern had been that eventually we would be evicted in favour of some local big shot. But the cooks made sure that their hosts were properly protected from anyone: they placed a guard on every corner of our property. Thus, we never had to fear a surprise appearance by an unwelcome visitor. Even the Dutch police found their efforts frustrated when they came to arrest me for blackmarketeering. The guard told the head cook, Fritz Bohlins, who in turn asked me if I was guilty of the charges. When I replied in the negative, the policemen had to swallow their pride and beat a retreat before the higher authority of the German head cook."

"How were you able to keep your Jewish wards out of sight?" Vicki asked.

"Whenever I was around, Jaap was sure to be close by. The Germans were just as nice to him as they were to us. Here and there, the kids would get a piece of sausage, a hunk of cheese, or a handful of cookies. They moved about as freely as any native of the village. No one knew they were Jewish and no one seemed to care. For example, they joined the Germans in their nightly sing-alongs in our garage like many others from the village.

"If they'd known that they were spending their fondest moments with Jews, they'd have swallowed their harmonicas.

"Marie took the same liberties as I did. At times, she proved to be as much of a prankster as I was. For example, one day one of the cooks was helping a soldier take an improvised shower in the back yard. Marie was hanging out the children's laundry in the back of the house. She whispered to the cook not to pour warm water on the shivering man.

"Sure enough, the dumb cook dumped a bucket of freezing water on the naked man and he almost jumped out of his skin."

"But Marie was not always in such a playful, carefree mood," Bertha interrupted her husband for the first time. "One day she even requested that John go pay them a visit down south."

"Did you say anything to her about the risks involved in taking such a trip?" Vicki asked.

"You can be sure of that." Mrs. Datema sounded indignant. "'I can't believe you'd make such an unreasonable request, Marie,' I told her. 'He's a young man; he could be caught in a raid and be hauled off to a camp, or worse.' John remained silent. Marie spent the rest of the evening locked in her room.

"But in the next room, I could hear her muffled sobbing through the night. I could not sleep either. Once again, I was torn. 'I know how the poor woman is tormenting herself over the fate of her parents,' I thought. 'But we've got our family to worry about. She can't accuse us of not caring enough. They really are like family, but I wouldn't want John to risk his life for anyone. For him to take a train ride to Almelo is sheer lunacy. And yet...'

"'All right, here's my plan,' John told Marie and me a week later. He sounded like an officer briefing his soldiers just before a mission. 'Bertha and I are going to take the train south; Marie, you stay here with all the kids. Our reserves have dwindled, so we need some additional income anyway. Marie, you told me that your husband hid some valuables and clothing with some farmers around Oss. We'll take a couple of empty suitcases with us and we'll bring them back full. On the way back, we'll stop by Amsterdam and see if your aunt and uncle are all right, Bertha.'

"Marie loved John's plan, but I was less enthusiastic. However, John knew me well and he used this knowledge with the cunning of a fox. I was easily given to bouts of anguish, but I also had another side to me. I was fond of adventure as long as John was there to protect me. I knew that it was mostly an illusion; in case of *real* trouble, what could my husband do? But I had this magic fantasy that John was smart enough to stave off any kind of trouble. I would have fought tooth and nail against John's travelling south alone. But if he planned to take me along, that was quite another story. Besides, stopping to check on my aunt and uncle in Amsterdam was not only a nice touch but also a kind one. I had had virtually no news from them since the war broke out.

"My baker may not have had a university education but he was a smart cookie." Warm pride animated her eyes.

"The next day, we boarded the train with one large suitcase containing a smaller one. The carriage was packed with NSB-ers. Wherever we looked the landscape was filled with Fascist uniforms. I hung onto John's arm a little tighter. John exaggerated the slight limp his accident had left him. As he was walking down the aisle, one of them noticed the limp.

" 'Where did you get the bum leg, brother?' he asked casually. 'On the Eastern Front,' John replied loud enough for everyone in the carriage to hear. As if he had pronounced a magic word, suddenly we were surrounded with cheering NSB-ers, all wanting to shake the hand of a real veteran, a hero. They showered him with cigarettes and chocolates. One of them even insisted on paying for our train ticket.

"Halfway to Utrecht, the train was stopped for a security check. When the four police officers reached our carriage, the only papers they wanted to verify were ours. But the NSB-ers shouted down the officers with insults.

" 'Leave him alone; he gave a leg to the Russians for the Fatherland; that's all the identification he needs.' The police did not insist.

"In Oss, we knocked on the door of Mrs. Molenaar, the name Marie had given us. She received us with cautious and cool politeness, from behind a scarcely opened door. When John mentioned that we were bringing news from Johanna van Dijk, the door opened wide and so did her smile.

Strange Bedfellows

" 'You must forgive my rude behaviour,' she apologized as she put on a kettle to make tea, 'but one can never be too careful these days. As for the van Dijks' things, we thought it would be safer to take them over to a farmer who could hide them without any risk. With all the traffic we have here, nothing and nobody is very safe. My brother will take you to the man who has their things shortly after dusk. You will join us for a modest supper, won't you?'

"John inquired about the de Haases, Marie's parents.

" 'My brother has connections in the underground at Almelo. He'll ask around tonight.'

"We spent the night at the farmer's house. In the morning, with both suitcases full, we were eager to get going. It was nearly ten o'clock when Albert Molenaar arrived on his bicycle with the news about Marie's parents."

John picked up the narrative. " ' "Everything was going well," the elderly pharmacist told me,' Mr. Molenaar said, his eyes full of tears. 'They were so safe for so long there. He can't understand how this could have happened. Someone must have found out something; how, but how else? For over a year they had a perfectly oiled routine: the de Haases spent the daytime in the hiding place beneath the kitchen floor. They even took their meals down there. At night, after black-out, they came up and sat with their hosts in their kitchen chatting about the day's events. But a couple of weeks ago, one morning as they were in the process of descending into the hiding place, a German soldier kicked the door open and caught them in the act. They were taken immediately. They must be in Westerbork right now, but who knows for how long? What are the chances of survival for a couple of old-timers? If he hadn't been one of the two pharmacists left in Almelo, he would have had to accompany them to the camp. But the chief of police told the Germans that he was essential to the survival of the town's population.'

"With heavy hearts, Bertha and I boarded the train for Amsterdam. Without saying a word, we were both thinking of Marie and her children. I was not in a talkative mood. I was too busy imagining what to say to Marie and how. 'I can't just say to her, "I'm sorry to inform you that your parents have been deported to Westerbork, on their way to death in Silesia. My sincere sympathies." If you take away all hope from a person, you'll leave her resourceless to carry on. Besides, there's got to be a way to rescue them, even from Westerbork.' I was deeply lost in thought but no idea came to me."

"What kind of reception did you get from your aunt and uncle?" I asked.

"After the initial outbursts of joyful surprise, Bertha, her aunt and uncle, and I sat around the dinner table over a cup of chicory to discuss what promised to be a grave secret. They were visibly nervous—the aunt seemed quite distracted, picking up things and putting them down without apparent purpose; the uncle was chewing on his meerschaum with a vengeance.

" 'These days, the less you know, the longer you live,' started Uncle Joerd, staring at the tablecloth as if he were looking at the blueprint for wisdom. 'But I know an older and just as wise saying: four heads are better than two. We're hiding two Jewish kids in...'

" 'STOP,' I interrupted forcefully, with my right hand raised for emphasis. 'I don't want to know where they are. It's bad enough that I know about them at all. The flesh is weak, Uncle Joerd. I would probably spill all my secrets if they tortured me long enough.'

" 'Well, let's just say that we know these people who had the bad fortune to be in Indonesia when the Japanese came in. They stuck them in a POW camp. Their two daughters happened to be visiting a family in Amsterdam and got stuck here. They're safe, but with these food shortages, we'll need some assistance soon. Can you kids come up with something?'

"I promised to work out something for them. Our reserves were quite low, but we Frisians can always put our hands on some food. As a baker, I was never too far from a few loaves of bread.

" 'I'll organize something in a few days, don't worry, uncle. But first I must attend to something more pressing,' I told them in parting."

"How did Marie cope with the news about her parents?" Vicki asked him.

"When she learned what had happened to her parents, the blood drained from her face," he replied. "First, she clung onto the kitchen counter. Then her hands lost their grip and she passed out. I barely managed to prevent her from banging her head against the stone floor.

"By the early evening, she had calmed down a bit. I pulled a chair next to her bed and she looked as if she would listen to what I was about to tell her. 'Marie, I can't tell you how sorry I am. So I won't even bother. What we need is action and not words. I know a guy who plays billiards with one of the NSB big-shots in Leeuwarden. I'll go right now to find him and see what kind of a deal we can strike to free your parents. I don't know if we can do anything at all, but if we can, it'll take a bundle. The bastards don't sell their principles or their favours cheap.'

" 'Take whatever you want, John. Do whatever you think is possible. If you need more money, there's plenty more with other farmers. And jewellery, too. Just don't let my poor parents die, please.... I'll do anything to save them.... I'll take their place in Westerbork, if that's what is needed....'

"An hour later, I was in Bergum, in my contact's stable.

" 'It won't be easy, but if anyone can do it, this pig is the one. I'll tell you right now, we're talking big money. Maybe even fifteen thousand guilders,' the man said as he continued to groom his horse.

" 'Don't worry about the money. I've got what we need. Instead, let's get going. I want to be in Leeuwarden before nightfall.'

" 'So you have a couple of rich Jews who don't like the accommodations at Westerbork.' The man's immense body rippled as he let out a monumental laugh. 'The pigs no longer appreciate the charms of the sty. Well, my friends, I'm a reasonable man. But I'm not a stupid jerk. Mostly, I don't come cheap. I'm the head of the Leeuwarden chapter of the NSB. Such distinction must earn respect and profit commensurate with the title. And what you're asking isn't easy. Here's my proposition....' He got up from his captain's chair and began to pace up and down the large, cluttered room. He poured himself a shot of gin and tossed it down his throat. After that he let out a loud belch, then picked up a billiard cue and continued his game. My partner and I followed him about, without a word. I felt the blood rush to my head. 'He's playing with us, the dirty bastard,' I was thinking to myself. My rage was building. Patience was never one of my principal virtues.

" 'Twenty-five thousand guilders, cash. Half of it in advance, half of it when they get out,' he finally blurted out without taking his eyes off the ball.

" 'Twenty-five thousand!' we echoed his words. 'You meant twenty-five hundred, didn't you?' the man from Bergum asked without much conviction.

" 'Twenty-five thousand guilders and a letter of guarantee,' the Fascist said and he made his shot.

" 'A letter of guarantee?' I knew what the rat was after.

" 'It should state that I voluntarily and heroically helped to rescue two top-level agents of the underground. Today, I'm captain of a mighty ship; tomorrow the direction of the wind might change. A little insurance can never hurt. If you know what I mean....' He seemed to have lost interest in the two of us.

" 'You've got a deal. But only if you can act at once,' I said.

" 'Hand over the twelve and a half thousand guilders and I snap into action,' he replied.

" 'What guarantee do I have that you are going to do anything at all?' I asked.

" 'None. But, then again, you have no alternatives, either. It's me or the old Jews croak, right?' He did not interrupt his billiard game for a second.

" 'All right, I'll take the risk,' I said to the man. 'But look me in the eyes while I tell you something. I want you to be clear on my terms of the transaction.'

"The NSB-er dropped the cue nonchalantly. He pretended to be bored.

" 'I'm giving you twelve and a half thousand guilders in cash for your efforts to free Mr. and Mrs. de Haas from Westerbork,' I said to him. 'Should you fail, you get nothing more. But we have ways to find out what you did or didn't do to free them. You want a letter guaranteeing your security once your crazy reign is over. You'll get it, for whatever it's worth. And I'll give you another guarantee, on this one you can count with as much certainty as on your day of reckoning. If you try to take advantage of the situation, I guarantee you in front of this witness that you will not enjoy a long life. Nor a peaceful one. Do we still have a deal? I haven't given you the money yet; you can still tell me that you overestimated your influence, and we'll knock on some other door. But once you take the money, you have signed a contract with your own blood. You are a Frisian; I suppose you know the weight of a Frisian's word, right?'

" 'Just fork over the cash and get lost. Come back at noon and I'll tell you what I did for the old yids.'

"Marie and the rest of us spent the night praying, biting our lips, and pacing up and down. Marie was tossed between despair and optimism.

" 'You'll pick up Mom and Dad today, tonight they can sleep free in a clean, crisp Frisian bed. You do have a place for them, don't you John?'

" 'If they're freed, they'll never need to worry for their safety again,' I said.

" '*If*, my God, you say *if* not *when*...you're not sure they'll be freed.... Maybe they won't.... How can we rely on the promise of an NSB shit?' We had never heard her use that kind of vulgar language. 'They're doomed, my poor old parents, what's the use? The pig is laughing at us without lifting a finger.... My children will never see their grandparents.... I want to die.... Oh, I want to die with my parents....'

"It was around four in the morning when, completely exhausted, Marie passed out, fully clothed, on top of her unmade bed. Bertha threw a blanket on her unconscious friend and prayed to the Lord for good fortune for her parents."

"Did the NSB-er do anything after all?" Vicki asked our host.

"In a way," Mr. Datema said darkly. " 'I kept my promise,' he said to me with a touch of sympathy on his ugly face. 'I put in a call to the camp commandant himself. It took him only a short time to come back with the news. Your Jews are no longer in the camp. There is nothing anybody can do for them now.'

"Marie retreated into a kind of silence that could be read as the death of the soul."

The tired old man stopped for a while. He allowed his pale grey eyes to go out of focus. Was he resting or paying tribute to a distant grief?

"When I regained consciousness after my accident," he said quietly after a short time, "all I felt was pain. I remembered nothing, I cared for nothing. The pain that screamed at me from every part of my broken body held my attention completely and I had no way to turn away from its grip. At one point, my tongue discovered a hole in my gum where, until the accident, I had had a tooth. From then on, the bloody void in my mouth held my attention, drowning into a low murmur all the other, much louder pains. The broken bones, twisted muscles, and jostled organs were at least *there*. That one lost tooth, though—a tooth that I had never noticed before because who notices a tooth until it starts hurting or until it's gone—that dark hole in my mouth nagged at me incessantly. Because that was something that was naturally mine and should have stayed mine until nature reclaimed it.

"Why am I telling you this now? I don't really know, except that I recall that on that night I tried my damnedest to make sense of what Marie was going through. And the only thing that came to my mind was the memory of that lost tooth. Marie had lost the people who gave her life. It's hard to lose one's parents, but we have to accept that life is only on loan to us. Sooner or later whoever imparts it to us will want it back. We mourn our losses and we let the eternal life of the soul console us. But to know that our parents were senselessly killed overwhelms everything a person can express in words. Marie had not lost her reason; she had just not yet discovered the words needed for living this new version of life. It took me ten months to dare to take a step after my body was crushed by a careless man. After that accident, I saw menacing faces everywhere. Marie must have felt all alone surrounded by a circle of strange faces, every one of them possibly that of a killer.

"And you know what?" Mr. Datema looked at me with some effort. "The craziest thing happened to me: as I tried to understand Marie's pain, my body began to ache all over again." And he grew silent again.

"Were you able to do anything about the food you promised to your uncle and aunt?" I asked after a few seconds of respect for his silence.

"We had two problems to solve about that." Mr. Datema lifted his head. "First, what to send and second, how to get it there. I knew the bakers would pull their weight. But we needed bacon, powdered milk, cheese, and flour, or else they'd starve. All this cost a lot of money. Not many farmers were willing to donate valuable foodstuffs to strangers. As we were lamenting the scarcity of funds, we were in for a surprise.

" 'I have money,' Marie said standing in the kitchen door. She seemed to wear on her face all the fatigue of an old country road. 'Use the money I had for saving my parents' lives to feed those Jewish children.'

"The next evening I came home exhausted, but I felt happy.

" 'It's all ready to go — bacon, cheese, flour, bread. I've got the whole lot in the two suitcases. With a lot of luck, we won't be searched; with a little bit of luck, we'll be able to blind the inspectors with some of this.' From a large sack, I produced four bottles of old Dutch gin.

" 'What do you mean "we" won't be searched, John?' Bertha didn't sound all that keen to hear the answer.

" 'I decided that Jaap needs a change of air. Besides, a child is always a good decoy. He speaks Frisian as well as any of the local kids; he'll do just fine.'

Strange Bedfellows

"Marie was not thrilled about letting her son come nose to nose with the Germans. But the boy was thrilled at the opportunity of doing something extraordinary. He was also bursting with pride that I had picked him. What boy would not have been jumping up and down with excitement at the prospect of being involved in a clandestine operation against the Nazis?

"The next morning, Jaap and I boarded the train for Amsterdam. 'Just keep talking to me in Frisian; no matter what you say, it's got to be in Frisian. You understand, Jaap?' I was not worried at all about my young accomplice's performance. Besides, I did not expect real trouble. If I had, I never would have taken the boy along.

"The journey was, indeed, eventless. At least until we reached the railway station in Amsterdam. There we were instructed by a couple of militia men to follow them to the inspection station.

" 'What for?' I enquired irritably. 'What the hell are you making me waste time with an inspection for when you can plainly see that we have no reason to be inspected, me and the boy? Don't you have anything better to do? We're in a hurry.' I quickly sized up the two young men showing off their brand-new authority with a childlike pride. 'Like two boys wearing their new shoes to church on Sunday,' I thought, as I moved within breathing distance of the shorter one.

" 'You could get into trouble for bothering the wrong people. Nobody told you that when you got your rifle and your handsome uniform?'

" 'To the inspection station, you Frisian bum.' The taller of the two wanted to stay on top of things. 'Enough of your gibberish. The Germans will take care of you, if you're lying. This is not your cow-shit patch, this is Amsterdam.'

" 'What a big man, this apprentice scarecrow,' I whispered to Jaap to reassure him. 'Don't worry, kid, we'll be just fine. You keep yammering away in Frisian, even if they speak to you in Dutch. For once, you can talk as much as you want to.'

" 'What have we got here?' the German soldier asked in his mangled Dutch. 'A couple of spies? Or perhaps a couple of blackmar-keteers?' He laughed. 'Or maybe even some contraband Jew.... Not bad...what do you think?' Jaap and I obviously did not impress him as dangerous individuals, standing there chatting in Frisian, carrying our weather-beaten suitcases. He was definitely in a playful mood. I could smell schnapps on his breath.

" 'What's in the suitcases?' he asked when he remembered his official duty.

" 'Mine has a bomb,' I whispered and winked at the drunk German. 'And my partner's carrying a short-wave radio. We're planning a sabotage action against Gestapo headquarters, tonight at twenty-one o'clock. If you don't hurry, we'll be late for our appointment.' And I winked at him once more, making a grimace that spelled clearly: 'You know I am fooling around, so why bother with this nonsense.'

" 'A bomb and a radio, *wunderbar*!' The German was obviously pleased at the opportunity to kill a few moments of boredom. Then he took another look at Jaap — a long, penetrating look. All of a sudden, I felt the weight of a cobble-stone at the pit of my stomach. 'Maybe he tricked me, this drunken pig, and this time the joke's on Jaap. I must act at once.'

" 'You look mighty thirsty to me, brother. How about something to wet your whistle?' And I slipped a flask of gin into his pocket. I did not want to attract the attention of another, more vigilant guard.

" 'Good man, you're an observant, smart fellow.' The bribe did the trick. 'A fine boy you have here'—he patted Jaap on the head—'and you can be proud of your papa.'

"I was twenty-three and Jaap had just turned thirteen...."

"What kind of reception did you get from your relatives when you arrived with the food?" Vicki asked.

"Well, the food was received with gratitude and jubilation. But when Aunt Lise and Uncle Joerd heard the story of the inspection, Aunt Lise's face grew sombre.

" 'You were lucky this time, John Datema, but don't you take another risk like that with a child. You could both be on your way to Westerbork by now. Have you lost your common sense? To fool around with a Jewish boy! How can you be so stupidly irresponsible?'

" 'There's no harm done, Aunt Lise....' I tried to defend myself. My face was purple with shame. No one had ever confronted me like that before. I felt thoroughly humiliated. Mostly because I knew that Bertha's aunt was right.

" 'Not another word from you, John Datema. You have acted without your brains. We're grateful to you for the food, but we won't accept it with a child's life in the balance. You've got to find another way next time.'

"Not only did I agree with her admonition about the boy, but I also realized that each trip was growing more and more risky because

the enemy was becoming more vicious. The country was hungry.
Everyone looked towards Friesland for food. I had to devise a way
that would not involve travelling.

" 'I've got a baker's solution to the food problem,' I told Bertha
one evening after work.

"I went to talk to Fritz, the head cook, after supper. We had a long-
standing, amicable relationship. I really liked that German polar bear
whose only concern in life was to feed his people the best he could.
He had been a fishmonger in Hanover before he had volunteered for
this job.

" 'War is hell,' he confided in me one evening, 'I don't like it any
more than you do, and I wish somebody up there agreed with you and
me to call this nonsense off. What business do our two peoples have
fighting each other?'

" 'What about the others, Fritz? The Poles, the French, the Jews?
What about them, Fritz?' I asked.

" 'I don't have anything against any of them. I have never hurt a
soul and no one has ever bothered me, not a Pole, not a Frenchman,
not a Jew. Don't ask me stupid questions, my friend. I don't want
to have to think up stupid answers. Germans are no worse or better
than anyone else. The closer you get to the head of a fish the more
it smells...take it from a man who has lived with fish all his life. Are
you catching on?'

" 'Fritz,' I began, 'I need a favour from you.'

" 'Anything, John, as long as it doesn't land me on the Eastern
Front.'

" 'I need a crate to send a package to my aunt and uncle for the
winter.'

" 'I have just what you need, my friend. And what is it that you
want to send? Nothing for which I could be charged with complicity,
I hope.'

" 'Fritz, my friend, how could you even ask such a question? What
do I have to ship that would be illegal? Perhaps a couple of loaves of
rye bread as a gift from their baker nephew, but that's all.' I was dead
serious. I did not want to expose myself to the whims of a German.
You could never be sure....

" 'Well, if you're sending rye bread, first of all, I didn't hear
anything about it. Second, if I sent rye bread in a crate by train, I
would make very sure that the bread was well moistened with water.

Who knows how long before it would reach its destination and in what shape.' He didn't need to say more.

"At six o'clock in the morning, when I set out for work, I found a large crate by the front door. When I picked it up to hide it, I found it heavier than expected. The damn old fool left in the crate two slabs of bacon and a sack of dry beans. And a note: 'Remember to water the rye bread.'

"With a little help from Fritz, the decent Wehrmacht cook, and a few generous local citizens, the first shipment was prepared according to specifications: foodstuffs inside, a couple of layers of old clothing and a generous blanketing of well-sprinkled rye bread on the outside.

" 'Fritz, one day this damn war will be over and I will personally nominate you for sainthood,' I told him with a lump in my throat. 'If you were not the bloody occupying authority, I would kiss you, you pink-hearted Nazi.'

" 'Don't be a sentimental fool, John Datema,' Fritz responded. 'What would you do in my place? You're sitting on the back of a people for years in their own country. You have plenty of everything except friends. Their teeth are getting soft from lack of chewing. What would you do?'

" 'The same thing you did.'

"A couple of weeks later, I got a hand-delivered message from Aunt Lise: 'Thanks for the clothes, they'll come in handy soon. Another winter is approaching. By the way, a lot of the pieces came full of holes.' "

"What about these holes?" I asked.

"You see, when a package arrived at the Central Station in Amsterdam, they first subjected it to an external inspection rather than ripping it apart," John explained. "They had these long needles that they stuck into the crate, reaching in as far as fifty centimetres. If they came out clean, they let it pass, but if something stuck to the needles, it was most likely blackmarket food. Mercy on you if your name was on such a package.

"Food supplies were running scarcer by the day. The winter of 1945 threatened the country with starvation. If it had not been for the German canteen in our home, we would have become acquainted with the ugly face of hunger. It was no longer possible to count on people's generosity to feed the folks in the city. Aunt Lise and Uncle Joerd were enduring lean days and long nights.

Strange Bedfellows

" 'Like it or not, you've got to contact the underground for help,' Bertha insisted. 'You have taken bigger chances than running the risk of gossip. Besides, Noordbergen is one large family of old neighbours. There is really not much to fear. Look how long we have had Marie and the kids. I wonder if anyone remembers that they are not locally born and bred. Come on, John, if you don't get in touch with the underground, I will.'

"I couldn't believe my ears. Was this my Bertha who had thought of all the reasonable and unreasonable excuses against having Jews in her house? She had become a regular warrior.

"Bertha was right, of course. We had already exhausted all our local resources. While Fritz always had a few morsels reserved for our family, it was no longer sufficient. 'What would he say if he knew that three of us are Jews?' I didn't want to imagine the answer. I told everyone in the household to be specially friendly to the cooks as our lives depended on them. But the war effort had been losing steam for a long time, and the Germans were feeling the crunch of Hitler's losing streak. The food gifts grew less and less frequent. And we had eight mouths to feed.

"So what do you think I did? I broke down and acted on my wife's orders, partly because we had inherited another two guests. One of Bertha's cousins from Amsterdam dropped in one night after blackout. He was feverish with hunger. And he had a Jewish friend with him who looked as if his body and his soul had already parted company. They had made their way from Amsterdam on foot, on stolen bicycles, furtively on the back of wagons and trucks. They had not eaten in days. This time, there was no discussion of the risks of harbouring fugitives."

"How did you manage to hide two young men without the Germans seeing them?" Vicki enquired.

"That was my main concern, too," our host replied. "But, you know, when you have no choice but to find a solution, you find a solution. So I did. Remember that I told you we had two hiding places, one of them outside? Well, that's where those two had to stay.

" 'You'll have to spend the day in the hiding place,' I told them. 'We don't have much to eat either, so a little will have to go a long way.'

"Swallowing my distrust for the underground, I finally made contact with a local man and asked for food stamps to feed my fugitives. I had a bad taste in my mouth the first time we met. The contact man mouthed off hatred for the enemy. He boasted with such promises that I began to fear that I had taken this enormous risk for nothing."

"Just why were you so distrustful of the underground?" I asked. "All the other rescuers have had nothing but praise for the movement."

"I was not too keen on trusting those jokers," John replied. "Too many of them knew one another. And once you have that many people involved, somebody is liable to wag his tongue just a bit too much. In the rescue business there was no room for gossip. I preferred going my own way as long as possible. I carried a smaller load by not having to worry about who knew what I was doing with whom."

"I see," I commented. "What happened with that man from underground?"

" 'Look, friend,' I told him, 'all I ask for is food stamps.' My voice was calm; my message, to the point. I tried to slow him down, but to no avail. I noticed that his right hand was constantly in his pants pocket, where the menacing outline of a gun appeared. 'You'd better take your hand out of your pocket before you shoot yourself in the foot. Relax, man, we're on the same side.'

" 'Just don't you forget who your friends are, Datema, and everything will be fine. But if you do, God have mercy on you.' We were to meet the next night.

"The next night a new contact man outlined for me the underground's proposal. The first man kept silent, still with his hand in his pocket.

" 'We give you food stamps. In exchange, you take in another man. He must disappear fast. No one would think of looking for him here, in the canteen.'

"Now there were three regular tenants in the cistern. As promised, I received food stamps regularly. The crisis of feeding all those mouths was over, but a new demon showed its face: the one I had tried to avoid by not dealing openly with the underground.

"A friend of mine came running to me one day to warn me about what he had heard with his own ears: 'While you guys sit on your asses, the underground never rests.' The loud-mouth contact man was showing off to a group of men sitting around swapping stories. 'Why, just a few days ago, I fixed up John Datema and his Jews with a good supply of food stamps. I'll be a hero one day in Jerusalem.'

Strange Bedfellows

"And as I feared, the long tongue of gossip whipped around the village. It fell on deaf ears most of the time because people had learned long ago to distinguish the harmless from the vicious. But, as I used to say, all it took was one little man with big plans and a pebble brain to stir up interest in NSB circles. There had been no action for quite some time and these bastards were itching to lash out and earn some distinction and have a good laugh.

" 'A rumour reached the storekeeper about you hiding Jews,' Willem, one of my teenage nephews, reported. He had been warned by several friends. 'He keeps mouthing off about how he's going to organize a raid on John Datema the Jew-lover and have the whole bunch arrested and shipped off to Poland.'

" 'I'll cut his throat tonight,' Sietske, Willem's older brother, muttered.

" 'You won't do anything of the sort!' I grabbed his arm hard enough to hurt the muscle-bound lad. 'That could be the signature on our own death sentences. We've got to do something just as final, but less dangerous.'

" 'He is a stupid jerk and a rotten bastard. I want to put him out of business,' my nephew insisted.

" 'So do I,' I agreed, 'but not by killing him. Sooner or later the word would get around that you did it, and then what? But here is something better. That creep is not only stupid but he is also a yellow-belly. He would never dare to do anything on his own account. He's too chicken for that. How about paying him a visit and threatening him with cutting his throat if anything happens to a Datema or his guest? Tell him that the two of you are speaking for all of your buddies and if harm were to find you, he may as well start putting together the guest list for his own wake, because somebody will get him before he has a chance to say *"Sieg Heil"*.'

"The boys decided to act on my plan that same evening.

" 'You won't believe what happened when we got to the bastard's store.' Willem was out of breath as if he had seen a ghost. 'As I was about to push in the guy's door, it popped open and who appeared, filling its frame, but Fritz the cook. I pretended not to recognize him, but he grabbed each of us by the arm and said quietly: "It's all been taken care of. Don't bother." '

" 'No need to make a big deal,' Fritz said to me when I asked about the incident in front of the storekeeper's house. 'Earlier during the day, I ran into the guy in town. He wanted to talk to me confidentially about you guys. I smelled a rat, so I told him that I was curious, but if he wanted to tell me something confidential, I'd visit him that evening. I also cautioned against mentioning it to a soul until he spoke to me. So I went to see the bastard. After a lot of garbage about doing his patriotic duty, he blurted out that you guys were up to no good. Before he had a chance to go into details, I grabbed him by the neck, and choked the rest in his throat.

" ' "Those people are my hosts and my friends. They are under my protection, the whole lot. Should any harm come to them, either I personally or one of the other cooks will chop your head off with a meat cleaver. Is that clear enough or do you need a sample of what I mean?"

" 'That's all. You won't have to worry about him in the future. And if you guys are doing anything illegal, you'd better stop it, because next time you may not be so lucky. Besides, I am the enemy, and I've got to act like it or I may raise a few eyebrows.'

"I read him loud and clear: we had to exercise more caution than before.

"Well, everything was pretty much under control." Mr. Datema looked like he was making a great effort to remember. "One day soon after the Fritz incident, when I got home from a food-searching journey, Marie was tearing her hair out and screaming, 'John, you've got to do something, you've got to do something...John, do something!'

" 'Something about what? Marie, calm down just long enough to tell me what happened so I know what I've got to do.'

" 'Do something, John...do something or I'll die right here.' She was hysterical.

"It didn't take a college degree to realize that something terrible had happened, but I also realized that I was not going to learn what it was from Marie. Next door, I found out that my two young nephews, Pieter and Renze, had snuck off to the woods with Jaap and that they had not returned. A neighbour saw the three lads being escorted by the police to the station. Marie could think only of the worst. She already saw her son deported.

"I stormed into the police station, pretending to be at war with everyone. 'You little bums, how dare you steal my saw. I need it myself every day. Now you're in a fine mess, arrested for chopping wood illegally—and I'm without my saw!'

"Then I turned to the police officer standing nearby, enjoying the show. 'You're a fine so-and-so, yourself! Can't you find anything more useful to do than to chase after little pranksters and arrest them for what you used to do yourself at their age? Their mothers are crying their eyes dry and I'm losing valuable time. And if the bread is not ready on time, you'll be among the first to shake your big policeman's finger at the baker for loafing on the job. For crying out loud, man, where is your horse sense?' Three minutes later the three culprits and I were on our way home."

There was a lull in the storytelling. I couldn't tell if the Datemas had run out of breath or if their stock of memories had been depleted. I proposed a short break. We had coffee and the ever-present Frisian honey cookies.

"Two weeks before Christmas, time had come for me to take the train south again, because our funds had just about run out. If I didn't get some of Marie's money, nobody was going to eat in a week's time," John continued, somewhat refreshed.

"One more time Jaap and I carried the old suitcases to Oss. This time around, the train ride to the farmers was peace-time dull.

" 'Good day, what can I do for you?' I'd never seen the man in the doorway.

"I was obviously confused and I didn't have the vaguest idea what to say. I was at the right place, all right. What I didn't know was what had happened to the farmer. And who was this man?

" 'I was here about six months ago on a visit with my wife. She's an old friend of the lady of the house. I'm in the neighbourhood with my nephew here to visit my brother in Wierden, so my wife asked me to make sure to drop by and say a friendly hello to her friend. But I am either at the wrong address, or they must have moved on, because I don't recall your face, sir. My name is John Datema, Datema from Noordbergen.'

"He invited us inside. 'You are looking for my sister-in-law, I believe. Now I'm living here all alone to look after the house and the farm. My brother and his wife...well...I don't know when they'll be back.'

" 'I hope nothing tragic has happened to them.' I relaxed a little, but I was still not sure of my man. Traps were all over the land; it was very easy to fall into them. For all I knew, this man was a detective. 'Nowadays, people come and go, disappear and reappear, it's very hard to make sense of all this, especially for a small-town baker like me. Would it be too bold of me to ask what happened to your brother and sister-in-law?'

" 'Well, they were denounced—without any foundation, of course—for helping Jews. I'm sure my brother would not stick out his neck; he was far too cautious a man. He just minded his farm and his family; he would never get involved with political stuff. And my sister-in-law has a heart condition, so she could not take on any excitement. The war has been stressful enough for her. I must say, I'm quite worried for her. They are in the detention camp at Vught. One hears terrible news from there.' He was visibly upset and nervous.

" 'I would never have said you two were brothers—you don't look alike at all.' I changed the topic to see where it would take us.

" 'You don't think we do?' The man perked up. 'That is quite remarkable, because people often say that we're carbon copies of our mother. Look here, Mr. Datema.' With that, he handed me a framed photograph of a mother and her two sons, both looking remarkably like the mother.

" 'Now that I see the two of you together, you're right, there is no doubt about the family relation. You are indeed your brother's brother. I didn't dare to reveal to you that I know a lot more than what I claimed before. But you can understand, I wasn't about to spill the beans to a stranger.'

" 'And I know quite a bit more as well.' He smiled sadly. 'I know that my brother and his wife were guilty of the accusations. He was always very conscious of other people's suffering, much more than of his own.'

"I related to him the purpose of our visit.

" 'Don't worry, young man. I know where everything is. That is one of the reasons I decided to stay here. Everything has been relocated, and you are not the first ones to come to dip into the well. I just hope that you all make it. Like my poor brother and his wife. I fear so much for her health.'

"We spent the night, once more, on the farm. By nine o'clock in the morning we were on the train. I had planned to go home directly, but the story of the betrayed farmers shook me up profoundly.

"The war was wearing thin even the sturdiest of nerves. 'Jaap, my boy, brace yourself for another stormy visit with Aunt Lise, but I feel like checking in on them to make sure that they are holding out all right.'

"I apologized for coming empty-handed, but I knew that they were happy just to see me. But I also noticed hunger in their eyes as they relieved me and the boy of the suitcases. 'This is an unscheduled visit. In fact, this is my last trip down south until the end of the war. The news is alarming from every corner. The occupation has lasted too long. Morale is sagging more and more. An empty belly is a merciless adviser.'

" 'People are beginning to turn on their own.' Uncle Joerd sounded tired. 'Not that it will get them one extra piece of bread or even a cup of hot water. Some are too disoriented to use their common sense. Others just need to spill their bile before it destroys them. Look at what the Jews are doing to each other. The Jewish Council has been turning list after list of names over to the Germans. They claim to save more lives by collaborating than by resisting. Does this make sense to you?'

" 'Don't the fools know better?' Aunt Lise's lips were quivering with anger. 'The Germans never keep any promises. All they care about is not having to deal with mass hysteria and panic. They will deport every single Jew they can get their hands on.'

"In my heart, I knew she was right. 'I often try to imagine what I would do in their place,' I said, 'and each time I come up with nothing. Nobody has been in their place. Who knows what is true and what is not? Each one is trying to survive the best he can. Survival is not always noble, or even fair—that's what I think, anyway. It's easy to be righteous and smart from this side of the fence. Some must be looking to God for mercy; others try to draw on whatever resources they can muster up; and others are looking to us to rescue them....'

" 'But you can only try to rescue people who are willing to collaborate in their own rescue!' Aunt Lise jumped to her feet. 'Some of these wise rabbis should have instructed their congregations that for the duration of the war, it's all right with God if they blend in with the Christians. They should have told them to dress like the rest of us, to mingle with us, to eat like us, to speak like us. Many more could be saved that way. But how do you hide an Orthodox Jew? I am sure that a lot more passive Christians would take a chance if more Jews were willing to cheat a little. After all, they would not be tricking God— for He must know what's in their souls—they'd be fighting for their lives. That's what God wants of all of us. There's still time for some, but I don't believe the rabbis will come to their senses.'

" 'I'm not so sure you're right, Aunt Lise,' I ventured a counter-argument. 'There are plenty of non-Orthodox Jews who look like you and me, who don't keep kosher, and who speak like any other native Dutch person to whom no helping hand has been extended. Worse: There have been plenty of Jews who were hidden or who blended into small Christian communities and who proved to everyone that they are not different from the rest of the population and so-called patriotic, honest Dutch Christians have ratted on them and they've ended up in the camps. It's not fair to blame the victim. Look at the case of this farmer and his wife....'

"This time around, I could hardly wait to be home with my family. I had witnessed more human suffering than I could cope with. I hated the war, I hated the famine and the excessively bitter cold. Above all, I hated the Germans."

"Did anything noteworthy happen on the home front while your husband was gone, Mrs. Datema?" Vicki turned towards our hostess who hadn't said a word for a long time.

" 'Things are definitely heating up in Noordbergen,' I told John upon his return. 'There were several raids in the area and the reverend never misses a chance to remind us of the importance of caution in what one says and to whom. "There are times when one proves one's wisdom by remaining silent," he keeps saying.'

" 'It's time for us to make sure that we won't get caught with our pants down,' John replied. 'We've got to work out a warning system.' This is how he thought of the idea of the password.

" 'With us being upstairs much of the time,' John explained to Marie and me, 'we are sitting ducks in case of a raid. I've got to convince Fritz that it's in their best interest to screen whoever approaches the property. I'll speak to him about a password system. I'll also speak to your cousin, Bertha, and his friend about stricter control of their comings and goings.' "

John took over the story once more. " 'Listen, boys,' I told them, 'you must observe the following rules of safety: you stay in the cistern all the time. You can come up only when you are told that it's all clear, late at night, after the Germans have retired. When you do come out, you have to wash and shave as fast as you can. You'll have to attend to your toilette in the dark. But do shave and wash every day; it's bad to let yourselves go. Then, stretch your muscles for fifteen minutes. There's plenty of room down there for exercising if you don't stand up, so use your heads to keep your bodies as fit as possible. Push-ups, arm wrestling, sit-ups, you name it. You will not be able to come up for your meals during the day. Every night, Bertha will prepare a basket for you that she'll leave under the sink, covered with a large rag. You'll bring up the dirties the next night. Bring up your WC bucket every night, as well, and empty it into the toilet.'

" 'I can't live like that,' the Jewish boy said, on the verge of tears. 'Even rodents have more freedom of movement than we do. I'm going to run for it.'

" 'Don't be stupid,' I yelled at the lad. 'You'd get as far as the edge of the village before someone would ask for your papers or order you to drop your pants! You've come this far; I'm not going to let you throw your life away. Karel, if your pal wants to do something stupid and you can't talk him out of it, you have my permission to knock him unconscious.'

" 'Fritz, I'm concerned about security around this place,' I cut right to the quick of things when I met him that night in the back yard. 'Too many people come and go without anyone really knowing if they have any business being here at all. Any riff-raff can wander in without good reason.'

" 'What have you to fear, my friend?' the German asked me. 'And what do I get out of these security hassles? I run a canteen and not an SS detail.'

" 'Well, do you recall how I saved a bunch of your boys' hides a few months ago?' I was referring to a raucous party. They were all singing and screaming about hanging Hitler from the top of the highest tree in Germany. My stupid brother was one of the gang. When I came in, there were a couple of detectives looking for my brother. They were mad as hell about the nonsense of hanging the Führer from a tree. I told them in no uncertain terms that there were no Communists in my house.

" 'These are German soldiers,' I told them, 'who have had enough of the war and they want to forget it. I'll deal with them my way.' I picked up one of the Germans' guns, put a cartridge in it and told the whole gang to go to sleep. 'The first one having any objection will get a bullet for his effort.' My brother was about to sneak out when I pointed the gun at him and ordered him to lie down with the rest of the boys. Then I locked up the guns. The next morning they didn't know how to thank me.

" 'Well, you did a big favour for my boys, and I've done a few for you,' Fritz said with a friendly slap on my back. 'You're right, if the wrong guys had come in that night, they would have shot them without blinking an eye. Some of those blood-thirsty SS are a bigger threat to us than the Allies.'

" 'In other words'—I came back to my original purpose—'you agree with me that it would be in our best interests to develop some kind of a low-key alert system, don't you?'

" 'Well, you've made your point as far as what we would get out of it. But what's in it for you?' Fritz was curious more than anything else.

" 'Let's just say that it's best for your health and mine if we can keep some control over who comes into my home. Besides, what you don't know can't give you nightmares.' That's all I was willing to say.

" 'Why do I have the sneaking suspicion that you have a plan all thought out just in case this old German fool had sauerkraut juice in his head instead of brains?' I couldn't tell if he was teasing me, or if he was a bit annoyed.

" 'You're the boss, Fritz. I just live here,' I responded in kind. 'But in case you're interested, I'd like to put into effect a password system. When someone wishes to enter the property, the guard will ask for the password of the day. Whoever doesn't know it will have to identify himself and state the purpose of his visit. The guard will then ask you for instructions. In case you think I should know about the visitor, you may want to alert one of us. That's all.'

" 'In other words, you want to transform my canteen into Gestapo Headquarters with an escape hatch,' Fritz replied. He didn't sound suspicious. Don't think for a moment he didn't know what all this was about.

"The first password was 'Baby Jesus'. It was December 23, 1944 — the fifth Christmas under German occupation."

"The day after Christmas, Fritz yelled into the kitchen while Marie and I were feeding the kids breakfast," Bertha intervened timidly.

" 'Baby Jesus, Baby Jesus!' John was out in the back looking for wood.

" 'Raid!' The two of us whispered. Marie freed the trapdoor by folding the carpet back. Jaap and Lise threw the dishes into the sink. I threw the extra food into the garbage.

"I told Rosie to go upstairs with the little ones and to stay quiet until the soldiers left. I explained to her that if they didn't behave the soldiers would take all of us to a terrible place where they might even kill us. I wasn't too sure of my words. In our preparations for a raid, we failed to attend to the matter of how to deal with the children."

"Do you recall the incident?" Vicki turned to Rosie, who had not said a word throughout the interview.

"I don't know if I recall it," the young woman answered, "or if I know it from having heard Mom repeat it who knows how many times."

"By the time I was back in the kitchen," Bertha continued, "John was inside. No doubt, he understood what was happening, for he pulled the big armchair over the carpet covering the trapdoor and motioned to me to sit down.

" 'Look very sick,' he whispered. I wrapped myself in a blanket covering most of my face, and settled into the chair. We were ready for them."

"The system worked," John said, picking up the story. "Fritz filled me in on the details later. When the four members of the notorious Black Police wanted to enter the house, the guard requested the password. They thought it was a joke. But the guard insisted on the password. They, of course, didn't know the password, only that they had their orders to search the house. The guard requested that they wait outside so that he could inform the NCO in command of their visit. Just to be on the safe side, the guard called out to his partner to relieve him while he was inside. Fritz told him to make sure their identification papers and their search warrants were all in order. He thought that would afford us the time for whatever we needed to hide from plain sight.

"What had begun as a thorough inspection of the premises continued with a sharp knock on the closed kitchen door. 'Police. Open up. We've orders to inspect your place for hidden fugitives.'

" 'Inspect whatever you want. We're not hiding anything or anyone,' I responded. 'Just be warned, my wife has a highly contagious disease. The doctor says it may even be some form of leprosy. No one knows, because no one dares to go close to her. She needs to be taken to the hospital in Leeuwarden, but I can't find a way to transport her. Here, look for yourselves'—I threw the door open for them to have full view of the shapeless mass wrapped in a blanket from which only a nose was visible—'We have to keep her all covered to prevent the spread of infection from her shedding dead skin. Anyway, go ahead with your search.'

" 'Well, all seems to be in order here.' They couldn't get away fast enough from the kitchen. 'By the way,' the leader of the pack asked me with a hint of suspicion, 'how is it that you are not catching it?'

" 'Who says I am not catching it?' I looked indignant at such a stupid question. 'It's just a matter of time. I'm her husband, that makes me the number-one candidate. So I don't even go near the kids these days. We have people from the church give us a hand with feeding the kids. Upstairs.'

" 'Leprosy, you say.' He wasn't entirely convinced, but he was not about to take any chances, either.

" 'That's what the doctor suspected. He can't be sure, but he is playing it safe. It may also disappear just as it came, from nowhere. But he doesn't want to take a risk with this. Would you if you were in his place?'

"They were out the door without having set foot upstairs. They sniffed around the yard for about thirty seconds and left shaking their heads.

"That week we had three more raids. One from the Germans. Someone was really eager to catch us in the act of breaking the law. But each time the system functioned like clockwork. Fritz and I were at the end of our wits.

" 'I'm going to have to pull a few strings of my own,' the irate cook said as on his way out. He came back a couple of hours later with the information.

" 'First of all,' he said, 'someone has it in for you really bad. So, you'll have to watch out. My guess is that it's the storekeeper. Go out as little as possible. If you get caught, I already took some steps to have you freed one way or another. I have a buddy in the SS; he is a decent chap, just as fed up with everything as you and me. He's regularly stationed in Leeuwarden, but he makes the rounds, checking to make sure that his local details don't step out of line, fomenting unrest in the population. He promised me to keep an eye out for anything that might have your name on it. You'll have to take care of the rest. He also warned me that they recently got the word from Amsterdam that when they go on a raid and they come back empty-handed, it doesn't mean that the suspects are innocent, but rather that the sabotage activities run deeper in the community than expected. The order, therefore, is to retaliate by arresting at least thirty adults of any age or sex they can find in the streets. Find a way to let the people know when to vacate the streets.'

" 'I'll take care of it,' I said to him. 'As for the other matter, I'd like you to arrange a meeting with your friendly SS man, but not here. It's too risky. It would be safer in Leeuwarden, where nobody knows me. I intend to find out who wants my head so badly and why.'

" 'But you may not even be able to board a train; they are watching the railways very closely,' the cook replied. 'They expect increased sabotage efforts.'

" 'Then have a couple of your men take me to the train at gun-point, so that they think that I've already been nabbed,' I asked. Pretty clever, *hein*?

"On the first Thursday of February, I was taken at gun-point to the train station. People in the streets whispered. Some quickened their steps, not daring to look. I boarded the train with the two soldiers, who got off on the other side of the tracks just as the train started to roll. I had an appointment with the SS man at noon.

"Two blocks from my destination point, I was scooped up in a street sweep by the police. I was taken to a school where I spent the night in the company of hundreds of men. All kinds of feverish rumours were running rampant.

" 'We're going to Westerbork.'

" 'They're taking us to Poland.'

" 'They want to use us as cannon-fodder on the front.'

" 'We're hostages.'

" 'They'll trade us for Jews in hiding.'

" 'They'll shoot us in retaliation for sabotage.'

"In reality, no one knew anything. After days and days, they took us to the Zalenschaaf, the largest hall in Leeuwarden. There were already thousands waiting to be processed. 'You men are needed to work in Germany to support the war effort.' The announcement finally dispelled our anxiety about our uncertain future.

" 'The train is ready to roll as soon as a transport has been processed.' That announcement didn't reassure me a bit. But knowing the painstaking bureaucracy of both the German and the Dutch officials, a lot could happen before boarding that train of doom. There were endless rows of tables manned by collaborators, attempting to register a chaotic crowd of thousands.

"I was in no hurry to hang myself. So I began to explore the place. I didn't know what I was looking for, but I was certain I would recognize a favourable opportunity, should one emerge.

" 'John Datema!' Someone yelled out my name. 'I'm Piet Postma. You probably don't remember me; I'm an old sea-faring buddy of your brother Rien's. We met once, but you were still a kid.' I come from a family of seventeen children, so I hardly recalled my oldest brother who had left home when I was three years old. He came to visit once every three or four years between long hauls on the oceans of the world. This man was a total stranger to me.

" 'Are you one of us or one of them, Piet?'

" 'I'm sort of in-between. I help out with the registration and other low-level joe-jobs, so they leave me alone. I don't want to be taken out of the country. It's safer here. But I haven't any good feelings for them, if that's what you want to know. For one thing, I can tell you that you're in the wrong place. Come to my table and I'll make sure that you get permission to go home.'

"He sat behind his table and slipped on his sleeve covers. At once, this adventurer of the seven seas was transformed into a meek clerk with ink spots on his fingers.

" 'I want John Datema's papers,' he snapped at a clerk. When he held my ID in his hand, he pretended to study it for a while. He then wrote something on a slip of paper, stamped it, and handed it to me together with my ID.

" 'This'll open the door for you. Good luck and try not to get sent back here.' "

"Did the experience of having spent two weeks in captivity mark you in any way?" I inquired.

"All in all, except for being covered with lice from head to toe, I went home unmarked by my two weeks in captivity. It was all over, no use dwelling on it. I needed to be thoroughly disinfected."

"Can you say the same thing, Mrs. Datema?" Vicki turned to our hostess. "Or were you more profoundly affected by your husband's absence? If I understand him correctly, he couldn't even get word to you to let you know that he was still alive and well."

"While he was on his 'holidays', we had five more raids. Marie and the kids were caught outside, so they had to hide in the cistern with the boys. Lise was terrified of Lazar, my cousin's Jewish friend, who looked and sounded like he had lost his mind. The poor lad would surely have hanged himself had he been left alone long enough. Anyway, Lazar yelled at Lise because of some silly accident. She wanted to scratch his eyes out. Then she decided she'd rather go to the Germans and tell them who she was than sit with this wild man. What

Strange Bedfellows

can I say? For two weeks I had hardly dared to breathe. Each footstep, each unusual noise—and suddenly all noises seemed unusual — each face was a potential bearer of tragic news about John. Now that he was home, I wanted him to hear all that I had stifled over those two weeks.

"After the second raid, we decided that it would be wiser for the whole bunch of them to spend the day in the cistern. The van Dijks would sleep upstairs but Marie and I would take turns staying up just in case of a surprise night inspection. The Gestapo ordered Fritz to stop the password game. When he protested he was reminded that there was always a shortage of cooks on the front. So we had to keep watching the road twenty-four hours a day.

"You remember Helmut Meissner, the young SS man who was so fond of Lise? He came over one day, and as usual, he asked for his little girlfriend. When I could not produce her because she was in the cistern, he began to ask questions about where a little girl could be all by herself. I did not dare to tell him a lie, because he was on a motorcycle, and he could easily have gone over to anyone's house, or to the church, or to the doctor and found out that something was fishy. So I told him, 'To tell you the truth, I don't really know, she must have gone out with Jaap for a stroll without telling me.'

" 'I'll be back in an hour,' he threatened. 'They'd better be back or I'll need some more concrete answers.' By the time he returned, I was able to extract Marie and the kids from the hole. He seemed relieved to see his little friend.

" 'I'm going to spank you for making me come back a second time,' the SS man said, grabbing the little girl, and pretending to carry out his threat. 'You damn little Jew,' he yelled at Lise as he wiped his bloody nose. In her effort to get away from him, Lise had punched him in the face. Fortunately, there was no malice or harm intended by either one of them.

"We had one more night raid, but Marie saw them coming on the road and made it to the crawlspace before they even knocked on the door. They found nothing, of course. But we had to keep up the vigilance day and night. I'd even got Jaap assigned to a four-hour shift."

"This was a totally new situation for me," John said. "My wife was calling the shots about strategy. She had definitely come into her own. I was very proud of her." He ventured a scarcely perceptible wink at his blushing wife.

"Did anything noteworthy happen before you were liberated?" I asked.

"Well, during the spring, raids became routine. Nothing changed and no one was caught. I even wondered why they bothered. Somebody really wanted to catch me doing the wrong thing, but not enough to come around and tear the place apart," Mr. Datema said. He began to sound somewhat winded. "The Black Police never came back after their first visit. They were not going to risk getting sick or looking like fools if in fact the whole thing was a trick.

"Lazar Wolff, the tormented young Jew, however, passed away. One April morning he just was not able to gather enough strength to awaken. If you want my opinion, he died of being useless."

"Tell us about liberation day, please." I decided to jump ahead in the interview as our host's energy was clearly fading.

"One day, mid-April, Marie and I took the kids for a stroll just to allow the children to feast their eyes on the peaceful spring landscape," Bertha answered. "As we were coming around a bend, walking away from town, we saw armoured vehicles rolling slowly towards us. We decided to retreat.

" 'No, mother, these are not Nazis. These are the liberators. They must be Americans,' yelled Lise. Instead of retreating, we ran in their direction, and in a couple of minutes we were all hugging Canadian soldiers. There was not a dry eye on the road on that mid-April afternoon. We were free.

"They gave the kids chocolates and chewing gum. Marie and I hugged like two sisters. We had never experienced freedom together.

"When we got back to the village, there was not a German in sight. They must have cleared out just minutes before, because their supper was still simmering on the stove. Above the stove, I found a note pinned to the wall with a kitchen knife: 'Goodbye, my friends. I'll see you in Hanover, if the victors don't string me up. Marie and the kids, you sneaky Jews, God bless you. I pray that you don't hate me. I was never a Nazi. Peace to us all—Fritz Bohlins, retired cook. P.S.: Tonight's dinner is on me.'

"Two days later, Johanna—that was Marie's real name—and the kids left to find out what was left of their home in Wierden.

" 'Now we'll find out,' she said to John and me, with tears in her eyes, 'if freedom can be relearned once you've lost it, or if it is gone for ever once it's been taken away from you.'

"At first, we didn't feel at ease in our home. We seemed to rattle in its sudden emptiness. No more Germans to endure. No more fugitives to populate our space. No more fear or anguish about unpredictable encounters or surprise visits.

"I even felt strange sitting in our room without having to whisper. The walls were still resonating with five years of foreign sounds. I couldn't figure out where their world ended, now that they had become invisible, and where ours started, now that we saw only ourselves within those walls. Then," she added after a moment's hesitation, "there was another thing. The war changed our lives. When we got married, we had planned to work hard, raise a family, and offer good, healthy children to God, just as our parents had when they got married. Instead, we had spent most of our best energies on dodging the enemy; we had become comrades first, and husband and wife second.

"But all the same, it was nice to have our home back." She seemed relieved, but not without a trace of sadness on her face. "Marie had entered my life so deeply, that when she left, I felt a special void—a kind of mourning. I knew that we'd see each other, but for the time being I was only aware of her absence. Often, I spent more time with her than with John. We shared the fears and dreams of women, thoughts and feelings I kept sheltered from his masculine scorn. In a very special way, I grew up with Marie during those years. Spending many hours trembling, planning, and letting our imaginations travel together unveiled a part of me whose very existence was unknown— a competent yet vulnerable me. I also felt myself to be a little Jewish. I learned what it meant to fear for your life and for your children's lives, I learned the taste of anguish for the consequences of a good deed. I also learned that there was nothing more Jewish than to live with the burden of an uncertain tomorrow, but not to abandon faith in that tomorrow. We Christians say that hope is last to die. Marie has taught me that for a Jew hope can never die." She stopped suddenly, as if she had become aware of divulging too much about herself.

"What was your life like after liberation?" I asked the Datemas.

"Soon, Noordbergen returned to its pre-war calm," our host answered. "For a while the streets seemed empty in the wake of the double exodus. Hunter and hunted vacated our tired village. An outside visitor would have found nothing to reveal that a bitter duel between life and might had been waged on the cobble-stones, on the dairy farms, and in our red-brick homes for five long years. But if he lent an ear to the softly spoken words of the inhabitants, he would have heard intense memories: anger towards the invader and his local boot-lickers, pain over our losses, sorrow over freshly severed friendships, and pride over small measures of victory. Noordbergen could never be the same again—a new kind of living and dying had drawn a few new wrinkles on its face.

"Some neighbours and I were among the first to remember those who hurt the community the most—the jelly-spined collaborators.

"A dozen men or so surrounded the storekeeper's house shortly after lunch one day. 'Come out, storekeeper. Your neighbours want a word with you. You will not be harmed.' There was no answer. The request was repeated several times.

" 'I think we've waited too long; by now he may be safely laughing at the whole lot of us somewhere in Germany,' someone said. Two men went to the door. It was open. They disappeared inside. The group drew closer in silent expectation. We all feared for their lives. If, in his despair, the bastard had wanted to shoot it out, those two would have been as good as dead.

"But, a minute later, the two emerged from the house, looking waxen yellow. 'We've nothing left to do here. The storekeeper judged himself guilty. He's hanging from a beam in the back room. God grant him serenity.' "

"What was happening in your own lives?" Vicki asked.

"Bertha and I had to start all over," Mr. Datema answered quietly. "The Germans had taken everything except the bare walls. We had to start from scratch. What was left of the bakery did not permit me to exercise my craft in my own shop. I've never owned a bakery again. How to forget what was lost when what was left kept rubbing my nose into what was taken from me? Where were the resources needed to make a second beginning?

"I looked around and I saw the way the past could have shaped our present. And then I wondered what kind of future was still possible for us there? I didn't want to become a beggar in my own home town, or even in my own country."

"I was afraid of what was going to become of us," his wife added in a near whisper. "When I think of all the dreams Marie and I wove...I guess they served their purpose—they permitted us to look at the future with hopeful eyes. But now, reality refused to conform itself to my fantasies."

"Bertha was, in fact, so eager to see Marie," Mr. Datema interrupted his wife, "that we decided to pay the van Dijks a visit down south.

"We were not prepared for the gruesome spectacle awaiting us. At the sight of their misery, Bertha failed to stifle an outburst of shock.

" 'I present a pretty sight don't I?' Marie was flu-ridden in a bed covered in rags and an old army blanket, propped up by a dubious object. An open umbrella in her left hand protected her from the rain drizzling through the leaky roof. In spite of her abject misery, the pleasure of seeing us painted pink flowers on her pale cheeks.

"I was speechless while the women lost themselves in a maze of memories. I preferred to remain silent, for otherwise I would have lashed out angrily at the victim for lack of a visible monster. It was not enough that this poor woman was deprived of everything except her bare existence, she was also cheated out of her own home. When she had returned to Wierden, her home town, a strange family had already grown deep roots in her house. She told them who she was and why she was away from home for years. They looked at each other as if the woman had lost her senses. 'This is our home. We have nothing to do with you.' And they shut the door.

"With her two kids in tow, she tried her luck at her brother's home, in Oss. A policeman had received it as reward for his patriotic services. What else was there to do but to seek out one of the farmers who still had some of her money? With it she rented a two-room hovel. That's where she received us.

" 'This can't go on. Something must be done about this.' The two women looked at me with surprise. 'I'm talking about the way you live. Not only do you not deserve this but it's just not right. Something will be done, for sure.'

" 'So what are you going to do, John?' Bertha knew me. By the time we were about to leave, I made it clear that I'd find some way to remedy the despicable lifestyle to which Marie and her children had been condemned.

"Bertha stayed with Marie for a few days to take care of her and I took Lise back with me. She was green as a frog. I began a forceful correspondence with the mayor of Wierden about the immorality of allowing this mother of two to waste away in a hole without even an adequate roof over her head while her family's homes had been donated to collaborators."

Our host seemed eager now to tell his story. He was slightly out of breath. "Perhaps he has heart disease," I thought with a touch of worry, "or perhaps he is just frightened that he will not be able to finish the tale the way he would like to."

"I didn't mince my words, you can be sure of that. I wanted them to convey not only my outrage but also a veiled threat of doing something more drastic should the mayor fail to act decently.

"The reply was no less direct. It curtly reminded me of the many hardships our nation suffered after five years of occupation, and that arrogant demands wrapped in veiled threats not only undermined the spirit of reconstruction but could also bring about lawsuits.

"However, a week after I received the mayor's letter, Marie was installed on the second floor of her brother's home, leaving the furious policeman the lower half of the house."

"But what about your own lives?" I had a distinct impression that they preferred to avoid that topic.

"Well, if you must know, we were not faring well, either. I abandoned the idea of making something out of the wrecked bakery. In fact, I was seriously contemplating leaving my profession altogether. There just was not enough work for me to support my family.

"Sometimes I couldn't help asking myself, 'Who won the damn war and who lost it?' I'd look in the papers or listen to the radio: who got the juicy jobs with the government? The former NSB traitors suddenly claimed to be double-agents for the resistance. 'Where are the true members of the underground—why don't they unmask these despicable impostors?' I was bitter and angry. 'Perhaps they're still underground. One had to have been an actual murderer to face prosecution. The simple traitor who kept the murderer supplied with victims is enjoying a more peaceful, more prosperous existence than we are, that's for sure.'

"More and more people shook their heads in disbelief, and began to wonder, 'What are we going to do?' The question echoed throughout Noordbergen and similar villages. Pessimism spilled into public meetings where alternatives were being discussed. A word began to make the rounds until it became a familiar idea to many families: emigration."

"Why emigration?" I asked.

"Our country had become too small for us in many ways. I wanted more freedom, more elbow room. I wanted our children to grow up in a country where they could work their own land if that's what they wanted to do, without fear that their ploughs might be blunted by some buried indiscretion of the war. I wanted us to settle in a land not likely to be ravaged by hunger. But do you know what? The damnedest thing is that all these reasons didn't amount to a hill of beans—the truth of it was that that day we went south to visit Marie, a restless snake seemed to have crawled inside me, and it made me fidgety and itchy to keep moving. I felt sticky and unclean. That snake inside me wanted me to shed its old skin and start growing a brand-new one. It doesn't make much sense, I know, but there was no turning back, even before we made the first step. No matter how harsh the winter is and how tenacious a fight it puts up, spring always has to win. That's the way it was with me. I didn't know if in a year, or in ten, I would curse that vicious snake inside me for luring me into a bottomless pit, but I had to take a chance or else I'd have suffocated as my country closed in around me. I know I acted like a madman. I forced my family to jump out of the window without knowing what was underneath.

"Very soon, it was no longer a matter of going abroad or staying at home. Rather, it was a question of where to go. I wanted to go to Brazil. It's a vast open land, with room for everyone regardless of tongue or faith."

"What did you think of Brazil, Mrs. Datema?" Vicki turned to our hostess.

"Brazil was far away," she replied with a sigh of relief. "Too far away, in more than one way. Luckily the fare was beyond our means. I would have preferred Australia, or any other English-speaking country. It was going to be strange anywhere. But I thought that in an English-speaking country, it would be a little less strange. Australia proved to be too far also for our pocket-book. We hoped to find a hospitable land that needed honest workers enough to subsidize their journey.

" 'We're going to Canada!' John burst into the house one late summer day in 1949. 'They want families there, and of all destinations, Canada is the cheapest to reach.'

"Five weeks later, we were on the S.S. *Volendam* together with a deck full of solemn Dutch emigrants, silently watching our country slip under the horizon. A quavering voice began to sing the 'Het Wilhelmus', our national anthem.

" 'For better or worse,' John made a clumsy effort to rise above the gloom of the moment, 'this is really the time to say that we are all in the same boat.'

"Mr. Harriman was waiting for us at the railway station in Waterford, Ontario. It was full of travel-weary emigrants, trying to be gracious guests for our Canadian farmer-hosts. Neither felt comfortable with silence, so we all spoke in our own tongues, being fully aware of the hopelessness of our efforts. To overcome our dilemma, we spoke little but loud. I can tell you, without being a mind-reader, at that time nobody thought of the uncertainties of the future. Was it faith? Optimism? Blind trust? No, sir. It was sheer exhaustion. We just couldn't give a damn about anything but rest.

" 'Well, here we are, for better or worse,' I whispered to John in the truck taking us to our final destination. 'We're out of the baking business and into chicken farming.' "

They grew silent. Like bookends, Bertha and John Datema collapsed in their well-worn armchairs. Neither of them seemed to be aware of our presence.

"Is there anything else you'd care to add before I turn off the tape recorder?" Vicki asked hesitantly.

"Well...I don't know. I think we've said more than enough...." Mr. Datema answered without even looking up. "We could tell you about our trials and tribulations in Canada, but then again, who cares about that? Let's just say we've struggled. But, by the same token, if you're alive, you struggle. But I don't mind that at all. Besides, we're Canadians now."

In the next half an hour, from reluctantly shared bits and pieces, we gathered the history of the daily ordeal that, after ten years, led to a measure of peace in their current home. In a quiet way, Burlington settled into their lives as the only home they would ever want. Gone were the days when they would call a whole town's population their friends and neighbours. Gone were the bonds that linked them to a Dutch identity. Gone was Sunday worship in the Baptist church. And yet, like so many of their former compatriots, and in spite of Mr. Datema's earlier pronouncement, they never fully became Canadian.

Illness has been plaguing both of them for quite a while. First Bertha was besieged by illness after illness. She appeared to have won the battle against cancer when breathing became an exhausting labour. Her lungs collapsed. She left the hospital on her own two feet, but she was never to enjoy the simple thrill of a deep breath again.

Deprived of vital air, Bertha mobilized the same kind of energy that had fuelled her struggle with fear when she found herself sharing her home with Nazis and Jews. With support from a physiotherapist, she organized a Breathing Club.

"Back home, all I needed for courage was my faith and my man," she told us. "Here, even though I had to close the door on the Baptist way of worshipping, I have to draw on my faith."

"I have faith in one thing only." John looked at me, but his words were really aimed at his wife. Ills and pills have been the only topic of conversation between them for a long time. "Acts of friendship. Don't come to me with big words. Shut up and do something. Then I'll take my hat off to you. Not because you deserve praise for what is your God-given duty, but because I respect people who go about doing their jobs quietly, without expecting medals, without checking around to see if anyone is watching. Life is taking care of business. And you can only take care of business alongside other people who are inclined to do the same."

"I agree with my man one hundred per cent." Bertha sat up so that she could breathe more easily. "We didn't do much, certainly not as much as we could have. You think you're doing the best you can or even better, but the truth of the matter is that you can always do better and more. And I'm the first one to admit how easy it is to think the contrary. But when you come to think of it, it's all very simple if you believe that people are born to help each other. That's what life is all about."

The Underground Butcher and His Wife:

Rudy and Betty de Vries

Rudy de Vries was waiting for us by the elevator on the fifth floor of his brownstone building in Welland, Ontario. He had a ceremonial air about him, as if he was expecting dignitaries. After a moment's silence, he extended an enormous right hand to me. "Welcome to my home," he said, and his rigid mask of awkwardness melted into a simple smile. "My wife, Betty, is expecting you inside. She has a bum knee, you know." He turned to Vicki. There was something paternal in the way he leaned towards her.

He ushered us into their apartment. Betty de Vries was standing in the living room, just beyond the tiny entrance hall. She was leaning on the back of a bulky armchair for support. A tall woman in her seventies, Betty carried her large frame with fatigue and visible pain. The struggle had etched a groove in her pale face. Beyond her thick glasses, however, her eyes showed strength and endurance. And a twinkle of feistiness.

"Rudy couldn't wait in here with me," she said as she shook hands with Vicki. "He was too excited. He may be pushing seventy-five, but he is still a boy." Her voice was loving rather than chiding.

"It's part of my charm." Rudy winked at us. He was now on home ground.

The Underground Butcher and His Wife

"Since Washington we've become regular celebrities," Betty commented once we took our seats. "All this attention is very touching, but tell me, is it really necessary?"

"Not only is it necessary, it's much overdue." I leaned forward to add more weight to my words. "In some cases the recognition has come too late."

"Well, the old guard is an endangered species." Rudy tried to make light of it. "We're highly perishable. Look at Betty, she can hardly walk."

"I'll need some surgery, and hope for the best," Betty sighed. She obviously didn't like to draw attention to her affliction.

"Well, thank the Lord, I'm in perfect condition," Rudy boasted. "And if you don't believe me, lend me your young wife and I'll take her dancing tonight."

While Betty and Vicki chatted about Betty's orthopaedic problems, I engaged Rudy: "What did you think of the meeting in Washington?"

"It was the best experience of my life since I set foot on these shores." His face turned red with the fever of excitement. "Not because of all the attention—I could have done without that part very well. It was wonderful because by turning the floodlights on the handful who helped, Elie Wiesel and his team brought to the surface how many didn't lift a finger to help even one single Jew. It was a very smart idea to open the meeting with your talk. The way I see it, those who spoke about the rescued and the rescuers covered only a small number of lucky Jews and an even smaller lot of Christians, whereas you spoke about the six million Jews who were massacred and consequently about the many millions of non-Jews who allowed the massacre to take place. I was very happy that this was made clear from the beginning."

"You seem to suggest that you don't deserve the recognition as a righteous Gentile," I ventured.

He jumped to his feet and started pacing back and forth, making the small room seem even smaller.

"That's the one thing that makes me mad about the whole thing," he said, once again dropping his large body into his chair. "What in the world is a Gentile? We don't even have a word for it in Dutch or in Frisian. As for being righteous, that is the exclusive domain of our Lord. The most we can do is to strive towards righteousness, but

183

we can never reach it. I know that no harm was intended, but still it bothers me when you refer to me with a term reserved for God."

"How would you like the world to refer to you after what you did during the war?" I asked.

"The same as before—as a man." He looked at me with disappointment. "I thought you'd know that."

"So according to you, you did nothing special. Is this correct?" I wanted to clarify what he meant.

"Well, yes, I did something, but it had nothing to do with right eousness or heroism." He became stiff again. With his back rigidly erect, he held on to the armrests of his chair as if he were bracing himself for an announcement. I looked in the direction of our wives. Betty had left the room.

"What I did differently from most others was that I chose to remain a man—a man fighting a system and not individuals. Most people lost their lives either because they stopped seeing themselves as individuals, or because they failed to see the man in their enemy." Rudy measured his words out cautiously. It must have been very important to him that I understand exactly what he meant. "They lost themselves in one trap or another set by the system.

"Jews or Germans—it made no difference to me, as long as I could see them as human beings. So when I saw a German soldier my stomach didn't start doing the goose-step of hatred. I would have been guilty of a grave crime against him if I hadn't made sure that he indeed was a Nazi. I didn't allow myself to fall into the trap of seeing an enemy in every German. That was special in those days.

"But I behaved exactly the same way towards the Jews. Once I knew of a Jew in risk of losing his life, nothing else made any difference. Our Lord had created the Jew just as He had created me. That was enough for me. Especially at a time when the Jew was running for his life. 'Hide the fugitive, and do not betray the refugee.' Does this sound familiar? It was my daily slogan in my underground rescue work. That, too, was special in those days.

"Let me give you an example. One October day in 1944, when I was up to my eyeballs in illegal Jews in the room above my butcher shop and I had enough TNT in the attic to blow IJlst off the map, a German soldier in full combat gear came into my shop. 'What in the world could he want?' I wondered. 'Is he going to conduct a raid just for fun? Or does he want a piece of meat for a sweetheart?' On a closer look, however, I read in his sagging cheeks a profound loneliness.

He seemed spiritually deflated. It was certainly *verboten* to weep in front of the captive population. And yet, that's what he looked like he needed to do.

"Finally, he looked at me. Then he bent his head in his embarrassment. 'Forgive me,' he seemed to be saying, 'for taking over your country.' He just kept looking at me without a word. His soul was on fire. Believe it or not, I knew I was dealing with a decent man.

"I took off my apron and went out to meet him in front of the counter. He followed every move I made. And you know what: this man of power, armed to his Adam's apple, was afraid of me, the empty-handed. But I knew what he needed: he needed to *be* with another simple Christian.

"I offered him a friendly hand to shake. He hesitated for a few moments. Then, with a decisive thrust, he shook my hand, cradling it in both of his bony palms, his fingers clutching on to my hand. He started nodding vigorously in hearty approval of what was happening: '*Das ist sehr freundlich. Das ist wunderschön.*'

"I invited him to come into the private section of the house. To alleviate his burden, I wanted to help him lift the rucksack off his back. He recoiled in fear. For a moment, I thought he might draw his revolver on me. I offered him a glass of milk. That was a small treasure in those days. And he looked like he knew it, too.

"I noticed his eyes resting on the crucifix in a corner of our living room. And his whole being seemed to relax. 'So that's what it is,' I thought in relief and on the edge of tears. I'm a butcher but, I'm ashamed to tell you, I am quite easily moved to tears.

"I invited the German soldier to kneel in front of the chesterfield to join me in prayer. And we knelt there for about half an hour or longer praying, he in German, I in Frisian. I could forgive him for being in the camp of my enemies because he let me know that he, too, belonged to Jesus Christ, our Lord. I had no hate for this German; he was a man, not a puppet wound up by an evil system. I needed him as much as he needed me.

"And it was that very same feeling that I experienced when one night, about eighteen months prior to the night I mention, I was awakened by a faint but insistent tapping on our bedroom window. There was a young woman standing there, motioning that I should come closer. I went around and met her in the shop, all the while wondering what in the world this whole thing could mean. We had two and a half years of German occupation behind us; we'd heard of all kinds of sneaky provocations. But why me? I wasn't aware that I had enemies. Had I sold a customer too tough a piece of meat? Had I accidentally short-changed somebody? Had I... Well, the questions were endless but she looked serious enough for me to take a chance.

" 'You don't know me, Herr de Vries,' she whispered. I detected a German accent in her voice. 'A mutual friend told me that if anyone is willing to help me, it will be you.'

" 'What is the matter, young lady?' I asked, still not all that sure that this whole thing was on the up and up.

" 'Please come to our house and it will all be clear to you. I was told not to reveal anything to you until we go back to the house.'

"As I dressed in haste, I weighed the situation. Was this a person in trouble or was I being manipulated? But there was something in her voice. She was either very scared or very, very good at her job. And why would they waste such a fine operator on a meaningless denunciation? I was a small fish in a very small pond. And the butchering business was too lean for anyone to salivate over and have me arrested.

"When we got to her little apartment, a middle-aged woman whose face looked familiar to me was waiting for us.

" 'I'm Helga Sachs and this is my daughter, Charlotte,' she said. 'We fled the Reich in 1938, when things were going from bad to worse for people like us. No, we aren't Jewish. My husband was a professor at the university in Tübingen. He openly protested against the barbarism of *Kristallnacht*. A week later, he was taken away to some camp near Munich for political prisoners. I believe it was Dachau. And I was advised by well-placed friends to take my daughter out of the country while it was still possible. With the help of an old Jewish colleague of my husband, this modest abode was arranged for Charlotte and me a couple of weeks after the first wave of violence against the Jewish community in Amsterdam began. He asked us to refrain from communicating with him because, as an outspoken Jew, he was a marked man. And we have been here ever since. You might have seen me a couple of times—I have been in your shop. I try not to attach myself to any particular neighbourhood merchant so that they don't become familiar with my face and start asking questions.'

" 'All this is very moving and fascinating, Mevrouw Sachs,' I said, most politely in spite of my impatience, 'but what is the urgent business for which you had me fetched?'

The Underground Butcher and His Wife

" 'Forgive me, Herr de Vries'—she sounded apologetic—'I must remind you of a war-time soup: lots of water and little substance, right? Well, the matter at hand is indeed very grave. Last night, we had an unexpected visit from an elderly Jewish couple from down south who were sent to me by...a person they know and I know...and the message they brought was, "please find a hiding place for these people in Friesland or they'll be taken on a transport to the camps." "How can I do anything for anyone," I asked myself. "But how can I turn away this frightened couple whose entire past and future is in a small suitcase?" Will you find a place for this couple who tremble in my bedroom about their fate?'

" 'I have never had the burden of holding in my hands anyone's survival,' I said. In my mind, however, things were not so clear. 'What business do I have with these people? I have never met them. Where will this all lead if I get involved today? If I look after one, by tomorrow night people will start taking numbers in front of my bedroom window. I've got a family to worry about....' My confusion lasted but a few seconds. When I was a little kid, I was taught to distinguish between right and wrong, justice and injustice, real Christian behaviour and phoney-baloney words.

" 'It is my privilege to help your Jewish guests,' I assured Mrs. Sachs. 'Thank you for giving me the opportunity to do our Lord's work in saving some of His people.' You should have seen the faces of those two German women. They must have thought I was making sport of them or that I was not entirely healthy in my head. I guess they had never met a genuine Christian who had an intimate relationship with Jesus Christ through the mediation of the Holy Ghost. They were too sophisticated to take my faith seriously. But it was my faith that motivated me to extend my hand to that German soldier in my shop and that same faith was behind my decision to extend a helping hand to the Jewish couple. My faith commands me as much as it challenges me to love my fellow man, without exclusions."

"Do you intend to treat our guests to a whole sermon, or will half of one do for today?" Betty de Vries scolded her husband. She had been leaning against the dining room wall behind Rudy's armchair for a while, signalling that she didn't wish to join us.

"Don't let him get away with his favourite trick," she said, turning to us. "He talks as if he had the flames of hell and damnation chasing him. The Lord has indeed provided us with a few miracles, but it's not right to boast about them. There is nothing more privately sacred than a miracle. So Rudy, you old wind-bag, keep it simple: tell about how you got involved deeper and deeper with hiding Jews, and skip the preaching."

"As usual, my wife Betty is right. I do have a tendency to give free rein to my mouth. You'd be better off if she told our story. Not only will she keep her tongue on a short leash, but also she knows more about hiding the Jews than I do. I wasn't around all that much while we had the Jews in the house, you see. I was too busy getting counterfeit or stolen food coupons, making arrangements for placing other Jews, or shipping illegally slaughtered meat down south. And after a while, I just had to vanish from the public eye. Doing resistance work was like taking a sunbath: too much exposure could get you burnt."

"There were plenty of times," Betty interjected, "when I wasn't sure whether or not I still had a husband. Loneliness and I were very close friends during most of the two and a half years of Rudy's involvement in the underground."

"Before all, you should know what we meant by 'underground' during the early days," Rudy cautioned us. "We're in 1942, some time during the fall. The people of IJlst had enemies among their own rank. There were at least ten known NSB-ers, but for the longest time there was no resistance movement of any sort. And when it did start up it was organized by four escapees from The Hague. They first set up a local resistance cell in Arnhem. When things began to heat up there, they retired to our sleepy little town. At first, they just did things as they needed to be done. Not knowing anyone, they proceeded gingerly. They posed as evacuees. No one knew that they had formed a cell—they never showed up anywhere together. It was from one of them that Mrs. Sachs got my name. Don't ask me how he knew of me. To this day I know precious little about that man, even though he and his three comrades, a few similar-minded people, and I went through many hot spots together. We placed over two hundred Jews, broke into a number of food-coupon distribution centres, and hid enough weapons to outfit a small army."

"You know, it's the darnedest thing," Betty changed the topic. "I can remember the day Uncle Ben arrived but I'd never be able to tell you how he got to us. And what's even more amazing is that I don't believe we ever knew. Today, if somebody wanted to come into my home, he'd have to have a very good introduction from someone I trusted before I'd open my door. But then, when everything was a potential danger, we just trusted our fate to invisible comrades and to God.

"One night, around six o'clock, we were still in the store when I noticed that Rudy was watching somebody through the window. 'What do you see, Rudy, that's so fascinating? You'll twist your neck into a pretzel.' 'He went past us, and he didn't seem to slow down,' he answered. 'I'll have to catch him before he runs into somebody not so friendly.' 'What are you talking about?' I asked him, but he was already in the street on his bike.

"About ten minutes later, the door opened and this enormous-looking man appeared in the doorway. His black, kinky hair and his unruly beard, not to mention his dark eyes sparkling with the alertness of the hunted, all pointed to the only possible answer. We had ourselves a Jewish refugee.

"My heart began skipping beats. I had known that it was going to happen. Rudy had kept staying out until all hours of the night. He had warned me: 'I think it's time for us to take in some Jewish people.' 'Ah, no,' I exclaimed, 'you know the punishment for hiding Jews— it's death if they catch you. And we have a family.' By then we had three kids. We were still young. And you know how it is, when you're still young you really like to live. '*If* they catch you, that's a very big *if*,' he said reassuringly. 'I didn't fall on earth with last night's rain. When we do it, we'll make sure they don't catch us.'

"He didn't convince me, but deep down I knew that he was right. With that decison a new era began in my life.

"So when I saw this giant in our door, wearing his flat cap like a Moses about to cross another sea, I thought, 'God, we'll need all Your help with this one. He is enormous, and he has the Old Testament tattooed on his face.'

"He came by boat on the canal from the sleepy village of Heeg. His wife and son would soon follow him. 'We'll keep the three of you, of course,' my husband said, carefree as if he were inviting someone over for coffee.

"Aunt Tillie and Wim, their mentally handicapped teenage son, looked obviously Jewish and I wasn't even sure what 'looking Jewish' was supposed to mean.

"They were delighted to live together again, within the bosom of a family. They had another son, hidden somewhere else. Wim had to stay with his parents because his mental abilities reduced him to the level of a young savage. The threesome moved into the room above the shop.

"When our house was built it had never occurred to anyone to soundproof it. We're very quiet people, anyway. So when our fugitives came to live upstairs, we had to insist that everyone whisper during business hours, upstairs and downstairs. During the day they had to avoid the tell-tale noise of footsteps above the store. Once we closed the business for the day and complied with the black-out laws, they came out of their cell and moved about freely. But, to tell you the truth, we preferred to visit them rather than having them roam about our home. We weren't used to the presence of strangers; we led very secluded lives. The front of the house was a marketplace, but beyond that our space was a sort of sanctuary where we rarely had spectators.

"I complained of loneliness during those years. Theirs humbled mine, I can tell you that. But at the time, the fact that their predicament made mine look like a summer vacation made no difference. I resented the whole thing: the war, the underground, the Jews, everything. Later on there were moments when I cursed even our faith, which demanded that we keep our door open. Remember, 'Hide the fugitive...'?

"In the beginning, they were quite pleased to come downstairs, just to breathe different air, to feast their eyes on the modest spectacle of another room, to stretch their muscles. They relished the illusion of being ordinary people in an ordinary house. But as time wore on, and their nerves wore thinner, they ventured out less and less. Our kids enjoyed their company so much that, at times, I grew just a touch suspicious that they might try to insinuate themselves into those little souls with their understandable need for acceptance. I was being silly and vulnerable; after all, the undertaking was running smoothly— most of the time, anyway. Still, I couldn't wipe the lines of anguish from my forehead until we were freed in 1945. That's a long time to keep company with anguish.

"A few months had passed by. News came to us about intensified activities against the Jews. One evening, Uncle Ben informed us of their decision. 'We believe that it's no longer safe for us to come downstairs. I hope you'll agree with our decision not to leave the relative safety of the second floor.'

"What could we say to people who feared for their lives? 'Come downstairs anyway; just ignore your fears? It's too much hassle for us if you stay in your own room?' Well, perhaps somebody else could have done it. I couldn't. Besides, whatever was the safest for them was also the safest for my family. There was no 'them' and 'us' in our household in those days."

"In what way did their seclusion inconvenience you?" I asked Betty. "Didn't you say that you found their roaming about your private space intrusive?"

"In practical terms, their decision meant that I became a chamber-maid in my own home. Morning, noon, and night, I served them their meals in their room. I didn't complain; it had to be done. I never mentioned to my husband that I didn't appreciate my predicament. I had enough work with my three small children and the house. And, on top of it all, for security reasons I had had to let go the young woman who came every day to help me with the chores. But I didn't complain— not because I was a martyr, but because I knew that it wouldn't do any good anyway. So I became the room service.

"If you detect a sour note in this, you're on the right path. In the beginning, I accepted my new role. The job needed to be done. I was there; I did it. You don't ask why the tree casts a shadow over the canal. It does so because they both happen to have been placed there by providence. My acceptance of my task, however, was not a straight road. I did come to a point where Christian charity and selfish rebellion intersected and I took the latter path without hesitation. Where was it written that I should go against my own dignity in order to protect strangers? I had no aspirations for sainthood. I was a butcher's wife with very common features. You couldn't have picked me out of a crowd of Frisian women any more than you could identify a particular fish in a pond. You could say I went through an uncharitable period.

"But even though I minded more and more my chambermaid role, I did convince myself that it was a very small price to pay for saving three lives. I used to close my eyes and see two alternative scenes: in one, we would be mourning the death of this Jewish family; in the other, I saw them free and tending to the business of everyday living. I kept insisting on these two mental pictures as I collected their dirty dishes and washed them with ours.

"But that wasn't all. I also had to do their laundry. The work itself would have been sufficient to break my back with everything else. But there was more. While we had no real reason to fear the neighbours, we had to be cautious. Rudy and I were both born on the block, so we knew all of our neighbours. My parents' house was right across from my father-in-law's butchershop. So, when we got married, Rudy picked up my suitcase, crossed the narrow pavement, and I was home again. All this to say that the neighbours held few mysteries or surprises for us. And yet, those were extraordinary times, and we were doing extraordinary things. For all I knew they all were hiding Jews. And by the same token, for all I knew, every one of them would be terrified to death to have a Jew next door, let alone in their own homes. It was best not to invite bad luck. We simply couldn't allow any visible evidence of newcomers to our household. Questions would have been as inevitable as the black spots on a Frisian longhorn."

"What does all this have to do with the Jews' laundry?" Vicki ventured.

"In those days we had no washers and driers. So how could I dry all those extra-large men's shirts and pants if I couldn't hang them on the line outside? (Uncle Ben's clothing was big enough for a bear, and Wim was no midget, either.) I had to dry them over several nights. I hung them after dark, and plucked them off the line before the neighbours would rise. I'd take them inside still damp and start over the next night and the next, until they were dry. You can't even begin to imagine the frustrating effort that I had to exert day after day just to keep afloat. At times I wanted to sink under that mountain of damp clothes.

"And there was even more. We had only one toilet in the house— downstairs. So, we provided our guests with a bucket that they kept in the room next to theirs. Once a day, it had to be emptied. So I began my day every morning by fetching that pail full of urine and faeces and carrying it to a nearby pond to dump it. And every step of the way, I struggled to keep my stomach from heaving. It was a vile chore that I couldn't discharge without revulsion.

"And if that wasn't enough, I still had to cope with the fact that most of the time I had no one around with whom to share my feelings. Rudy spent the day in the shop: I could hardly engage him in a conversation about my troubles. In the evenings, he wolfed down his meal, he kissed the kids and me, and he was off to fight against the warriors of darkness. To him the resistance movement seemed exhilarating and adventurous. Rudy and his comrades often saw the fruits of their work. A family was placed...on to the next task. A child was spirited away from a risky spot...on to the next task. A weapon cache was stolen right under the eyes of the Nazis...on to another accomplishment. And all that time, I was panting at home with three little children to whom I was mother and father, and three big children to whom I was everything. Who was there for me? Where was my reward? Where was the fuel for my sagging energies? I needed something concrete, something I could grab with my tired fingers and say, 'Hey, that was worth getting up for at half-past five in the morning.' "

"How did all this burden make you feel about your Jewish family?" I asked.

"I had no ill feelings towards the Hembergers. In fact, they turned out to be kind and considerate friends. There was a regular love affair between them and my kids. My six- and four-year-olds and Wim had glorious moments together. Uncle Ben was a fabulous story-teller, with a bottomless repertoire of tall tales. He would keep them spellbound with his words and his pantomimes. Aunt Tillie cuddled them as if they were her own. But they could not alleviate either my solitude or my despair. They had enough to contend with, living at the mercy of total strangers who looked after even their eliminations. A word to them would have upset their already precarious sense of worth. It would have been distasteful of me to burden them with my troubles. But I knew that something had to give—and soon.

" 'Rudy, I'm giving fair notice to you,' I said to my husband one night when I felt that the edge was but a step away."

"What did that mean for you at the time?" Vicki asked. "Do you recall?"

"I guess I feared that I would collapse. One day I discovered that praying no longer sheltered me under the umbrella of my faith. I was slipping away from Jesus. For me that was a sign of approaching disaster. That is why I called my hero's attention to the brewing crisis in his own home. 'I know that for tonight you must have a full program,' I told him, 'but I need to speak to you. So I want you home tomorrow night.' "

"How did those words affect you?" I turned to Rudy.

"I had never heard her speak with so many clouds in her voice," Rudy answered, after a long silence. "I knew that life had to be hard for her with all those people and no assistance to speak of. Look, her own father across the street couldn't be told what was going on in our home. He could have been caught and tortured. Or he could have been tortured in a different way by Betty's stepmother, who didn't have much of a warm spot for the two of us. I wouldn't have put it past her to denounce us anonymously. That would have been her revenge for Betty marrying out of the church. When Betty disobeyed her stepmother and married me, she filled up with bile against us. This is just to show you that I had no illusions about what Betty's everyday life must have been like. But not knowing the details allowed me to slip into a kind of passive caring."

"How did you let him know the details of what you were going through?" Vicki asked Betty.

"What I did was simple and to the point: I gave him a minute-by-minute account of my day from the moment I got up until the moment when, unconscious, I collapsed for a brief night's rest. Then I told him to multiply that by thirty to arrive at the grim picture of my month."

"I was speechless," Rudy reminisced. "And I was also caught in a conflict without a solution. I couldn't let my family down, but I couldn't let down the people who were counting on the underground to rescue them, either. That would have been a betrayal of my God. What could I do?

"Not a great deal. But, after reflecting for a time, I suggested, 'Let's have a sink installed upstairs. That way, they can do their own dishes and their own laundry. You will be spared the labour and the red hands. And Uncle Ben can afford to pay for it. After all, we're not taking a cent for their keep.' That was all I could do. But it seemed to work. Or at least I like to think it did. She didn't complain after that."

"It wasn't just the sink, Rudy." Betty turned towards her husband. Her voice was rich with young love. "It was much more important that I felt pampered for a long moment just because you took care of me. I told you my problem and you found a solution to ease the sting of the wound. It was romantic having a knight in shining armour come to rescue me, a damsel in distress. My butcher was my Prince Charming. After that, even the daily latrine detail was more tolerable.

"After the sink was installed, my life began to run more smoothly again. That didn't mean that I no longer had to battle with the phantoms of loneliness."

"How did you cope with that loneliness?" Vicki asked Betty.

"I prayed a lot. I prayed mostly for my children. They were so young and so miserable. How could they recognize a trap, even if they were to see one? Can you imagine? I didn't dare to send them to the barbershop. You know how kids are. They like to impress adults with stories. Mind you, they had an uncanny sense of discretion. They never bragged or boasted about the mysterious hidden guests on our second floor. But one time, Rosie and Pieter went to play with the neighbour's kids.

" 'We played as usual,' she told me in a bored monotone in answer to my motherly questions. 'Piet told them about Auntie,' she added as if she spoke of the afternoon rain. I squatted so that I was eye to eye with my seven-year-old.

" 'What did he say *exactly*? It's very important that you remember it word for word.' To add more weight to my words, I grabbed her by the shoulders and looked very sternly into her lovely sea-green eyes.

" 'That's no big deal,' her voice was still unmoved. ' "We have an Auntie upstairs"—that's what he said word for word, and nothing else.'

" 'And then what?' I interrogated my poor child like a detective.

" 'I said to them, "Oh, it's just some dolls we have upstairs that he calls auntie and uncle," that's all.'

"I hugged my bright little girl with a ton of relief. She was so smart, my baby, she knew...she knew....

"But I was angry with the world. Why should a seven-year-old be called upon to save the day? Why should the simple statement of facts by a five-year-old be thought of as an indiscretion with eight lives in the balance?

"However, the children picked up from us without ever being told that we lived an existence governed by whispering. When Auntie was hungry, she would send Piet down to me to ask me for a piece of bread or a few potatoes. He would quietly snuggle up to my ear, whether I was in the shop or in the yard hanging up the wash, and whisper the message.

"As if hiding Jews wasn't dangerous enough, Rudy then decided to hide dynamite and guns in our attic.

" 'Dynamite? Are you crazy? Do you want to blow us up? I don't want explosives in my home. It's explosive enough with just the Jews.' I was furious. But I knew my man: the only thing I accomplished with my ranting and raving was to blow off the excess steam of anxiety. But you know what? I was speaking to a lifeless mass — one hundred kilos of exhaustion. He was fast asleep.

" 'Where did you hide the goodies?' I asked him the next morning before we opened the shop. 'I don't want to accidentally stumble over something that might kill me. I hope it's all out of the children's reach.'

" 'There's no cause for worry,' he said, without looking at me. He knew I was not at peace with the new development. 'I hid everything in the ceiling.' With that he closed the matter.

"I tell you one thing, Rudy," she said, turning towards her husband with a counterfeit cantankerous tone, "our war-time acrobatics were good for one thing. You were much less chatty those days. But then, I would have preferred your long-winded lectures on silent nights. At times I even wondered what in the world you could be doing out in the night all the time. Nothing that earthshaking was happening in IJlst, so what could you have been up to?"

"Let me tell you a bit about what went on while the womenfolk were warming their fannies in their comfortable homes, cuddling up to their babies." Rudy seemed happy to have a chance to tell his side of the story. "We had our hands more than full. It's true that if we just had to deal with the needs of the local population, we would never have spent an evening away from our families. There were no Jews in our town, and most folks were clever enough to keep to themselves. But the underground was set up to help those who came from other areas—from the cities of the industrial south. There were infinitely more Jews whose survival depended on whether or not the underground could get to them fast enough—or the other way around—than there were active members in the movement. We could reach out to a minute group of people; the vast majority of them died. For every Jew saved, ten perished. That's a sad record to keep remembering."

"How did you find the Jews you helped to save?" I inquired.

"Most of the time, they came to us. But not always. Once I went as far as Amsterdam to fetch a Jew. I'll never forget that one.

"One night, in the summer of 1943, I was to meet with a couple of the boys for a planning session to secure some food-ration coupons. There was more to rescuing Jews than just placing them, you know. They had to be fed also. By then, we were running out of coupons and our main printer of phoney coupons had been shot just the week before. I should add that in those days, the deportations and killings were in full swing.

"When I got to a shed on the outside of town where we met occasionally (not very often, because we were constantly on the move just to minimize familiarity with our faces), there was a bit of excitement. There was a young woman who looked like a cow had chewed her, swallowed her, and then spat her out. She had come from Amsterdam on foot, travelling only at night.

" 'She hopped from field to field, from doorway to doorway.' One of the boys began to recount what he knew of the young woman's ordeal. 'And still it was a miracle that she made it. She is a young Jewess. She saw her older sister get abused and arrested under her very eyes as she was watching from behind the curtain of their apartment in Amsterdam. Her nephew is hidden in the city. But with a cruel turn of fate, a truck full of captive Jews turned into the street and the NSB-ers tossed her on the back of the truck. She was on her way to Westerbork, no doubt about it.'

" 'I knew somebody in Amsterdam whom I could count on,' the young woman said, continuing with her story. 'He helped me out of town and to meet up with a series of nameless people. The last link in the chain led me to you.'

" 'Is there anything that we need to attend to right now to help you? Unfortunately, your sister is beyond our reach. Only the Almighty can intercede in her favour. But is there anything that you want from us? Do you need a hiding place? Do you need to see a doctor or to contact somebody in particuliar?' I asked. I felt sorry for her, but we had business to do.

" 'I need you to rescue my nephew. He's only eight,' she said without the slightest hesitation. She could have been ordering a ham and egg sandwich and a beer, it came out so naturally from her mouth.

" 'Didn't you say that he was in a safe place in Amsterdam?' I inquired. 'Just where is the boy?'

" 'My sister left him with a...with the owner of a bawdy house in the red-light district. She bought the address from somebody she knew from work—a fellow who offered her a chance to save herself from going on a transport. He had connections in that line of business. If she was willing to prostitute herself, he told her, she would be quite safe: the Germans had the strictest orders to stay away from the Zone.

" ' "I'm not interested in saving myself that way, but can you possibly arrange for me to hide my son in the Zone with someone trustworthy?"

" 'They struck a deal: two thousand guilders for him to stick his neck out and whatever his contact would charge to keep the child. The greedy pig ended by asking for five thousand guilders a month. At that rate, we could buy about three months' safety for little Paul. But we agreed the deal must be made. Before she left with her boy, she showed me the address: "Sylvia, if anything happens to me, this is where Paul will be hidden. Memorize it." It was written on a tiny piece of paper glued to the inside of her undershirt. Now I want to rescue my nephew from the red-light district and have him brought to Friesland. I have ten thousand guilders to give to the person who brings him here and keeps him safe.'

" 'I'll go get your nephew,' I said without hesitation. 'And I don't want your ten thousand guilders, either. You'll need it more than I do. I'll find him a family who will treat him as one of their own. They are not in the habit of making money out of other people's misery. Whatever food they can't raise on their own farm, we'll provide through food stamps. Let me have the address and I'll take care of the rest. It's best that you don't come back here again. Where are you going to hide out?'

" 'I already set her up with a friend near Dokkum. She'll be on a dairy farm,' Karel told me. 'I'll arrange for a way to notify her about the success of your mission.'

"Sylvia shook hands with me like a man. 'Thank you, thank you in advance. I guess the rest is in the hands of fortune.'

" 'No, Sylvia, fortune has nothing to do with it,' I told her. 'The matter is in my hands, and I'm in the hands of the Lord.'

"Next day, in the early afternoon, I was in Amsterdam. I wasn't your typical country-bumpkin, thus the bustle of the big city didn't unnerve me. What I did find distressing, though, was the constant presence of oppression and hostility. In our town we never forgot that we were under enemy occupation, but it was, most of the time, a quiet war in IJlst. In Amsterdam, I was assaulted by the clang of military transports, the huff and puff of heavy trucks loaded down with weapons, and the sound of enemy troops marching through the city. Soldiers and militiamen paraded around, consumed by self-importance. Others just loitered, patiently stalking a victim to give meaning to their otherwise boring days. At one point I caught a glimpse of a small crowd making sport of a branded middle-aged woman. From afar, I said to myself, 'I know that silent, stubborn, desperate gait, that refusal to accept that the sky won't be blue for long. The head squared between the shoulders, sizing up the adversary just below the eyes. I know that stance. I've seen it every time I've taken a steer to the slaughterhouse.'

"I had no idea where I was. Nor did I know the direction to the red-light district. I had been in the capital only twice before — once

with my mother and once with Betty just after we got married. I had
to ask for directions. Now you should know that I have always been
terribly shy. It's quite amazing that I could participate in all sorts of
dare-devil stunts in the underground. Because above ground, I was
as brittle as a mimosa. How was I going to ask for the address of a
bordello? I felt like hiding under the pavement. I could imagine the
spiteful reply to my inquiry. 'At a time when so many Dutch men are
suffering in labour camps or hiding with their bellies to the ground,
you — big Frisian oaf—have the gall to make a long trip from up
north to the capital for *this*?' I was in quite a pickle, wasn't I?

"I shuffled my feet around just to look like I was moving. I feared
attracting unwelcome attention if I remained motionless. After about
twenty minutes, I saw my man: dressed in rags, he was hunched
over from the habit of scanning the pavement and perhaps from life's
fatigue. He *had* to know the direction to the red-light district, and he
wasn't in a position to judge me harshly.

" 'Can you be of help to me, *Mijnheer*? There's a ten-guilder note
in it for you if you can tell me how to get to this address.' I slipped
him the crumpled cigarette paper on which I had copied the address
of the bawdy house.

" 'This is the easiest ten guilders I've ever made. I know all the
whorehouses in the Zone. Unfortunately my current state of finances
prevents me from becoming a customer. I tell you, there's nothing
like poverty to guarantee a chaste life. I hope there's a reward in it
for me in the hereafter, otherwise it would be a shameful and unjust
pity. Anyway, you seem impatient. So here you go.' He gave me the
directions and continued: 'Think of me in the moment of ecstasy;
perhaps I'll feel it through the air waves.' I was purple to the roots of
my hair in my embarrassment.

"It was nearly three o'clock when I rang the bell at the address I
got from Sylvia. Madame Rosa appeared at the door in her dubious
evening splendour. A repulsive blend of sweat, smoke, and cologne
reached my nose from her direction.

" 'Well?' She snapped at me. 'Life is short, and time is money. So
in or out?'

" 'I came for the boy,' I said curtly.

" 'Which one?' she snapped at me once more, 'I have several.'
Then she sized me up from top to bottom and, as if a light bulb turned
on under her mop of greasy hair, she said, 'On second thought, I don't
have any. I don't want any filthy peasant in my house. I bring together

lovers, men and women, you understand, you rotten satyr. Get out of here you bum.'

"She went to slam the door, but I stuck my foot in the doorway. It took me a while before I caught on to what she thought I was after. If the consequences hadn't been so serious, I would have hit that whore-monger.

" 'Your dirty business is of no concern to me,' I hissed at her. 'All I care about is little Paul; his mother paid you five thousand guilders for a month, you leech. I've come to take him with me. You still have two weeks out of the month unused; keep the money. I just want the boy right now, or else I'll be back tonight with a half dozen buddies to burn this place down with you in it.'

" 'Take him, take him! I have no use for the little bastard anyway. Take the creep for all I care.'

"Two minutes later, I was walking with the boy's trusting hand in my baker's shovel-sized paw.

" 'Your Aunt Sylvia sent me to fetch you. This is no place for you. I'll take you to a good family of farmers in Friesland where fresh air, good food, and affection are waiting for you. We're going to take the train tomorrow morning back to Friesland. Then we'll take a bus. Then we'll walk a bit and you'll be home, near Harlingen. I have a false ID for you.' Then I gave him the particulars of his new identity.

"We spent the night in a comrade's place in Amsterdam. She put fugitives in transit up for the night. She was nearly one hundred years old.

"The next day, by three o'clock, Paul Krause was taking a bath in his new foster parents' home, a stone's throw from the fishing port of Harlingen.

"Call me an old softie, but the miserable lot of such a young orphan touched me so deeply that in his case I decided to bend one of the strictest rules of rescuing: place your ward and forget you ever met him or her. Otherwise, the thinking went, you risked a greater chance of discovery by the enemy. But there was an even deeper wisdom in that rule: we were confronted with so much misery, so much pain, such magnitude of fear, that if we had allowed all that suffering to get too close to us, it would have destroyed us.

"So, I dropped by the farm where he was enjoying the vigours of country life. I had unveiled the little fellow's sad story to his hosts, the Sytsmas. In spite of their hard-boiled reserve, they opened their heart to the boy as if he had been afflicted with a terminal illness.

"I was wrong, I'm delighted to say. Little Paul bounced back after the war with remarkable resilience. No one will ever know how deep are the grooves of pain in his soul, because he chose to cover them up. He became a children's physician, a healer of young bodies and souls. There are few truly happy endings, even among the rescued, but there are some.

"I remember little Paul's story better than the others, but when I think of those times, I see other faces, as well.

"Take, for example, that elderly couple—I never knew their names. They were smuggled out of the Jewish quarter of Amsterdam in caskets. Their friends staged a real memorial service for them. One of them was connected with the underground. They arrived at Vredenburg's farm on the back of a makeshift hearse. They even had death certificates, according to which they had committed suicide.

"I could have killed that Vredenburg that night. And you'll see why. When the 'remains' arrived, only he and I were present. He knew that the boxes contained live Jews; I didn't. So the dirty so-and-so says to me: 'Okay, butcher, you've had plenty of experience with stiffs, you open the caskets and we'll have to transfer them into Christian-looking coffins. These will never do. I already took care of all the paperwork; you do the rest. You handle meat every day of your life; you see only meat, where I see dead flesh. You be a good comrade, and you take care of the transfer. While you open them up, I'll go fetch the substitute caskets.'

"With that he left me in the unlit barn with those two pine boxes and a crowbar. Now, I want you to know that, in spite of being a butcher, I have always been rather squeamish when I was forced to touch a cadaver. It doesn't make sense, but it doesn't have to. Nothing is sensible about the dead. I had this clumsy fear.... I'll ask you not to laugh, either one of you, because this is very awkward for me to say. I guess you could call it a superstition, but I believe that if your skin touches the frozen flesh of the departed, you might die too. Whatever killed him may be contagious. I know: it's very primitive like most fears about the dead, but that's my belief. So there I was with the two cadavers in their coffins, my superstition, and the night that wasn't growing any younger. And we had plenty of work ahead of us.

"I took my courage in my two hands, but not without first wrapping them tightly with a couple of rags I found in the barn to protect them from the cadavers. I murmured a couple of prayers for my soul just in case I became contaminated, and I proceded with my task of opening the boxes. The soft wood and the clumsily fastened lid offered minimal resistance. In less than a minute, there they were, exposed to the darkness.

" 'Good job, butcher. I knew I could count on you.' I didn't even notice that Vredenburg was leaning against the wall of the barn behind me.

" 'Okay, Okay, just bring out the real caskets so we can finish this ghoulish job as fast as possible. I don't mind risking my life for the living, but I don't want to get shot trying to save a couple of bodies.'

" 'As you wish,' he said off the cuff. Then he approached one of the open boxes and tapped it on the side.

" 'All right, old-timers, this is the end of the line. Time to get out.'

" 'This is in very poor taste, even from a country bumpkin like you.' I was furious with him. 'I thought you were a decent Christian.' But the words froze on my lips. In the stillness of the night I could discern something like the noise of stiff muscles being stretched and joints cracking.

" 'Thank God, it's over,' I heard a tired voice sigh with relief. 'I have been in this creepy box for so long I was beginning to wonder if, in fact, I was dead or alive. Mother, are you in there?' he called over to the other casket.

" 'A bit shaken up, but I am fine. But if I don't get to empty my bladder soon, I'll be so embarrassed that I won't want to come out of this box ever again.'

"They were flippant and alive. Vredenburg was rolling in the hay, and I was still dumbfounded, not knowing whether *I* was dead or alive.

" 'I got you,' my comrade said, tapping me on the shoulder. 'We have to have a few laughs here and there or the tension will crack us wide open. All right, so this wasn't very funny for you. I owe you one, and a big one, right?' It took me a while to see any humour in the incident.

"Finding the couple a place to stay was relatively easy. They had papers and they had money—although the latter was mentioned to the potential hosts only as a last resort. As a rule, we didn't trust people who inquired about the financial aspects of their involvement. Everybody was likely to get cold feet, but the shakiest of all were those who had agreed to hide Jews for financial gain. For all we knew, the money could run out before the war ended, or their greed might be tempered with fear."

The Underground Butcher and His Wife

"Did you do any screening at all?" I asked. "And if you did, how did you go about it?"

"In fact, one of the most delicate aspects of our work was the proper screening and selection of prospective hosts. You couldn't just go door to door the way peddlers in Canada come to your door to make a pitch for your money. You had to be most cautious about whom to approach. One wrong choice and we could have found ourselves on the receiving end of a fast bullet. So the very first doors we knocked on were those of people with known religious backgrounds. The most stable were those who had made a commitment to Jesus. They were at peace, unlikely to crack under pressure. Mind you, not every religious person was able to conquer his panic at the thought of risking the safety of his own home, even if innocent lives hung in the balance. When you are faced with someone who can only picture doom while you speak to him of salvation, you know you have knocked on the wrong door. Boy, wouldn't it have been magnificent if every God-fearing Christian had agreed to take a stand on the side of the victim! I don't believe that the Nazis would have had a chance.

" 'Look,' I would tell every one of the candidates before accepting to collaborate, 'here are the facts. I'm not going to hide them from you, or minimize the serious nature of the consequences of your involvement. First of all, you *are* taking a risk that could land you in a torture chamber or in a ditch, or even worse. Most of the time you'll be alone, without help when a crisis threatens. You may not even be able to contact anyone from the underground to help you, and, if you can, you may find yourself talking to deaf ears, because the movement must go on; we can't endanger the whole rescue operation in this area for the sake of one person.' Often that was the end of it.

"That was in fact the most common scenario. In fact, our warnings were an exaggeration. The truth was that the underground was very active in helping people in case of trouble. That's why we kept moving so many people from place to place, some as many as twenty-five, thirty times. We helped them with warnings, with advice, with food coupons, with false papers; whatever we could do, we did. But there *were* times when we could do nothing. Either we had no resources at a particular moment of crisis or our comrades were also on the run. Anyone trusted with the lives of Jews had to be prepared to handle the worst on his own. If they were prepared for that, then when the crunch came, we were there. Most of the time, anyway.

"But I'm sad to say that in spite of this very rigorous screening process, there were plenty of hosts who got cold feet and wanted to stop playing. For many the association ended up leaving the sour taste of panic in their mouths at the first sight of German soldiers or at the faintest rumours of an impending raid. Towards the end of the war, when nerves were frayed because of hunger and despair, many people wanted to get out. 'I've had enough of this cat-and-mouse game, I want you to rid me of these people,' they'd say. I would try to calm them down. 'You can't just dump your guests; you've got to face the music like the rest of us. We're all scared but we all hang on. There is no other choice, there are lives at stake,' I used to tell them."

"Yak, yak, yak," Betty cut in. "You just go on and on, but you forgot to tell about how you placed the elderly couple. Your stomach is going to catch a draft if you don't keep you mouth shut for a while."

"The end of that story couldn't have been more routine. They were lovely people, educated and healthy. And in the placing of the elderly, health was a big factor. Not many people wanted to take on a sickly or debilitated Jew, old or young; it meant a lot of contact with doctors, nurses, pharmacists. Not to mention how much care and work the sickly require. And the hosts were seldom people of leisure; they were most often farmers.

"Anyway, it was one o'clock in the morning by the time we were ready to move them. Hardly an appropriate hour for dropping in on people who get up with the rooster. But the underground had its own schedule. If you had agreed to host Jews, that agreement included permission to be awakened or bothered at any time of the day or night, weekday or Sunday. This wasn't a social game; we were dealing with saving lives. So, exhausted as I was, I hopped on my bike, and by 2:30, I was back at the barn with an address for the pair.

"We borrowed two bicycles from Vredenburg and off we went. Without bicycles, I tell you, the resistance would have been altogether different, perhaps impossible. Every comrade had a surplus of 'flets' as we called them, for expected or unexpected travellers. In Amsterdam, Jews had to surrender their bikes to the authorities. I wonder how many of those bicycles found their way back to their original owners strictly by accident. After the war, the underground could have opened the country's largest used-bicycle store.

"Then there were two kids. I don't recall a great deal about them. One night a couple of months after I placed the elderly couple, I heard the familiar tap tap on the bedroom window. It was Damsma with two youngsters.

" 'These kids are a real problem,' my comrade said once they were inside. 'Someone squealed on the farmer who had them. His daughter helped them get away through the barn and took them to their doctor. He wanted no part of the kids, but he gave the girl an address. That address happened to be my father-in-law's. He had no one available so he brought them to me. I'm in exactly the same position, so I thought of you. We've got to act at once because by morning the bloodhounds will be sniffing these kids' footsteps.'

"I offered to keep them in my attic, but Damsma didn't like the idea. 'These days the walls, the pavement, the trees, everything has ears and eyes. The raids are getting more penetrating. Somebody must be bucking for a promotion at German or Dutch headquarters. We have to find a virgin for these kids.'

" 'I thought of the Mennonite minister whose name was mentioned to me as a new recruit for the first time the day before.

"Twenty minutes or so later, I knocked on the back door of the parsonnage.

" 'I've been expecting you,' the Mennonite said, to my great surprise. 'Not you specifically or tonight precisely, but I knew that once I made my offer it would be just a matter of a day or two before someone would need my hospitality.'

" 'They're contagious,' I said. I thought I should inform the good man. 'The bloodhounds are already sharpening their fangs. If you have other birdies in your barnyard, don't let them mingle.'

" 'Young man, you look tired,' he said with a faint smile on his face. 'Where these lambs are going to rest tonight no man or hound would ever find them.' "

"While he was playing second fiddle to the archangels"—Betty took over the story—"things were not quiet on the home front all the time. I had a crisis or two on my hands. Nothing life-threatening, mind you, but in those days you couldn't tell a war from a tiny skirmish.

"One day Aunt Tillie shocked me by showing up in my kitchen. She hadn't been downstairs for months. 'Betty, there's big trouble. I don't even know how to put it into words. I'm so ashamed, and so scared.'

"That's all I needed. Suddenly my stomach felt like a piece of laundry being twisted to squeeze out the last drop of water. But I couldn't show her my feelings. Somebody had to look like she was in control. To boot, Rudy was gone for a couple of days.

" 'Well, let's hear what we're up against,' I said. I knew I sounded put out. And she picked up on my exasperation.

" 'Believe me, Betty, I wouldn't bother you if it weren't a major problem. I have no one to speak to about this. If I mention it to Ben, he'll go berserk.'

" 'Don't worry about me.' I tried hard to sound charitable. 'I'll be fine. I'm almost as tough as the meat my husband sells.'

" 'You call us Aunt and Uncle. But Ben is only forty-seven and I'm only forty-three. We're still young, we have...urges.... And we share a room with Wim. He has the mind of a small child but the body of a young man. Confined to the four walls, we try to be discreet. Still, I know that Wim lies awake every night and he listens. Oh, my God, it's so hard to put these things into words, even to another woman.'

" 'It's not exactly easy to hear them, either,' I replied, feeling the salty taste of nausea well up in my mouth.

" 'I have been telling Ben to refrain from intimacy for the sake of our boy. But the longer we're cooped up in our room, the more amorous he seems to become. He promises each time, but a day or so later, he begins to press me to give in to his advances and I always do, partly because I think he'd make more noise if I didn't, and partly because I, too, am weak. And Wim's glands are working overtime...

" 'Last Thursday night, I was awakened by a warm breath on my face. In my semi-conscious state, I took it for granted that it was Ben. But then a second later, I realized that I could feel my husband lying against my back. I wanted to bolt out of bed, but I was held down gently but firmly. Betty, it was my own son—he was holding me down. I could feel his breath against my breasts. Imagine! If I made a scene of it, Ben would have killed all three of us. And I certainly couldn't allow Wim to continue with his assault on his own mother. When his hand began to creep down to my belly, I just had to stop him.

" ' "Wim, you're having a nightmare," I said out loud. "Everything is all right. Go back to sleep, dear." Ben woke up, asking if everything was under control.

" ' "Wim had a bad dream," I told him, "and he crawled into bed with us." I escorted my son back to his own bed. Betty, that boy was sound asleep. The next morning I asked him if anything remarkable had happened during the night. He had no recollection of anything.

" 'But the following nights, the same thing happened again and again. Ben decided to tie the boy to his bed. But he makes horrible noises so we have to untie him. As soon as we go to sleep again, he starts his advances again. Last night he bit my breast while I was asleep. I woke up with a scream. What am I going to do, Betty? You've got to help us, because this could be the end of us. I have refused Ben's pressure for over a week with the excuse of feminine problems. But he won't believe me for ever. What am I going to do?'

"I just sat there with my mouth open, my insides in a state of siege, holding onto the edge of the wooden stool, digging my nails into the wood to prevent myself from screaming in horror. That night, I gave into hatred. I hated this sick family; I hated my husband for getting us involved; I hated the Germans, the Dutch; I even hated God. Most of all, I hated myself for not being able to stand up and say: enough. I wanted Rudy to relocate them. I didn't want to put up with this madness anymore. I couldn't live with them, but I couldn't live with throwing them out, either.

" 'This is above my head, Aunt Tillie.' I tried to pull myself together. 'I really pity your family. But you'll have to wait until Rudy comes home tomorrow night. He'll find some solution. Until then, Wim should sleep on the floor in the little room next door.'

"When Rudy came home, before he could even sit down, it all gushed forth. The next day he came home with a powder. We put a teaspoon of it in the boy's tea and it dulled his overactive glands.

"The night I was going to bring up the subject of relocating our guests, Rudy brought home another Jewish woman.

" 'This is Tony. She has no place to go. It's either us or the camps.' By then we knew everything about the transports. 'Some choice,' I thought. 'I go insane or I send someone to her death.' "

"So much of this is news to me, Betty." Rudy was profoundly moved. "I knew that the workload was stiff, but I also had confidence in the strength of your faith. I was so caught up in everything else, and you told me so little. You wanted to spare me, I'm sure. For nearly three years, only my body went home to visit; my mind was constantly going clickety-click. Even in my dreams, I was devising new tricks, new strategies, new hiding places. If I only knew then.... Well, who am I kidding? If you had told me then, I would have talked you out of your misery. I was obsessed with the rescue work. It was so selfish of me. I don't even dare to ask for your forgiveness.

Quiet Heroes

"You are right, though, it *was* inspiring to know that day after day I drew a small measure of blood from the monster. But that was only a bonus, the reward for a job well done. That certainly wasn't my aim. In the meantime, you had to dispose of their refuse, to tolerate their presence, to solve their problems and—to top it all off—you couldn't even count on me. As for relocating our guests, I would have convinced you to go on enduring them. There were no open doors. That's why I had to bring Tony home. Her brother had been caught in a raid. There was no doubt that they were going to try to get out of him her whereabouts.

"The darnedest thing about this underground work was that it snowballed. First you hid someone, then you had to procure identification papers and food coupons for him. They had to be taken by breaking into a distribution centre or by ferreting out a counterfeit artist. Then in '43, when they started rounding up our youngsters for work in Germany, our clientele swelled tremendously. I'll never forget, in one week I had to find ten places and ten ration cards. That's what I'm trying to explain so that you and our guests can understand what was responsible for the neglect of my family.

" 'I think I have gone too far,' I confided one evening in my best buddy. 'I have four Jews in hiding, all the weapons and TNT that the English dropped by parachute are stashed under my roof, and I now have a reputation of never saying no to anyone. But what am I to do? No one was willing to take that much TNT; I was the only fool.' I was scared like a deer in the middle of a circle of hunters. But there was no way out. And I could tell that to my buddy, but I couldn't tell it to my wife."

"You're quite right," Betty cut in, "you would have gotten little sympathy from me in those days." Betty's face was dark with memories. "I would have offered you one solution: get out of the movement and return to a normal life. I would have even settled for allowing the Hembergers to stay. But when Tony came I was fed up. I didn't have the right stuff to do a saint's job. But my back was to the wall. I had to learn to cope better, and with some help around the house, I could fight off my bad feelings. And I knew you. If you said that there was no other solution, I took your word as gospel. You had never lied to me, and that was good enough. I only wished you would have attended to some of the practical details. And I told you that much.

The Underground Butcher and His Wife

" 'Tony looks Frisian,' you said. 'She'll blend in like milk into coffee. She'll be of great help to you, even in the store, since she doesn't have to be invisible.'

" 'I speak German like a native. I can be of help with your German customers,' she said. She immediately won my heart. She assessed what needed to be done and plunged into doing it without being told, 'do this, do that'. She was a warm breeze on a cold spring day. Sure enough, German boys would come into the shop to buy something and she would chat up a storm with them. No one ever suspected that she was Jewish. At times, she accompanied me into town, if I had to go out on a visit or to buy something. We claimed that she was a friend of my cousin's from Amsterdam. She fit in perfectly. We rebaptized her 'Rita' because that's what her fake ID said.

"In 1944, I was expecting again. Sometimes I wonder how—I saw so little of this gentleman. Rita took over the store when I rested. More and more often Rudy was spending even the days with the underground; he came home as a visiting ghost. In fact, there was this one rabid NSB-er in our neighbourhood who would come into the shop and try to weasel information out of Rita about the butcher's whereabouts. But she was smart.

" 'The boss is out but he'll be back later; if you tell me what you need, I'll have him prepare it for you so when you return it will be waiting.' Now and then he would leave an order that I would fix up for him. So when he came back, his order was always ready, even when he came sooner than we had agreed. He wasn't going to pull a fast one on Rita.

"It was Rita's idea that we should have a hiding place since we had heard that raids were becoming more frequent in the area. The Germans and the NSB knew that our region was perfect for hiding fugitives. 'Without a hiding place, we may all be sitting ducks,' she insisted. When Rudy came home, she spoke to him about it. He fully agreed with her.

"What foresight! About three weeks after the hiding place was inaugurated, we had several raids in rapid succession. One time, Rudy was home, on one of his rare appearances. He and Wim were cleaning guns in the tiny room with the stove. Suddenly, we heard loud banging on the front door. I peeked downstairs from the second-floor landing and I could see several men in uniform. My heart stopped beating.

" 'The Germans!' I exclaimed. I thought I was going to pass out.

Quiet Heroes

" 'I'll go to stall them,' Rita volunteered. She went to open the door. We didn't move a muscle upstairs. The only thing that prevented us from all getting caught was Rita's cunning. How bizarre when you come to think of it: she was the illegal Jew hiding in our home and she was the one protecting us, her Christian hosts. Well, the war had the world on its head; nothing really made sense the way you'd expect.

"Rita did a splendid job. First, we heard some unfriendly sounds, then some laughter and then lots of levity. And then the door slammed behind them.

" 'They forgot that there is another war going on, one that they'll never win,' she said when she joined us upstairs. 'The war between the sexes. A well-aimed wink can still disarm the bravest soldier. These boys hadn't had a woman flirt with them in German for a long time. They even forgot the reason for their visit. One of them promised to come back for me to take me out for a stroll along the canal. I said, "I won't be here later. I'll have some Jews to hide, weapons to pick up, trains to sabotage; the work of the underground is never done." And I winked at him. They thought it was a great joke. He asked me for a guided tour of the underground. I told him only after he had been buried. They just loved it. What can I say, the best strategy with them is to tell them the truth. It sounds so absurd when you say it, especially in the Swabian dialect, that they have no alternative but to take it as a big joke.'

" 'Rita, you know too much to tease them that way.' Rudy was furious and he let her know it. 'You've got to watch yourself, because one of these days you're going to be unmasked for what you are. You make a fool out of them, and we may end up paying for it with our lives. You joke around about the underground and they may think it's a good laugh. But when they tell somebody else about this cute girl who fed them these funny lines about this and that, that person may take your careless words seriously. And then the whole thing will blow up. Next time, I'll move you to a farm where you can't play your little games.' She didn't like to be told off in front of everybody, especially when she was so proud of herself.

"A couple of days later, a friend from the Town Hall came to see us. 'This is not a social occasion. I saw your name on a list of places to be searched tomorrow. Be prepared my friends.' Uncle Ben rolled the piano slightly off to one side so everyone could climb in. Rita pushed it back, placing a cigar box on top of the piano. It was full of money. We had prepared it as bait to distract the raiders, should their curiosity attract them to the piano.

"They found nothing. A couple of the local boys accompanying the Germans made it all the way to the piano. They found the slightly open old cigar box with the money. They helped themselves to a couple of hundred guilders. Like kids who reach into the cookie jar secretly, they disappeared with their bounty as fast as they could. Rita's plan worked down to the last detail. But some of the credit goes to the Lord, because this was a miracle. Look, the raiding party consisted of about ten rascals. They searched every nook and cranny of the house. With all the weapons and TNT in the attic and four Jews in the house, they left empty-handed. Then they went next door. There they found an old radio and for that they ripped the place apart. Think what you want, but I see the Lord's hand in our good fortune."

"How could we not attribute some of the things that happened to us to divine providence?" asked Rudy. "How else to explain that ordinary folks like us came up with schemes and solutions for which one would have required a keenly trained mind? I tell you a story so that you see what I mean. One night, early in 1945, we learned that a whole warehouse full of cheese was going to be shipped to Germany. You might have heard of the great famine of '45. It came to be precisely because all our food was shipped to Germany.

"We weren't about to allow this blatant robbery to take place. But how to prevent it? After a lot of crazy schemes, each less feasible than the last, I saw the light, *and I mean exactly that*! It must have been about three o'clock in the morning and I was half asleep. My eyes were closed when a bright light appeared on the inside of my eyelids: I saw the image of a German officer. I was no longer sleepy, that's for sure. And then it came to me.

" 'I've got it, boys. This is it!' No one lifted an eyebrow: we'd heard similar outbursts in the course of the past night dozens of times.

" 'But this *is* the winner. All we need is a friend among the local Germans. The rest is as easy as taking a piece of cheese from a child.'

" 'That's all? Maybe we should put in a call to the SS to send us a traitor at once,' one of the boys quipped. My idea was not taken seriously at all.

" 'I know a German,' I ventured with self-assured bravado. I told them the story of the German who prayed with me in my house. 'If he were around, he would help us. There must be others like him. Come on boys, give it a chance. We must find someone who'll help.'

No one was laughing any more; they were trying to conjure up the portrait of a decent German.

" 'I don't know if he'd do it,' one of them said hesitantly. 'There is this fellow who has been sniffing around my sister for quite some time. She tells me that this guy is quite clean and that he's fed up with his country's treatment of its own soldiers. Well, if my sister is willing to play along with us, she might convince him to help us, but that's a lot of *ifs*.'

"Then I told them the rest of my plan. But may I turn into a pillar of salt if I had thought it through even once before. The words came to me as if a secret voice were prompting me. And I believe that's exactly how it happened.

" 'But what if the scheme doesn't work?' one of the not-so-convinced comrades interjected.

" 'It will work,' I said firmly. I had faith in the outcome, otherwise why would I have received that message?

"The next morning, around ten o'clock a young girl came by. 'My sister's friend will pay you a visit this evening. She doesn't know when exactly, but you should wait for him, he will come for sure.'

"At nine o'clock in the evening a truck stopped in front of our house. Seconds later, we heard an impatient banging on the door. 'Are these guests or is this a raid?' Betty whispered to me. Our Jewish guests had already taken their positions in the hiding place—including Rita.

"I turned off the lights in keeping with the black-out regulations. Then I opened the door. There were three Germans standing there, fully armed. They pushed their way in past me. They were led by a lieutenant.

" 'Shut the door.' I heard the crisp command and I obeyed it.

" 'We've got a truckload of cheese,' one of the Germans informed me in Frisian. Boy was I shocked! It turned out that the young officer and one of the foot soldiers were from the underground and the other soldier was the German sweetheart of my comrade's sister. Somehow he put his hands on the two disguises and a requisition order. They took the truck to the warehouse and filled it with cheese, with the supposed intention of taking it to the Fatherland. Instead, it was sitting in front of my butcher shop.

" 'Now you have lots of cheese and a runaway German soldier,' our new ally informed us in broken Dutch. 'I can't show my face any more, because I'll be kaput.' He didn't look or sound heartbroken.

"'Obviously, we can't unload the cheese in front of the whole neighbourhood. But I know someone who'll take care of it. I'll put on my coat and you guys make believe that you're taking me away. Otherwise, if someone sees me all chummy with the Wehrmacht, I could be in big trouble. As for you, Fritz, welcome aboard.' And I shook the German's hand.

"The incident ended as perfectly as a summer sunset over the North Sea.

"We started to think the war would last for ever. Our numbers were shrinking, thanks to treason, exhaustion, and the apathy of the masses. I certainly could no longer keep up with the diabolic tempo. By the beginning of 1945, I just about gave up on going home. It was a rare treat when I could afford a moment with my family. Betty was running the shop as well as she could. Mind you, there was so little meat that the additional chore didn't overtax her. Even sleeping only a couple of hours a night, I still needed another ten hours to the day, and even that wouldn't have sufficed. Nothing would have, short of a bunch of new comrades to relieve us.

"One night I fell asleep while riding my bicycle and nearly killed myself. That brought home the message: something had to give. I decided to take on subalterns—to decentralize, so to speak. I took inventory of the size and nature of my resources. I considered what factors worked against me and what ones helped me, and I decided to set up a network of lieutenants, runners, couriers, liaison men, infiltrators, escorts. I definitely had to fade into the background. In spite of all the precautions, my face had been overexposed. I had become one of the nerve centres of an invisible creature, and my assistants had become its hands."

"What did that mean in practical terms?" I asked him.

"Well, as I said, people didn't just show up at your door and ask you to hide them," Rudy explained. "There were regular channels, like underground rivers, in whose beds ran the blood of refugees. And for them those last few months took the shape of a slalom race: they zig-zagged through a jagged course studded with NSB-ers. There was hardly a day when we would not lose a comrade or two. But with our new organization, we improved our rescue activities while decreasing our chances of fatalities. The most important tasks focused on monitoring the lifelines that linked the hunted to us. One would monitor our radio contacts with the south, telling us in code of the imminent arrival of new exotic birds. Another would keep his

Quiet Heroes

ears to the ground to pick up whispered names and places where people had to be met and dropped off. A third would haunt the halls of public offices where rumours could be picked up by a trained ear, telling of unspoken dangers. Each came back with a different piece of the puzzle which, when put together, meant safety and survival for another fugitive."

"Oh yes, I remember his subalterns," Betty commented playfully. "I remember one night during the last winter of the war Rudy and one of his couriers came home unexpectedly to hide another load of ammunition. There was no room on our property any more, so what did they do? They dug out a bush on our neighbour's land and sank the crate in there and replanted the bush. The Lord must really love him, because the neighbour didn't stir."

"That must have been quite close to the end of the war," I remarked.

"Quite so," Betty replied, "because soon after, he came home one night quite late and proceeded to dig up his crate of ammunition. It was a slippery Sunday morning. Rudy wanted to let me know that there was a chance that we would be liberated later on that day. He made his way to our bedroom window in his clay-covered boots. When he tried to attract my attention by the window, he slipped in his wet boots and flew head first through the glass. It sounded like a bomb had hit the house. I was sure the fright was going to make me go into labour. But it didn't. Rita came dashing into my room to see what on earth had happened. When she saw my husband half in the window and half out, covered in mud and clay, she burst out laughing. That was the first genuine laughter I had heard in years—you know, the kind that explodes inside of you from your belly all the way up to the top of your head.

" 'Instead of splitting a gut, come out and help me quickly,' he called out grouchily to Rita. 'I dropped some ammo on the ground. Come pick it up before somebody else comes around and finds it. Hurry up, for goodness sake.'

"You must understand. Rudy takes himself very seriously when he has a mission. For him, there was nothing laughable about his accident."

"Women don't take manly commitments seriously," Rudy came to his own rescue in earnest. "And this was as serious as they come. I had my entire back yard planted with ammo under a large patch of onions. I even had that crate under my neighbour's bush. I thought in those last days we might lend a hand to the Canadians in flushing out the rats. I came home to dig up the ammo. I also had a lot of rifles to give to the boys, even a couple of machine guns. Two couriers were with me to take that materiel to where it could be distributed. By the time I was all done in the yard, it was 6:00 a.m. I thought Betty would like to hear the good news about being liberated on the Lord's day. I didn't expect to scare her. 'The war isn't over yet, but by tonight there will be freedom,' I told her.

"We still had to be cautious, however, because the enemy was not going to surrender easily. And I hadn't slept for three nights. It was so tempting to just climb into my warm bed next to my wife, but that had to wait. So, instead, I went to sleep at another woman's house. No need to raise your eyebrows; I had a regular hiding place at an elderly widow's house. So I decided to stretch out for a couple of hours.

"But just as I got off my bicycle, whom do I see about five metres from me? That no-good NSB-er, the one who kept coming to my shop when I wasn't around. I knew that he carried a gun. And I had no weapon with me at all.

" 'Well, if it isn't the butcher,' he said sarcastically. 'Are you bringing the widow a piece of illegal pork or picking up an illegal Jewish pig?'

"I didn't like his tone. He was inching his way closer to me. I had a large key in my pocket which had a long shaft, like the barrel of a gun. I reached into my pocket and pointed the key tautly against my pants to intimate that I was ready to shoot before he could reach for his weapon. The NSB-er wasn't about to take a chance. He turned around, got on his bike, and he shouted at me: 'I'll get you, butcher, before the war's over. I'll even the score with you—Jew-loving pig.' I never saw him again.

"I fell on the bed in my hiding place. All I wanted was two hours of rest.

" 'Rudy, wake up,' the widow called out. 'It's eight o'clock in the evening.'

" 'Eight o'clock? How could you do that to me?' I jumped to my feet, ready to bite her head off. 'I had commitments, and the guys were counting on me.'

" 'Not any more, my boy. We're free. The Canadians are in town. Go home and kiss your family. This is the moment we have all been waiting for.'

"What can I say? Even now I can't find words for the feeling of freedom that took hold of us that Sunday in April 1945. We were jumping up and down in the street; we laughed, we cried, we kissed, we slapped each other and the liberators on the back. I tell you, all the pent-up emotions of five years erupted like lava from a volcano. There were so many feelings; no matter what we did, we just couldn't calm down. Those Canadian boys looked tired, but their dirty faces beamed with pride, knowing that they brought freedom and life to so many people."

"What memories do you have of that day, Betty?" Vicki asked our hostess.

"When I saw the first Canadians through the shop window"—tears glistened in Betty's eyes as she recalled that glorious moment—"I yelled from the bottom of the stairs (because I was in my ninth month), 'Outside, everybody outside. You're alive and free. The Canadians are here.' They piled down the stairs as fast as their feet would carry them. They hugged and huddled. I'll never forget those three faces crushed against one another in a perfect circle as they wept their relief and joy. I know what freedom meant for me, but I can only imagine what they felt as they turned their backs on years of humiliation and anguish.

"The Hembergers left the next day to return to their home and to look for their other son. Tony—there was no more reason to call her Rita—proved herself to be a loving friend to me. I don't know if we mentioned that she had been a nurse in Naarden before the war. Well, she was, and she intended to return to her town and to her position at the hospital—but not before seeing me through my last month of pregnancy. So she stayed more than three weeks longer than she had to. And don't think she wasn't eager to get going: she had a twelve-year-old child whom she hadn't seen for nearly three years.

" 'You have been my sole support all this time, Betty. I won't leave you until we deliver your baby. I waited for years to see my little girl. I can survive a few weeks longer, especially since she is no longer in danger.'

"I admired her so much for her generosity. You see, here was a Jewish woman who in my eyes acted like a perfect Christian and we know how many Christians acted in a God-forsaking manner. It just shows you that boundaries between Christians and Jews are not drawn through the churches and temples. They go right through our soul.

"So she stayed and helped me bring Annemarie into the world. And I was very proud of my friend's loyalty. Especially because loyalty was a scarce commodity in those days. Suddenly, I found myself surrounded with friends who hadn't given me the time of day for five years. Still, it was a warm experience to hear and see people who no longer could harm you."

"Not so fast," Rudy interrupted glumly. There was indictment in those three short words. "There were those who tried to blacken my name because of the bogus German operation. Remember the truckload of cheese? Well, some neighbours saw the truck. Did they ask me about it? Did they try to find out what it was all about? No, they denounced me anonymously, in the most cowardly way. And their words were given the same credibility as those of my comrades who vouched for my record! Then, there were those who loudly beat their chests with phoney pride about all the underground work they did, all the lives they saved. I can guarantee you that those of us who were in the thick of things would have known about anyone who was involved in resistance in IJlst and its surroundings. Well—they kissed the boots of the Germans without shame and without conviction, so why wouldn't they do the same with the Allies and the new regime? And so many managed to dazzle our new administrators with their hypocritical fireworks. It made me sick to my stomach. I no longer felt at home in IJlst. I needed to cleanse myself of all the dirt those bastards heaved in the air, because it kept falling back upon my head.

"What can I say? After the waves of joy, I quietly slipped into a sort of depression. I couldn't see or feel clearly any longer. I didn't know what was right. All I knew was what didn't feel right. I began to feel more and more like a pig wallowing in infected mud. The hostilities might have been ended but there was no trace of peace in my soul.

"I sold the shop in an attempt to put the past five years behind me. I didn't know where to go. And I didn't really care. It was a reckless move for a father of four, but I had to loosen the grip of my bitter disgust.

"We thought about it a lot. Finally, Betty and I agreed that, if we were so unhappy in our country, we must leave it behind and start over somewhere else. But you know what? It took me all these years to realize that all my life I was chasing a rainbow that only I could see. There is no such thing as a just, human world. It's not possible to bring about and to preserve it against corruption—not in Holland, not in Canada, not in Israel. But I needed to spend most of my long life to discover this simple truth. That's why we thought that things could be radically different in Canada."

"Why Canada?" I asked him.

"Because I was blinded by a romantic mirage. The Canadians had crossed the ocean to free an oppressed country. That appealed to me. It was very naive of me, naturally. I focused in on one steer without noticing that it was standing in the middle of large herd. How could any one country be that different from any other? There is good *and* bad everywhere."

"What was it like leaving Holland?" Vicki turned to Betty.

"We decided to leave our country," Betty replied, "but there was no way to get going. You had to be a farmer or a tradesman to emigrate, because the prospects were dim in war-torn Holland. The economy was limping just as badly as I do these days. And it looked like it had about as much chance of recovering as I have with my decrepit knee. But our Jewish friends, the Hembergers, came to our rescue. Remember we told you that in addition to Wim they had another son? Well, the family who hid Abraham had already resettled in Canada. Uncle Ben sent a letter to them asking them to sponsor us. Those people agreed to sponsor us, and here we are."

"Did you derive any wisdom from your wartime experiences?" I asked first looking at Rudy, then at Betty.

"My wisdom can be summed up in a very few inexpensive words." Rudy had the answer on the tip of his tongue, as if he had been expecting the question. "If you want to save your life, you will have to lose it.

"If you are prepared to lose your life for somebody else, then you'll save yourself: physically and spiritually. Either way, you have to face the consequences of your choice. We have done just that, Betty and I. We thought it over, and we made a decision. We never stopped shaking in our boots, but we also knew that the road we chose allowed for no return. And what we accomplished is a very small measure of success. There is no heroism in carrying out actions for which your faith has prepared you all your life."

"If what you did was not heroic, then can you give us an example of what you consider heroic?" Vicki asked our host.

"Do you want me to tell you what heroism is about? I'll tell you one final story.

The Underground Butcher and His Wife

"When I was doing my military service, there was a fellow who was giving instructions to us about the use of weapons. One day, he was demonstrating the use of a grenade—you know, the kind with a pin in it. He made a terrible oversight: he forgot to check if the grenade was 'on system' before he pulled the pin. He pulled the pin and let the lever go when all of a sudden, he discovered his terrible mistake. He looked out the window to see if he could throw it outside. But there was a company right underneath the window. You know what he did? He turned his back to us fellows in the room and he pushed that damn thing against his stomach and he detonated the grenade to shield us from its destruction.

"That's a hero. He offered his life in order to save the others.

"What did we do that could compare to that? Nothing, absolutely nothing."

Over a year has passed since I met the de Vries. We stayed in contact. Betty is now in a wheelchair. She never had the much-needed surgery. There were too many hurdles to overcome for her and, this time, Rudy could be of no assistance: he suffered two heart attacks in six months, which rendered him debilitated and vulnerable. He also grew anxious to see his story published—not for glory or praise: in fact, he was most adamant about using fictitious names. "When I begin something I like to see how it turns out. But if I'm not around when the book comes out, good luck with it."

But Rudy is not about to lie down and die. In a few weeks he is off to visit Israel, thanks to the generosity of one of the Jews he rescued. When I asked him if he was physically up to this long trip, he replied: "Of course I am. And if I happen to die, I couldn't have picked a better place to meet my Maker than the Holy Land."

Defiant Outsiders:
Albert and Wilma Dijkstra

The Dijkstras' home was not easy to find. Their tiny community is nestled in the landscape of rural Ontario, without much regard for the convenience of a hesitant visitor from the city. To be sure, we left Toronto armed with what we believed to be adequate directions. The rustic landmarks that loomed as large as the lake itself for the Dijkstras failed to reveal themselves to Vicki and me on more than one occasion. For us, one dirt road was like another, and an unmarked county line evoked only doubt and concern about arriving on time.

We were an hour late when I parked my car on the Dijkstras' property. We were surrounded with nature rampant; our feet trampled grass that had never been fussed over, and generations of weeds rebelliously co-existed with other vegetation. We were, to say the least, surprised. According to our information, the Dijkstras were gardeners and landscape architects. As such, I imagined a home surrounded by carefully placed flowers. That our hosts were Dutch added to the picture I had in my mind that their residence would be in meticulous order.

"You're more than an hour late, I'm sorry to say," an angular woman, grey and brown in appearance, stood at the entrance of a greenhouse I hadn't even noticed before. "It's not that punctuality is all that important, but there is a big party at the hotel today and I'm doing all the flower arrangements."

Vicki and I muttered excuses about getting lost, but we quickly desisted. Our hostess was already heading towards the house. What difference could our explanations make anyway? She had business that couldn't wait to attend to. Anything we could have said would have slowed her down.

"I was watching the two of you through the window," the man of the house said, with a twinkle in his clear blue eyes, after the introductions. "I bet you were saying to yourselves, 'My, what a blooming mess. How can gardeners let their yard go to seed like this?' Am I right?"

"To tell you the truth, I was wondering...." Vicki started to say.

"You can stop wondering," Albert Dijkstra interrupted her with a fatherly tone in his voice. He seemed to enjoy his own coyness. "One man's messy, neglected yard is another man's expression of respect for nature's way. Weeds have as much right to live as grass. So Wilma and I just let them fight it out without taking sides. It looks like the weeds are putting on a stronger show. But it's all part of a higher order than manicuring lawns and colour co-ordinating flower beds. Now, if you want to take a look in the greenhouse, you'll see an entirely different world. There our plants are kept with the same care we would give to our children. That's business; we must deliver the healthiest plants and flowers we can to our customers. That's what they pay for, after all."

"I don't mean to be rude," his wife joined us in the spacious living room, "but we should get down to business. I simply can't be late at the hotel."

We all settled into over-stuffed armchairs. A quick survey of the room gave evidence that we were being received in a real "living" room. Nothing seemed to have been accorded a place, and yet everything seemed to belong where it was.

"Perhaps, Mr. and Mrs. Dijkstra, we could begin with you telling us about what stands out the most vividly in your memory about your rescue activities," I proposed as I saw Vicki's finger push the "record" button.

"I'd like to preface the story of our rescue activities with a few facts," Mr. Dijkstra replied. "They'll help you understand who we are and what we did. And my wife's name is Wilma and people call me Albert."

With a nod, I invited him to proceed as he wished.

"My father was an alcoholic. As such, as a child, the first thing I had to learn was to go without—without security, without direction, without love. But perhaps the worst was to swallow with my daily bread the fact that violence was always just around the corner. Then later there came the day when I reached a crossroad. 'Do I stay on the familiar track of hopeless questions, or do I start making decisions about how to go on?' I took the latter path."

He was gazing out his lakeside cottage window, but his eyes were not focused on the landscape. Rather, they scanned the soundless surface of the water — one of his two loyal companions and advisers, the other being Wilma, his wife of forty-five years.

"After alcohol played havoc with my childhood, I was relieved to find that inner peace was still available to me. I just had to recognize it and be hospitable to it. You look mystified. I'm referring to nature, of course.

"When I saw puzzlement on your faces, I realized that I should tell you something right now. My wife and I, we don't believe in words; we believe in actions. We have never stopped to sort out our life philosophy. Somehow we always knew what to do. Even when we weren't sure, we just took a chance and jumped."

"Oh, it's certainly not because we're so smart." Wilma's words joined us softly, like a cat entering a room full of people. "We just take our clues from nature. And the most basic wisdom that flows from nature to man is that life is sacred. Every life taken before its natural term is a criminal, shameful waste."

"What we learn from nature," Albert continued, "is an economical treatment of life. Nature spares from extinction all living creatures except those whose sacrifice is essential for the maintenance of balance and harmony. Spoiling this grandiose plan is the handiwork of man, the social creature. Boy, you're making me into a regular blabber-mouth." Albert winked at Wilma. "Whatever is good in man and society comes from nature, and what is evil is his own invention. You'd better get this straight because without this the rest will make no sense to you."

"Just one more thing before we get down to the nitty-gritty." Albert sounded serious now and perhaps a shade embarrassed. "We'll open for you the private storybook of our lives. You'll read in it some details that will appeal to you because people nowadays seem to be impressed by simple acts of decency. I want to ask you to be very cautious with our story. We don't think that our involvement in the rescue operations merits any attention. But you claim that stories like ours possibly can help future generations. So, why not? But, please, choose your words carefully. I'm referring mostly to words of flattery and praise. Those don't belong in our mouths.

"Now, I've said more than a mouthful. I'll let the wife do what comes naturally to women. Besides, she knows more than I do, because the lion's share of the work and the risk fell on her back."

Wilma was fidgety and a faint blush glowed on her cheeks.

"Well, I'll try to put it in modern terms. Let's say that as a child your brain is a computer and it is fed facts, day after day. As you keep growing, more and more facts are put into the computer, then one day, as an adult, along comes 1942 and you learn that your Jewish friends are in danger and need a place to hide. Things couldn't be simpler for you. You push the right button of the computer and out comes the clear answer: 'Yes.' 'Sure.' There were no 'ifs' or 'buts' in our computer, just 'Yes'. Now I'll translate this into our language, the language of the soil; we were in the right place at the right time. You could say we were very fortunate to be where we were needed."

"You forgot about Albert Schweitzer," Albert prompted his wife, "and Gandhi, and the Youth Organization."

"I'll get to that, don't worry." She was composed again. "We're now in 1942, towards the end of August, minding our own business. We had been struggling for a kind of survival ourselves. I used to be a psychiatric nurse at Het Apeldoornse Bosch. Have you heard of it? No? Well, it was the largest Jewish mental hospital in Europe, with over one thousand beds. When we married in the spring of 1940, just a couple of months before the German occupation, Albert was in bad need of help with his organic farming. We had a piece of land just a stone's throw from the hospital. I quit my profession to give him a hand. Cultivating our land in this peculiar way, and not being from Apeldoorn didn't exactly establish us as household words in the area. To ease our burden, we took in a lodger, a retired nurse from the hospital. And we worked and we worked and we worked. Mind you, we were never happier than in those early days. Every day was a challenge.

"We were so busy that we couldn't even take time to think about the occupation of Holland. We had a radio; we knew what was going on; we heard the low rumble in the sky as the warplanes rushed towards Rotterdam. We even saw the Germans march by our own front door, a mere two months after we were married. Our farm was right on the main road from the border through Winterswijk and Zutphen. None of that compelled us to put down our tools and do something about the occupation.

"In those days, we wanted no involvement with any aspect of the war effort. Albert and I had both been active in the pacifist movement from as early on as our teenage years. So for us it made no difference on whose side one fought—it was still a matter of killing. We didn't want to hurt Germans any more than we wanted to be hurt by them. Perhaps we were not good patriots, but our concern has always been with human life and not to whom it belongs."

"So how did you get involved with hiding Jews?" I asked.

"Late in August 1942, we received an unexpected visit from a man called Grootendorst. He had come from Albert's hometown, Winschoten, with bad news.

" 'Our Jewish friends are in trouble. They need good hiding places fast. I don't know if you have been following what Hitler's boys have been doing to the Jews in Germany.'

" 'Well, we have not kept abreast with everything,' Albert admitted. 'We know that they had been treated rather roughly; we heard, of course, of *Kristallnacht*, but not much more....'

" 'Well, a lot has happened since *Kristallnacht*. That was almost four years ago. That was mob violence. Now, they are on a well-organized campaign, carried out with efficiency, order, and detachment.

" 'In Holland, the hunt for Jews has been officially open for over a year. You know how it is: if the original is bad, the imitation is even worse. We fear for our Jewish population. We've got to act fast. In our small town, we have only four Jews. Do you remember any of them, Albert?'

" 'I certainly remember Dr. Hellman and his wife,' Albert replied.

" 'Excellent. Can you find a place for them here, or with another farmer? Their chances are far better on a farm than in town.'

" 'Send them to us,' Albert answered without hesitating, without consulting with me, even with his eyes. He knew what my answer would be.

" 'Just one thing, though,' Albert said, blushing like a bride. 'We've just started out in life doing strange things to our produce in a strange neck of the woods. Naturally we're as poor as church mice. Our home is open to the doctor and his wife, but we would need some financial assistance with their keep. How about eighty guilders a month?' "

"What did that buy in those days?" Vicki asked.

"Eighty guilders would buy, on the black market, a twenty-kilogram bag of potatoes or half a kilo of butter. Anyway, two days later, in the evening, the elderly couple appeared at our door to settle into our lives for the next thirty months.

"When I think back, I don't really know how we managed. We were not at all prepared for underground work. We had no idea what we were getting into. For one thing, who was to know how long the war would last? And with the Germans, it was impossible to know what they would cook up next. As they grew more threatening we had to rise to the occasion and become more clever. But in the meantime, we did an awful lot of silly things.

"The day after the doctor and his wife arrived, we built a fence around the house and the barn. None of our neighbours did that. What a terrific way to signal to one and all that the Dijkstras had something to hide. Then we hung a large cow bell on the front gate to alert us if someone had entered the property. Because we were outsiders, we hardly ever had visitors. And when someone did come, we had two very loud dogs who made so much noise that we couldn't even hear the bell over their yapping. The bell was just another eye-catcher.

"One thing that we did decide, however, even before the couple arrived, was that we weren't going to tell anyone about who was living upstairs. Then we decided to avoid having visitors as long as we were hiding Jewish people in our home. But one day, Albert's father wrote that he wanted to come for a visit. He hadn't seen us since our wedding in 1940; how could we tell him not to come? We stalled him with clumsy excuses, but one day he just showed up. The Hellmans were his friends, and yet he didn't know that they were hiding on our second floor.

"The dogs made their usual ruckus, so Albert and I went to meet him along the little path between the gate and the house. 'You go upstairs, Father. There's a little surprise waiting for you.' You should have seen him; he looked as if he had seen a ghost when he was nose to nose with his friends who had disappeared from Winschoten without a word, without a trace.

"Our everyday life changed very little with the doctor and his wife in the house. We didn't get into all sorts of gymnastics, like hiding beds and dragging them out again. After the initial few mistakes, we became quite fatalistic: 'If your number is up, it's up. And if it isn't up, why bother anyway?' Albert used to say those days. Later on he, too, adapted his tune to the music of the day. 'Maybe you can't cheat destiny, but perhaps you can cheat the Germans.' Well, we'll get to that soon.

"Fortunately, our guests were very considerate. They fit into their displaced existence with the ease of a spade slipping into moist soil."

"What was life like for them?" I asked Wilma.

"I couldn't tell you what it was like for them to be cooped up in that room like chickens. To a great extent they had become dependent on us. How can an adult relearn how to lean on someone else for the basic necessities and decisions of everyday life? He was a doctor and was used to having people come to him for help. And his wife used to be a homemaker. How was she to make herself useful, to feel vital and healthy? I don't know, because they spared us the burden of their anguish. Had I been in their place, I wouldn't have been able to cope. I'm sure of that. They had to have some secret resource which allowed them to be pleasant and unassuming, never unreasonable or intrusive.

"But just as I knew nothing of their plight, I don't think they ever realized what hardships we had to face. Not only did we have to make do at home, but we also had to navigate in the troubled waters of the outside world."

"What did that mean in concrete terms?" I asked her.

"We had to stay clear of malicious or just plain idle gossips; we had to disarm dangerous rumours; we had to feed all of us; and we had to worry about our safety. In more ways than one, for nearly three years, we, too, were captives.

"As I said, we were lucky with our guests. Some friends of ours hid a Jewish couple who insisted on having breakfast in bed every morning. Can you imagine that—expecting farmers to stop their daily labours in the fields just so they could laze around in bed! They constantly complained about the food. After a week these crazy people just got up and left. They had been warned about the world outside, but it was beneath them to stay with such inconsiderate people. Need I tell you that they got caught before they could leave the village? Fortunately, nothing like this ever happened to us."

"But even they slipped up," Albert interrupted. "We kept reminding them to lie low because the fields had eyes. They would hold to it for a day or so, but then they would reappear again. After a while we

stopped reminding them, and hoped for the best. How can you forbid a human being access to the fresh air? I couldn't, and my wife
couldn't either."

"What do you mean by 'the fields had eyes'?" Vicki asked.

"Our house was right on the main road between the German border
and the heart of Holland. We had a constant procession of soldiers
and equipment," Wilma continued, taking over from her husband.
"As a matter of fact, we had Germans in our house quite often.
They used our house during their manoeuvres and their childish war-
games, making themselves right at home: they set up headquarters
and telephone lines, or they would request us to make tea for them.
As occupants, they had the right to demand anything of us."

"And I want you to know," Albert cut in once more, this time
quite energetically, "that I was very fond of the Germans. I had spent
a couple of years in Germany in the early thirties. That's where I
acquired much of my knowledge and enthusiasm for organic farming.
I spent two years with hard-working Germans at the agricultural
school. I just bicycled right into the country; they didn't guard the
border. You should have seen them work and work. And I worked
with them. They made me feel at home. What a contrast to my
previous trip to England. I had to apply for a permit to enter the
country and they never let me forget that I was a visitor. People
hardly ever addressed a question to me. I spent two years in England
without making a friend. When my time was up, I got up and left;
nobody cared. The folks at the agricultural school near Bremen were
all thinking people, lovers of land and life. There was not one Nazi
among them.

"This is to say that I wasn't one of those who was prejudiced
against the Germans. I lived with them in peace time, so when they
came to our home, I was not full of hatred or even anger. But I
always separated the Nazis from the Germans. A lot of people have
a hard time making such a distinction. Take my own wife: we have
always seen things very much through the same eyes, but we always
disagreed when it came to our feelings about the Germans."

"Well, I'm not going to start a whole political argument here."
Once more, Wilma seemed uncomfortable. "But don't make me into a
German-hater. I don't hate anybody. Nationalities make no difference
to me. They are barriers people put up between themselves, and I
have no use for them. I would have been angry with anyone, not just
the Germans, who showed such contempt for the sanctity of life.

"To come back to our Jewish guests, though. They had to hide not only from the Germans, but also from the neighbours. We had a small community of six farms and we all worked together. We'd trade machinery and horses and stuff like that. Because we were not from the area, we worked with them but never really got to know them as friends. We had no idea about their feelings towards the Nazis. So we told the Hellmans to keep away from the big doors upstairs in the back of the house where the hay was put. But since the summer heat was stifling in their rooms, the doctor and his wife would stand by the doors at night to cool off. But here I'd like to tell you something you might want to hear. The last time we were back in Holland, we went to visit our old neighbours in Apeldoorn. We spent an evening in their company, reminiscing about the old days. Somehow the topic of hiding Jews came up. And you know what? They all knew about it all the time. So you see, just as we told you in the beginning, we did nothing special. The neighbours saved them as much as we did. We were just the tip of the iceberg. One bad neighbour, and that would have been the end of all of us."

"We were just an instrument," Albert said with a youthful vigour in his voice, "in the right place at the right time. The history of Holland, the history of my own family, especially my grandfather, my own childhood experiences, they all helped us in our actions. What frightens me, though, is that, if this is true of our side, it has to be true of the other side as well. They had to be programmed to hate the Jews. And if that's the case, then how can one remain free of bias against other people? At times like these I wish I had more education, to better grasp the problem. This way, I am confused. I can't be sure of anything. Because if what I fear is true, with the right programming and the right circumstances..."

"Well, let's just stay with the facts." Wilma sensed her husband's fear mounting. "You remember the lodger we took in before the Germans came, to help us with the bills? Well, soon after the Hellmans came to us, she asked us how we would feel if she took in, entirely at her own cost, a five-year-old Jewish girl. We had no objection, even though we were liable since she was in our home illegally. But we already had two illegal guests. So what's the difference between two or three, or even twenty? The only meaningful distinction is between none and one. Besides, what choice did we have? They needed the place, we had the place; you tell us, what choice did we have?

"One day, let me see...in July 1943, we heard the infernal barking of our dogs. Albert and I both went to see who was coming. We liked to meet people outside—it was more prudent. In case of trouble, it gave our Jewish friends a little extra time to hide upstairs. Well, that particular time, it wasn't trouble at all. A stranger came; he muttered some name and asked us if we could chat inside; he had something important to discuss with us. We were a touch guarded with him, but we were also curious."

"Did he turn out to be friend or foe?" I asked.

"He was from the underground with a message from our friend Elly Weiss. We had known her for quite some time, through the organic-gardening movement. Everyone in the movement was well acquainted with everybody else. We were a small bunch of enthusiasts.

" 'Did you know Elly was Jewish?' the visitor asked, as if he was testing our trustworthiness.

" 'So?' We weren't born with the last rain, either.

" 'Well, I came on her account,' he ventured.

" 'Keep talking,' Albert replied.

" 'She led us to believe that you would be likely to hide a couple of Jewish boys if she asked you nicely. Was she right or wrong?' "

"What a dilemma! How could you know what to say?" Vicki exclaimed.

"Precisely." Our hostess flashed a rare smile at Vicki. "You catch on fast. We had never seen this man nor heard of him. He could have been telling the truth. But what if he was a provocateur? Those days there was every chance that what looked white was in fact black, or vice versa. Even asking him to prove that he was sent by Elly would have been too risky. It could have betrayed our inclination towards hiding Jews, and in those days, the intention of lending assistance to a Jew was sufficient cause for a trip to one of those camps. I looked at Albert. His colourless cheeks spoke clearly of his worry. Finally, he took the bull by the horns: 'Look, what you are asking of us is of course illegal. For less than that we could be expedited to Germany or to Poland. But tell Elly that if she is in danger, or needs something that we can do for her, to get in touch with us.'

"The man didn't insist. He *was* from the underground. He knew the score."

"Did you hear from him again?" I inquired.

Quiet Heroes

"Two days later he returned with a pamphlet penned by Rudolf Steiner, the founder of the Anthroposophical movement, in his hand." Albert took over. A big grin lit up his face. He was visibly proud and pleased with the outcome of the incident. "I had given that pamphlet to Elly some time before the war."

" 'Elly asked me to return this to you whenever I was in the area. She also asked me to tell you that if you are interested in her response to the man's writings, reread it, and you'll find her response in the text itself. I'll be returning to Utrecht later tonight; if you care to send a message to her, I'll be glad to pass by before I leave. It's no trouble at all.' He was already by the door, with his hand on the knob, when Wilma stopped him with a question: 'Just where is Elly right now? How is it that you can freely meet with her if it's true that she's Jewish?' It was one of those rare occasions in our forty-five years when I felt like pulling her by the ear and making her stand in a corner like a kid." He looked at his wife with affectionate disapproval.

" 'How could I answer that question?' the man replied, with an apologetic smile."

"Well, I was very curious and it just slipped out." Wilma defended herself lamely. "You can't imagine how hard it is to monitor your tongue all the time. It's inevitable to make a slip here and there. What's more human than to make a mistake? It just shows you what we had to cope with: there was little room for our basic imperfections without putting our own hides on the line."

"Anyway, Elly was a smart woman." Albert was itching to finish his story. "At first, I saw nothing. Then I noticed something that looked like a piece of wood in the cheap paper. I got out my magnifying glass to discover that it was a tiny pinprick in the paper. I searched for other such marks—they were all over the pamphlet. I turned to page one and put together Elly's message letter by letter, each bearing a tiny pin mark. It was: 'The bearer of this pamphlet is a friend. I'm active in the underground. Peace, E.' "

"Well, to make a long story short," Wilma said, eager to move on, "Elly's friend sent us two Jewish boys. They were poor labourers, and we were delighted with that."

"What was the difference?" Vicki asked.

"We would have opened our home to anyone, but we were not eager to receive wealthy people. For one thing, it was easier to share our meagre resources with our own kind—people had no fancy expectations. And for another, we knew that rich people could always pay their way with less trouble than the poor. These boys had nothing to their name.

"Shortly after their arrival, I got a note from a dear friend of mine from the Jewish hospital. She was safe where she was, at the Jewish Hospital of Amsterdam. Here I've got to explain something. My friend Rosa fell into a trap shared with many other Jews: she thought that hospitals were safer places than anywhere else. She had arranged for her twin brother to get a job at our old hospital. But they were sadly wrong, and we knew it. So when rumours of evacuating Jewish hospitals reached us, Albert and I began to wonder about Rosa and her brother. We decided we shouldn't leave the matter to chance. But before I managed to get a message to Rosa, we received a desperate note from her: 'The dark clouds are closing in above our heads. I see only three alternatives for me: to wait to be taken on a transport, to commit suicide, or to find a hiding place.' Well, what do you think?"

"You offered her shelter in your home, of course," Vicki answered. "What was to happen to her twin?"

"The twins belonged together," she answered without hesitation.

"A week later, she joined us. Her brother came a month after that. With them, our permanent Jewish family was complete, with six members.

"We had others, also, but they were there only for short periods— some so briefly that we can't even remember if in fact they were with us or if we just imagined it. There was one other person there for sure whose face I recall with clarity—a Jewish teacher of mine from my home town. She had so many former pupils who were willing to put her up that she came to stay only for two weeks and then went on to her next host. Albert and I tried to explain to her that each time she undertook a journey, she exposed herself to untold risks. We wanted her to stay, but she didn't want to disappoint the others, all of whom wanted to help her. There were also a couple of teenage boys from Amsterdam—who knows what their names were? These two youngsters were the only ones who gave us trouble. There was hardly a day when Albert didn't have to drag them inside to take shelter from possibly risky encounters. And the next day, the whole thing would start all over. So for their sakes, and for ours, after two weeks, Elly's friend found another place for them.

"Karel was a remarkable man. According to a modest count, he helped, one way or another, seven hundred Jews. He lives in Australia now. When we were in Holland in 1978, he was visiting too. We asked him if he remembered those two boys.

" 'I don't know what happened to most of the Jewish people I helped,' he told us. 'Out of the seven hundred, only one let me know after the war that he was alive.' He was quite melancholy about the silence of seven hundred Jews. 'It would've felt good to know the outcome of four years of risking my life for theirs.' "

"How did you feel, hearing his words?" I asked the Dijkstras.

"He was definitely speaking our minds," Wilma replied. "Who they were mattered not. They were alive; they deserved to stay that way; and we needed them to keep our consciences clean. In a twisted way, during those days, we needed them to let us stay relatively blameless. It's a magnificent feeling for us to know that our faces are free of dirt."

"How did you manage to run a household full of all those strangers on top of your regular hard work?" Vicki asked Wilma directly.

"Luckily, all the six regulars got along fine with one another. To be held captive for so long, even by a benevolent warden, had to become a hell on earth—let alone the tension of knowing what was going on beyond the walls of their hiding place. They knew everything because the doctor listened to our radio every day (which we failed to surrender to the authorities as requested). He borrowed my school map and marked with pins all the positions of the Germans, keeping track of their whereabouts. We still have that map full of holes. Anyway, the six of them made everyone's life as tolerable as possible under those circumstances. Albert and I were working in the fields all day long. They could have done anything they wanted but they remained wise and considerate, more than anyone would have expected.

"It took us a little time to get organized, because we were rank amateurs, but we made it. I had another Jewish girlfriend who was in the underground. She got phoney identification papers for all our guests. Not that they would have been of any use if anyone had taken a close look at them, but they put us in line for food coupons. Don't forget, with our six permanent customers, our lodger, and the little Jewish girl she was hiding, we had ten mouths to feed. We were all very slim those days.

"We baptized Rosa, 'Riek', and her brother Moishe became 'Mau'. Riek helped around the kitchen, making my life easier, and Mau assisted Albert around the barn. I was delighted to have an old girlfriend in the house to whom I could tell everything without lies and stories. I know our troubles were minor compared to those of our Jewish friends, but still, they weren't negligible. To live a life of lies day in and day out wasn't my cup of tea. But with Rosa I could put all my cards on the table. On the other hand, to my great surprise, I found her quite secretive and unwilling to reveal what was on her mind. Most of the time, she walked around with a long face. She became more and more silent. And we had been so close during the two years we shared the same tiny room at the Jewish mental institution! We had no secrets from one another then.

"So I began to censure myself for fear of overburdening her. After all, I thought, she had enough on her mind. I was beginning to suspect that she had some deep, dark secret. At other times I imagined that I had offended her by prying into her private world. Since I have never been a person of intrigue, when I found the rapport too strained, I brought up the subject.

" 'Riek, you and I have to have a heart-to-heart talk, like we used to have in the good old days. Once more we live under the same roof; nothing has really changed. Except that you and I no longer speak to each other like we used to. What happened?'

" 'Wilma, please, don't burden yourself with me,' she struggled with every word. Watching her torment herself silently confused me for a while. But then it came to me as a lightning bolt out of a cloudless sky: she was ashamed of something! But of what? How to help her get that ugly mask off her face? We had been too close for too long to play this silly game.

" 'What are you ashamed of?' I asked quite insistently. 'I can't tolerate that you live in my house and feel that there is something that you must hide from me out of shame. Out with it, come on!'

" 'I have never been a useless human being in my life,' she whispered, covering her face as she was weeping quietly. 'Since I have been in your house, I contribute next to nothing to anyone's welfare. I don't even earn my keep. My life used to have meaning; I made myself useful to those in need. But, now, it's the other way around. I'm helpless and I just take and take. I'm ashamed of being a leech, syphoning away vital substance from you and Albert who are working your fingers to the bones.

" 'I feel so devalued,' she went on. 'Whose fault is it? The Germans', no doubt about it. And perhaps we Jews aren't blameless, either. How could we be reduced to this pitiful state? We don't even go to our death fighting, if death is what the world has decreed for us. We cower; we hide under the skirts of our generous Christian friends; we bow our heads as we board the cattle trains; or we close our eyes as we utter a last prayer asking forgiveness before they tighten the noose around our necks. You are putting your life and your backbone on the line for me, the superfluous person? All you need on top of that is the burden of my shame and anxiety. The least I can do is to make myself invisible, to take the least amount of space and time from people who have a purpose to their existence, like you, Wilma....'

" 'Is that all?' I interjected. 'If you weren't like a sister to me, I would be furious with you. As is, I'm dumbfounded. Since when do we derive the meaning of our lives from what we do, whether for others or for ourselves? The real meaning of our existence is and has always been the same—yours, mine, Albert Schweitzer's, Gandhi's. What is this meaning? We don't know. It is not something for our limited brains to understand; it's locked in the infinite plan of nature.

" 'The meaning of my life resides in the very fact of being alive. And for me the meaning of your life—and Hitler's life, for that matter—is exactly the same. To say that you are less deserving of respect because your life has been put in danger by political evil is indeed astounding. If you have any reason for shame it should be for collaborating with the Nazis in your own degradation. As for my life, I live it without question, without merit. To say that there's any merit in working harder when there is need for it is about as absurd as saying that you deserve praise for breathing heavier when you run than when you walk.'

"She listened to me without a word, without a muscle twitching in her face. When I finished, I hugged her and left the kitchen. I knew that she needed time alone. I knew I made sense, and she knew it, too, but somehow she had to hear it from me. Whether my words seeped in deeply enough, I couldn't tell, but I had to say them for both her sake and mine.

"I told Albert about what had happened between Rosa and me. 'You are a fine one,' he chastised me in a half whisper. 'You can never understand or feel what she has been going through because you are not in her situation. If you keep feeding slop to a person for long enough, she just might end up seeing herself as a pig! After a while, it's being *human* that no longer makes sense to her—not having changed into a pig. The doctor tells me enough for me to conclude that the biggest massacre in the history of mankind is being conducted around us. And we continue working the land, eating three meals a day, sitting around the table and chatting, making babies, and everything else that points to our complicity with the Nazis. How can we go on with our ordinary business-as-usual existence when on a windy day our mouths may be full of human ashes? And yet, what else is there to do?'

"I didn't sleep a wink that night. That hadn't ever happened to me before. My conscience had always been clear enough for me to abandon myself to a well-earned night's rest. But not that night. Morning comes early on a farm, but that night it couldn't come early enough.

"I had to wait until the following night to have a chance to speak to Rosa alone. I made blunder upon blunder that day, but the evening finally came. 'I was stupid to put up barriers between you and me,' my friend said to me softly and with a touch of embarrassment. She sounded like a child apologizing to her parents for something really silly. 'Please, understand that for me to feel like a real person I have to be able to act like one.'

" 'I wish I could tell you that I know what you mean, but I can't. I have never had your experience,' I told her in a very clumsy way. 'I wish I had some understanding of what goes on inside you. For lack of a better alternative, let's aim at a compromise: let's just try to pretend, you and I, whenever we're alone, like right now, that all the horrors of the world out there don't exist. Let's just try to be Rosa and Wilma.' "

"Earlier you praised your Jewish guests for their exemplary behaviour," I said to our hostess. "Did you mean to say that you never had any altercation worth recalling?"

"As time wore everyone's nerves thin, our guests began to lose their composure," she replied. "It was then, as they were coming a bit unglued, that we realized how much effort it took for them to spare us their miseries. These poor souls, in addition to coping with the constant procession of Germans just along the edge of our property and a much reduced scope of existence, they also had taken it upon themselves to shield us from the spectacle of their personal troubles. But how can you contain all that anguish without allowing it to spill over onto anyone who stands next to you? In other words, tempers were flaring.

"Whenever we thought we could no longer just swallow our frustrations with the war, the shortages, the cramped living, or the increasingly frequent tantrums of our guests, Albert and I would go out and chop wood, or break bricks, or dig up a patch of hard soil. We'd come back into the house spent, and that would be the end of a potentially explosive situation. But what kind of safety valve was available to our Jewish guests? There was no way for them to blow off steam. They could either stew in their own juices or complain to an ally about someone who had committed an offence of some sort— a careless accident, a rough word, an edgy tone, a minor violation of routine."

"Can you give an example or two of these altercations?" I asked.

"Take for instance, the matter of the bathroom. We had one bathroom upstairs for the six of them. Its use required a careful routine. And it worked most of the time. But more and more often, people would stretch their allotted time just a tiny bit, by a couple of insignificant minutes. By the time it was the third person's turn to use the facilities, there would be a delay of, say, ten minutes. What's ten minutes when you have your whole day to do nothing? But that wasn't the issue. For the violators, that minute infraction of the unwritten rule was the sole area where they could exercise some control over their lives, where they could sabotage the system. It became the only safe form of rebellion against the regulation of every aspect of their existence. It was a declaration, without having to actually say anything offensive or openly hostile, that 'in spite of everything, in this particular moment I'm still in charge of my life and the rest of the world can go to hell.' For those out there in the hallway, it became another instance of their being treated disrespectfully, with no concern for their rights, with no consideration for their needs.

"As the war wore on, the 'bathroom guerrillas', as Albert and I referred to them, became more and more aggressive. One day, even Dr. Hellman lost his habitual self-control. He appeared to have forgotten about time. Mau was to follow him.

" 'Mau couldn't have been waiting for more than five minutes, if that long,' Rosa, said, reporting the incident to me that evening. 'Why did he have to make such a case out of a few miserable minutes? It's not as if he had an important appointment to keep! The longer the war lasts, the nastier we become. The time might come when we'll resort to some form of cannibalism. How can I not cover my face in shame? I can't think of anything more demeaning to me than this gradual erosion of our decency.'

" 'You have a lot of nerve to make me stick around like a piece of lumber. How can you be such an uncouth, inconsiderate bastard?' And with that Mau stormed into the bathroom and slammed the door hard.

"Dr. Hellman retired into his room and remained there for over twenty-four hours. He didn't appear even for his meals. Neither did his wife. Albert and I were worried. Mau refused to speak to anyone about the incident. He paced up and down like a wounded tiger. When I learned the details from his sister, I related them to Albert, who went to convince the angry young man to present his apologies to the doctor. Mau would not even gratify my husband with an answer. He just shrugged his shoulders and walked away from him. A lot of wood got chopped that night, I can tell you that much.

"The next morning, Albert heard from behind the Hellman's door the kind of whimpering one would only expect from a horrified child. 'What shall we do? What shall we do?' we kept asking ourselves. At first the others paid little attention to the Hellmans' absence. But the following morning, everyone began to whisper, as people do at a wake.

"By noon, however, the doctor reappeared. I'll never forget his eyes: there was a dry red flame burning in them as if they had been painted in the middle of his bloodless white face. He spoke to no one at lunch.

"The doctor sought Albert out when he came back from work with the dirt of the field still on his hands. The two men locked themselves in our bedroom."

"What did the doctor tell you, Albert?" I turned to our host. He looked a bit hesitant, but his wife flashed him an encouraging smile.

" 'Albert,' Dr. Hellman began, 'you know that my wife and I have always taken extra care to keep our private worries from Wilma and you. You're overloaded as is. But now something has changed. When I think of this banal incident with Mau taking on crisis proportions, I realize that you deserve some explanation. This is your house; responsible adults are beginning to behave like rotten brats and it's time to let you know what's behind it, at least on my part. And I would be surprised if Mau didn't have a similar story to tell. I learned in my medical practice that patients afflicted with the same illness always recognize one another. There's a fraternity of pain, one could say, a secret society whose symbols are unintelligible to those who haven't been initiated.

" 'You know, Albert, that we have three daughters. We never spoke to you of them for fear that you might run off to fetch them from wherever they might be and perish in the process. We thought all three of them were out of danger. Remember that message we received a few days ago? You asked me about the nature of the news and I told you that all messages are lies nowadays. Well, my friend, that news was devastatingly true. We have been informed that our youngest girl was caught in a raid and she was taken to Westerbork. She tried to escape and she was brutally punished....'

"At that point his tears choked his words in his throat. He wept out of control for nearly an hour. His shoulders continued to heave after he ran out of tears. I was awe-struck before so much raw emotion. Also, I'm a very shy person, very ill-prepared for tears...." Albert was struggling with his own emotions as he spoke.

"I was very stupid: instead of just keeping my mouth shut, I asked in desperate frustration, 'But why didn't you tell me that your daughter needed a place?' As I finished I realized that I just plunged the dagger deeper into his heart. I have never felt so ashamed of my limited intelligence before or since that incident.

" 'Well,' said the doctor, 'I'm sorry to have burdened you with our tragedy, but you had to know what really happened. I spent the extra few minutes in the bathroom because I needed to weep alone; my wife is teetering on the edge of nervous exhaustion, and I must appear strong before her or else she'll lose control. I promise you it won't happen again.' "

Albert sat there, on the edge of his armchair, spent, wearing his washed-out sweater and faded farmer's work-pants. His eyes searched out his wife's, saying, "I couldn't help it and I still can't help it. The past is supposed to be the past but that pain is still present. What am I to do with it?"

Wilma quickly resumed her narrative to escape the painful memory. "After hearing the doctor's story, I wanted to find out what was bothering Mau. It was so unlike him to raise his voice. I spoke to Riek that night.

" 'My brother had a very trying experience the day before the bathroom incident,' she told me in the kitchen. 'He could no longer cope with the confinement, he confessed to me today, so he stole a stroll down the road. He snuck under the fence in the back. He went along the road towards Apeldoorn. As he was nearing the mental hospital, he noticed a long line of people in weird get-ups: it was a brigade of the camp police from Westerbork. They were poor Jewish devils who had been brought in to do the dirty job of dragging off to the camp the inmates of the institution. He caught a glimpse of a fellow who used to work with him in the hospital. Recklessly, he went up to the chap to find out what was going on.

" ' "What the hell are you doing here?" the other asked him in total shock. "You want a one-way ticket to paradise?"

" ' "I just need to find out what's going to happen here, then I'll make myself invisible again. What will happen to the patients?"

" ' "Not much good." When Mau pressed him for some details, he said: "They'll be loaded into trucks, then into trains, then away they go to Poland.... "

" 'Mau ran back to the farm, seized by panic as if he himself was about to board the train of death. But since then he has been possessed by visions of hundreds of demented people being ushered to their deaths. One of those was a young boy he used to care for and who was his friend.

" 'My brother lashed out at the doctor because he was an available target. You see, we are reduced to our barest limits of humanity. We can no longer vouch for our behaviour. We are beginning to devour one another.'

"That night, all of us gathered in our dining room. There was a respectful silence when the doctor rose and began to pray. Our Jewish friends all dropped their chins on their chests and their heads bobbed silently as if blown by a wind only they could feel. Some of them moved their lips at a feverish pace as if they were afraid of running out of time or running out of breath. The others' lips were frozen tight.

" 'He's saying Kaddish, the prayer for the dead,' Rosa whispered to me. I was startled by the chill in her breath. 'This time the Kaddish is for us.'

"She was wrong, however." Wilma raised her chin and looked me straight in the eyes. I felt warned to pay particular attention. Albert rose from his armchair as if that were his exit cue, and with unexpected agility he rushed out of the room without a word.

"The Kaddish was for our loss, too. I hadn't told you yet that I had been expecting. I was due in January 1944, but perhaps under the effect of all the emotional energy, I went into labour the week after our last crisis, just at the beginning of my seventh month of pregnancy. We were not happy about the turn of events. We hoped that our child might be born a free person, but more concretely we feared that a crying child might attract unexpected visitors.

"We had already had to clip little Elsje's five-year-old wings because the ways of childhood made us too vulnerable to intrusive questions."

"Who's Elsje?" I asked. "That's the first time you've mentioned that name."

"She was the little Jewish girl our lodger was hiding. How do you keep a five-year-old quiet and motionless? So we had to curtail her freedom and insist that our lodger keep her indoors at all times. But how do you tell a newborn not to cry? I know, she was my child and not a Jewish child, but, still, the sound of a child crying always attracts more attention than one would prefer. We, too, were beginning to fear for our fate.

"Did you know that in Holland babies are not always born in hospitals? Often a midwife assists at the birth. But, in fact, we had Dr. Hellman in the house. And Rosa was a nurse. And we even had a retired nurse as a lodger, so we had plenty of medical help. Still, just to make things look right, we arranged with the local country doctor to come to deliver our baby. He had to be let in on our secret but that proved to be just fine. In spite of all that medical staff in my house, I still had to be taken to the hospital because of the premature arrival of the babies. Yes, I had twins: a girl and a boy. They lived for a few hours. They made some faint little noises, then, exhausted, they surrendered the life for which they were ill prepared. Albert keeps saying that today they would be kept alive, but medicine then was not advanced enough to save them. So many of them died. Ours succumbed, too. In a matter of a few hours, we discovered the black face of senseless, unnecessary death. We began to really understand the things our Jewish guests had gone through; we had become Jewish.

"After that, the pace of our household picked up. Something was happening all the time. We didn't have the time to catch our breath for long or to wipe the sweat away from our foreheads. I had just started to work in the fields again when we had the fright of our lives.

"It started with the rumours of impending searches to ferret out hidden Jews. There was palpable danger in the air. We had to send away our Jews.

Defiant Outsiders

" 'How can we go to relocate six people at a time when everybody will be under the same gun as ourselves?' I asked, echoing Albert's very concern.

" 'Not only that,' he added, 'how are we going to move them at a time when every turn on the road will have German or NSB eyes waiting for the flushed-out rodents? How are we going to break the news to these people whose resistance is worn paper-thin?'

"Albert pulled all the strings he could, and he came up with precious little. There was one farmer closer to Zutphen than to Apeldoorn who was willing to take the Hellmans in for a month for two hundred guilders. But he would not commit himself to a day longer for any amount of money. But nothing materialized for the others.

" 'They'll have to join the underground and float around in the forest, in the bushes, in cellars, attics, ditches, boats, what have you,' Albert informed me. We agreed that our friends had to be told what was waiting for them.

" 'They're all young people'— I was trying to put my mind at ease about their fate—'some of them are itching for action, even Rosa has been speaking of violence.'

" 'My friends,' Albert began, looking around the pathetic assembly, 'you're all going to find temporary alternatives to staying here. We're expecting to be raided in the next few days. You have all become our brothers and sisters. But you cannot be found here when the Germans come. It's fortunate that we received so much advance notice, allowing us to make inquiries, and to eliminate potentially hazardous alternatives.'

"The next evening, around nine o'clock, a comrade from the underground came by with a moving van full of old furniture. Albert and the comrade unloaded the lot. The doctor and his wife climbed in. At the very back of the cabin, they left a chair for each. They reloaded all the furniture, thereby barricading the fugitives.

"By the time Albert came back, around one o'clock in the morning, the others had disappeared into the darkness. I went to bed as usual.

" 'Good night and see you soon; try to come back in the same shape as you leave or perhaps better.' I purposefully didn't say farewell. Albert had arranged for each of them to be picked up by someone from the underground near the back of the property. To make sure that the dogs wouldn't bark, Albert took them with him in the truck. The only guest who had to remain with us was Elsje, because nobody would take a Jewish child in those days. Normally, a little girl would have been easy to place, but not while 'razzia fever' was on. So we decided that at all times she was to remain in the old nurse's room. She did have a fake ID for her and they rehearsed over and over again that if anyone came, she was to jump into bed and pretend to be very sick, unable to speak."

"What was it like for the two of you remaining at home?" Vicki asked.

"Albert and I were rattling around in our suddenly empty house. We never used to have company before. But our Jewish friends had stopped being company; they were part of us. We worried and we kept guessing who was where and how he or she fared in the 'underground wilderness'. We ended up feeling displaced in our own home. Does that make sense to you?

"As it turned out, the rumours ended up being just that—rumours. We were never raided. We did have our share of unwelcome visits from the Wehrmacht and the SS, but they were of a technical or operational nature. They were not searching for anybody; our place just happened to be conveniently located for them. Thus, after one month, when the Hellmans' welcome had worn out, Albert 'repatriated' them. One by one, our friends returned unharmed and relieved to be home.

"For most of them, the experience had proved to be a lot less harrowing than all of us had expected. The only one who had some unpleasantness was Mau, the only ardently religious Jew among the six of them. As bad luck would have it, he spent three days with a fanatical man who wanted to convert him. When Mau resisted, he began to threaten him. Mau left his house. He retraced his steps to his previous hiding place where he was received with open arms. From then on, everything went smoothly.

"With all our friends back in their rooms, we thought we could relax for a while. But our tranquillity was short-lived. First, we received an unscheduled nocturnal visit from our underground contact, Karel.

" 'We need you to take in two more boys immediately. You are our only chance.' Albert and I looked at each other.

" 'Where would we put another two people? There's no way we can accommodate anyone else. If we take in any more people, we would endanger the safety of the ones we already have in our home.'

"He left without a word. We were tormented for a long time about that. We had never said 'no' to anybody in danger. In our minds we knew that we had done the only thing we could do, but in our hearts there was doubt. We never found out what happened to them. To this day, every time the incident comes up, I feel goose-bumps and chills at the thought that they might have perished because every door was slammed in their face. I read about a Swiss film some time ago called *The Boat Is Full*. Did you hear about it? Well, that's what we did to those people: our boat was full; another two could have made it sink. You see, that's what made those days unique: no matter what you did, you couldn't do enough, and, you couldn't know if what you did would lead to good or to evil. The Nazis had us coming and going.

"And they had us in more than one way. In the middle of the summer, one day, just after lunch, we were all sitting in the kitchen when we heard the dogs raise holy hell. Albert and I jumped to our feet; the others froze. I peeked out and I, too, froze for a few valuable seconds.

" 'Two German soldiers! Everyone get out!'

"As planned time and time again, the Hellmans ran upstairs and Albert dashed after them and hid in their room."

Albert returned just in time to recount first-hand his part in the incident. "I pulled the armoire in front of their door and rolled out the carpet to cover the floor. Then I ran out through the barn towards the back of our land. I don't know if you've ever seen our barns but they are attached to the house so that you don't have to go outside to get to them. There was a large hole in the ground, sheltered from view by a cluster of brush. We kept a big tarpaulin rolled up out there just for such an emergency. The Jews hid in the hole, and then I rolled out the tarp and shovelled hay on top of it at devilish speed. In thirty seconds, nobody would have said that there was anything noteworthy underneath. Then I ducked under it."

"Why did you hide?" I asked Albert.

"Those days, I, too, ran the risk of being scooped up for forced labour in Germany. We just waited silently. We always wondered how we would behave if we were caught."

"They poked around everywhere without saying what they were looking for," Wilma said, taking over again. "By the time they looked in the kitchen, there was no evidence of any sort that ten people had just finished a meal in there. After they opened a door here, a cupboard there, they left without a word. We never found out what the whole thing was about, but it certainly had a lasting effect on us.

"In September, shortly after the Battle of Arnhem, we received a note from the Town Hall that everybody had to take in four evacuees.

" 'This is great,' Albert said, fuming with anger. 'We couldn't take in two Jewish fugitives for lack of adequate space. Now, we'll *have* to make room for not two, but four more bodies.'

" 'That's the smaller problem. What are we going to tell the evacuees about our guests?' I was shaking like a leaf I was so anxious. We tried on all kinds of stories, one more absurd than the other. The day of their arrival everyone was near panic. Including us.

" 'You'll have to tell them the truth,' Dr. Hellman decreed, 'and hope for the best.' No one liked the idea, but no one had a better alternative.

"And they came, a family of four: the parents, about the Hellmans' age, and their two daughters, in their twenties. We had emptied the living room and put down mattresses for them. Our Jewish guests were to remain in their rooms until they were told otherwise.

" 'Welcome to our home,' Albert received them with genuine warmth. After all, it wasn't their fault that they had to abandon their home; they, too, were victims. 'Please, bring your things in and settle them in your room.' Albert ushered them towards their quarters.

"They were speechless, partly because of the awkwardness of their situation and partly as a result of their shock at what accommodations awaited them.

" 'Please, forgive us for the very primitive and very cramped quarters we have available for you. It's the best we can do under the circumstances.' Albert sounded as clumsy as the others looked.

" 'But this is a huge house,' the father said, without taking his eyes off the room full of mattresses. 'Our understanding was that you were a childless couple.' There was no anger or any suspicion in his voice; he just couldn't make sense of what he saw.

"From a quick, superficial assessment I could see that they had a subtle polish to them. I caught a glimpse of his hands; they were soft and white. The women were modestly dressed but quite well groomed. Both daughters had somewhat worn but stylish clothing.

" 'I'm sure that you're accustomed to far better accommodations than we can offer you, but if you'll just sit down with us in the kitchen, we'll explain the whole thing to you.' Albert's voice was quavering as it had done the day he proposed to me. 'Indeed, we are a childless couple. But that doesn't mean that we have any vacant space in our home; in fact, we couldn't even contemplate having a child until after the war, when everyone can go back to his own home.'

" 'You have more evacuees?' the man asked politely.

" 'In a manner of speaking, yes. We have six evacuees and a child, and also a lodger.'

" 'So there are ten of you living here?' his wife spoke for the first time. 'That's quite a crowd at bath time, not to mention at dinner.' Her husband threw her a mildly disapproving glance.

" 'Look, Mr. and Mrs.... I don't believe I caught your names...'

" 'Van Dam,' the man said. 'This is my wife, Wilhelmina, my daughters Juliana and Beatrix, a regal family, one might say....'

"One could tell that he was used to making the loyal reference to the first names of the female members of the royal family. 'A note of encouragement—these days signs of loyalty to the House of Orange can be read as opposition to the current rulers of the land,' I thought.

" 'Well, look Mr. van Dam and family,' Albert sounded a little more resolute now, 'our evacuees are in some way different from you people. They're Jewish, except the lodger. We have had these people staying with us for years now. They are like family to us. They are wonderful people, a doctor and his wife, a nurse and her brother, and two young labourers who want a chance one day to become old labourers. They are just like you and us, Dutch people. Now our fate is in your hands. My wife and I have no political or religious allegiances. All our lives we have been pacifists. We respect all forms of life without distinguishing between Christian and Jew, German and Dutch, animal or human; we are all part of the family of nature.'

"The van Dams looked at each other in silence. Their glances were hard to read.

" 'That's all right,' Mr. van Dam finally said resolutely. 'Don't worry about us. We have nothing against the Jews. We don't care one way or another. We don't like the killing either. I am a teacher and I like the idea that all the children who go through my classes grow up to become decent human beings. Even the Jewish kids. I'm not particularly thrilled to have to share the roof over my family's head with Jews—not because I think they are inferior to us but because it's dangerous. Should you be raided, we might well be held responsible along with you, at least for complicity. We couldn't exonerate ourselves of the charge that we should have reported them and you to the authorities. Just for that, we could be sentenced to forced labour. But I'm neither a squealer, nor a collaborator. Besides, I hate the Nazis with a passion. It'll be a thrill to help to undermine their cannibalistic efforts.'

"The crisis was over. We had survived one more time. But it seemed to have become our life's pattern that no sooner would we emerge from one panic, than we would find a new one brewing.

"One evening, about two weeks after the van Dams came to us, Wilma and I came in from the field to find two German soldiers sitting in our kitchen, peacefully smoking. None of our guests were visible. It turned out that the soldiers had a flat tire and no spare, so they had decided to wait at our place until reinforcements could arrive later that night. They asked if we could give them something to eat.

"Wilma offered them some bread and a few carrots. They ate their snack politely, they had a smoke, and they left.

"We were about to retire for the night, when we heard the dogs barking. Wouldn't you know it, it was our two German soldiers. They had gotten tired of waiting and were also just plain tired; would we let them stay until morning?

"What were we to say? They were polite at least; they didn't just requisition our bed and have *us* sleep wherever....

" 'It'll have to be the hayloft if you promise not to smoke or make any light because of the black-out.

"They were eager to agree to all of my conditions. Our worries were not about fire or black-out at all. We feared a surprise encounter with one of our two boys, Dik and Kareltje who were also sleeping in the hayloft. What if one of them sneezed, or snored, or had a nightmare, or had to empty his bladder? What if...

" 'Let me go ahead and clear some space for you,' I told the Germans. 'I'll come down for you two when I'm ready.' They looked half asleep already.

" 'Boys, you'll have a couple of bunkmates for the night,' I whispered to Dik and Kareltje. 'They're Germans. Be very careful. Put a piece of cloth in your mouths to make sure you don't make any noise during the night.' The boys spent the night awake to cut down the chances of making tell-tale sounds.

"The two soldiers fell on the hay as if they had been shot and lost consciousness before I could find my way downstairs. Their sonorous snoring was a reassuring sound. Dik and Kareltje spent the night staring into the darkness."

"How did you spend the night?" I asked our hosts.

"Without closing our eyes, right Wilma?" Albert turned to his wife with a tender smile on his face. "But all ended well because in the morning they left without even asking for a glass of water. That was a close call.

"One day, around mid-November, I was out in the field and everyone else was in the house.... Well, you tell it, Wilma, since you were there."

"I had the fright of my life!" Wilma sounded winded, as if she had been running away from the memory of that day. "A German officer came to look for my husband. 'He went to town shopping,' I lied.

" 'Let me see,' he said, and he proceeded to look around. He opened the door of our lodger's rooms and saw the old woman and the little girl in bed, seemingly asleep; he saluted and closed the door. Then he opened the door of the evacuees. He asked for their IDs and demanded to know what they were doing there.

" 'We were evacuated from our home in Arnhem; our home was hit by an enemy shell.' The German saluted and, without a word, he closed the door on them. In the meantime I was trembling because our friends upstairs could hear every word, especially Mau and Riek; their room was right above the kitchen. There was a door at the foot of the stairs that we sometimes kept closed, but sometimes it remained open. Every muscle in my body was tensed as I tried to remember whether it was closed or open.

"It was closed. He passed by without noticing it. I'm not ashamed to admit it, but I was close to wetting my drawers I was so frightened. He walked out through the door leading to the barn. A few minutes later he came back in.

" 'Your husband has to report to the marketplace tomorrow morning at seven o'clock sharp. If he isn't there, we'll come for him and shoot him for desertion.' With that he left. Albert came in from the fields about thirty minutes later. He had heard the dogs bark and had seen the German come and leave.

" 'Everybody is in one piece?' he asked with a big grin on his face.

"I gave him the message word for word. 'Perhaps, you should go, or he'll come back to shoot you,' I suggested.

" 'Are you crazy?' he answered, looking at me to see if I had lost my mind. 'I'm not going to report and they're not going to come to shoot me.'

"Well, if he wanted to scare me, he succeeded, and, without further ado, I fainted. That was the first and only time in my life."

"Our friends were all terrified," Albert said. "They stood there like organ pipes in an empty church. They thought that Wilma had died of a heart attack or something. I myself had quite a fright too, but luckily she opened her eyes in a few minutes. The doctor gave her a sedative of some sort and sent her to bed; the next morning she was as good as new. Of course, I didn't report to the marketplace, and it was a good thing. We knew somebody who did go and he was taken to Germany.

"By the winter of 1944–45, Holland was starving. That was the winter of long teeth. People were dying of hunger in the cities, especially in the west, and Amsterdam had it the worst. Every day we saw strangers on the road—some on their bicycles, some on foot—begging for food. We gave very little because our supplies were seriously down as well. The food coupons were not worth the paper they were printed on, because the shelves were empty in Apeldoorn. You know what happened to all the food? The Germans loaded everything on trains and they painted on the wagon '*Liebesgaben*'—'gift of love'—from Holland. They stole all our food. We couldn't complain, though, because we had hidden reserves of grains, potatoes, some dry vegetables, milk, and eggs. I can't remember a day when we went to bed hungry. But we could not afford to be too generous with the people who knocked on our door because the news would have spread like a forest fire in August that the Dijkstras had food to spare and in no time we would have been plucked clean. I'm afraid those days we had to become selfish.

"Then spring brought the Canadians to Apeldoorn. But before they came, we had another addition to our household. This one was most welcome: our son, Frank, was born. With the assistance of the local doctor and Dr. Hellman, Wilma delivered a plump, vigorous child with lust for life in his lungs. He was definitely the messenger of a new day. And the 'new day' dawned in the middle of April."

"How would you assess the years of occupation?" I asked the Dijkstras.

"You know, it's quite amazing: on the one hand, we can't complain—we survived, and so did all our Jewish friends. That's more than a lot of people can say. But on the other hand, nothing came to us easily. Some people just sat through the war and nothing happened to them and then, one day, they were liberated. For us, it was a struggle to the very end. Even liberation came with a loud bang and a boom; in fact, lots of very loud bangs and booms."

"What sort of bangs and booms?" Vicki asked.

"Liberation day was the 13th of April, a beautiful, warm, sunny day, and that doesn't happen every year. April is often chilly in Holland. The wind was still and there was absolutely no noise. We knew the Allies had to be on their way. First of all, there was no traffic at all, when on a normal day the road would have been in a constant rumble with all the German military hardware and troop movements. About mid-day, a German soldier was passing by on a bicycle; he was a wrung out, middle-aged man. He asked for a drink. I gave him a glass of water."

"He looked like he lost the war," Wilma commented.

"Soon after, the party began. First, there was a screeching, metallic, whistling noise. Was it the Germans trying to stave off the Canadians or was it the liberators chasing the Germans towards their own border? There was a constant barrage of shells; the sky was buzzing with giant iron bees. We couldn't hear explosions, only the whistling. It was an eerie, unnatural sound. Would you believe that the starlings of the area heard enough shelling that they learned to imitate its noise? Isn't that the most pathetic lesson man could impart to nature? Anyway, later in the afternoon we saw black columns of smoke dividing up the sky—each black pillar was a tombstone to a farm reduced to cinder. But the smoking countryside signalled the rapidly approaching moment of liberation after five long years of war. Around five o'clock in the afternoon, we saw Canadian soldiers coming through the ditches, moving closer and closer to our house. Inside, we could hardly contain our excitement. Everyone was kissing and hugging. Mau was praying fervently. The doctor and his wife were silently weeping. I was beside myself with joy, I wanted to hug one of those sweaty messengers of freedom. Without thinking, I flew out of the kitchen door, running towards the nearest soldier.

"If the guy had been a little faster on the trigger, this story would not have a happy ending. He had his rifle pointed at me but he didn't fire. Minutes later, we had Canadian soldiers in our house! We were ready to forget our cares and just celebrate until we dropped from joyful exhaustion.

"There was no time for celebration, though. Seconds after the Canadians came inside, all hell broke loose. Not only were we in the firing line, but we had become part of the target. We dashed down to the cellar.

"There was not a moment's lull. It continued well into the next day, when the Canadians decided that we should flee. I wasn't fond of the idea, but I had to listen to the military wisdom of the liberators. After all, if they came all that distance, risking life and limb for our freedom, the least I could do for them was to not give them a hard time while they tried to save my life.

"We were told to wait until the cover of night. We had no car, just a horse and a wagon. We loaded everything we could on it. Dr. Hellman insisted that he carry three-month-old Frank and go on foot with the others, while I had to perform all kinds of gymnastics with the horse and wagon, hoping to avoid getting blown to smithereens. I was shouting like a mad Turk because the shooting wouldn't stop. In all honesty, I was scared out of my wits, and shouting ceaseless profanities at least distracted me from my panic. Enemy bullets were buzzing around me like flies around a honeycake. But, in the end, we all made it to a barn where we set up our emergency headquarters. It wasn't more than two kilometres from our house, but it seemed like we had just crossed the Sahara Desert. We were all shell-shocked, literally.

"Then, suddenly, Mau exploded in laughter. That brought us to our senses.

" 'No wonder you couldn't keep up with the rest of us,' the doctor chided his wife. All eyes were on Mrs. Hellman: in her white fur coat, she looked like a fuzzy, pudgy snowman. She had put on seven dresses! Human nature, what can I tell you? If it can be imagined, somebody will do it. And if it can't, someone will do it anyway. It annoyed me, though, that while we were trying to help one another save our lives, she took the time to put on seven dresses. Of course she could not help with carrying anything; she would have needed a crane for herself."

"When were you really liberated?" I asked him.

"The next day, finally, brought us a tranquil, friendly sky. We went home, where a very sad spectacle was waiting for us. I hesitate to recount it because I don't like to speak ill of anyone, and especially not of our liberators. But the truth should not be shaped to suit people's sensitivities.

"But first, a preface. We had lived under the Germans for more than three years. They never took a thing from us. They might have stolen all the food the country produced, but they never stole from us personally. Once, we left a can of milk and a basket of apples in the barn. The Germans came and took the milk and the apples. But in the empty basket, they left more money than the whole lot was worth. The Germans stole on a grand scale, but individual soldiers exercised great discipline in respecting personal property. You may want to argue about the value of this noble honesty in soldiers who killed and tortured in cold blood, true. But facts are facts.

"When we returned to our home after one day's absence, the Canadians had stolen everything of any possible value—the camera, gadgets, knick-knacks, teaspoons, everything. Wouldn't you say that it's noteworthy to contrast the two experiences? The Canadian government wouldn't steal anything from the enemy or the people they liberated, but their soldiers did. For the Germans, it was the other way around. Go, make sense of this.

"Our only casualty was our horse, who got a piece of shrapnel in his leg and had to be destroyed. I shed tears for that poor beast who had no business being caught between two shooting camps. He was a victim like anyone else who got shot. And he suffered before he could be put out of his pain."

"How did you celebrate your liberation?" I asked.

"We didn't celebrate. The rest of the country wasn't liberated for another two or three weeks. When the last German was chased from Holland, our friends left. The doctor was expected back in his home town. They were going to receive him with a parade, brass band and all. But he insisted that such plans be abandoned. He was still mourning the murder of his daughter. Oh, how I wish they would have asked us to take her! What a tragic waste: one life for sure could have been spared, but they never asked us!

"And there was another strange thing. I knew the doctor and his wife, since they were friends of my parents. We had been through a lot together, but once they left us, they wrote us only one brief letter and that was it. During the hours of the occupation, when we kept insisting to them that they were like family to us, we really meant it. Obviously, they didn't, but then again it was only we who kept saying it, not them. They came to visit us once for a quick goodbye, just before we took off for Canada. They brought us a camera as a farewell gift. I always found their quiet distance strange. Perhaps we reminded them too much of the war, of their grief, but still...."

"What happened to the others?" Vicki inquired.

"The boys left the day after the country was officially free. They returned to their home and took up working practically immediately.

It was as though the war hadn't forced them to interrupt their lives. We received a card from them a few weeks after postal services resumed. Look, I still have it: 'We're all right, working, eating, living, but mostly we're free, Salomon and Karel.' "

"I heard from Rosa regularly," Wilma joined in again. She had a faint smile in her eyes as she recalled her lifelong friend. "My friend never wasted precious time. She offered her services at a hospital in Amsterdam and threw herself into her work. Of their family only she and her brother lived to see liberation. She longed for her mother and father. Not one of her Jewish friends survived.

"Moishe—Mau—was offered a position in the new hospital administration. He, too, was driven to work by his memories and by loneliness. His star rose very fast: in no time he was appointed *burgomaster* of a considerable town.

"And then there was Elsje, little orphan Elsje. She was so tiny when the old nurse took her under her protective wing. Neither one of her parents came back and the only mother or father she ever knew was her war-time guardian angel. We lost track of them quite soon. Oh, yes, the van Dams thanked us for the modest hospitality we extended to them. They disappeared from our lives without a trace, like so many others with whom we had quite vital connections during the occupation. And that was all right with us. You attend to the needs of the moment and when your business is done you move on to the next thing."

"What about you?" Vicki asked Wilma. "How did you pick up the pieces?"

"We, too, had a life to remake in that house that, once again, echoed with silence. But we did have Frank to take care of some of the excess quiet. We had definitely not fallen out of grace with mother nature: she blessed our soil and our home with fertility. Frank was not even a year old when his brother Arno entered our lives.

"Freedom didn't come cheap to us. When I say 'us' I mean Holland—not just our family. We had to rebuild so much with so little. But hardship was not enough to discourage us. The war had no effect on our way of life. There was one thing, however, that changed our vision. In 1940, it was just Albert and I. The two of us confronted anything without fear; we were wonderfully and foolishly optimistic and invulnerable. But by 1946 our two boys became a source of caution and concern.

" 'Look at this desolate land, defeated, sucked dry, plucked bare under five years of devastation.' We contemplated the portrait of post-war Holland. We didn't mind the back-breaking struggle with the soil, provided that it kept up with its share of the bargain. But we didn't want Frank and Arno to live on the barricades. They should have time and energy left to enjoy other beauties of life besides working.

"And then there was another thing: we were *not* going to raise cannon-fodder. Europe had been plagued by wars for so long; so many millions of youthful lives had been wasted. How long would it take the Germans or another power to take another stab at dominating what was left of the continent? Actually, I was more scared of the Russians than of the Germans. They had millions of lives to toss into the fire without blinking an eye. We didn't want our children to grow up in the shadow of military monsters.

"One day, late in 1948, we decided enough was enough. All things considered, it was time to pack it in and try our fortune elsewhere, before it was too late."

"That was the one time in my life that I made the wrong decision, one that I'll never stop regretting," Albert's voice was strong, decisive, bursting with vigour. He was giving testimony before a mighty tribunal—no ambivalence, no guilt, just remorse for an error in judgement for which he accepted a self-imposed life sentence.

"To what are you referring?" I asked Albert, somewhat confused.

"All my life, I kept repeating the same thing: never do anything for money. Do it because you like it. We went through the war—that's a fact; we had some bleak memories—that, too, is a fact. We worried about future wars—once again, a fact. But what kept us going when we should have been resting in peace was the economic situation. We thought of the boys' future, and, yes, we thought of our own future comfort. So we chose Canada. I'm not ashamed to admit that it wasn't for the love of Canada that we left everything behind. We wanted it to surrender to us just a small parcel of its untapped wealth. You see, we didn't mind putting our sweat and blood into the land as long as it would pay us back in kind. But our land was tired and anaemic. Canada's, on the other hand, seemed to be overflowing with vitality and opportunity. And its frontiers could be contained only by oceans, not by men.

"We were impatient and our faith and trust, severely undermined. No wonder our eyes were no longer able to see what lay beneath the rubble. Those who clung to their roots with determination came out of the adventure invigorated, with their muscles and their coffers bulging. Take my brother: he's doing fine, just as well as we are, if not better. The competition is fierce over there, but only the lazy are deterred from entering the race. So maybe it's harder to get into university in the old country than it was for our boys. But I know them, they would have made it there, too."

"In 1954, our third son was born. Eric was a Canadian, a modest gift to this country for the many lives left behind in Dutch soil." Wilma spoke with pride. "It's good to know that we didn't just take from this country, and that we have also planted more than just vegetables and flowers. We have invested our offspring in Canada: from Ontario to British Columbia, the Dijkstras have done their share of building the empire."

"Well, it's only natural," Albert added. He was eager to have his say in this matter. He seemed enthusiastic about unravelling the part of the yarn that touched the New World. "Our children know that their first allegiance is to people, wherever they see the light of day. But beyond that, they are indebted to this land. In many ways, Canada has made sense to us from the moment we decided to leave crusty old Europe. It did not appear to be an aggressive land; it didn't even have a conscripted army. We liked that. You see, for instance, I could never have gone to the United States, never. Somehow they always manage to vote in governments who just can't resist the temptation to seduce the poor and vulnerable nations to surrender their soul for dollars and guns. U.S. political history is pock-marked; there seems to be some deep-seated need for the country to flex its muscles abroad. I could never live in a country where my taxes would contribute to killing. But don't think that I'm a blind fool: I know that it's only an illusion that Canada is pure and the U.S. alone is tainted. Wherever Americans are spreading venom, you'll find Canadians lending a helping hand. The age of innocence is over. In one way or another, we all contribute a brick or two to the construction of hell on earth."

"Don't misunderstand us, Canada has been great for us, we don't want to bite the hand that has more than fed us." Wilma didn't seem comfortable with Albert's candour. "When we arrived in this community in 1949, we were penniless. The cost of transplanting the family from Holland to Lake Simcoe exhausted our meagre budget. But we were better received than we expected. After all, nobody owed us anything. When we moved into this house, there was no electricity, no storm windows, nothing but an empty shell. Oh yes, we had water, plenty of it; unfortunately it came in through the roof directly. We had to collect it in buckets because we had no plumbing. The first two weeks were scary. I felt like we had just moved into a cave. We were, indeed, at the mercy of an unfriendly nature.

"But then, two weeks later, somebody knocked on our open door. It was the local welcome wagon. Their hands were loaded with coffee, cakes, cookies, fruit, you name it. Every neighbour had something to offer. At first, I was most embarrassed. I thought they had come out of charity. When we moved into our house in Apeldoorn, nobody came to welcome us; we just lived side by side, everybody tending to his own business. But in this foreign country, people who had no idea what sort we were, good or bad, came and took a chance on us. I had tears in my eyes I was so touched. That day we didn't even have to tell them that our entire treasury consisted of two little boys. They saw for themselves—no poultry, no cattle, no cars, no tools. When our neighbours saw how bare our cupboards were, they snapped into action. The next day, one brought a couple of chickens, another a bag of grain, a third, material to fix up our home. The next morning, we had our first eggs. Each day, from that morning on, life became just a hair more friendly, a shade more jovial. I tell you, that visit from our neighbours did what it set out to accomplish—it kindled the first fire in this shell of a house, and ever since then we have never been really cold here."

"You look like you have something else to say before we turn off the tape-recorder," Vicki said, turning to Albert.

"You're right, my dear," he replied with a paternal smile. "I want to tell you about our trip to Israel. Mau paid for all the expenses. It was one of the most important experiences of my life. I think you should hear about it."

Wilma cleared her throat to attract her husband's attention. Without a word she glanced at the cuckoo-clock on the wall.

"Well, you go look after the flowers. I'll tell the rest." There was a childlike eagerness in his voice. It reminded me of occasions when my children seemed more than happy to have us out of the house, leaving their activities unsupervised, unwitnessed.

Our hostess shook hands with us hastily and she left without a word. Something about her departure suggested to me that in addition to her professional concerns, there was another reason for which she chose to exit in a hurry. "Perhaps, there is something she doesn't want to hear in Albert's narrative," I thought.

"One day, around the beginning of April 1977, we got a letter from Mau." Albert sounded relieved that Wilma had left him in charge of finishing their story. "My, what a surprise! I had to sit down to reread the letter, I was so excited. In fact, I saved it—I save everything. Would you like me to read it to you?"

"Yes, of course," Vicki and I said in unison.

"Fine, but first let me give you a few background comments about them. Mau was among the very first to take his place in the new Jewish homeland in 1948. Since then he has been as happy as his memories would allow him to be. Soon after his sister, Rosa, and her husband joined him on the kibbutz where he lived.

"Poor Rosa wasn't around for long to enjoy the milk and honey of Israel. She died very young of breast cancer. She did, however, leave three children. By the way, Mau and his wife, Yetti, had three kids too.

"Well, back to the letter before my wife comes back. She doesn't like to hear me speak about some of my experiences and thoughts after the war. She thinks I'm boasting. We spoke about this very thing until late last night. But I'm quite stubborn about telling the whole truth. So this is what Mau wrote:

Dear Albert and Wilma,

My wife, Yetti, and I, as well as the rest of the family, want to see you in Eretz, Israel. We know that such a trip is not within your means. So Yetti and I have the pleasure and the honour of inviting you at our expense. The German government gave me some money to compensate me for the murder of my father. First I thought I really owe this money to make the life of the kibbutz a little easier. There is so much we need here. But then Yetti and I spoke about the matter and we also spoke with Rosa's kids, and we all agreed that we couldn't spend the money better than by offering you an all-expenses-paid holiday in Israel. We want our children to meet you. And we want to show you our country. We're very proud of what we have accomplished. Without people like you, it couldn't ever have become a reality. Shalom and God bless you, my friends, we'll see you this year in Jerusalem.

P.S. We have a surprise for you for when you get here.

Defiant Outsiders

"I tell you, Vicki and André, that letter knocked the wind out of me. I couldn't have imagined anything more moving. And you'd never guess what I thought of as I sat in this chair, staring with teary eyes at the sky above the lake. I thought of my friend in Australia who had received one 'thank you' out of the seven hundred he helped save. I can think of countless ways Mau and Yetti could have spent that money on themselves. But instead, they chose to spend it on expressing their gratitude to us. As if they owed us anything at all. We had no thoughts about 'rescuing' nor 'righteous behaviour' nor 'heroism'. These are all your words.

"Once we got to Israel, and we spent one week on Kibbutz Naan, I understood what Mau and his family were doing and saying. I loved those people more than any other people, because they made my dream come true. They created a commune where money was of no importance, where only communal happiness and raising their kids in peace made any sense at all. Taking care of one another, regardless of family boundaries, was their priority, and there was really only one family, the community. Once I was there, I understood Mau and Yetti's gesture, and also Rosa's kids'; because they chipped in, too. They wanted to show us what they had done with the lives that they had trusted to us for safekeeping. And we couldn't have been more honoured.

"I take my hat off to those Israelis, because they made something come true that has been tried in so many places and has always failed. But not there; in Israel they were going strong and growing stronger day by day. If I had been younger, I could have seen myself living on that kibbutz."

"What was the big surprise Mau announced in his letter?" I asked.

"That was some surprise! First Mau said: 'We'll take you to Jerusalem because that's the soul of both your faith and ours. It also has its own magic for us—without Jerusalem, Israel would be without a heart.'

"And we visited Jerusalem. Then, we went to a magnificent hill. It was breath-taking; it felt like we could see the whole world from up there. And there was a shady corner reserved for us Christians who took in Jews during the war. 'The Avenue of the Righteous', they call it. I don't know about the word 'righteous', it has little meaning to me, but I tell you, if our friends and the State of Israel wanted to make something of our feeble efforts, they couldn't have picked a more meaningful way to do it. They plant young trees in that garden with the name of a rescuer underneath each. For gardeners and nature-lovers like Wilma and me, that was a greater pleasure than anything else in the world. And I planted our tree with my own hands. Life definitely will continue to flow from us to the land of Israel through that one tree that I put into its soil."

"How did Yad Vashem hear of you?" Vicki asked.

"I'm glad you ask." Albert was nearly breathless in his excitement. "There was a ceremony, which I could have done without. There is one thing from that speech that I want to tell you about. That's when we learned how Yad Vashem—the Israeli War Memorial Authority—had heard of us. After all, the Dijkstra name is not on the six o'clock news every night. (Even our own children didn't know a great deal about what we had done during the war. After we received the invitation to go to Israel, we told them the story of our Jewish friends. They were impressed with their Dutch farmer parents—especially Eric, the youngest one, the one who was Canadian-born, without a direct link to Holland and its people.)

"It was all Mau's work. When he found out about The Avenue of the Righteous, he contacted the proper authorities and not only set out to document how we hid him and Rosa—that would have been enough for us to get our tree and the plaque that hangs over there on the wall, as you can see—but he tracked down Salomon, who was still living in Holland. His brother, Karel, after a short restless struggle with his displaced existence in Holland and his inability to make a firm commitment to Israel, died very young. But Salomon, or, as we used to know him, Dik, recalled both of their stories and sent it in writing to Mau. Then our friend tried to reach the doctor and his wife but they were dead. He managed, however, to find his way to a cousin of the Hellmans who lived in Israel and who knew all about what had happened to his family during the war.

"What can I say: if I had died right after that honour, I would have closed my eyes with a sense of eternity in my veins. I had our brand-new tree growing in Israel. I know for sure that my soul will go to thrive in that tree when I return to the earth. You see, that is our version of faith and religion."

"When you think back from the distance of forty years, how do you feel about your rescue activities?" I asked our host.

He turned his gaze away from me to contemplate the lake as if he wanted to draw his answer from its silent wisdom. Then, he turned towards us, looking each of us straight in the eyes and he said: "It was the most important experience in our lives—actually, the best thing that ever happened to us. The negative aspects faded into a meaningless fog. But the rewards are enormous. And I don't mean material rewards or even the recognition we have received in Israel and in Washington. That has just been the icing on the cake. The real reward, what we couldn't have achieved any other way, is the immense peace of mind that has kept us daily company since the end of the war. The happy feeling that we know that when the chips were down, we did the right thing. There is nothing else like it, for this peace of mind is the ultimate and perhaps the only achievement of our lives."

Sanity in Madness:
Salie "Sake" Bottinga

"I witnessed a lot of petty anti-Jewish incidents before the war,"
Sake said, reaching back into his well-manicured memory, "but
nothing that would have permitted me to forecast the black blood-
bath that took place." His teal-blue eyes—a perfect match with his
V-neck sweater—scanned the Frisian horizon for images and words
stored away for more than half of his eighty years. "You know, after
the war I *ordered* myself to forget everything as quickly as possible. I
took meticulous care to leave room only for beauty and service. The
horrors of those five years had to vanish in an unlit corner of my past.
They had grown on me as an unavoidable blemish; the best I could
do was to drape them in harmony and affection."

A quick survey of Salie ("just call me 'Sake' like everybody else
has for the past seventy-seven years") Bottinga's private domain in
rural Friesland allows no doubt about the outcome of his life-long
battle against ugliness. His unmistakably bachelor home emerges
before the visitor like a lavish oasis. We passed by the anonymous
path that led to his pseudo-Mediterranean villa three times before
finding it. I drove along the only road that sliced the tiny hamlet
of Wouterswoude into two thin halves. After a meticulous process
of elimination, we rolled onto a winding dirt road. My interpreter,

Sanity in Madness

Louisa, and I passed by modest cottages overflowing with countless children. Rusted-out automobile carcasses, stray barnyard animals, and weedy vegetation comprised the road-side panorama. After ten days of criss-crossing through Frisian dairy farms, our eyes and our noses no longer remembered a world without cattle or the heavy, fertile aroma blanketing the landscape. Just before turning around in frustration—the road seemed to have come to a dead end—I made a slight turn to the right, as wide as the skimpy path would allow for, and there it was.

Our host, in immaculate, white patent-leather moccasins and white linen pants, was tending to his painter's-palette garden, a garden which assertively separated his sun-drenched, red-tiled, and white-stuccoed residence from the ubiquitous grazing land and its countless black and white ruminants.

"I'm so glad you're here; Coco Chanel and I were beginning to wonder if you got lost in our Garden of Eden. I'm also glad to hear you enjoy my garden. These flowers...these flowers are my dearest friends.... They are genteel and discreet.... Oh, no, please don't expect me to pose for a photo. I would be an unsightly intrusion in this lovely panorama. Besides, I've spent years of my life erecting an invisible shield between the world of men and this modest hideaway. Please, my dear lady, present my apologies to the professor. But he's welcome to photograph my flowers; they thrive on attention, the vain creatures. You may tell him that a picture of my garden would have to include the best of me. And why bother with the rest, right?"

We followed an exuberant long-haired black dachshund into the spacious home. As I feasted my eyes on the dozens of cut flowers, the quietly elegant furniture, the rich textures, for the first time in days I felt happy to breathe freely through my nose. We settled into armchairs between an imposing marble fireplace and a generous French window, affording us layers of visual peace.

"'Oh, he's just a Jew,' or 'Why are you so surprised to have been gypped; what else could you expect from a Jew?' Does this sound familiar? I never paid any attention to such comments. I never gratified them with any response. To tell you the truth, it never occurred to me that Jews would notice them. It's like a wart: it's unsightly, but if you focus on the unblemished skin around it, your sense of beauty won't be offended. If you choose to concentrate on it, that's all you see. Then you'll spend your days tormented by

261

the imperfection of life. I had a patient in the Sint Joris Gasthuis, in Delft—it's a psychiatric hospital—who would lament every day: 'You don't know how much I've suffered for being a Jew; you don't know how horrible people can be when they know you're Jewish.' His constant complaining annoyed me because I didn't believe him.

" 'Come on, Max; it can't be all that bad. We're just not that kind of a people,' I'd tell him. I have always been very patriotic. I found it distasteful to hear these derogatory insinuations against my fellow Dutchmen. And this was only a couple of years before Hitler came to Holland! But you see, ever since I was eighteen and I moved from Dantumadeel—not too far from here, where there were no Jews—to bigger towns like Ermelo, Delft, Zwolle, I always had Jewish friends. Not that I sought them out. Did I tell you that I used to be a psychiatric nurse? I worked in a number of institutions. In mental hospitals there seem always to be some Jews among the staff. It's that simple.

"You know something; you may find it shocking, but for quite a while, we were rather enthusiastic about Hitler and his Nazism. Even the Jews thought that he had something to offer.

" 'He has a message, that Hitler,' this Jewish friend of mine used to tell me. 'There's a masculine magnetism to him that promises big things.' But then, the news began to filter through to us on the radio, in the press, from people who came back from visits to Germany, about the nature of his message. Most of us either didn't pay attention to the whole matter or just couldn't believe the truth.

"I worked day and night in the mental hospital, and I had no time or interest in those days for anything but my patients. As much as I enjoyed my profession, I was not happy working for someone else. My only goal in life was to operate my own convalescent home. You could say I had only one love—my dream of owning my own hospital. Being immersed in the world of the insane, I failed to notice the madness that began to infest the continent. Once I had my own chronic-care home in Blaricum (a stone's throw from Amsterdam), in 1937, then it started to sink in that something very foul was happening to the Jews. I had a couple of Jewish patients and some of their relatives came from Germany and told me about what Hitler was doing to the Jews, to mental patients, and to others. It would have been preferable to just shrug it off, but the news on the radio was malignant. When I heard about *Kristallnacht*, I felt sick to my stomach, literally.

Sanity in Madness

"My unusual first name, 'Salie', comes from 'Solomon'. I have a Polish Jewish ancestor on my mother's side—Solomon Levi. According to the family lore, he had many wives and countless children. My mother was one of them. I was named after him, but that's all. Religion never penetrated my parents' home. They were neither for it nor against it. We didn't even own a Bible. Dantumadeel was dominated by the Christian Reform Church, a very strict version of Calvinism. And since all my friends went to Sunday school, I wanted to go, too.

" 'If you start going,' my mother warned me, 'you'll have to complete the year.' I went for three years. I liked the teacher. I also liked the Bible. My parents just shrugged their shoulders. 'Children need stories, whether they come from the Bible or anywhere else. What's the difference?' they said.

"Why am I telling you all this? Ah, that's right, we're back in 1938–39, when the Nazi campaign against Jews was heating up. For the first time in my life, I asked myself the question: 'Am I Jewish?' The answer was a quick and irrefutable: 'No'. I was too busy running the home to scatter my attention on non-essential concerns. I had fourteen patients and the staff to worry about.

"Then, one night, I came in direct contact with the disease of the day.

" 'Tinus, wake up'—that's what my patients called me, 'Holy Tinus'—'Holy Tinus, you've got to get up.'

" 'What in the world are you doing up at four o'clock in the morning, Hilde? What's happening? Why aren't you in bed?' My patient was beside herself; she could not calm down enough to tell me why she had awakened me at the crack of dawn. Finally she blurted it out. 'The Germans are here, Tinus. They're coming to take the Jews away. Tinus, I'm Jewish. I don't want them to take me away....'

"I was nearly undone by the news. I had to keep splashing cold water on my face to keep myself from panic. But then I got hold of myself in front of the bathroom mirror. 'You've got a hospital to run, people have to be treated, fed, taken care of, Germans or no Germans.' So I decided to go about my business as if nothing had happened. But I could not chase the thought from my mind: 'The Germans have entered Holland; they're going to occupy us. What's going to happen to us?'

"The next day brought more news. 'Hilde Herzog has run away.' One of my nurses caught me with the news by the front door. 'She left the message that she was going to England tonight. Should we try to do something?'

" 'No, let her take her chances. If she doesn't make it, she'll probably come back to us one way or another. What's waiting for her here anyway? She's Jewish you know. With the Germans on our backs, she's better off in England....'

"Two days later, I came face to face with the Wehrmacht. It was a horrible vision. I lost my composure. I couldn't tolerate the sight of them. I buried my gaze in my chest and ran through the yard of a stranger. It was like the onset of an epidemic, I tell you. Just thinking back I get the shivers. And that was just the beginning. If I had known what was waiting for us, for me, I tell you, I don't know what I would have done, I just don't know....

"Things began to happen very quickly. Dr. Krygers Janssen, one of the two psychiatrists on our staff, came to see me about a week later.

" 'Sake, I've got a problem; I need your help. I have a patient, Walter Dozeman. He's taken the news very badly. He's gone into a deep depression. Can you put him up here for a while?'

" 'But, of course! Have him come today. The doors are open; it's business as usual,' I said, a bit surprised. I didn't understand what the problem was.

" 'He's Jewish, Sake. You should know that.'

" 'Why should I know that, Doctor? What business is it of mine? Is Jewish depression different from Christian depression? He's not the first Jewish patient in here nor will he be the last.'

"Walter moved in that evening. His wife was there all the time. And so were his parents. He stayed with us for months and months before he began to feel sufficiently reassured to go home to Bussum. Shortly after, in 1941, the Jews were ordered to evacuate the area and to move to Amsterdam. That didn't mean, of course, that I let them slip out of sight. I grew more and more anxious about their fate. They had to share a small flat with Walter's in-laws. For poor Walter the endless list of laws restricting the most mundane activities of Jews proved to be less and less bearable. He was emotionally and morally shrinking, his psyche was withering away. When it came to pass that Jews could not even shop for food except in the late afternoon hours (when the shelves had already been plucked clean) I had to step into action. I bought them fruit and vegetables in Blaricum and took them to their home day after day.

Sanity in Madness

" 'Walter, Betty, why don't you come back to stay with me? It would be so much safer and so much healthier for you, my friends,' I implored them each time I saw them.

"And each time the answer was the same. 'No, Tinus. That's just not in the cards. You don't really imagine that we would venture out beyond the boundaries set for the Jews? We would never make it past the city limits. Oh, my God, how could you even think of it. If you were a Jew, you'd know that it would be suicidal for us....'

"However, Walter managed to find a vacant room in a boarding house.

"One night, I was awakened by a strange sound. It was nearly eleven o'clock. I couldn't imagine what it was, but it sure sounded like plaintive laments, sobbing and weeping. I thought I was dreaming. Since we had black-out orders, I couldn't turn on the light to see if there was anything unusual happening underneath my window. I put on a night jacket and went down to the front door. When I opened it I couldn't believe my eyes. Walter and Betty were standing there, crying hysterically.

" 'We just couldn't bear sitting in that wretched room any longer, waiting for the inevitable.' Walter said, after regaining his composure. 'We know that they are going to kill all the Jews one way or another. You sit there and do what you are told, hoping that obedience will bring its fruit, but there have been too many examples to prove the contrary. But since the prison door is open, enticing you to escape, you want to trust your fate to God or to luck since you can no longer count on people. But that's exactly what they want you to do! They want you to go crazy in your open cell and make a run for it. And they wait for you outside to pluck you like a ripe plum. What kind of a world is this anyway, where people are not even given a chance to live within the limits of the law? What constitutes law-abiding today is defined as law-breaking tomorrow. So, we've had it. Betty and I decided that if we're doomed anyway, we might as well try the only chance we have to survive—make a run for it to Blaricum, and here we are.'

" 'We never expected to make it all the way here'—Betty took over from her breathless husband—'but we were past caring. Anything would have been better than rotting in our own anxiety. Last night, a bunch of hoodlums gathered in front of our house and pelted our window with excrement. When they ran out of their foul projectiles, they produced a Torah scroll. They set it on fire and whirled it against our window. Walter was so enraged that he wanted to run down with a kitchen knife and go on a suicide attack....'

" 'I'd rather die than endure this kind of debasing day after day. I've reached the end of my spool, the thread of my patience has been unravelled.'

" 'Well, here we are, Tinus. We have done what you've been urging us to do for such a long time. Is the offer still good, Tinus?' Her eyes were imploring, untrusting.

" 'You're welcome, of course. This is now your home for as long as you want to stay.'

"So that's how I started my illegal career of hiding Jews. They were the first, but they certainly were not the last. Soon after that night, the same doctor who introduced Walter and Betty to me, Dr. Janssen, came to my room one morning to tell me about another Jewish couple. 'Sake, can you help me again? If you had the space for one more couple it could mean the difference between life and death for them. Have you heard about the camp at Westerbork in Drenthe? Have you heard about the death factories in Poland and Germany: Auschwitz and Mauthausen?'

" 'Dr. Janssen, you don't need to sell the idea of hiding your Jewish couple. My home is open to anyone in danger. I can always find extra beds. Besides, if we get caught, what's the difference between having one couple or two? But we can't think of getting caught. I have to go on with the assumption that we can always outfox the dimwits. The rest is a game of chance. However, I have one question for you, Doctor. Are you connected to the underground?'

" 'My dear Sake, these days you couldn't ask a more dangerous question of anyone, even if you wanted to. If I answered in the affirmative, one day it might be the death of both of us, not to mention all our protégés. What would you do if you were caught and tortured or were offered your life in exchange for the names of all the people you knew in the resistance movement? So, even if I were, I wouldn't tell you. But as it happens, I'm not. I work on my own initiative. It probably has something to do with my personal repulsion for suffering. Let me repay your curiosity in kind, Sake. What about your staff, do you trust them? You can't have people taking up space and not getting treatment. What about their loyalties?'

"His question jarred me. I had a hard decision to make. I *thought* I could trust all of my people, but it was more a guess than a certainty. I had never had to test their leanings, their courage, their commitment, so how could I judge what they might do? Really?

" 'I trust Dr. Kees Emmer, our general practitioner, like I trust myself, but everybody else is an enigma,' I told him. 'The only thing I can do is to have the Jews stay in one wing of the villa, confined to their rooms during the day. I will have to find an accomplice who'll look after their daily needs.'

"Lines marred Dr. Janssen's smooth Nordic features. 'Sooner or later, there will be talk. It's inevitable. The place is not big enough to hermetically close off one part without it attracting suspicion,' he said.

" 'I propose, Doctor, that you leave the worrying to me. I have nearly fifteen years of experience in working with people in the mental-health profession. I think I can handle them.'

" 'What about the patients?' he asked.

" 'Well, as you know, most of our current patients are demented. Who would ever ask a "lunatic" for information? The general public, including the authorities, are petrified in the presence of a mentally ill person, as if their condition were contagious. So we don't have to worry about the patients. But we do have to keep in mind their visitors. During visiting hours, therefore, I will insist on the absolute confinement of our Jewish friends to their rooms.'

" 'Well'—the doctor's eyes were still overcast with doubt—'I guess these days there is no guarantee for any of us. We have to wager on the side of hope and, by the same token, give hope a boost with some good old common-sense cunning. Tell me, Sake, aren't you scared?'

" 'Come on, doctor,' I answered. 'What do you take me for? A hero? I'm shaking in my shoes and socks. Of course I'm terrified. If I weren't, I would check myself into my own clinic as a patient. But you can be sure of one thing: when this is all over, I'll have a well-earned hysterical fit. Until then I'll keep myself under control, I promise....'

"The Wassermans moved in the next night, after the household had retired for the day. They settled into our lives like two shadows. They glided on weightless feet during the empty hours of the day.

"I never really got to know them. They slipped into their new role of the living dead with ghostly ease. I certainly respected their inclination to vanish into the walls of our little institution. In my profession you quickly learn to take the cue from the other as to how close to draw the boundary between you.

"The most curious event that I recall in connection with the Wassermans—I don't know if I ever knew their first names—was Walter's reaction to their joining us. I thought that their presence was going to be a beneficial experience for Walter and Betty. You know what I mean? Another couple with whom to share the vicissitudes of internal exile and the dreams of a better day. Well, I was very wrong.

" 'You mean, this place is known about as a safe harbour for wayward Jews? That has to lead to some notoriety in certain circles. Once that happens, it will be just a matter of time before the Germans will kick your door down, Tinus. You can't let that happen. You must do everything to safeguard our secret.'

" 'Calm down, Walter,' I told him, still somewhat stunned. 'Except for our common friend, Dr. Janssen, no one knows about the Jews in my home. We want to stay healthy, don't we?'

" 'But the doctor,' he continued in a whining nag, 'he travels around a great deal, making contacts everywhere. Just as he found out about this couple of interlopers, he will find others. Where will it end, Tinus, I ask you, where will it end? Is your home going to become a private club for illegal Jews? Dr. Janssen must be in the underground and you know and I know that the movement is infiltrated with spies. The underground will bring doom upon our heads.'

" 'Stop it right there, Walter!' I lost my patience with his selfish fears. 'Don't get your feathers all ruffled on the doctor's account. He's not in the underground. As for the rest, just trust me. Don't you think I want to survive, too? After all, if you get caught, so do I; and whatever happens to you, I'll have the dubious pleasure of sharing your fate.'

"But, as you might have already guessed, Walter was who he was and nothing I could have said would have calmed him down. He regressed into infantile narcissistic concerns. He obviously couldn't help it. There is nothing more frustrating for me than seeing someone in the grip of anxiety and not being able to do anything. You may say that this is my little obsession, and I wouldn't argue with you. Nevertheless, I feel worse when I find myself helpless in front of another person's pain than when I myself suffer. I'm not trying to put on saintly airs, that's just the nature of the beast that I am. Well, let's glide over my little peccadilloes, they're neither here nor there. You didn't drive to this end of the world to be entertained with the petty follies of an old fool....

"You can imagine my shock, when a couple of months later, Dr. Janssen grabbed me by the arm ever so gently, but with authority in his touch.

" 'Sake, I don't like what I've been hearing in town,' he whispered to me as we were walking down the steps. 'Rumour has it that the Wassermans are hiding in Blaricum. I heard it from a couple of different sources. One of them intimated that they might be hiding in a medical facility of some sort. They didn't seem to be malicious rumours, but all rumours have the tendency these days to turn to malice. So what do you say?'

" 'I'd be happier if you could find greener pastures for them, that's for sure. If you can't, you can't...but from here it certainly looks to me like the witches' brew out there is beginning to bubble.'

"The following day, when I saw the doctor open the front door, I knew there was trouble. You see, he was not scheduled for that day and we had not put in a call for an emergency visit.

" 'Sake, they've got to go tonight.' He cut to the heart of the matter even before I shut the door behind me. 'I heard your name mentioned this morning in the context of the vanished Wassermans. We can no longer take a risk, they'll leave tonight. I'll come by to get them myself at nine o'clock.'

"Just as silently as they came, and just as silently as they stayed, they disappeared from our lives that night at nine o'clock sharp. I never asked him about them. I assumed that he preferred it that way. Sometimes, half a word was enough to get you into more trouble than you bargained for; at other times, even silence might have been too much.... Those days...aye, my dear lady, what a way to live...

"As you might have guessed, when Walter heard the news of the Wassermans' departure, he was relieved. Of course, I didn't tell him that they had had to flee because of gossip.

"The next day, Betty came forth with an amazing request: 'What would you say about a little stroll, just the two of us, after dinner, you and I, Tinus? I need some change of air, even if only for a few minutes. Do you realize how long it has been since I set foot outside? How about it, Tinus? Just fifteen minutes off for good behaviour.'

" 'Why not, Betty, why not?' I thought it was completely safe for us to venture out in the neighbourhood. Betty was the embodiment of the young Germanic woman. About thirty years old, with a large frame, and thick straw-blonde straight hair, the open rectangle of her forehead inspired confidence and a clear conscience. She had azure-blue eyes to instill envy in all aspiring young Loreleis.

"Walter was quite another story. He was so typically Jewish, if I were to draw his portrait, you'd accuse me of anti-Semitism. Walter wouldn't have wanted to leave the protective cocoon of our home for anything in the world. After the Wassermans left, they resumed their habit of coming down after curfew for a chat in my room, an occasional game of cards, or for a session of clandestine radio listening.

"After a while, Betty and I became bolder; we strayed farther and farther away. We presented the image of a serene young couple, enjoying the fresh air and the simple pleasure of each other's company in the midst of a very noisy world. Later, we took advantage of the peaceful lull of Sunday afternoons and we left Walter home for his afternoon nap.

"But I'm digressing again. I guess you just have to put up with a senile old man's undisciplined ramblings since you've already come all this way to hear about those times. Frankly, I believe you attach more importance to them than I ever did, but then again, I don't really know what is of interest these days and what isn't. As you see, I'm so far removed from the hustle and bustle of life that I hardly know what day it is...but then again, Coco Chanel and I have no need for the calendar—one day is exactly the same as another, so why bother? Oh, my Lord, what kind of a host am I? I should be truly ashamed of myself. You've been here for a couple of hours and I haven't even offered you a cup of coffee.... How inhospitable of me...not to mention unpatriotic. You can't visit a Dutch home without being offered a cup of coffee. The French have their wine, the British their tea, we Dutch have our daily coffee.... We'll take a moment's respite, all right?—just long enough for me to serve a nice cup of espresso and a slice of lemon cake which I baked in your honour...to sweeten the task, so to speak."

" 'Tinus, I can't sleep nights from worry about my poor old parents,' Walter confided in me one day. 'The man who's hiding them in Bussum is also sheltering all kinds of smugglers and black-marketeers. The host doesn't upset me too much; he obviously doesn't care if he let them come. But any one of those shady characters might sell them to the authorities for one hundred guilders if they suspected them of being Jewish.'

"For once I agreed with Walter's concerns. I knew of the place—I had been there myself and I almost got jaundice just watching some of those hustlers. I had already suggested to Walter's parents that they move in with us, but the father was no different from the son—he was petrified of the thought of setting foot in the unsafe streets.

" 'I know what we can do. Betty and I will ride our bicycles over to Bussum and see if we can talk them into some healthier arrangement,' I suggested.

"When we entered the large, neglected house, I thought I was in some sort of underworld locale. The salon was swimming in bluish smoke; the acrid stink of alcohol and unwashed bodies was screaming for attention. The crooks were dealing openly in illegally obtained merchandise: coffee, cigarettes, cocoa, gin, you name it.

" 'We can't leave you here, Mr. Dozeman. This is hell. Come on, make an effort. We'll get out of here in the evening and walk calmly back to my house in Blaricum, the four of us.'

"The only thing we could accomplish that day, though, was to agree on a system. The owner had a young girl who for a couple of guilders was glad to deliver messages and do other little chores.

" 'If we think it's time to evacuate the premises, we'll send little Anna over on the the bike with the message: "Danco needs to be taken to the veterinarian." Then you come at once,' Dozeman senior suggested. Danco was their dog. He was one of Coco Chanel's ancestors.

"Sure enough, a couple of weeks later, we got the message, 'Danco needs to go to the vet; come fetch him immediately.' I went that night alone on the bicycle. I can't tell you why, but that night I felt safer without Betty. As it turned out, I could have taken her. Anyway, when I got to the house where Walter's parents lived, I decided against walking out with the old couple into the midst of that crowd of throat-cutters. If they saw the two carrying their suitcases, they were sure to stick their long noses into the matter, just to see if there was any profit to make. In fact, I decided to have them leave behind everything they couldn't carry on their persons or in Mrs. Dozeman's handbag. Those days there was no greater attention-getter than a suitcase in the night.

" 'You'd better climb through the window,' I advised the Doze-mans. 'It's safer that way. I'll help you from the outside.' And so they did. I walked my bicycle back to Blaricum with the two Jews, not exchanging a word on the long promenade. Their tongues turned to stone under the weight of fear. You see, the poor souls were caught in the web of an intolerable paradox: they knew that according to the law they were supposed to wear the yellow star on their chests, but they couldn't follow the letter of the law because that would have been the end of everything. On the other hand, they were terrified to be in breach of the law.

" 'We felt naked without the star all along the walk from Bussum to Blaricum. We were convinced that our faces would betray our true identity. With the star, we would have been doomed, without it, we were *sure* we were doomed,' they reflected in the safety of their new home.

"So, now they were four. And soon Len made five. She was an old friend of mine from The Hague where she had been a purchaser for a large notions' firm. I had told her, too, many times, that she would be better off at my place than anywhere else. But, what can I say— even though she was a woman of the world, educated and refined, she just didn't feel at ease with my general clientele.

" 'As safe as anyone can be in a lunatic asylum. No offence, Sake, but I'd have to be crazy to move into your jolly home.' She ended up hiding with a wonderful couple near Amsterdam. They treated Len like family. There was one problem: the wife was Jewish.

" 'A most explosive situation, my dear,' I told Len on my first visit to her new residence. 'You're sitting on a dormant volcano that can erupt any minute under your posterior. Think it over, my place is a lot safer than this fly-catcher.'

" 'Sake, you're very sweet to worry so much about me, you old fuss-budget,' she responded with a gentle tease. 'It's so typical of you old bachelors to blow up every little thing into a major intrigue. I'll be just fine here, don't worry.'

"But I did worry because I had known of several mixed couples who had been denounced by nasty neighbours, bounty-hunters, and NSB turncoats. If you're scared of the lion, you don't hide in a river infested with alligators, am I wrong?

"One day, Len went for a stroll in town bold as she was, without papers, without care. On her way back, as she rounded the corner, she saw her hosts being brutally ushered into a Gestapo vehicle. She made an instant about-face, leaving everything behind. She didn't stop until she reached my address in Blaricum. Once she allowed her exhausted body to drop into my armchair, she felt safe enough to give free flow to her fear. She was heaving and weeping, shrieking and whining—she went through a rich repertoire of panic reactions. When the fire finally blew itself out in her wrung-out body, she asked for my handkerchief.

" 'Just think, Sake, if I had stayed home, safely hidden in my room, I would now be on my way to Poland via Westerbork. I'm here because of an absurd stroke of luck: I refused to play it safe, by the book. The reward for my insolence was reprieve. Go explain divine or human justice to me after this! In any event, you won. These days it *is* safer in a madhouse than in the world of the sane.'

"Ella Boas was number six. She joined us almost the same day as Len did. It doesn't make any difference whether it was one day or one week later, does it? Ella Boas came to join us towards the end of spring 1944. We had already endured four long years of the heavy German diet. And there was a lot more to come. But to come back to Ella, of all the Jews I hid, I felt the most devastated for her. Some friends of mine spoke to me about this woman who had been blown about like a feather in the wind. She was in constant motion. For some reason, she had been ushered from one hiding place to another. By the time my friends brought her over, she was shivering with fear. She wouldn't take her coat off.

" 'Ella, come on, make yourself comfortable. From now on, this is going to be your home. Come on, let me hang up your coat.' But she just held on to her lapels as if she would drown without them. She fell asleep on top of the bed, without even folding down the covers, without even taking off her shoes.

" 'Do I have to leave next week?' she asked the next morning.

" 'No, of course, you don't.'

" 'That's a switch. I've been on the road every week, at least once. So when do I have to leave? In two weeks?'

" 'No, not at all. Don't even think about leaving. Come on, I'll introduce you to Len. She's about your age; she's all alone too. The two of you can cheer each other up. Then you'll meet the others.' I briefed her on the house rules. But she didn't seem to listen or care.

" 'Ella, why don't you pay attention to what I'm saying? These are very important matters. They have to do with security. Doesn't that interest you?'

" 'Not really,' she answered with a shrug of her shoulders. 'By the time I remember them all, I'll have to leave anyway.'

Quiet Heroes

" 'Can't you get it into your thick skull that you don't have to leave unless you want to leave?' I lost my patience.

"Later, I felt quite ashamed of myself: 'Of course, she can't get it into her head that there is such a thing as a safe place. It's your head that's thick, not hers. Why can't you appreciate her predicament? Stop judging her! You can't possibly know what makes sense to her. Shame on you, Sake Bottinga.' I really gave it to myself for coming down hard on poor, abused Ella. I tell you, it was a most valuable lesson for me, as a man and as a professional. There are times when paranoia is the only healthy way to assess the situation at hand. When you are constantly hounded, if you don't keep looking over your shoulders there's something wrong with you. They should teach that to anyone who has to work with victims of persecution. More coffee, my dear lady? What about the professor, would he like another refreshment, or perhaps another slice of lemon cake? I always stop for coffee when I need to distract myself from an unhappy thought....

" 'I'm so sorry, Ella,' I apologized to her the next morning. 'I have the sensitivity of a rhinoceros. After what you've been through no one can blame you for not trusting anyone. But I promise you, you're finally at home. You will not be moved again—not next week, not the following.'

" 'So when am I going then? Next month?'

" 'No, you're going after the war is over.' But do you think that was the end of it? It took her over a month to finally relax and to stop living in combat readiness. It was a real exercise in humility for me to accept the fact that I couldn't do more for her than shelter her, and to be patient with her persecution delusions. If I had the time, I would have sat with her day after day, the whole day, holding her hand until she would have finally felt safe in my home. But I didn't have that kind of time. I had all the others. Not to mention the operation of the home. And I didn't have a full house yet. I still had number seven to come.

"One day, in the middle of the summer—to be quite exact, on July 31—I went to visit a married couple in Blaricum. They were very good friends, and they had invited me for my birthday—that's why I remember the date. They lived in a tiny home, more like a dollhouse than a place fit for two adults. That day, I arrived at my friends' house thirty minutes earlier than expected.

" 'Something is strange about this room, Bertil,' I said. I couldn't put my finger on what it was, but I felt a strange presence. 'It's as if

274

there was somebody else in here. You know me; I'm very sensitive to bodies.'

" 'Why, Sake, I don't know what you're talking about. Who on earth would be here besides Friso and me? Sometimes I think some of your patients' habits are rubbing off on you. Have you become just a tad paranoid, my friend?' She was gently chiding me but I wasn't fooled by the mock levity in her voice, it was tinged with a hint of anxiety.

" 'Cut it out, Bertil. I may be all wrong, but I don't think so. Perhaps you're right about picking up some peculiarities from my clientele, but not necessarily those that you so flippantly attribute to me. Sometimes the mentally ill are gifted with an eerie sense of awareness. At times I, too, possess a keener power of perception than the ordinary mortal.' As I was speaking, my antennae were out like those of a prowling snail.

" 'Well, Sake, if that's so, perhaps you wish to offer your services to the Gestapo or the NSB; such powers are invaluable nowadays.' I couldn't fail to pick up a suddenly sharpened edge to her tone. Now I was sure that something was not quite kosher in the home of my friends.

"I decided to continue on my reconnaissance expedition. If soft-spoken, even tempered Bertil was in a morose mood on my birthday, there must have been something rather serious bothering her. As a good friend, it was my duty to ferret out the problem and to help. There is a thin line between sticking one's nose into other people's business and sensing that the other is in trouble. I like to think that I can find that thin demarcation line, most of the time, anyway.

" 'Bertil, don't play games with me, please,' I said to her as she was pretending to have lost interest not only in the topic of conversation but also in me. She began to leaf through an old magazine—it was upside down! 'There's nothing in that upside-down magazine of yours that could possibly hold your attention. I'm sure you're in some sort of trouble and you don't dare to trust me with it.'

"Before she had the chance to answer me, my eyes that hadn't stopped scanning the tiny room during our conversation, fell on what I was looking for, the proof of an unknown person's presence. On top of a dark-brown armchair I noticed a piece of silver hair glistening with secret information. 'Just tell me one thing, Bertil, and after that I'll drop the whole subject if you so desire. Since when do you have wavy grey hair, either one of you fine specimens of young blond Aryans?'

"She looked at me with raw terror in her face. 'Sake, I can't stand it any more. Stop interrogating me like an SS officer; if you can't do that much for me, just go home and don't come back; forget that you even know us.'

" 'As a matter of fact, you're right,' Friso said, as he came from the kitchen. Of course, he had heard every word. In that tiny house there were no secret sounds. If you had had an extra heartbeat, everyone in the house would have heard it.

" 'Friso, no, just keep your mouth shut.' Bertil jumped to her feet, reaching out with her arm as if she wanted to put her hand across her husband's mouth.

" 'It's all right, my dear. Sake is a friend, and we need at least one ally or we'll go crazy.' He put his arm lovingly around his wife, who was trembling like a trapped creature in the forest, face to face with her fate. I felt a pinch of envy, my dear lady. There are certain inconveniences that go with the solitary life of the bachelor. But there I go again, off on an other tangent....

" 'Sake, my friend, my mother-in-law has been living with us for a while.'

" 'Your mother-in-law has been living here? Where? You have no other room but this one and the kitchen. And there is certainly no room in the kitchen for a bed.'

" 'The truth is that she has been sleeping under the kitchen floor. I took out some boards from the floor, then I dug out a hole large enough to lower a mattress in for her to lie on. When she retires, we place the boards back and no one is the wiser. You have been here many times when she was in the hole and you didn't notice anything. That's why I'm so surprised that you caught on to something today.'

" 'But why is she hiding in there? For goodness sake, what has she done?'

" 'Done? I'm surprised at you, Sake.' Bertil's voice was quavering, but the edge was gone. 'Since when do you have to have done something to be in danger?'

" 'You must bear with me, my friends, but I don't follow you at all. Only Jews have to hide like that—and conscientious objectors.'

" 'So, where's the inconsistency?' asked Bertil, a shade paler than usual. 'I'm Jewish, and obviously, so is my mother.'

"'You're Jewish? Come on, you're teasing me. This whole thing is a practical joke. You almost had me convinced. There's nobody here; there's no hole; you're just pulling my leg because I dared to be pretentious enough about my sixth sense.'

"'No, Sake, she's Jewish all right, Jewish from Hamburg. That's where her mother ran away from five years ago.'

"'You're not going to tell me that she's being living in that hole for five years,' I said in disbelief.

"'No, she's been living there for the last two years; she was hiding at different people's homes before. It became too risky to keep moving her around, so we thought this could work. And it does.'

"'But why did you keep it a secret from me that you're Jewish?' I harboured a touch of hurt because of their obvious lack of trust in me.

"'Did you ever ask if I was Jewish?' she retorted. 'Since when is it worthy of conversation among friends whether they're Jewish, Christian, or Buddhist?'

"'Since friends have to stick their mother in the ground while she is still very much alive. You know that I have a big house with all kinds of people in it. If I had known that your mother needed shelter, I would have insisted on having her take up residence at my address.'

"'You're very sweet, Sake,' Bertil said in a whisper, wiping a tear from her eye, 'but these days, you don't have the right to burden your friends with such indiscretions. It's best that nobody know our secret.'

"'I don't ever want to hear such nonsense. I want you to dig up your mother from under the ground and we'll transport her to my place at night.'

"Grandma Spier, as we used to call her, was a frightened little woman, dressed all in black. She reminded me of a large prune. She carried deep chagrin in every one of the countless wrinkles on her face. 'Bertil is about twenty-five, so she can't be as old as she looks,' I thought to myself. Later I learned that she was in her early fifties.

"Did I tell you that Friso and Bertil were dear friends of mine? I had known them ever since they moved to Blaricum, a couple of weeks after they got married. Friso was studying with Heidegger in Heidelberg. That's where he met Bertil, who was studying French literature at the same university. So far it's quite trivial—boy meets girl during university studies, they fall in love, and get married in a hurry. Friso returned to Holland with his new German bride just before the Dutch-German border was closed. When I met the two at a mutual friend's house, he was looking for some sort of gainful employment.

"I'd never even thought of putting two and two together at the time about their hasty marriage and the sudden interruption of their studies. I chalked the whole thing up to young lovers' impulse. Who would have thought of a life-and-death flight from Germany during those early days of Nazism? A Jew, perhaps, and even then, most of them didn't think of it.

"From the first time I met Grandma Spier at that rather momentous birthday party at Friso and Bertil's house, it struck me how, every once in a while and for no apparent reason, she would bury her face in her knobby, shaky hands. What was left visible of her face turned grey, like the earth that had sheltered her for two years. The creases in her visage grew deeper and darker. She made a desperate effort to be discreet about her tears, which resulted in a muffled moan of agony with occasional peaks of pain expressed in a chilling wail. After about ten minutes of this inner torment, she would regain a veneer of composure and, without a word to anyone, she would remove herself from our midst—not physically, but mentally and spiritually. I looked at Bertil for some silent encouragement, but her cheeks were still, with a dull ache glazing her motionless eyes. Friso turned his gaze on the table, cutting himself off from the rest of us. Later, once she was in my home, I learned the poor soul's story. She confided in Ella Boas. Ventilating her scathed memory afforded her a touch of relief.

" 'She and her husband were Orthodox Jews living in Hamburg,' Ella informed me. 'They had a small dry goods' store. The couple was devoted to their daughter and to the love of God. The turmoils of modern European cosmopolitan life were disconcerting for them. To protect themselves from the confusing influence of secular forces, they redoubled their fervent vigilance over the purity of their practices and their faith. The six hundred or so laws outlined in Leviticus were not sufficient for this fragile couple because they felt that their spiritual edifice was built on slippery terrain. So they drew the boundaries of Orthodoxy even more strictly, even more narrowly than required.

" 'But neologism was sweeping Germany. Bertil was no different than the majority. She wanted to be German first and felt she was Jewish only by accident. Tolerance of their only child's leanings caused them great suffering, but they were so enamoured with their otherwise dutiful daughter that they accepted with wise resignation that the Almighty wouldn't let go of her vulnerable soul if He found her to be in danger. They gave her their blessing when she went off to university to study literature. Bertil had never disappointed them in any way. But she wanted to fit in rather than be on the fringe. One November day in 1938, all their joy came to an ear-shattering crash that planted broken glass in Grandma Spier's memory for the rest of her days. Every now and then, she felt her face lacerated by visual memories that demanded her stoic attention.'

"The way Ella Boas related the rest of Grandma Spier's story has such a destructive power over me that I hesitate to recall it. You might have noticed that I'm really hedging and delaying the account of what caused the old woman to cover her face and what brought inarticulate pain to her lips. I'll skip the details. Let's just say that Grandma Spier met the devil face to face on *Kristallnacht*. And he ravished her husband that same night. The wretched storekeeper weaned on Torah and Talmud, had no defence available to him other than just that, the words he had learned all his life. The hateful thugs literally tore the miserable Jew to pieces. And if that wasn't bad enough, they forced his wife to watch from close up how they were extinguishing the life in her husband, spark by spark. It was that ghoulish spectacle that kept haunting her with merciless stubbornness.

"I tell you, my dear lady, there are times I'm ashamed of being a human being, if I have to share that dubious title with degenerates who commit such acts of violence. What they did to Herr Spier and by extension, to his wife, goes beyond violence. Indulge me for a moment, please. In my opinion and in my experience with the demented, violence has its inner logic, its meaning, and even its esthetic. When people shred to pieces a defenseless old man just because he *is* or just because they feel like it, it's a wasteful gesture of self-mutilation as much as maniacal homicide. You look at me and you see me with my face, my arms, my feet, my eyes imploring you to see in me a brother, a fellow human being, but you fail to see sufficient similiarity between you and me. Instead, you assert your right and might to dispose of me in a manner for which there is really no known word.

"You don't act like a beast, because animals kill only to satiate their hunger; they are economical and free of greed in their destruction. When an animal kills, it's to sustain life. I'd hate to be a gazelle who may end its earthly existence as a meal for a hungry lion. But from the comfort of my safe distance, I can reconcile myself to that killing.

"How can a person do that and remain a person? How can a person do that and be a person to begin with? How can it ever occur to a human being to do something that exiles him beyond the boundary between man and his nameless enemy?

"I am sorry, my dear lady, to get so carried away. My doctor would certainly disapprove of such blood-pressure–boosting emotional acrobatics, but I can't return to my memories of the war without visiting with Grandma Spier. And when I do recall her gruesome tale, I lose all self-control.

"Call me a degenerate, but I can cope with less revulsion with the hallucinatory reality of the piles of victims. At least I know that they had no choice but to submit to a force beyond their control. The victims make more sense to me than their assassins do. So when I think of the gangs of those monsters in human skin I lose all civility myself. You see, the victims bring tears to my eyes and force me on my knees to beg for forgiveness, but in a very real sense, they are beyond my horizon.

"But those who transformed them into victims *are* my concern. I want them to account to me, because they implicated me in their cannibalistic consumption of souls. I don't want the murderer's blood; I want his banishment from my blood, from my face. I want to be able to walk freely among Jewish children and not to have to worry that they may mistake me for the murderer. I never hurt a soul in my life, I know that; but, my dear lady, after those five years of black plague, the knowledge of one's own innocence recedes into darkness in the light of the guilt that blankets us from beyond the barbed wire. Did you wonder what I am doing in this austere corner of the continent, sheltered from a busy Europe? How is it that my sole companion and witness is this forgiving four-legged friend, Coco Chanel? I don't have the audacity to show my face where its moral validity might be put into question just by its mere chronological endurance. I am hiding, my dear lady, in shame for all those assassins who are so busy in their freshly painted skins. Oh, my God, I don't believe how I have been carrying on like a fish-wife when there is still so much more to tell you, things that are of interest to you and the professor, rather than what I think or don't think. But you see, when one loses touch with human rapport, one is likely to slip into self-important poses assuming that just because one hasn't said much

for a long time, one in fact does have a lot of worthy things to say....
How about some more coffee before I continue with the story that
interests you? Let me get you a fresh cup. In the meantime you and
the professor may wish to stretch your legs...."

"Grandma Spier was smuggled into my home. She became a
patient for most of her tenure among us. Need I say that her Jewish
identity was not revealed to anyone? Some might have guessed it
anyway, just from seeing the suffering etched into her face. But you
must wonder how we got this debilitated old woman from Friso
and Bertil's abode to my house. Walking the streets was out of the
question. She had neither the will nor the strength to step outside. I
had no access to any vehicle in which to transport her— except for the
hearse that we had to call upon every now and then. Well, I thought,
this time we'll reverse the order of things (an activity most befitting
the times). Instead of removing a body from the clinic, we'll take one
in. All we needed was a piece of credible fiction. Before the night was
out, we were in possession of one.

"I called upon the driver of the hearse and asked him to help me
out in a delicate matter and I intimated that he wouldn't find me
ungrateful.

"'You need transportation for a Jew. So what's in it for me?' He
inquired bluntly, without even waiting to hear my story.

"Needless to say, I wasn't about to trust him. I wasn't born with
the last rainfall, either.

"'No, it's not at all what you think,' I protested, but not too
vehemently. 'You know my clientele; they're not all working with
a brand-new hat on their heads, if you know what I mean. Most of
them are harmless; they just have a slightly richer fantasy life than is
healthy, for them and for us. But at times we have to indulge them just
a bit so that we can procede to the next step in their cure. What's the
harm in entering a little game now and then if it will lead to helping
a sick person, you tell me?'

"'Well, I wouldn't know.' He sounded disappointed. Those days
nothing was more lucrative for someone with a vehicle than smug-
gling Jews. 'By the time folks get to me, nothing really matters.'

"'Well, here is my scheme,' I continued in a fine conspiratorial
style, making him my accomplice. 'I have a patient who is convinced
that his dead mother is quite alive and that they are having nightly
conversations in his room, just the two of them. I want to play a

little trick on him that I believe will help him realize that he has been imagining those visits with his mama, who has been dead for many years. Once he comes to terms with her death, we can go on with his treatment. So, this is what I want to do. I have a friend whose mother has agreed to play dead for my patient. We'll put her in a casket that you'll lend us for the occasion. You'll deliver her at the back door where you usually make your pick-ups. We'll have to do it after the patients have retired, because, as you know, you are not exactly the most popular man in the neighbourhood. Then we'll take the casket upstairs. You'll get it back in fifteen minutes. Instead of a body, there will be one hundred guilders in it for you. What do you say?'

" 'For a hundred guilders I will not only deliver the phoney stiff, but I'll also pick her up when she's ready to go home.' He was obviously satisfied with the deal.

" 'You're more than kind, but that won't be necessary. I'll put up the old lady for the night and in the morning she can go home on her own.'

"Everything was in order, we just needed Grandma Spier's collaboration. How was anyone to tell this lady, who had been living in the shadow of death, about our macabre plan?

" 'We'll give her a sleeping pill and we'll transport her asleep. When she wakes up she'll be in a nice clean bed with soft pillows and you and Bertil smiling at her. The rest we'll tell her when you think she is ready to hear it,' I assured Friso.

"The following night, Grandma Spier rode, unconscious, in a casket in the belly of a hearse, to what was left of freedom in 1944.

"My house was full like a *pensione* on the Riviera in August. It was time to take stock. With seven Jewish fugitives under one roof I could no longer trust my fate to the wind. When we said farewell to one patient, we didn't open the door to a new one. Instead we replaced him with an already resident Jew. Thus, one by one, our circle got smaller. With fewer people to care for, I cut down on the number of care-givers. Some of my guests were only too glad to pitch in. Ella Boas and Len worked far more than I would have expected.

" 'I'm virtually penniless,' Ella admitted. 'I want to repay you for my keep with work.' Len echoed her words.

" 'The last thing I worry about is money,' I reassured the two. 'All I care about is that we all survive unharmed; the rest has the relevance of a bee's feather in the wind.' Still, I recognized that they had to determine for themselves what was sufficient to balance the two sides of their moral scales. Not being equipped for entertaining healthy guests, work served as a lacklustre but adequate pastime.

"A much greater concern of mine was food. We were painfully enduring the 'winter of famine'. In every sense it was a relief that our numbers shrank simultaneously with the reserves and supplies in our pantry. I also tactfully said goodbye to those members of the staff about whose loyalty I had a shade or two of doubt. Still the portions we placed in front of us were less and less copious. No one complained out loud, but here and there I caught the muffled sound of a grumbling voice belonging to a growling stomach. I had to take drastic measures. We had plenty of food coupons without even tapping the resources of the underground. Betty and Walter were registered with the Town Hall of Bussum as Mr. and Mrs. van Wetering. For a long time I fetched their coupons and redeemed them in the local stores. But by January 1945, the shelves were all but empty in Blaricum. All the merchants knew me and liked me. More important, they sympathized with my predicament of having to feed so many mouths. But when the cupboards were bare, I couldn't expect miracles of them.

" 'I don't have anything of note to sell you Sake,' one of them whispered to me one day. 'But I know where I can put my finger on some good stuff, for the right price, if you know what I mean.' Black-marketeering had become a way of life. I hated the bloodsuckers with a religious fervour. But you don't turn your nose up at a slab of bacon just because the pig wallowed in mud. 'Later, you greedy leech, later you'll pay for your profiteering,' I thought gritting my teeth. 'What would a gold Omega watch fetch me?' I asked with a hungry smile.

" 'A week's supply of everything you need for your rather large household, home delivered at night, so quietly that even the alley cats won't know a thing.'

"Only a week's reprieve for the gold watch I received from my father on my twenty-fifth birthday! I felt a churning in my stomach. Was it the involuntary encouragement from an empty stomach, or a warning sign of anguish about parting with a very dear symbol of affection from my dad? No matter, I thought, this is not the time to get sentimental. Tell that to the famished assembly in my home: 'Folks, no food for a while because I couldn't get myself to convert my father's gold watch into bacon, cheese, potatoes, and flour.'

" 'You've got yourself a deal,' I told the man without hesitating. 'I hope you'll take good care of it. It's more valuable than you can ever know.'

" 'Oh, it's not for me,' he hurried to defend himself. 'It's for the Frisian farmer who's building a legendary fortune this winter.'

" 'Sure enough—like I'm the daughter of the Prince of Wales,' I thought bitterly. 'I'm not a Frisian for nothing. I know those farmers; they are not likely to rob us blind.'

"A week passed and we were still hungry and the war still ravaged through our empty plates.

" 'What would your famous farmer give for a fine concert piano?' I asked my secret supplier.

" 'Well, that's quite a deal you're proposing there. I'll have to look into what the market value of such a prize object is.' He was good and cagey about his dark profession.

"He gave me the answer the next day. 'Three weeks of a full table for all.'

" 'I want five.' ('To end up with four,' I added silently.) I was a fast learner.

" 'Well, my contact told me, if push came to shove, he'd be willing to go to four, but not higher. He's dying to offer it to his daughter for her sixteenth birthday.'

" 'He's right.' My sarcasm was growing rapidly. 'No Frisian farm-girl should be without a baby grand by the time she reaches sixteen. He is dying to offer the piano to his daughter. My patients are just plain dying of hunger. I want five weeks' worth of food or I'll take my piano to another farmer. Yours is not the only fine soul in the province, you know.'

"We got five weeks of ample supplies.

"Our household calmed down again for a while. We had enough empty space to allow everyone to have his own room. The two couples, of course, shared one each. Ever since I had started harbouring Jews, I had admitted only elderly patients enduring the quiet ravages of senile dementia. We didn't have to worry about their verbal indiscretions. This afforded my Jewish guests a greater freedom of movement when there were no visitors of any sort in the building. But we did have to be very careful when an outsider came. Hunger oiled people's tongues.

"One morning I ran into one of the cleaning ladies at the bottom of the steps. 'What are you doing this morning, Willy?' I asked, just to make sure that she wasn't heading towards the Jewish wing before it was all clear.

" 'I'm going to start on Jodenbreestraat.' And she winked at me. She knew! She was, of course, making allusion to the street in Amsterdam with the highest density of Jews in the country.

" 'Well, so you know about our special patients,' I told her. 'I'm glad to learn of your commitment and your decency. Thank you, you're a good woman.' 'I've started my day in the Jodenbreestraat ever since you opened it to traffic.' She obviously was referring to the arrival of the two Dozeman couples.

"The incident with Willy the cleaning lady steered me towards assessing the situation: who knew that we were sitting on a keg of gunpowder and who didn't? Dr. Janssen knew of his own protégés but not of the others. Dr. Emmer, our house physician, knew everything about everybody. The other members of the custodial and nursing staff might be aware of some illegal presence, but they couldn't know anything for sure. I had no evidence, nor even cause to suspect, that any of my employees was likely to betray me. I had always been very good to them, and they reciprocated in every way they could.

"As for the neighbours, I enjoyed a rather peculiar, mixed blessing. As I told you, my home was located in a large villa, situated at the bottom of a large garden. I had only one neighbour, the wife of an ophthalmologist. He was never to be seen. She was not only always around, but she was an ardent follower of Mussert, the pale Dutch copy of Adolf Hitler. The woman was a bloody NSB-er. What do you think of that, my dear lady? However, that didn't deter me from continuing to have with her a more than amicable neighbourly rapport. I paid regular visits to her, but she never crossed my threshold.... Ah, wait a minute, I think I see in your eyes, my dear lady, that you understand something that I didn't imply. When I said our rapport was more than amicable, I didn't intimate any romantic inclinations, not at all. I would never have allowed myself the audacity or even the curiosity to transgress the boundaries of platonic friendship. But that's precisely what I was referring to, a true platonic friendship which was not tainted even by the fact that she was a Fascist. Call it insensitivity. It's such an overused cliché that every Jew-hater had his pet Jew who was 'not like the others'. Well, I had my pet Fascist who was, perhaps, like the others in some ways, but in others she was a refined lady with a misguided but generous heart. With her as my neighbour, I always had the impression of being observed with golden eyes. From a less idealistic perspective, it was strategically wise to continue the rapport. Its interruption might have aroused some unwelcome curiosity.

"One day, she came to my door. She rang and asked for me, refusing to set foot in the house. I met her on the threshold. Her face was a shade redder than usual.

" 'As you know, I'm a member of the NSB. As such, I have certain privileged sources of information. I don't want to know what's going on in your house. Suffice it to say, Sake, that I would be very worried for you if you ventured out into the streets today. Should you get caught, no matter how much I would like to help you, I would be powerless.'

"So she knew, too. What a well-guarded secret! Who else was too well-informed about the little congregation I was hiding under my roof? On the one hand, I was surprised because I had told no one. On the other hand, I wasn't too surprised because I didn't have to say anything; people did the talking on their own initiative. I can't tell you the exact number of hidden Jews and their hosts who were expedited to the gas chambers of the east as a result of harmful gossip. Many, I can assure you of that. And some other times, people just put two and two together. Some of them were malicious; some of them just whiled the time away by saying 'Do you know what I saw today? I saw a Jew sneaking through Bottinga's back door....' That was more than enough to start the avalanche.

"Not everyone was as decent as my neighbour, alas. When I visited my family, my father warned me in a flat voice, 'Beware of your sister. She has taken the path of shame: she has joined the NSB.' This was about a year after Walter and Betty came to me. The news knocked me senseless. I had always thought of my older sister with affection and respect. She was a fine woman with high ideals and concern for everyone in need.

" 'The most important goal of any society, of any leader of any political movement, should be to put bread and butter in the mouths of everyone. There's no excuse for hunger in this world.' And how I admired her for her generous idealism. In fact, I am quite sure that I learned my tendency to be idealistic from her.

" 'Hitler will do just that—he will feed all the poor, all the disenfranchised,' she told me when I asked her about her espousal of Fascism. 'We have to do everything to implement his plans for Germany in our country.' She married another NSB member and they moved not too far from me. From what my parents told me she had a very comfortable existence, devoting all her leisure time to supporting the regime of doom. I never exchanged another word with her. Should I see her walking in the street today, I would cross to the other side. I disowned my sister and, with her, just a sliver of my own idealism.

"But do you want to know the darnedest thing? In the village, I somehow acquired the reputation of being an NSB sympathizer. In addition to my frequent contact with my NSB-er neighbour, I often exchanged friendly chitchat with Mr. Dorrius, a restauranteur from Amsterdam who was another enthusiastic supporter of the ruling ideology. I would often meet him in the street in Blaricum, and sometimes I would have Ella or Len with me. He would harangue me about the incomparably better future awaiting us on the other side of our current horizon. I never contradicted him. But I never openly espoused his incendiary vision, either.

"One time, about three months before the end of the war, Mr. Anoli, a mild-mannered NSB sympathizer, came to my rescue. He knocked on my door one morning.

" 'Sake, if I were you, I would make myself very scarce today. The Germans are conducting a house-to-house search for hidden fugitives. The woods might be worth a short visit at the tail end of winter.'

" 'Well, for one thing, a good captain never abandons his ship,' I told him gratefully with a touch of flippancy in my voice, 'and for another thing, I have nothing to fear from the Germans. Let them come and inspect my patients. They'll find nothing but a bunch of depressed folks wallowing in their dementia.' He couldn't know anything about my hidden Jews, so I wondered why he had come to alert me, given that he was on their side, the side he thought I shared with him. Can you figure that one out, my dear lady? It has always been one of the major enigmas of the occupation for me. But anyway, after I thanked him for his gesture of solidarity, he left. I stood behind the door for a few minutes, trying to figure out what this was all about.

"He wasn't off my path yet when, indeed, a bunch of Germans jumped out of a truck and started walking in my direction. Mr. Anoli engaged them at the foot of my property. They seemed to be involved in a heated discussion, for the Germans were gesticulating wildly. Every once in a while they pointed at my house. In the meantime, I just stood there mesmerized by the encounter between a bunch of apparently animated Nazi soldiers and the enigmatic Mr. Anoli. But instead of coming to search my house, they appeared to have been appeased by taking Mr. Anoli with them. I was relieved, I must confess. It was only after a few minutes of breathing again that I thought of worrying about this man who took my place and willingly went with the Germans, heaven knew where. I felt guilty but I tried to console myself: 'Anoli is a resourceful chap; he'll find a way out.' I spent many a tense moment until I heard from him that same afternoon. Around five o'clock he came for a quick visit.

" 'I thought you might be interested to know that I'm at large again. They gave me a hard time about a report they got from a source they were not about to divulge that I was hiding illegal fugitives in the clinic. Need I say that they had me confused with you? I figured I might as well go along with their dumb mistake for a while. And by the same token, it distracted them from bothering you. I know you're not the type to stick your nose into some dirty business, but with all that you have to attend to with your patients, you didn't need them coming to poke around.'

" 'That's what I call a real humanitarian gesture, Mr. Anoli. I'm truly grateful to you on behalf of my patients. Some of them do tend to get frightened by the shadow of a fly on the wall. But tell me, if I'm not too nosy, it was my impression that you approved of the operations by the occupying forces and their domestic counterparts. Why did you risk rubbing them the wrong way?'

" 'I approve of national socialism, but not of all national socialists. There's a lot of nonsensical nuisance being perpetrated upon us in the name of our ideology. Remember one thing, Mr. Bottinga, I'm first a man, and only second a national socialist. When you think of all the abominable crimes committed in the name of Christianity, it serves as a stern warning that we don't fall into the same trap with national socialism. Being a bit of a trouble-maker and a practical joker, I thought, well, we may as well have a little fun with these "Mofs". So I went along with their insistence about hiding illegals in the clinic. I said, "You know what, I surrender to you. You can take me in as a hunting trophy. But don't be too surprised when you get your pants dusted for interfering with the operation of a health facility. In fact, you've got me hot and bothered, so I demand that you take me in so that I can file an official complaint of harassment."

" 'They, were much less sure of themselves, but they were not entirely at ease with letting me go, either. So we went in. They couldn't have been any more polite if I had been Mussert himself. So I told this desk hero, bedecked with all kinds of colourful hardware on his chest, "So what is this nonsense for which I have to interrupt my very busy work at the clinic in the middle of the day."

" 'He looked at me as if I had dropped in from the moon.

" ' "I have absolutely no idea what you are talking about. I don't even know why my men went to your place. For that matter, who are you?"

" ' "That's not so important." I stayed on the offensive, hoping to confuse him even more. "It's more important who you are to send your tin soldiers to my hospital to create havoc with some heavily guarded mental patients who can blow up in a second. They are like time bombs; you obviously don't know the first thing about these conditions. So do I come to bother you with nonsense about how to run a war? No. Well, why don't you follow my example and stay away from what you don't know? You leave me no choice but to report to the family of a high-level German diplomat, who is our patient and who shall remain unnamed, of course, about the rights of the mentally exhausted. I want his son, the SS colonel, to tell you personally that he doesn't mind if you molest his demented father and the people who take care of him day and night. Shall I tell the colonel to drop by tomorrow morning for a little chat with Hauptmann Muller or would Herr Hauptmann prefer that I arrange a little informal meeting at my facility? You are very welcome to visit with him. So what's your pleasure, sir?" He was fidgeting on his seat as if he had been bitten by a squadron of bees.

" ' "Well, I mean, well, it's not all that clear. I mean we have no specific objectives with all the mentally ill. Of course, those who have reached a decline in their faculties after a life of...of...patriotic service, they should be honoured and not relocated. I don't want you to misrepresent to the colonel our aims here.... Look, how about being a good fellow, and just chalk this one up to a misunderstanding. I won't make a report and you won't mention your little visit to anyone, especially not to that colonel. In fact, I would be just as happy if this visit became our little secret. It can be handy to know that an assistant bureau chief of the occupying forces in Bussum owes you one. You never know when you can collect such a debt...."

" 'And here I am. I don't think you're going to be bothered again. But if you are, just let me know. Or if you can't, just ask for Hauptmann Muller and refer to today's incident. Just say that you're my silent partner. They have a lot of nerve, these country yocums; they deserve to have their backs stiffened a bit by putting in them the fear of God. They sure can dish it out; let them learn the taste of their own diet.'

"We had a good time with Anoli's story for weeks. Until we had another, this time unannounced, visit from the Germans. One night, around nine o'clock, I had just tucked my books away for the night and I was about to make myself a cup of ersatz coffee, when I heard noise at the front door. I went to see what was happening. There were three German soldiers making a lot of ruckus. They looked and smelled quite drunk.

" '*Wir suchen ein Puff*,' one of them blurted out and the others chimed in, '*Ja, ja, ja, wir suchen ein Puff* ....' and the general mayhem continued. They wanted to push past me. I had no idea what they wanted. I slammed the door on them and ran upstairs to ask Friso what a 'Puff' was. (He was spending a few days with us since he was running the risk of getting picked up and taken to a forced labour camp. After all, he was a strong young man.)

"Friso broke out laughing. 'They think this is a whorehouse, Sake. Let them in, take them to a couple of patients' rooms and see how their amorous ardour responds to what they'll find.'

"I followed his advice. The drunken Germans piled in on top of each other like pigs at the trough. They all wanted to be first. You should have seen their faces when they ripped open the first door and found a stony-eyed old man staring at nothing on the ceiling. And the second, and the third... Well, the spectacle of these spent old folks sobered them up fast. They looked ashamed; they didn't know how to hide their embarrassment. They began to fight in German among themselves. They even exchanged a few blows. Then suddenly they stopped and remembered me. In their shame, they vented their anger on me and one of them decided that I should be taken to headquarters in Bussum for questioning about where I had hidden the prostitutes.

" 'I demand to see Hauptmann Muller,' I kept repeating with dogged determination.

" 'You'll get to see the Hauptmann. Don't worry about it,' my arrester reassured me with a mocking menace in his half-sober, half-drunk voice. 'Just wait for him right here in his office. He will have a few questions to ask you. There's something definitely fishy about a Dutchman who can make a bunch of whores change into half-dead old prunes.' They left me there in Hauptmann Muller's office.

I waited and waited, trying to figure out what I was going to say. How was I going to clear myself of this absurd charge without them wanting to raid my place? How was I to benefit from Anoli's bluff? As I was sitting there, I became aware of a cold draft on my neck. I turned around and saw an unlocked window. I jumped to my feet and observed that the window was facing an alley. We were on the mezzanine, so letting myself drop onto the ground would not be hazardous. But how could I prevent the Nazi from sending his hound dogs after me? Then it came to me. I took a sheet of paper from his desk and left him a note: 'Hauptmann Muller, it seems that you and your men are determined to interfere with the operation of my psychiatric clinic. You leave me no choice but to inform SS Colonel X of your stubborn determination. I have been waiting for you for over thirty minutes to inform you of my decision, but you rudely made me waste valuable time. I am leaving now so that I can catch the colonel before he leaves his father's bedside for the night.' And I affixed to my note a characteristically illegible signature. I took leave through the window. I was concerned about his men catching up with me to take me back for a session of pleading, negotiation, or even bribery. I had to get off the street.

"Remembering that Willy, the cleaning lady, lived in the neighbourhood, I made my way to her home. She already knew about the Jews in my clinic. She would help, I was sure. I knocked on her door. She looked like she had just seen the ghost of an ancestor.

" 'Look Willy, I may be in trouble. The Germans may be after me. I know you're a sensible and a decent person. Help me out.' I made a hasty verbal sketch of my flight from German headquarters in Bussum.

" 'What can I do, Mr. Bottinga, to help you?' She was trembling like a plate of jellied pig's feet.

" 'Take off your clothes right now.' When she heard my order she forgot to close her mouth.

" 'But Mr. Bottinga...I'm willing to help, but just what do you mean?... I'm a virtuous woman.... I mean...'

" 'No, you don't understand, you silly goose.' It suddenly dawned on me that the poor soul thought I wanted to climb into bed with her to hide out for the night. Heaven forbid! 'I want to borrow your clothes and disguise myself as a woman. If they're out looking, they'll be after a man. It would never occur to them to stop a woman.' She was visibly relieved, even though the idea of allowing a man to get into her clothes didn't exactly thrill her. None the less, I made it home without incident. 'Oh, my Lord,' exclaimed Ella Boas, 'is that you, Sake, in that awful get-up?' I took off Willy's kerchief and I lit a match to expose my unabashed face. 'None other than yours truly.'

"Oh, I tell you, my dear lady, we had some laughs that night, some celebration—as if we had won the war, and not just a tiny skirmish. We laughed and we suffered. But the longer the war went on the less we laughed and the more we suffered.

"Did I tell you about Walter and Betty's baby? I've been filling your head with so much babbling that I no longer remember what was said and what still remains to be related. I didn't? Well, I'm not surprised. It's probably the single saddest story of the whole period. No wonder I have conveniently 'forgotten' about it.

"Well, Walter and Betty had been married for about five years when the war broke out. They had been speaking of starting a family but then the whole débâcle fell upon them. Obviously, it wasn't the time to bring a child into the world. But Betty was yearning for a baby.

" 'I'm getting on in age. How much time do I have left to start having children?' At times, she sounded like she wanted my permission to go ahead.

" 'Betty, it's your life, your body. Only you and Walter can make that decision,' I told her. 'I just want you to know that I will stand by you no matter what.'

"And one day, towards late August, Walter told me with anguish clouding his joy: 'Betty is carrying our child. What shall we do, Sake, what shall we do? What if we get caught and the baby falls into Nazi hands? It will end up in smoke without the shadow of a doubt. Do we have the right to bring a life into this world with such a prospect in the balance? What if for some reason the clinic is closed down and we have to move somewhere else and Betty has a belly full of baby? Where are we going to hide? Isn't it a form of suicidal madness to create life out of decay?'

" 'I have never been given to believe in any form of mysticism,' she told me one evening in confidence, 'but I feel that this child has been sent to me as a sign to reinforce our sagging courage and faith in life. How can one allow hope to wither with a baby on the way to start anew?'

" 'Betty, my friend,' I said, reaching for her hand. I wanted her to believe me more than ever. 'By the time your baby comes, the war will be over. But if you and Walter decide against keeping it, I know a doctor who will help you with your decision. You and Walter should not think of anyone else in your deliberations. Take your time, quietly. Just let me know when you have made up your minds one way or another so I can take steps with the doctor.'

" 'We're going to have the baby, Sake,' Betty whispered to me in the hallway a week later. She was radiant.

"I can't tell you how much it hurts me to recall the night many months later when Betty pounded on my door hysterically. 'Sake, Sake! My baby is very sick. Please come. She is dying.' First I thought I was having a nightmare. But the pounding and the panic just didn't fade away. I jumped out of bed and ran in my pajamas to their room. The four-month-old child looked pale and waxy. She didn't look like she was getting enough air to sustain that tiny light of life flickering in the night. I called Dr. Emmer immediately.

" 'Take the child as soon as you can to the hospital in Bussum. I'll meet you there,' the doctor ordered me. I had to take the baby from her parents, who were tearing their hair, wringing their hands in terror.

" 'I've got to go with my baby. I'd rather die than let my baby go alone. I'll never see her again. Let her die in her mother's arms at least.'

"But for once I had to do the cruel thing, for all our sakes. I took the tiny bundle that was already cooling off. After I fastened her little basket on the back of my bicycle, I rode off with her into the night. For the first and only time in my entire adult life, I didn't stop praying from Blaricum to Bussum for the salvation of that child who was supposed to lead us all into a better world. And there she was, breathing pathetically as if she just couldn't make the effort required for such a tiny person to live beyond the horizon of atrocities. 'For the sake of all of us, please Lord, keep this child alive. Don't let her die on the back of a bicycle in the middle of nowhere. Please, my Lord, I beg of you, deign to take this child under your wing and breathe some vigour into her chest. Don't let her slip away. Oh God, anything but that....' By the time I got to the hospital the frozen tears clung to my cheeks like two candles, but the baby was still breathing. Dr. Emmer and a pediatrician friend of his received us. They admitted her and put her into an oxygen tent. I took the empty basket back to Blaricum, dreading the encounter with the poor mother and father. By the time I got back to my house, the message was waiting for me: she had

given up the struggle for which she had been so ill prepared. I...I....
Forgive, my dear lady, the tears of an old soul who could never accept
the useless death of a child.... She was so tiny...and so vulnerable....
She deserved to live. There is no valid excuse for the death of a four-
month-old. She didn't even have a chance to work out the kinks in
her little body.... I'm devastated, even after all these years.... I'm so
sorry.... I'm so sad.... Please, forgive me....

"I think I'll be all right from here on. You've been very tolerant,
my dear lady. But you see, I loved that child not only because she was
my friends' child and the first and only child born under my roof, but
because she was a child. And to see her go just like that, her minute
body lost in a loveless hospital bed.... I bicycled back to the hospital
the same night and claimed the stiff little bundle and took it over to
Dr. Emmer's house. I spent the night there, keeping her company.
The next day, the town hall gave me a grave for the poor.

"There's very little to report after that tragedy. We all seemed to
have died a little with Betty and Walter's baby. We had hardly any
patients left. Instead we had three people from the underground who
came to us to hide out for the rest of the hostilities. They didn't
know anything about the Jews when they came, but they soon found
out about them. We encountered no problems on that front. Nothing
seemed to matter any more. Our well-organized existence gave way
to a more chaotic form of surviving one day after another. We all
slept wherever we felt like collapsing. Nobody bothered any more to
return to their rooms for the night.

"And then one day we woke up and we were free. I don't even
remember how we learned that we had been liberated. Isn't that
something? I have no trouble with all the stories of gloom and doom,
but I didn't bother to retain the moment of joy when we learned that
we could live again. We didn't know how to celebrate it. First, I recall,
we were disoriented by the news, as if to say 'Now what? Where
do we go from here? What does a free person do?' But then there
was hugging and kissing and dancing and crying—lots of crying—in
the house, in the streets, everywhere where people emerged from the
darkness of war. There were as many tears as there were smiles.

"Around noon time, I knocked on the door of my next-door
neighbour, to wish her good luck in our new world and to let her know
how much I appreciated her loyalty in spite of her affiliation with the
NSB. But she didn't answer the door. I tried to open it. I don't even

know why. I certainly didn't expect it to be open. But to my great surprise, it gave under the pressure of my hand.

" 'Nettie, are you home? It's Sake Bottinga. Nettie!' But there was no answer. I looked around in the tiny garden cottage, but there was no sign of her downstairs. With hesitant steps, I climbed the stairs. I had never been past her public domain. I didn't know if that was all right with her.

"There she was, in her bedroom. What a sight, my God! I almost lost my stomach right there and then. She shot herself in the head. Fresh red bloodstains sprinkled her elegantly appointed bedroom. I could not get myself to look at her exploded head. I fell into a chair, feeling lost and devastated. Another wasted life, another friend ravished in the struggle between ideologies. My poor friend Nettie. NSB-er that she was, she still couldn't let her neighbour take the risk of getting caught in a raid by her own associates. Can there be a better testimony to the bonds people make to one another as compared to the fragility of one's commitments to causes?

"Well, there I was with Nettie's inert body. Something needed to be done. Her husband was an opthalmologist in Rotterdam; he spent only the weekends with her. He had to be notified at once. I went back to my house and arranged for a courier to be sent with the sad message to the widower. What a way to greet freedom!

" 'I just don't feel it's right to leave the poor woman's body without anyone to keep vigil over her.' It bothered my sense of propriety to know that she had renounced her life because she feared the solitude of the vanquished.

" 'Well, I don't feel any pity for her,' Walter sounded off about his profound contempt for Nettie. 'She was a Nazi, so what! She took her life rather than face the justice of men. I think it would be very wrong to pay her any last respect, she who had no respect for us, Jews.'

"I quite understood his bile. I would have felt similarly had I been in his shoes, and yet I didn't have it in me to continue to wage a war against the dead. For me, she was not a Fascist but a friend and a neighbour, a fine lady. Amid bitter protests from my Jewish friends, I went over to her house to sit wake with her.

"The next morning, when her body was removed, was when I felt for the first time a whiff of real freedom.

"What followed the war, my dear lady, was nothing to be proud of. There was too much vengeance in people's hearts. I was quite content with being free at last. For me, it was sufficient to know that good had triumphed after all, although I don't think we can speak of triumph ever again when we think of the number of victims. But still, to punish the culprits was only fair and square; after all, there are consequences to anything one does, especially if what one does is written in blood. And yet, at times I was profoundly sad. So many of these youngsters were victims of their own gullible idealism. They *wanted* to believe that what they were doing was building a better world. They were so eager that they failed to see the harm they did by sustaining the enemy of man. For that they needed to be pitied, to be re-educated, to be disciplined. Instead, they were shamed in public. That was just not right.

"You don't know what I'm referring to? I'm recalling young women having their heads shaved for collaborating with the enemy. There were two sisters, for example, whose own brothers put them through this villainous ritual that proved nothing, except that the victors could be just as mean as the losers. At the risk of ruffling a lot of feathers, I allege that there were plenty of collaborators who were among the loudest judges on the streets!

"There was one incident I'll never forget. I saw this mob near my house one day. Being of a curious nature, I wanted to see what was on the program that time. The streets those days were always rich in eye-stopping events, but after five years of oppression and suppression of vital energies, people were purging themselves of all their tired blood and venom. This time, once again, it was a young girl who was being accused of having sold her body to German soldiers. In the heart of the circle, the terrified young creature—she couldn't have been even twenty years old—was being tightly pinned against the wall by two vulgar-looking, unwashed young lads. They claimed to have the goods on her.

" 'I know the days and the names of the Mofs for whom you opened your legs. You must be punished for making the enemy feel so wanted and so loved.' The crowd cheered. 'And I even have witnesses from parties this little strumpet organized for her Nazi lovers. You should never be allowed to love anyone ever again.' The crowd cheered again even more menacingly.

"The two youngsters seemed more and more intoxicated by the approving bystanders' support. And mob power does have its own magic seduction.

" 'Let's shave her head.' The first one produced a razor. He grabbed the young girl's dense reddish mane and yanked on it as if he was going to scalp her with his bare hands. She cried out in pain. I was getting indignant.

" 'This is not right,' I told a man standing next to me. 'This is exactly what they used to do to the Jews.'

" 'So what else is new?' the man responded, with spite on his face. 'I'm Jewish and I suffered plenty of humiliation and torture. I want to know what it feels like to be on the other side for a change.'

" 'It's just not right. We can't live by the eye-for-an-eye law of revenge. When will the violence ever stop?'

"He was not interested in my lecture. The crowd was rhythmically applauding the young man as he was shaving the poor girl, who looked like she was going to faint any second.

" 'Just a minute'—the other one grabbed her by the neck—'who said we're finished?' As he was holding her, choking the life out of her fragile neck, he addressed the crowd with an evil twinkle in his eyes. 'In the middle ages, they used to punish criminals by cutting off the part of their body with which they committed their crime. I propose that we revive this fine old way of carrying out justice and that we shave not only her hair, but also her—' and he used the most vulgar term for her sex our language knows. The crowd loved it. The young woman seemed more dead than alive. 'Kill me first,' she said bearly audibly. 'You'll have to kill me first.' Two thugs grabbed her arms and another two got hold of her legs in spite of her kicking like a captured frog.

" 'Take it off, take it off, take it all off,' some people began to chant rhythmically. I couldn't stand it anymore. I pushed my way to the front and I screamed: 'STOP! STOP RIGHT NOW!' The crowd was stunned by the unexpected interruption. I had to speak fast before they recovered their bloodthirst: 'Before you participate in such harsh judgement, I think more evidence is needed. I want to ask our two young heroes here a question or two. If they answer to your satisfaction, perhaps she should be punished lawfully, but not by a mob. That's not the Dutch way of bringing justice.' Before I could lose momentum and become a target of violence myself, I turned to the two: 'How do you know all these accusations so well? Where is your proof? Where does it come from? How do you know so many details about what she did with whom? Were you watching? Come on, let's hear the facts.'

" 'Who the hell are you anyway?' One of them turned towards me with dark threat in his eyes. 'Are you the avenging angel of justice or a leftover Nazi?'

" 'Answer the question!' I heard first one voice, then another one, then pretty soon, they were all chanting: 'Answer the question! Answer the question!' Crowds are fickle, my dear lady, and my gamble paid off, because they rallied behind me once the bug of doubt was planted in their ears.

" 'I will answer the question for them.' We heard a faint voice everyone seemed to have forgotten. It was the young victim's. 'I'll tell you how they know so much, in fact more than what really happened. They were with the Germans who gang-raped me. They participated in the fun, didn't you, you scum? I was a good girl until then. After that I said, well, one is a virgin only once; it was taken from me brutally, so now I will put it to use. And the Germans paid handsomely for my services. And so did these two fine Dutchmen.' The crowd drew tighter around the two hoodlums. In no time, they too were shaved. If I hadn't intervened, they would have been beaten to death.

" 'STOP! LISTEN TO ME! You were so willing and eager to bring justice upon this innocent young woman, now you're doing the same thing to these two traitors. Who really knows their story? Isn't it really the job of the police and the courts to bring about justice and not the streets? How about taking them to the police and leaving them in their expert care?'

"There were other scenes like this all over the land. I can only deplore such brutality. There was a young woman in her early twenties whom the crowd was about to chastise in its usual fashion. She was a proud female—the kind that has always scared me, the kind I have always secretly admired. She grabbed the scissors from the hand of an older man and shouted her self-incriminating confession to those assembled to see her on her knees: 'Yes, I've loved a German. I still love him and I'll always love him. The fortunes of the war can do nothing about our love. As a symbol of my unshakable love for him, I'm glad to shed my hair. Somebody has got to show in these spineless times that just because the Germans have been beaten doesn't mean that we can no longer love individual human beings. If we were to close our eyes to all Germans and treat them as if they had a shameful disease, how would that make us different from the Nazis? I will not break my allegiance to my love: and here is the proof.' With that she proceeded to crop close to her scalp her fine blonde hair.

Sanity in Madness

"The crowd assembled around her grew silent, as if they were witnessing a funeral. I bowed my head before her in shame. I knew that I would not have had the courage to make a statement on behalf of a forbidden loyalty.

"Well, how about if we take another breather, I don't know about you, but I've spoken more at one sitting today than I have in thirty years. And I can tell that my poor friend Coco Chanel is in bad need of a romp in the field. Shall we take the lead from my four-legged companion? Come on, old girl, you've been very patient. You didn't interrupt your old friend who has become a wind machine in his dotage. That's it, you're right to get excited; fresh air and the magic scent of flowers in the garden deserve our exuberance...."

"Now isn't this better? My dear lady, I don't know about you and the professor, but I certainly feel a surge of renewed current in the old wires. Perhaps that's alarming news for you. Rest assured, there isn't that much left to tell. But I do want to make a point that occurred to me outside. I don't want you to think for a second that I would have let the NSB traitors go unpunished for their despicable opportunism and voluntary servitude to the masters of our fate for five horrible years. Far from it. I was glad to see them being ferreted out, tried, and put behind bars. After all, we do live in a society that must cleanse itself of its infectious elements. My sister, for example...You may think I'm a heartless man, with unctuous words in my mouth but vengeance on my sleeve. No matter. You should know that I was just as delighted to see her spend some time in prison as I was devastated when I learned that she had sold her soul to the devil. Not that I think it taught her a lesson, or that while incarcerated she and the other NSB-ers took the trouble to take a hard look in their inner mirror and see the light of wrong-doing. I didn't expect them to return to their communities purged of the poison—far from it. I don't believe for a second that penance visited any of those misguided people's minds long enough to claim squatter's rights on their consciences. But they had to be imprisoned anyway, not just as a consequence for what they did or didn't do but also as a message to their victims that we didn't forget about them.

"Some steps had to be taken, and as depressing as it may sound, only evil is infinite; the horizon of the just has rigid boundaries. Thus, what else could have been done to the traitors but to remove them from their homes, their communities, from free movement and enjoyment of the same atmosphere they polluted with their acts of cruelty?

"As for my own sister, I can't see into her heart—nor did I ever have the urge to venture a peek for fear of what I might see—but I could have lived out my long life without ever forgiving her. I did hold her hand, however, a couple of years after liberation. My mother was on her death bed. She called my sister to her side and told her, 'Stay with me, my girl, and when Sake comes, offer him your hand and he will not refuse it.' When I got there, my sister executed my mother's wish. I didn't refuse. She just looked at me with eyes that revealed no remorse and said, 'I know we did wrong.' And that was that. It wasn't an apology, a promise of redress, or a recognition of guilt. They had done wrong because they lost, that's all. Call me an uncharitable man, but I found no road that led from me to her. It was beyond my means to climb over the obstacle she placed between us.

"Well, I've jumped ahead of myself a bit, haven't I? My life didn't return to normal with liberation. I don't think it ever did completely. I was definitely marked by the ordeal of my Jewish friends. They hadn't all started out as my friends but when they were ready to leave, I was knocked senseless by the emptiness they left behind. The Dozemans were the first ones to say goodbye, first Betty and Walter, and then his parents. They were lucky to be able to return to their former homes. So many people were denied the right to repossess what was rightfully theirs. (That injustice embittered me.) Then Ella, Len, and Grandma Spier all returned to whatever was left unfinished in their lives.

"I was seized by a profound depression. I had no direction; there was no purpose to my life. I was choked by a version of mourning. My clinic was empty. I had nothing to get out of bed for in the morning. And, indeed, I remained depressed. Dr. Janssen wanted to send me a patient, but I let him know that I had no vacancy. I just lay in bed, pretending to stare at the ceiling, but, in reality, my eyes were as blind as my heart was blank. One day, one of my former patients came by to visit and found me unshaven, slovenly, in a disheveled room.

" 'I can't believe my eyes. Maybe returning to this place makes me imagine things again! Tinus, how can you be like this? You should be ashamed of yourself. Get out of bed this instant! Do your toilet and get out of this depressing mess. You have a clinic here and you take no patients. What kind of nonsense is this?' And she just carried me out. She literally evicted me from the hole I had dug in my depression.

Sanity in Madness

" 'No, you're wrong about that, Corrie,' I told her limply. 'I'm as happy for the end of the war as I was when I got my first pair of real shoes. Oh, yes indeed, I'm happy about the end of the war. I'm just not happy, that's all, not happy at all.'

"I don't think she understood what I meant, but she didn't seem to need to understand—she saw that I was in a desperate rot and she dragged me out.

"Eventually, I reopened the clinic. My Jewish friends kept very close contact with me—all of them except for Grandma Spier, who passed away before the first anniversary of our liberation. There was nothing left to keep her alive. A week after her funeral, Bertil ushered into this tentative world a baby girl. She named Sarah after her freshly buried mother.

"My Jewish friends made lots of publicity for my clinic. I could easily have made it into an exclusively Jewish institution. I even made a joking comment about that to Ella. 'Don't you dare to start making selections. We know where that leads.'

"Everything was in place for me to rediscover the passion for my work, and yet my heart was no longer rooted to the home and its guests. The past was intruding with too many memories. I resented the world for soiling what had started out as a perfect, immaculate relationship. It was becoming clearer by the day that I had to take leave from everything that tied me to the years of fear.

"I became a private nurse for various families. I never again grew permanent roots. The home, meanwhile, was being managed by Friso and Bertil, with the able collaboration of Drs. Janssen and Emmer. I was never unhappy, but I never had the chance to enjoy my life either. I devoted all my waking hours to caring for others. I offered them flawless nursing but I stingily withheld my feelings from my patients and their families. In short, I became another person.

"Then I met the Hamburgers. I tell you, my dear lady, there was no kinder man on earth than Mr. Hamburger. He was mentally quite alert but physically stagnant. He had come back from Auschwitz, where his body had been broken. Nobody could find out what his real condition was, but I knew it. It was nothing that could be seen under a microscope or with an x-ray machine. Auschwitz had sapped his vital energy. And yet, he was free of all rancour, all hate. We spent countless hours together, just he and I.

" 'What was it like, Herman, over there?' Those days I was too squeamish to even utter the name of that hell.

Quiet Heroes

" 'No, Sake, don't.' He would look at me with a sheenless light in his placid eyes. 'Don't make me go back there; it was enough to have lived through that excremental assault once. Don't plunge me in that world once more. Let's speak about something beautiful.' He banished from his ears the sound of death and replaced it with fine music. This is how he exorcised the demons from my soul as well. We spent precious time in each other's company, delighting our weather-beaten souls in the splendidly festive Venice of Vivaldi, or the opulent elegance of Haydn's Vienna, or the mischievously romantic Paris of Offenbach. In fact, our musical escapades blossomed into many foreign journeys. I was immeasurably grateful to Herman Hamburger for opening for me the gates of charm and beauty; I cultivated a thriving affection for this truncated lover of life.

"We roamed the world for years. One day, after a lengthy residence in Toronto...wait a second, that's where the professor lives, isn't it? What a coincidence.... Well...anyway, I asked him: 'What about going back home, Herman?'

" 'Sake, my friend, "back home" is only on the map of the homeless. Here or there, we don't fit in anywhere. Do you hate me for dragging you to this anonymous shore with me?'

" 'I could never hate you, Herman. You're the only good man I have ever met; my home is where you are.'

"He spent the last couple of years of his Canadian residence in a state that I could describe only impressionistically as 'self-inflicted coma'. Everything hurt him, and yet the physicians found nothing significantly untoward. I spent many hours trying to figure out what had successfully undermined his robust appetite for aesthetically pleasing experiences. It was, of course, his memories of Auschwitz, a very private pain.

"Twenty hours a day, my dear lady, twenty hours a day I spent with that lovely man. He would lie there with his eyes open, but he saw nothing because his soul was already dead. However, quite extraordinarily, should I have to leave his presence, if only to attend to my bodily functions, he would stir—ever so imperceptibly (even to his wife, but not to me)—and his masklike lips whispered: 'Don't.'

"When he passed away in that room facing the peaceful ravine in his Rosedale residence, I felt that I, too, had expired.

"It was time to return to Europe where, in fact, no one expected anything of me and I owed nothing to anyone.

Sanity in Madness

"I found solace in finding my Jewish friends in good health and enthusiastic to have me back in their midst. I keep in regular contact with Ella. In fact, I spoke to her just two days ago. I even spent some private time with Walter and Betty, whenever he succumbed to a bout of depression. Len and I lost each other and then found each other off and on. She never married, either. Her soul was on fire. She ran from one end of the world to the other to search for the hand that could put out the flames.

"Friso and Bertil have been the closest to me. At a birthday dinner, when I turned seventy, I gave all of us a present: I turned over to them the deed to the clinic, which they had been running for me over the years. It was really theirs; my ownership was purely historical. Divesting myself of my former home populated by so many gigantic moments was a present to me, too. I could close the book for good. For one last time, we were all together under the same roof—all the Jewish friends, Mr. Anoli, the two doctors, and Willy, the cleaning lady who was nearly a hundred years old.

" 'What you did for all of us,' said Friso when he stood up to toast me for the dubious achievement of having lived for a long time, 'was pure heroism. There is no other word for it. To Sake Bottinga, our friend, our saviour, our hero.'

" 'You don't know what you are saying, my friend,' I retorted with scarcely controlled embarrassment in my voice. 'There was nothing heroic about hiding one's friends. I was scared just as much as you were. We were in it all of us with equal merit. If I was a hero, then so were you. But I tell you, I was no hero. There was only one thing I did in my life that I would consider heroic. I had a patient in this very house before the war who was a heroin addict. No one wanted to go near that poor man. "What can you do for a wretch like that?" my staff asked, and even Dr. Janssen asked—right doctor? You remember him? "Well," I said, "I will lock myself into a room with that man and when we emerge he will no longer be a heroin addict." Three days later, we staggered out of that room, the both of us free men. I will spare you the details of what the room looked like. But I can tell you with pride that that was an act of heroism. For three days I was a hero. The rest...the rest is you, my friends, and history.' "

Epilogue:

A Personal Inquiry

I was eight years old when the Nazis marched into Budapest, Hungary—my city of birth. With enthusiastic assistance from the Arrow Cross party—the Hungarian Fascist party—they killed nearly sixty members of my family, including my mother. I was tortured and left for dead by three Arrow Cross thugs in the ghetto. My sister and I survived thanks to the self-denying determination and cunning of my aunt. Upon liberation my father came back from a forced labour camp, blind and broken in spirit. Without much optimism, the three of us succeeded in starting our lives over. Confusion about what had happened to us, however, stayed with me for forty years.

I was able to arrive at one conclusion about the events of the Holocaust: in its abandonment of the Jewish people, humanity has incinerated its own heart. Such a tragic conclusion afforded me no optimism about the future, about my children's fate. To be sure, I succeeded in developing a "normal" way of life: a home, a family, a career. Under the surface, however, my memories forced me towards pessimism: there was nothing to convince me that finer days were ahead for my family and for the human family at large. While I was resigned to my dismal outlook, whenever I allowed myself to dream I kept repeating: "If only there were one person whose deeds unveiled a kinder, more trustworthy face, then I could dare to hope."

In September 1984, in the halls of the U.S. State Department, in the wrinkled, vulnerable faces of Albert, Wilma, Bill, Margaret, and the others, I did discover another version of being human. "Bill, how could you take your wife and children on that perilous ride to Amsterdam with a Jewish woman in your car?" I asked. "How else could I have gotten her to the doctor? How else would she have survived?" Not an answer, just more questions. "Betty, what fuelled your steps, day after day, for months, from your home to the site, blocks away, where you disposed of the excreta of a whole family of Jews hiding in your home?" "What else was I going to do with their bodily wastes?" Yet another question. Thus equipped with only a list of questions, I set out on a quest for heroes. This volume was born out of one of those questions: How did these glamourless Dutch people become rescuers?

Three years of dialogue and reflection have failed to uncover an answer that I could put forth as a blueprint for human goodness. But at the end of my journey through the world of the rescuers, I learned that before I can find any credible answer about the nature of heroism, I must first learn who I am. I learned this simple wisdom from Bill, the potato farmer, when he related to me how he became clear about what was the right way to react to the Nazis' "Final Solution to the Jewish Question". It was only after having heard Bill's story that I realized that all the lofty questions about human nature, about good and evil, amounted to nothing more than rhetoric. The fundamental issue really lies in the answer to one question: what do *I* do when *I* am faced with the need to put my life on the line for a stranger?

It took Bill just a few hours of pacing on the dike across his farm, struggling with his confusion about risking his and his family's life to save a total stranger, to find an answer to that question: "If I had done anything else, I would have had to be somebody else." Period. Some readers may share my initial disappointment upon hearing Bill's conclusion. When one is, as I was, on a mission to find heroes, such a revelation is likely to be seen as a banality, a commonplace. And yet, it turned out to be the most fruitful insight I learned. First, it demonstrated the survival of good at a time when all pointed to the opposite. Second, it pointed out with irrefutable authority, that goodness, as personified by the rescuers, was—and is—within the means of all of us. All it requires is a measure of authenticity. What I find so striking is the double nature of this discovery. On the one hand, if it is available to all, then goodness can be seen as a commonplace occurence. On the other hand, since most people opted for either committing or allowing the perpetration of evil deeds, must I conclude that the rescuers' goodness, grounded in austere authenticity, is another version of the extraordinary? I don't have a way to resolve this dilemma. I find nothing common, however, in participating in the massacre of human beings. In fact, I see a threat to our survival if we accept with resignation the trivialization of mass murder. And by the same token, I find it equally dangerous to demote authentic goodness to the rank of the commonplace: there was nothing common in the rescuers' risking their lives and their children's lives to save strangers. There was nothing trivial about their defining their personal moral rules in such a way as to include the willingness to die in order to remain who they were.

The rescuers insisted time and time again that what they did had nothing to do with heroism. Instead, it all had to do with who they were and what, being who they were, was required of them in order to remain unchanged. I dismissed these disclaimers as evidence of their shyness and humility. Now, I know better. They, of course, were right all along. Rescuing the fugitive at the risk of one's own life has nothing to do with being superhuman. On the contrary, it has everything to do with being ordinary.

But what about all those extraordinary risks the rescuers took? What about John and Bertha harbouring Marie and her two children in their home, which was also a German canteen? What about Pieter sheltering the Lezer family for over a year in a bunker dug in the forest? Every time I posed this type of question to a rescuer, their answer was just another question: "What about it?"

Could it be that what appears to be extraordinary to me, was for them just as ordinary as tending to a potato farm or a butchershop— all in a day's work?

When Bill found his answer, it allowed him to go on hiding Edith and, later, the others. But that's not all. It also bestowed upon him the peace of mind that only that kind of clarity can provide. In this connection, I recall Wilma's parting words to Vicki and me: whatever else she and Albert have or lack, they always have their peace of mind to keep them company. When it was time to act, they knew what to do, and they did it. Not because of any ideology, not because of any religious principle. Just because she was Wilma and Albert was Albert. Could it be that the most valuable wisdom resides in such simplicity? I am reminded of Michel de Montaigne, the 16th century French thinker. After the death of his friend, La Boetie, people asked, "Why did you and La Boetie love each other so much and why is your grief so profound?" "Because," replied Montaigne, "he was he and I am I." The rescuers are saying nothing more, nothing less.

I have come to some small understanding of the heroism of these noble people, yet I remain confused and strangely unmoved. Instead of sighing with relief, instead of allowing my heart to fill as a reward for my completing my quest for a hero, I find myself in the grip of "Tevye's dilemma". In *Fiddler on the Roof*, the milkman Tevye had to make peace between the demands of tradition and his heart's desire, because his oldest daughter and her intended decided to get married without the mediation of a matchmaker and without asking Tevye's permission. While he wanted nothing more than his daughter's happiness, he also felt bound by the rules of tradition. Unable to solve his dilemma, he turned his face to the sky and, in the presence of a silent God, he weighed the pros and cons. He was searching for clarity so that he could act as himself. Then his second daughter presented him with a dilemma that was a variation on the same theme: she decided to marry a godless student of Jewish birth and, upon his arrest, follow him into Siberian exile. Once again, Tevye, aching to see his daughter find happiness, was torn between his heart's inclination and the edicts of tradition. In both cases, he ended up giving his daughters his blessing. As for his breach of tradition, he managed to find rationales which allowed him to remain himself. When his third daughter presented him with her wish to marry outside of the faith, after having weighed all arguments he came to a tragic conclusion: "If I bend any further, I'll break." That is what the rescuers would have had to do if they had buckled under all the considerations that conflicted with who they were. And this has been precisely my dilemma since I have understood the rescuers' commitment to themselves. On the one hand, I have my memories that allow neither for trust nor for hope—they have exercised as rigid a power over my outlook as age-old tradition exercised over Tevye's decisions. On the other hand I desired nothing more than to allow the rescuers' wonderful humanity into my world, a world whose burden has been breaking my back for over forty years. But how to allow new wisdom without betraying the memory of my precious dead? How to find some hope without clouding the clarity of the past, a past that demands of me unbending loyalty?

On the one hand, can I allow myself to lose sight of my mother's anguished glance as she disappeared from my life? She must have summoned all her strength to reassure my sister and me that everything was going to turn out just fine. But I knew better. I felt, more than I saw, the terror of a final farewell. Bergen Belsen was already moving into her eyes, sunk deep in their sockets. Each time this memory enters my soul, I feel as if I have taken my last breath. On the other hand, how can I not recall the story of Sake Bottinga's bicycle-ride through the night with a dying Jewish infant on his luggage rack? Each time I recall how he bargained with God to take his life in exchange for that brand-new one, a burst of air unclutters my chest.

On the one hand, how can I forget the faces of the onlookers watching our procession through the streets of Budapest, towards the stifling space of the ghetto? I recall the panic on an old man's face when he faltered under the weight of his belongings: he saw from the corner of his eye a young Arrow Cross hoodlum's rifle poised to shoot him. I recall the shock that registered in his eyes when, a second later, he was felled by the assassin's bullet. I recall how excluded I felt from the ranks of the living as my glance shuttled from the silent bystanders to the murderer. And what I recall more vividly than anything else is my question: was the murderer older than my thirteen-year-old sister, Agi? On the other hand, how can I ever forget Pieter Miedema's journey into the forest twice a week, month after month, to give Latin and Greek lessons to the Lezer children? How can I not think of Rudy de Vries' descent into the red-light district of Amsterdam to yank a Jewish boy—exactly my age—from the fate the Nazis had for him?

I know only too well all the terrible images that clutter my mind, even after forty years. But in my quest for heroes what I have discovered is that, in fact, there is another view! When I unclench a still hesitant fist what I see is the new light of hope.

Like someone living a subterranean existence, I find the first contact with light to be disorienting, even undeserving of trust. New questions rush to my mind. "Is this light's radiance another version of darkness? Is it going to vanquish the night?" As a child emerging from the rubble, I was not moved to question. Before I have a chance to reflect on the child I was, my mind is filled with the vitality of little

Epilogue

Sonja in the streets of Ternaard on the day of liberation. One of us was abandoned; the other was preserved by Bill's mother. These images are not sufficient to erect a theory about what happens to a child's innocence after surviving an all-out assault. But Sonja's version of survival provides some new insights: her story has enriched me, even though, in my case, Christians were unmoved to lift a finger for me. I feel sad, jealous, and angry when I think of how I was abandonned. And I feel relieved, grateful, and joyous for all the Sonjas and their rescuers. Learning about Sonja's fate doesn't change the pain of my memories, but her story has a soothing effect. And hope gets a shot in the arm.

Today, as I conclude this volume about John and Bertha, Lidia and Willem, Albert and Wilma, and the other rescuers, I have nothing but questions. Did knowing them rekindle the child's curiosity in me? Perhaps. Did learning about their efforts for the friendless Jews of Holland move me from despair to hope? I'd like to believe it did. Two years ago, when my sister Agi passed away, in my grief I sought out a rabbi for solace. "If you can't believe that there is a just God and eternal peace in His company, do you, at least, hope that such a God and such a peace exist?" he asked me. "Of course, I hope so," I answered without a moment's hesitation. "Then you are half-way there," he replied with a smile.

A month after my sister's death, I met Joekje Miedema from whom I learned that, for the desperate and the optimistic, hope is last to die.

So now I welcome this tentative light and the confusion it has ushered into my life, even if I don't have Joekje's courage to always stand on the side of hope. Nothing has ever been able to shake this Frisian woman's trust in hope, not all the evidence of hostility, cruelty, betrayal. For her, to be human is to hope. For me, hope is a welcome visitor. I am willing to believe that it is possible that, living with realistic hope, the quality of my life and that of my children will improve. With this presence in my life, it is less painful to endure the moments of despair when I revisit my losses.

How comforting it is to know that I shall never be alone again in the night. The rescuers will keep me company. But living with tentative hope reminds me of how flawed human nature can be. This, of course, is not a new discovery. But having met the rescuers makes me wonder if there are at least slivers of goodness in humankind. I cannot go on considering evil as an absolute. And if that is so, what prevents yesterday's bystander, or even perpetrator, from becoming tomorrow's rescuer?

Still, I must question my trust in hope. All I have to do is open the newspaper: Biafra, Bangla-Desh, Cambodia, Soweto, Lebanon, Ireland, Israel... Children are still being killed and maimed; their faith in a just world, and perhaps in a just God, is taking a strong beating. As the gruesome images wax and wane in my mind, the face of Joekje Miedema emerges before me. "So what about absolute hope?" I would like to ask her. "Can I afford to rely on such an elusive moral support? After all, the facts don't lie." Then I surprise myself, for I not only remember Joekje's words about hope, but I also invoke them: "Can I afford *not* to hope exactly *because*—and not in spite— of a world that continues to be cruel to children? Of course I can't. Despair breathes death. Hope holds the door open for a better future."

One final question remains. Engraved on the medal bestowed by the State of Israel upon the rescuer are these words, taken from the Mishnah: "He who saves one life, it is as if he saves the whole world." I am not comfortable with these words. He who saves one life, has saved just that: one life. By this I don't mean to minimize the exemplary deeds of the rescuer. But just as I can't conjure up the image of millions of dead victims, even though I feel that image in the depths of my most private pain, the picture of the whole world saved by one human being eludes me. How can anyone save the whole world? Saving the world is given only to the superheroes who inhabit our television sets every Saturday morning.

On their very ordinary human scale, what the rescues seem to have in common is a direct link with their fellow humans, regardless of who those humans are. They see the suffering, and in a reflex-like fashion, they take action. They don't lobby, negotiate, implore. They act. The protagonists in this volume saw the fugitives, and they did something. Each of these rescuers saved at least one life. But they didn't save my mother's life, nor the lives of the members of my family who perished nameless, in mass graves. No rescuer reached out to me while the torturers were tearing at my eight-year-old body. Why wasn't my life touched by them? "He who saves one life, it is as if he saves the whole world." No, the rescuers didn't save humankind, and in the the matter of saving or not saving lives there are no "as ifs". Or are there?

Epilogue

When I come to think of it, the child whose life the rescuer saved grew up and most likely he or she had children and they, in turn, have their own children, and so it will continue, one hopes, for countless generations. Thus, that one life saved on a distant Frisian farm will have blossomed in a few generations to a whole community which, in turn, in a few subsequent generations, could populate the earth. No, the rescuers couldn't save the whole world in the past. But they certainly have offered humankind a fighting chance for the future. One by one, on their farms, in their stables, behind their pianos, they thought of only that one life, and they acted to save it. Perhaps in some mad vision they fantasized a world populated by the innocent and the peaceful. In the meantime, however, the rescue work had to be done. And they did it—naturally.